MW00882496

The Old Testament Historical Books: An Introduction

Israel P. Loken

PRESS

The Old Testament Historical Books: An Introduction
by Israel P. Loken

Printed in the United States of America

ISBN 978-1-60647-238-5

www.xulonpress.com

Dedication

To Eugene H. Merrill, who helped instill in me a deep love for Old Testament history through his teaching and writing.

Acknowledgments

The author gratefully acknowledges the following individuals who have made this study possible. I am most deeply indebted to the faculty of Dallas Theological Seminary for providing me with the training necessary to accomplish this task. Of special note is the Department of Bible Exposition, which has provided me with the opportunity to teach seminary students what I have learned. I am also deeply indebted to the administration of the College of Biblical Studies for providing an environment in which I am able to study the Word of God and share with college students what I have learned.

Contents

Introduction: The Method of Literary Analysis

Narrative is the dominant art form in the Bible. It comprises roughly half of the Old Testament (Genesis, half of Exodus, Numbers, Joshua, Judges, Ruth, Samuel, Kings, Chronicles, Ezra, Nehemiah, Esther, Daniel, and Jonah as well as various portions of Job, Isaiah, Jeremiah, Ezekiel, and Hosea) and half of the New Testament (Matthew, Mark, Luke, John, and Acts). In fact, the entire Bible is essentially one long story. Ryken observes, "Taken as a whole, the Bible tells a story that has a beginning, a middle, and an end. The Bible is above all a series of events, with interspersed passages that explain the meaning of those events."[1]

The stories of the Bible share three major characteristics. First, they are Biblical. In other words, Biblical stories are true to God. They are theologically sound; an accurate reflection of God's character, attributes, and actions. Each of the books listed above is in the Biblical canon, a fact that means that they have already been deemed theologically accurate by the Church. In fact, one of the major reasons that many of the Apocryphal and Pseudepigraphical books did not make it into the Biblical canon is because they were regarded as theological unsound. Second, they are historical. The stories of the Bible are historically factual. They are not myths or legends created in the minds of an imaginative storyteller. The characters portrayed in the Bible really lived; the events recorded actually took place, facts proven accurate time and again by archaeology. Third, they are literary. The Biblical accounts are written to communicate something to the reader. As a result, they share features common to all literary stories. These features include setting, characterization, plot, point of view, and style. Tremper Longman identifies six functions of biblical literature; historical, theological, doxological, didactic, aesthetic, and entertainment.[2]

Before the investigator can perform a thorough literary analysis on a narrative book of the Bible, it is necessary to propose a methodical plan for accomplishing the task. There is at present a great deal of disagreement among scholars as to the exact nature of literary analysis, what it is, what it can do, and what it cannot do.[3] There is also a great deal of disagreement among scholars as to the proper method of biblical literary analysis. However, a few works have stood the test of time and are now largely considered to be the standards in the field. These include the works of Shimon Bar-Efrat,[4] Meir Sternberg,[5] and Robert Alter.[6] Of special note is the work of Sternberg. His literary approach has been widely accepted by literary scholars and he appears to have provided a standard for modern biblical literary analysis. The following list, taken from Sternberg, details the features of narrative which are to be examined when conducting literary analysis:

1. Temporal ordering, especially where the actual sequence diverges from the chronological.
2. Analogical design: parallelism, contrast, variation, recurrence, symmetry, chiasm.
3. Point of view, e.g., the teller's powers and manipulations, shifts in perspectives from external to internal rendering or from narration to monologue and dialogue.
4. Representational proportions: scene, summary, repetition.
5. Informational gapping and ambiguity.
6. Strategies of characterization and judgment.
7. Modes of coherence, in units ranging from a verse to a book.
8. The interplay of verbal and compositional pattern.[7]

This comprehensive list involves a study of every level of a text, from the most basic element of individual words and phrases to the higher levels of scenic structuring and plot formulation, and must necessarily make up the groundwork for any discussion of literary analysis. I believe that this extensive list can be narrowed down to the following five categories: setting, characterization, plot, point of view, and style.[8]

Setting

Setting is by far the most overlooked and undervalued element in literary analysis of biblical narrative. The setting quite often makes a significant contribution to the message that the author is trying to communicate to his audience. As such an integral component of the narrative, it must not be overlooked by the interpreter. The interpreter must analyze every detail of setting that the author includes in the narrative. Biblical authors rarely include irrelevant details in their stories. In fact, just the opposite usually holds true. Biblical stories consistently supply only those details necessary to gain a proper and accurate understanding of the meaning of the text.

The literary analyst must also investigate the relationship between the setting and the elements of characterization and plot. This relationship often enhances both character development and plot structure. This relationship may also be the key to fully understanding the overall message of the narrative. Additionally, the setting can sometimes function as a leading element of structure and unity (e.g., geographical notations in the Gospel of Luke and Acts).

The setting of a narrative is the space in which the story unfolds. This space routinely involves a specific historical time period with actual characters, places, and events. As a result, the setting is simultaneously physical, temporal, and cultural. The physical setting is the environment in which the action occurs. While the most common physical setting in the Bible is a city, other popular settings are houses, palaces, temples, gardens, jails, boats, rivers, seas, lakes, mountains, caves, deserts, valleys, roads, and battlefields. In addition to their literal meaning, physical settings often take on a thematic or symbolic meaning in biblical stories.[9] For example, spiritual revelations often take place on mountains (e.g., Moses' meetings with God on Mount Sinai, Elijah's encounter with the prophets of Baal on Mount Carmel, and Jesus' transfiguration on the Mount of Olives).

The temporal setting is the historical era in which the story unfolds. The temporal setting often has a dramatic impact on biblical stories because the fate of the Jews so often lies in the hands of foreigners (e.g., Egyptians, Babylonians, Assyrians, Persians). The temporal setting also helps to explain the behavior of characters (e.g., the fact that the book of Esther takes place during the period when the Jews were in exile in Persia explains the apparent lack of cultic sensitivity in the story).

The cultural setting is made up of the beliefs, attitudes, and customs that prevailed in the world of the story. The cultural setting is oftentimes implied rather than explicitly stated; yet it can have a significant impact on the events of the unfolding story. The cultural setting explains why Sarah offers Hagar to her husband Abraham, why Abraham lies about his marital relationship with Sarah, why Abraham doesn't question God's command to present Isaac as a burnt offering, and why Laban is unwilling to give his younger daughter in marriage to Jacob before the firstborn.

The setting of a story is the element that gives the story reality. It allows the reader to picture the events of the narrative in his mind. However, since we are centuries removed from the original audience, we quite often miss details of the story which were obvious to the original readers. It is quite important, therefore, that the analyst searches for related details on the setting from outside the text of the story in order to see the picture in as complete detail as possible. For example, the book of Ruth takes on whole new levels of meaning when the physical setting (Bethlehem in Israel and the land of Moab), temporal setting (time when the judges judged), and cultural setting (Israelite customs such as the allowance of gleaning in the fields, the prescription of a kinsman redeemer, and the exchanging of a sandal to signify a pact) are taken into account.

Characterization

In the overwhelming majority of narrative literature, the characters are the main objects of interest for both the storyteller and the reader. Characters are so interesting because they are filled with those characteristics common to everyone. Even when the main character in the account is an animal or an inanimate object, the storyteller routinely endows it with human characteristics.[10] Through characterization the author is able to transmit the significance and substance of the literary narrative to the reader. Bar-Efrat explains:

> Many of the views embodied in the narrative are expressed through the characters, and more specifically, through their speech and fate. Not only do the characters serve as the narrator's mouthpiece, but also what is and is not related about them, which of their characteristics are emphasized and which are not, which of their conversations and actions in the past are recorded and which are not, all reveal the values and norms within the narrative, and in this respect it makes no difference whether the characters are imaginary or whether they actually existed. The decisions they are called upon to make when confronted with different alternatives, and the results of these decisions, provide undisputable evidence of the narrative's ethical dimension.[11]

It is the characters of a story that most attract the reader's attention as well. The reader often feels an emotional attachment with the main characters, whether positive or negative. The reader participates in the experiences and fortunes of the characters, feeling elation in their achievements and dismay in their misfortunes. The friends and enemies of the narrative's hero or heroine are quite likely to be the friends and enemies of the reader.

The audience learns about the central characters of a narrative through their appearance, their actions, and their speech (both words spoken by the characters themselves and those words spoken about them by other characters). As a result, it is absolutely critical that the storyteller fully develop his various characters. Shaw elaborates on the importance of character development: "It is difficult to identify with a character whom one does not know or understand. This is why characterization is important in fiction. Before a writer can make his reader sympathize with or oppose a character, that character must come alive. The reader wants to be able to visualize him—to see him act and hear him talk. Characterization, no mere by-product, is an essential part of plot."[12]

Since our understanding of a character is wholly governed by the narrator, it becomes necessary to analyze each character in order to determine what the narrator is trying to communicate to the reader in the way he portrays his characters. The storyteller will often communicate his message through characterization rather than by direct narration. Reynolds writes, "By manipulating the characters and their various perspectives, the author influences the reader's response to the different elements in the story, thereby insuring that the reader will leave the text with the correct interpretation of the narrative."[13] I disagree with Reynolds' assertion that the reader's correct interpretation of the narrative is insured. For whenever the narrator decides to communicate his message through characters, he places the burden of interpretation upon the reader. Oftentimes this interpretation is quite subjective. Ryken explains,

> Whenever a storyteller decides to let a character's actions do the talking, he thereby places a burden of interpretation on the reader. Often we know exactly how to interpret an action because we can place it into the context of moral commands elsewhere in the Bible. When Cain murders Abel, when David commits adultery with Bathsheba, or when Ananias and Sapphira lie, we have no difficulty in judging their characters negatively on that point. Conversely, when Abraham exercises faith in God, or when Joseph resists sexual temptation, we do not need to take a Gallup poll before concluding that they are examples of moral virtue.
>
> But there are many other places in the stories of the Bible where the assessment of what a character is like is open to alternative interpretations. Is the youthful Joseph's telling Jacob about his brothers' bad behavior an example of moral courage or ignominious self-serving? Why does Joseph manipulate his brothers before revealing himself to them? Did Esther compromise her religious principles when she fit in so well at the Persian court that she even managed to keep her Jewish identity a total secret? Many of the stories of the Bible raise interpretive questions like these, and we need

only read around in the commentaries to see what a lack of consensus there is on some of them.[14]

Making the task of interpretation even more difficult is the fact that the variety of techniques employed in biblical narrative makes it impossible to set general rules for interpreting characterization. For example, good looks usually indicate a favorable character, but Absalom and Saul become major exceptions to the rule.[15] Sternberg further illustrates this concept by observing the element of old age in the patriarchal narratives. While arrival at old age routinely indicates a time of blessing (e.g., Abraham, Jacob, Joseph), for Lot and Isaac old age becomes a period of heartbreaking betrayal and deception.[16] It thus becomes the formidable task of the literary analyst to produce sound interpretations based on the correspondence of individual elements with the entire narrative. Inevitably, blurred characterizations become clear when analyzed in the illuminating light of the author's point of view.

The composite portrait of any literary character is developed in three manners.[17] First, direct definition refers to statements made about the character, whether by themselves, the narrator, or another character. Rimmon-Kenan writes that direct definition is "akin to generalization and conceptualization."[18] The narrator almost always designates this type of definition. For example, we know that Boaz was "a man of standing" (Ruth 2:1), David was "ruddy, with a fine appearance and handsome features" (1 Sam. 16:12), and Esther was "lovely in form and features" (Esth. 2:7) because we are told so by the storyteller. These epithets or characterizations invariably prove crucial to the plot.[19] A character within a literary account may also specify this type of definition. For example, Matthew 23 records an extensive discourse given by Christ describing the teachers of the law and the Pharisees. Direct description as a whole, however, is relatively rare in the stories of the Bible. Second, indirect presentation is characterization that is accomplished through a character's speech or actions. We know that Elihu is wise while Eliphaz, Bildad, and Zophar are fools because of the record of their speeches throughout the book of Job. This is by far the most common form of characterization found in biblical narratives. Third, reinforcement by analogy is characterization that is accomplished by means of a foil, another character used to emphasize unique, similar, or contrasting behavioral traits. Rimmon-Kenan elaborates, "When two characters are presented in similar circumstances, the similarity or contrast between their behaviour emphasizes traits characteristic of both."[20] For example, David's lust and treachery are all the more dishonorable when compared to the honor and integrity of the consistently faithful Uriah (2 Sam. 11).

Characters themselves usually fall into one of three categories.[21] First, protagonists are the main characters in a story and it is usually their perspective through which the story is told. Protagonists, whether sympathetic or unsympathetic, are meant to invoke a response from the reader. Another form of the protagonist is those secondary characters who aid the main protagonist in his quest. Second, antagonists are the ones who stand against the protagonists and attempt to prevent them from realizing their desires. Third, foils are characters who stand in reinforcement or contrast to either the protagonists or antagonists.

An additional category of characters is that of the archetypal character. A major aspect of the universality of the Bible is its utilization of recurring master characters.[22] Literary analysts have traditionally identified these recurrent characters as archetypes. Archetypal characters are of considerable importance to the literary analyst because they bring to the narrative an extensive body of characterization which need not be fully described in the text. Frye explains, "Some symbols are images of things common to all men, and therefore have a communicable power which is potentially unlimited."[23]

The biblical literary analyst must be especially aware of the presence of archetypal characters in the literature of the Bible since the biblical authors routinely make extensive use of them. In fact, Ryken calls the Bible the "great repository of archetypes in Western literature."[24] Frye adds that the Bible is "the major informing influence on literary symbolism" and argues that familiarity with the Bible is the prerequisite for understanding literature as a whole because of its extensive archetypal content.[25]

Archetypal characters in biblical literature tend to fall into two categories, positive characters and negative characters. Chief among the positive archetypal characters is God. When a reader encounters the character of God in a narrative, he automatically assumes certain things to be true. For example, the reader believes God to be fair, just, holy, and active in human affairs. The storyteller need not describe God in this manner in his characterization of God. These qualities are assumed to be possessed by God by everyone who reads the text. Other positive archetypal characters include angels, wise men, true prophets, virtuous wives, innocent children, and benevolent kings or rulers. Chief among the negative archetypal characters is Satan. The reader who encounters Satan in a narrative immediately assumes that he is deceitful and wicked. Other negative archetypal characters include demons, soothsayers, false prophets, temptresses or prostitutes, witches, and oppressive kings or rulers.

Plot

If the characters are the lifeblood of the narrative, the plot is the body.[26] Plot in a literary narrative is the organizing force through which the meaning of the narrative is communicated. This organization involves the sequence of scenes which together form the story.[27] It is essentially a series of cause and effect relationships. Plot is almost always characterized and motivated by conflict.[28] Ryken writes, "The essence of plot is a central conflict or set of conflicts moving toward a resolution."[29] This conflict can be physical (e.g., the shortage of food and water in the Exodus account), characteral (e.g., Cain vs. Abel, Jacob vs. Esau), or personal (e.g., Job's spiritual conflict, Jesus in the Garden of Gethsemane). The presence of conflict is the element that gives narrative suspense,[30] and it is the element of suspense that arouses the reader's interest and emotional involvement, encouraging him to finish the story to see the resolution of the conflict.

Many of the stories of the Bible contain archetypal plot motifs. These are general plot structures that commonly recur throughout the literature of the Bible. Ryken has identified twelve common archetypal plot motifs:

1. *The quest*, in which a hero struggles to reach a goal, undergoing obstacles and temporary defeat before achieving success.
2. *The death-rebirth motif*, in which a hero endures death or danger and returns to life or security.
3. *The initiation*, in which a character is thrust out of an existing, usually ideal, situation and undergoes a series of ordeals as he or she encounters various forms of evil or hardship for the first time.
4. *The journey*, in which characters encounter danger and experience growth as they move from one place to another.
5. *Tragedy*, or the more specific form of *the fall from innocence*, depicting a decline from bliss to woe.
6. *Comedy*, a U-shaped story that begins in prosperity, descends into tragedy, but rises to a happy ending as obstacles to success are overcome.
7. *Crime and punishment*.
8. *The temptation*, in which someone becomes the victim of an evil tempter or temptress.
9. *The rescue*.
10. *The suffering servant motif*, in which a character undergoes undeserved suffering for the benefit of others.
11. *The Cinderella* or *rags-to-riches motif*, in which a character overcomes the obstacles of ostracism and poverty.
12. *The movement from ignorance to epiphany* (insight, illumination).[31]

The underlying purpose of these archetypal plot motifs, according to Ryken, is "to help us organize what we encounter in stories by placing a given story into a familiar landscape."[32]

An analysis of a story's plot involves much more than a simple recitation of the events of the story. These events only take on their complete significance when viewed in relation to the other events recorded in a narrative. Bar-Efrat writes, "The events of the story in their mutual relationships make up the plot. The plot always has a structure. Contrary to real life no accidental and irrelevant facts are included and the incidents are connected with each other both temporally and causally."[33] It is therefore the investigator's responsibility to determine how each scene contributes to the narrative as a whole. The interaction of the various scenes essentially constitutes a series of cause and effect relationships. As a result, each scene must be analyzed in terms of its relationship to the other scenes, especially the one preceding it and the one following it.

Point of View

The narrator and the narrative are integrally related. The narrator is the one who controls the story and provides unity throughout the narrative. It is the narrator who decides how characters are portrayed,[34] which elements of the setting are indispensable, and how the scenes are arranged to form a plot.[35] It is through the narrator's point of view that we observe and evaluate the events of the story. Bar-Efrat explains: "The narrator is an apriori category, as it were, constituting the sole means by which we can understand the reality which exists within a narrative. The nature of this reality, and the essence of the narrative world, with its characters and events, and, above all, their significance, is entirely dependent on the narrator, through whom we apprehend. Consequently, the character of the narrators and the way in which they mediate is of supreme importance."[36] It is the narrator's point of view that predominates over all others since it is he who determines how other points of view emerge.

The narrator's point of view[37] is developed through either first person or third person narration. In first person narration, the storyteller serves as a character in the story, usually the protagonist. The books of Nehemiah and Habakkuk are examples of first person narratives. In third person narration, the storyteller relates what is happening from a distance. The storyteller does not appear as a character but the story is told through his perspective. The books of Ruth and Esther are examples of third person narratives.

Both forms of narration usually give the impression of an omniscient mind standing behind the story. The narrator is aware of secret conversations and actions. He is conscious of the inner thoughts and desires of the characters. The narrator is omnipresent, seeing everything that relates to the narrative, no matter where or when that event occurs. The breadth of the narrator's omniscience may even extend to the feelings and thoughts of God (cf. Gen. 6:6, 8; Ex. 4:14; 2 Sam. 11:27). An additional aspect of the narrator's omniscience in biblical narrative is the total reliability of the author. "The Bible always tells the truth in that its narrator is absolutely and straightforwardly reliable."[38]

While the narrator speaks of the characters and events in a factual manner, he is clearly not indifferent to them. The interpreter must be familiar with the techniques employed by the narrator to correctly determine the author's intended message. The narrator's point of view is expressed in various ways.[39] First, the narrator may insert direct comments about the characters or events into the narratives.[40] The author's references to the events of Christ's birth as being the fulfillment of prophecy in Matthew 1 and 2 is an example of this kind of overt narration (i.e., Matt. 1:22-23; 2:15, 17-18, 23). Second, the narrator may allow the narrative to speak for itself. This more subtle form of narration is most obvious in the doctrine of retribution found throughout the Old Testament. When the Israelites obeyed God good things happened to them while bad things happened when they disobeyed God. The narrator often does not have to state whether something was pleasing or displeasing to God. It is evidenced by the blessings or judgments that occur as a result of the action. Third, the conversations of the characters are often clues to the narrator's point of view. However, this is usually the most subtle expression of the narrator's point of view. Joshua's discourse in Joshua 23 is an example of the narrator expressing his point of view by means of the speech of the protagonist.

Style

The narrative style of a story involves the various techniques utilized by the author in the account of his narrative. These techniques help to form the structural unity of the narrative. Narrative techniques include repetition, word play or paronomasia, parallelism, chiasm, inclusio,[41] irony, chronological ordering, and omission. Repetition involves a repeating of key words, themes, or motifs and serves to give coherence and rhythm to a story (e.g., barrenness in the patriarchal narratives, the phrase "I am the Lord" in Leviticus 19, banquets in Esther).[42] Whereas English prose composition tends to avoid repetition, ancient Hebrew prose uses it quite extensively.[43] While the extensive use of repetition in biblical literature has caused some scholars to discredit the biblical text (e.g., documentary hypothesis, synoptic problem), the effective use of repetition unites rather than fragments biblical literature. Reynolds explains, "The common occurrence of repeated information with numerous variations in style, found in a text characterized by paucity of facts, can only indicate the presence of a literary structure with specific meaning."[44]

Word play is used by the author to give coherence and interest to his story. Word play involves techniques such as pun, irony, and other figures of speech. An example of word play occurs in Genesis 40 where Joseph is called on to interpret the dreams of the cupbearer and the baker. The interpretation of the cupbearer's dream was that Pharaoh would "lift up your head," a restoration to the office (v. 13); but the interpretation for the baker's dream was that Pharaoh would "lift up your head," an execution (v. 19).

Parallelism is a structural element used by the author to show symmetry, variation, or contrast between two or more components. While parallelism is most commonly found in Hebrew poetry, it is often an integral component of Hebrew narrative as well (e.g., Israel's cycle of sin under the judges). Ross observes the parallel development of Exodus 13:1-16:

> this day you came out (4)
>> when the LORD shall bring you into the land of the Canaanites (5)
>>> you shall keep this service: seven days eat unleavened bread (6-7)
>>>> show your son that this is because of the Lord's victory over Egypt (8)
>>>>> it will be a sign on your hand, and memorial between your eyes (9)
>>>>>> for with a strong hand he brought you out (9)
> you shall keep this ordinance year by year at this time (10)
>> when the LORD shall bring you into the land of the Canaanites (11)
>>> you shall keep this service: set apart all males (12-13)
>>>> tell your son that this is because the LORD brought us out of Egypt (14)
>>>>> it will be a token for your hand, and frontlets for your eyes (16)
>>>>>> for with a strong hand he brought us out (16)[45]

Chiasm is a structural element utilized by the narrator to add unity and structure to his narrative as well as to draw the reader's attention to the center of the chiasm, in which is commonly emphasized the author's main theme in that particular episode. A chiasm occurs when the storyteller arranges his material in an X pattern with parallel material in the outer and inner positions to form an ABCBA pattern. For example, Ross identifies a structural chiasm that unifies the flood account presented in the Book of Genesis:

Introduction: Noah's righteousness and Noah's sons (6:9-10).

> **A** God resolves to destroy the corrupt race (6:11-13).
> **B** Noah builds an ark according to God's instructions (6:14-22).
> **C** The Lord commands the remnant to enter the ark (7:1-9).
> **D** The flood begins (7:10-16).
> **E** The flood prevails 150 days and water covers the mountains (7:17-24).
> **F** God remembers Noah (8:1a).
> **E'** The flood recedes 150 days, and the mountains are visible (8:1b-5).
> **D'** The earth dries (8:6-14).
> **C'** God commands the remnant to leave the ark (8:15-19).
> **B'** Noah builds an altar (8:20).
> **A'** The Lord resolves not to destroy humankind (8:21-22).[46]

Inclusio is another structural technique used by biblical authors. Inclusio involves the use of similar or identical phrases, motifs, or episodes to begin and end a literary unit. Inclusios are most commonly found in Hebrew poetic literature (e.g., Psalm 8 begins and ends with "O Lord, our Lord, how majestic is your name in all the earth").

Irony is a literary device that expresses contrasts for literary effect or impact.[47] For example, Haman is identified as an Agagite in Esther while Mordecai is identified as a descendant of Kish, epithets that bring to mind the ancient conflict between Saul and the Amalekites. This device includes the reversal-of-fortune motif so prevalent in the Old Testament. For example, Haman is hung on the very gallows he built for Mordecai while Moredecai inherits Haman's position, estate, and the king's signet ring.

Chronological ordering is another structural technique used by biblical authors. Quite often, the biblical author will change the sequence of events when telling a story. This change may be done to organize an author's work, emphasize certain themes, create suspense, or develop foreshadowing.[48] For example, Mark and Luke arrange their Gospels around geographical rather than chronological episodes.

Finally, omission is the intentional neglect of an author to include events that occur during the setting of a story but are not of significance to the unfolding of his specific narrative. Recognizing the omission of certain events often helps reveal the author's purposes in writing his narrative (e.g., the omission of the grievous sins of David and Solomon in the book of Chronicles, the omission of parables in John).

Conclusion

The proper method in literary analysis is crucial to the investigator's conclusions based on their study of the text. The various elements used by the author in composing his narrative must fit together to achieve the effect of bringing the reader's attention to the key themes or ideas that the author wants to communicate to the reader. These elements include setting, characterization, plot, point of view, and style. Since these parts are only significant when their relationship to the whole is shown, the literary analyst must analyze each of these elements in order to ascertain the message of the narrative as well as to show the unity of the story. The process described above has formed the foundation of my study of the historical books of the Old Testament. What follows is the fruit of my labor.

CHAPTER 1

Joshua

"No man will be able to stand before you all the days of your life. Just as I have been with Moses, I will be with you; I will not fail you or forsake you. Be strong and courageous, for you shall give this people possession of the land which I swore to their fathers to give them. Only be strong and very courageous; be careful to do according to all the law which Moses My servant commanded you; do not turn from it to the right or to the left, so that you may have success wherever you go. This book of the law shall not depart from your mouth, but you shall meditate on it day and night, so that you may be careful to do all that is written in it; for then you will make your way prosperous, and then you will have success" (Josh. 1:5-8).

The book of Joshua serves as a bridge between the Pentateuch and the Old Testament historical books. The book is closely related to the Pentateuch. The land promises of the Abrahamic Covenant recorded in Genesis are fulfilled in Joshua (cf. Gen. 12:1; 15:7, 18-21). The great work of redemption from bondage in Egypt (Exodus) is naturally followed by the inheritance of the land that God had promised (Joshua).[1] This was, after all, the twofold reason why the Lord came down from heaven to speak to Moses; "So I have come down to deliver them from the power of the Egyptians, and to bring them up from that land to a good and spacious land, to a land flowing with milk and honey, to the place of the Canaanite and the Hittite and the Amorite and the Perizzite and the Hivite and the Jebusite" (Ex. 3:8). The instructions concerning Levitical cities and cities of refuge presented in Leviticus are executed in Joshua. The appointment of Joshua to replace Moses as leader of Israel is presented in the book of Numbers. Many of the great predictions found in Deuteronomy are fulfilled in Joshua (e.g., Deut. 6:10-11; 31:3). In fact, the parallels are so great that the book has been commonly regarded as the conclusion of the Pentateuch, giving rise to the idea of a "Hexateuch," a literary unit composed of six books (Genesis-Joshua).

However, the book of Joshua is also closely related to the historical books. The book records the conquest of the land that is later lost in Kings and regained in Ezra. Joshua himself serves as the forerunner of the great judges and kings of Israel who come after him. His leadership role is markedly different from that of Moses. He is not called a prophet nor is he the recipient of God's laws. He is a military commander who is instructed to keep the law in order to achieve success. Although the book of Joshua is itself inspired revelation, it consistently refers to a previous revelation, the Book of the Law (e.g., 1:8; 8:31-32), i.e., the Pentateuch. These factors indicate that Joshua is better seen as the first of the historical books of the Old Testament rather than the final book of the Pentateuch.

In the English Old Testament, Joshua is placed first amongst the twelve historical books (Joshua-Esther). This grouping follows that of the Greek Septuagint, in which the Old Testament is divided into four sections; namely, Pentateuch (Genesis-Deuteronomy), History (Joshua-Esther), Poetry (Job-Song of Solomon), and Prophecy (Isaiah-Malachi). In the Hebrew Bible, Joshua is placed first amongst the Prophets, one of the three divisions of the Old Testament (i.e., Law, Prophets, and Writings). It is unknown why Joshua is placed among the Prophets. Perhaps he held the office of prophet.

The book receives its title from its chief character, Joshua. The name Joshua means "the Lord saves." Joshua was originally named Hoshea (meaning "salvation"), but Moses changed his name to Joshua (Num. 13:16). The Septuagint translates the name as *Iesous*, the same word used for Jesus in the New Testament. Joshua, a member of the tribe of Ephraim, is routinely identified as the son of Nun. Nun appears to have been a man of faith; he evidently placed the blood of a lamb on the doorpost of his house on the night of the first Passover (it is likely that Joshua was the firstborn son of Nun based on the genealogy recorded in 1 Chronicles 7:27). Joshua is one of the most popular figures in the Bible; he is mentioned in ten different books (Exodus, Numbers, Deuteronomy, Joshua, Judges, 1 Kings, 1 Chronicles, Nehemiah, Acts, and Hebrews).

The life of Joshua can be naturally divided into two parts. In his earlier years, he was the servant of Moses and military commander of Israel's armies. In his latter years, he served as the successor of Moses and political leader of the nation. As the servant of Moses, Joshua ascended Mount Sinai with his master to receive the words of the Lord. As a result, Joshua was providentially absent from the Israelite camp during the Golden Calf incident. Joshua also served as guardian of the tent of meeting when Moses met with the Lord "face to face" (Ex. 33:11). Joshua was chosen as one of the twelve spies sent into Canaan in preparation for the conquest of the land. Along with Caleb, Joshua advised the nation to enter the land to possess it. Unfortunately, the two visionaries were outnumbered by their fellow spies who were in favor of a return to Egypt. As the military commander of Israel's armies, Joshua achieved a great victory against the Amalekites at Rephidim as the nation of Israel was on its journey from the land of Goshen to Mount Sinai. In this battle, the fortunes of Israel turned with the rising and falling of Moses' arms. As the leader of the nation, Joshua was able to guide the Israelites in their conquest and settlement of the Promised Land. He also led the people in a covenant renewal ceremony at Shechem.

Author

While the Bible does not identify the author, Jewish tradition has long held that the book was written by Joshua, the successor of Moses.[2] The traditional view has been criticized by liberal scholars in recent years and many now hold that the book was compiled by the Deuteronomic School around 621 B.C. This view is improbable for several reasons. First, the book was assuredly written by an eyewitness (cf. the "us" reference in 5:6). Second, Rahab was alive at the time of writing (6:25; though this could be a reference to her descendants). Third, the Jebusites still inhabited Jerusalem (15:63; David conquered Jerusalem around 1003 B.C.).[3] Fourth, Tyre had not yet conquered Sidon (13:4-6), an event which dates to the twelfth century B.C. Fifth, Gezer was still inhabited by the Canaanites (16:10; 1 Kings 9:16 reveals that an Egyptian pharaoh defeated the Canaanites at Gezer and gave the town to Solomon's wife as a dowry, an event that dates to the middle of the tenth century B.C.). Sixth, Canaanite cities are mentioned by archaic names (e.g., Baalah for Kiriath Jearim in 15:9 and Kiriath Arba for Hebron in 15:13).

Since some parts of the book seem to have been written by Joshua (cf. 24:26), it seems best to ascribe authorship of the majority of the book to him. It is probable that certain portions of the book were added by the high priest Eleazar and his son Phinehas after Joshua's death (*Baba Bathra* 15a). These include the record of Joshua's death (24:29-30), the conquest of Hebron by Caleb (15:13-14; cf. Jud. 1:1, 10, 20), the conquest of Debir by Othniel (15:15-19; cf. Jud. 1:1, 11-15), and the conquest of Leshem by the Danites (19:47; cf. Jud. 17-18).

Date

Assuming Joshuaic authorship, the book that bears his name was likely completed within a decade of Joshua's death. The chronology of Joshua's life can be determined based on the dating of the Exodus. The chief dates proposed for the Exodus are 1446 B.C. (during the reign of Amenhotep II) and ca. 1260 B.C. (during the reign of Rameses II).

The following arguments are used to support an early date for the Exodus:

1) In 1 Kings 6:1, the time between the Exodus and the beginning of Solomon's temple construction was 480 years. Solomon began to build the temple in the fourth year of his reign, i.e., 966 B.C.; hence, the Exodus took place in 1446 B.C.

2) In Jephthah's day (ca. 1100 B.C.), Israel had been in the land for 300 years (Jud. 11:26). This would place Israel's entrance in the land around 1400 B.C. (1446 B.C. for the Exodus plus 40 years in the wilderness).

3) Archeological evidence from Egypt during this period corresponds with the biblical account (e.g., though Thutmose IV succeeded his father, Amenhotep II, Thutmose was not the eldest son).

4) Events in Palestine about 1400 B.C. correspond to those of the Conquest (e.g., archeological evidence suggests that Jericho, Ai, and Hazor were destroyed at this time).

5) The Amarna letters speak of a widespread invasion of the land of Canaan in the early fourteenth century B.C. by a group called the 'apiru, a possible reference to the Hebrews.

6) The events recorded in the books of Exodus, Numbers, Joshua, Judges, and Samuel cannot fit within a period of only 300 years, the time frame proposed by the advocates for a late date.

The following arguments are used to support a late date for the Exodus:

1) The 480 years of 1 Kings 6:1 is a cryptic reference to twelve generations, each lasting forty years. Since a typical generation is about twenty-five years, the actual number is closer to 300 years, thus indicating a date around 1266 B.C.

2) Jephthah is not referring to the Israelite conquest as a united nation. Rather, he is referring to a preexodus occupation of the land by those tribes who later associated themselves with the Israelites.

3) A number of archaeologists, including Nelson Glueck,[4] have concluded that there was no sedentary population in the Transjordan and Negev areas between 1900 and 1300 B.C.

4) Exodus 1:11 reveals that the enslaved Israelites built the storage cities Pithom and Rameses (or Raamses). Since the city of Rameses was named for Rameses II, the city must have been built during his reign (1304-1236 B.C.).

5) Archaeological evidence indicates that a massive and wide-spread destruction of cities in central Canaan, including Jericho,[5] occurred in the thirteenth century B.C.[6]

The early date takes the biblical evidence at face value and is to be preferred. The arguments for the late date can be adequately refuted. First, there is no evidence to suggest that the Israelites ever used the generational method to reckon time. Second, the Jephthah passage unequivocally identifies the conquerors of Sihon with the nation of Israel who came up from Egypt (cf. Jud. 11:13, 18-23). Third, the findings of Glueck and others have been invalidated by conservative scholars.[7] Fourth, if the city of Rameses was named for the pharaoh of the same name, then the date of the Exodus would be much later than ca. 1260 B.C. (the pharaoh's reign must include the years of construction, the years between the building of the cities and the infanticide decree, and the first eighty years of Moses' life, a total of well over one hundred years).[8] Fifth, there should be no evidence of a massive and widespread destruction associated with the Conquest. The Israelites were specifically told to spare the Canaanite cities and towns that they conquered (11:13-15; 24:13). The only cities destroyed during the Conquest were Jericho, Ai, and Hazor. The massive and widespread destruction in the thirteenth century B.C. is a result of the repeated invasions of Israel during the period of the judges.

Assuming one accepts a date of 1446 B.C. for the Exodus, the book of Joshua can be dated to within a few decades of the completion of the conquest of Canaan in 1399 B.C. (the conquest of the land took about seven years—cf. Josh. 14:10 with Deut. 2:14). As a result, the final draft of the book should be dated no later than 1360 B.C. The book was written in the newly conquered land of Israel, possibly in Timnath Serah, the home of Joshua (19:50).

Historical Background

The conquest of the land took place between 1406 and 1399 B.C. In 1446 B.C., the nation of Israel escaped from the land of Goshen after living in Egypt for 430 years. The climactic moment came when the Lord parted the Red Sea (Reed Sea), thus allowing the Israelites to cross this body of water in safety. Following their escape, the nation entered the Sinai Peninsula, journeying for three days through the Desert of Shur to arrive at Marah, where the bitter waters were made sweet. The nation then continued their journey, entering the Desert of Sin about forty-five days after leaving Egypt. It was in the Desert of Sin that the Israelites were first provided with manna sent by God. The nation next journeyed to Rephidim, where they were attacked by the Amalekites. Under the leadership of General Joshua, the Israelites were able to achieve a great victory. The nation then continued their journey, arriving at the base of Mount Sinai about three months after leaving Egypt.

At Mount Sinai, the Lord gave Moses the portion of the Covenant found in Exodus 20-40. After the construction of the tabernacle, the Lord gave Moses the portion of the Covenant found in the book of Leviticus. In all, the nation spent almost a full year at Sinai. On the twentieth day of the second month in the second year after leaving Egypt, the nation began their journey from Mount Sinai to Kadesh Barnea. When they arrived in Kadesh Barnea, the nation set up camp and sent twelve spies into Canaan. The spies returned to Kadesh Barnea forty days later with evidence of the abundant fruit growing in the land; but also with tales of the awe-inspiring inhabitants of Canaan. Although most of the spies were for abandoning the planned invasion, Joshua and Caleb argued for an immediate attack. The Israelites, swayed by the negative report of the ten spies, decided to select a new leader and return to Egypt. At this very moment, the Lord came down from heaven and announced that the nation would spend the next forty years wandering in the wilderness for the forty days the spies were in the Promised Land.

Almost forty years later, in 1406 B.C., the nation once again found themselves at Kadesh Barnea. This time, the Israelites were determined to follow the Lord and allowed Him to guide them from Kadesh Barnea to the Plains of Moab. After defeating the Canaanite king of Arad and the Amorite kings Sihon and Og, the nation finally arrived in the Plains of Moab directly across from the central Canaanite city of Jericho. While encamped in the Plains of Moab, Moses delivered the series of sermons which together comprise the book of Deuteronomy. Following the death of Moses and succession of Joshua, the Hebrews invaded the land of Canaan and successfully conquered the land seven years later (1399 B.C).

There is quite some disagreement as to the exact nature of the conquest of Canaan. The first view is the traditional view and is known as the conquest model.[9] Proponents of this view see the conquest as a large-scale, hostile invasion, resulting in a major extermination of the Canaanite tribes who occupied the land. This view identifies the Israelites as a distinct ethnic group who journey to Canaan from Egypt. The second view is the settlement model. Proponents of this view[10] see the conquest as a peaceful, sedentary infiltration into the land, with the Israelites settling amongst the Canaanites. This view identifies the Israelites as a group of pastoral nomads who gradually infiltrated Canaan from the desert. The third view is the revolt model. Proponents of this view[11] see the conquest as an internal upheaval, a sort of peasant revolt. This view identifies the Israelites as an internal group made up of the lowest classes in Canaanite society. These peasants revolted from their Canaanite lords, perhaps provoked by the entrance into the land of a small band of Yahweh-worshippers who had escaped slavery in Egypt (hence the Exodus account). The conquest model best fits the biblical records and should be regarded as accurate. The two alternative views regard the biblical accounts with skepticism and are instead constructed using archaeological findings as primary evidence.

Because the history of Israel is routinely impacted by those foreign countries with which the nation comes into contact, a brief review of the three major powers in the Ancient Near East during this period must be provided. The first major power is Egypt. The land of Egypt is strategically located at the northeastern tip of Africa, forming a land bridge to the continent of Asia. The most significant feature of the land of Egypt is the Nile River. In fact, Egypt is often called "the gift of the Nile." Because the Nile River flows from south to north, southern Egypt is known as Upper Egypt while northern Egypt is known as Lower Egypt. The Egyptians are probably the descendants of Ham, the son of Noah; Egypt is sometimes identified as the land of Ham in the Old Testament (Ps. 78:51; 105:23, 27; 106:22).

Like Israel, Egypt was a land of religion. Herodotus notes, "They [the Egyptians] are beyond measure religious, more than any other nation. . . . Their religious observances are, one might say, innumerable" (*Histories* 2.37). The chief god of the Egyptians was Ra, the sun god. However, many other gods were regularly worshipped including Osiris, god of the Nile, and Isis, goddess of children. These gods were shown to be inferior to Yahweh through the ten plagues sent upon Egypt. These plagues demonstrated that the God of Israel is the most powerful Being in the universe. While the various gods were certainly important to the Egyptians, the single most significant ingredient of Egyptian religion was the pharaoh. The pharaohs were regarded as divine and were always the focal point of Egyptian religion. Notable Egyptians in the Bible include Shishak, the pharaoh who invaded Israel during the reign of Rehoboam (1 Kin. 14:25-26), and Neco, the pharaoh of the army who met Josiah in battle at Megiddo; a battle in which Josiah was fatally shot by the Egyptian archers (2 Kin. 23:29; 2 Chron. 35:22-23).

During the entire period of the Exodus and Conquest, Egypt was governed by Dynasty 18. This dynasty was founded by Amosis (1570-1546 B.C.), the pharaoh who expelled the Hyksos from Egypt. Amosis is probably to be identified with the "new king . . . who did not know Joseph" of Exodus 1:8.[12] Having recently defeated the Hyksos, Amosis took steps to subdue the Hebrews, a people group closely related ethnically to the Hyksos. The new pharaoh enslaved the Israelites and used them to cultivate fields and construct storage cities. Amenhotep I (1546-1526 B.C.), the successor of Amosis, was most likely responsible for the genocide program described in Exodus 1:15-16. It is also possible that Thutmose I (1526-1512 B.C.) was the culprit. Moses was born in 1526 B.C., the year of Amenhotep's death and Thutmose's rise to power.

The pharaoh of the Exodus was Amenhotep II (1450-1425 B.C.). Having recently lost a significant portion of his slave force (Hebrew Exodus), army (drowned in the Red Sea), and population (firstborn of every family), Amenhotep was unable (or unwilling) to occupy the area of the Sinai Peninsula, a territory normally under Egyptian control. This allowed the Israelites the freedom to wander through this region for forty years. Amenhotep was succeeded by his son

Thutmose IV (1425-1417 B.C.). Thutmose was likewise disinterested in Sinai and Canaan, as was Amenhotep III (1417-1379 B.C.), who was busy fighting against Nubia to the south.

The second major power in the Ancient Near East during the period of the Exodus and Conquest was the Neo-Hittite Empire. The Hittites were the descendants of Heth, the son of Canaan (Gen. 10:15). They are identified in Deuteronomy as one of the seven nations in the Promised Land "greater and stronger" than Israel (Deut. 7:1). Many scholars consider the Hittites as the third most influential people group of the Ancient Near East, rivaling the Egyptians and the Mesopotamians.[13] The Hittites dominated Asia Minor. Their capital was located on the Halys River at a place called Boghaz-keui in central Anatolia. Groups of Hittites migrated south, eventually settling in the hill country of Canaan near the city of Hebron (Gen. 23:19; Num. 13:29). Notable Hittites include Ephron, from whom Abraham purchased a burial site (Gen. 23), and Uriah, one of the mighty men of David (2 Sam. 23:39). Esau married two Hittites (Gen. 26:34) and Solomon had Hittite women in his harem (1 Kin. 11:1).

In ca. 1440 B.C., the Hittites were able to extend their borders south and southeast by capturing Aleppo from the Hurrians and much of Syria from the Egyptians. The southern edge of the Hittite Empire effectively formed the northern border of Canaan. By 1370 B.C., under Suppiluliumash, the Hittite Empire became the preeminent force in the eastern Mediterranean world. The Hittites eventually destroyed the Hurrian Empire in ca. 1350 B.C. and probably would have attempted to conquer the newly formed state of Israel if not for the rise of the Neo-Assyrian Empire to the east.

The third major power in the Ancient Near East during the period of the Exodus and Conquest was the Hurrian Empire of Mitanni. The origins of the Hurrians are unknown. They are probably closely related to the Kassites. The Hurrians settled along the Balikh and Habor tributaries of the upper Euphrates, effectively controlling northern Syria. As a result, Mitanni became a buffer state between Assyria to the east and the Hittites to the west.[14] Since archaeologists have never discovered any records or inscriptions written by the Hurrians, our knowledge of their kingdom comes solely from

Assyrian, Egyptian, and Hittite records. The nation gained wealth primarily as a result of sheep breeding; Hurrian wool was exported throughout the Ancient Near East. The chief god of the Hurrians was the storm god Teshub. The war chariot of Teshub was led by the bull gods Seris ("Day") and Hurris ("Night").

The Hurrian Empire reached its peak at precisely the time of Israel's conquest of Canaan. By 1400 B.C., the territory ruled by the Hurrians stretched from the Mediterranean to the northern Zagros Mountains. Because of its indefensible location Mitanni was constantly overrun by first one major power and then another.[15] Naturally, the Hurrians enlisted the support of the Egyptians against the Hittites and Assyrians. To solidify their treaty, the Hurrian kings Artatama I and Shuttarna II married their daughters to pharaohs Thutmose IV and Amenhotep III respectively. When the Hitittes finally overthrew the Hurrians in ca. 1350 B.C., the Neo-Assyrian Empire filled the void and occupied the territory of Mitanni.

These three powers fought to control the trade routes between Africa, Asia, and Europe. These included both sea routes governed by major port cities (e.g., Byblos, Ugarit, Sidon, Tyre) and land routes (e.g., Way of the Sea, King's Highway) governed by significant city-states (e.g., Gezer, Hazor, Megiddo, Damascus, Hamath, Aleppo, Babylon). The relative stalemate between these three powers ca. 1400 B.C. allowed Israel the opportunity to conquer the Canaanites without foreign interference.

Since the Canaanites play a prominent role in the book of Joshua, it is necessary to provide a description of this significant people group. The Canaanites were the descendants of Canaan, the son of Ham. They are identified in Deuteronomy as one of the seven nations in the Promised Land "greater and stronger" than Israel (Deut. 7:1). The Canaanites lived along the eastern Mediterranean coastal regions from the River of Egypt to the area of Lebanon (Num. 13:29). The Canaanites, caught between the cumbersome writings of Mesopotamian cuneiform and Egyptian hieroglyphics, were the inventors of a simplified method of writing, the alphabet.[16] Biblical Hebrew is derived from the Canaanite language. The Canaanites were also known as artisans, bronze metallurgists, potters, and merchants. However, their most significant impact on Israel came in the area of religion. The Canaanite fertility cult was perhaps the most immoral and vile religion known to man. The chief god of the Canaanites was Baal, god of thunder and lightning. Other gods included El, the patriarchal deity who was the father of Baal; Yam, the god of the sea; Asherah, the wife of El; Mot, the god of the underworld; and Anat, the sister of Baal. The Canaanites worshipped their gods by engaging in sexual immorality involving male and female prostitutes and sacrificing their children. The Canaanite religion proved to be too attractive for the Hebrews to resist. Israel's worship of Baal seems to have been the most significant sin among those that led to the nation's deportation (cf. Jer. 11:17; Hos. 2:1-13; 11:2; Zeph. 1:4).

The Amorites are routinely linked with the Canaanites; the result being that the two groups are virtually synonymous (cf. Deut. 1:7; Josh. 5:1). The Amorites were the descendants of Canaan, the son of Ham (Gen. 10:16). The name Amorites is derived from the Akkadian *Amurru,* meaning "west;" the Amorites lived to the west of Mesopotamia and thus were called "westerners." The Amorites had their origins in Syria and later migrated south into the land of Canaan. There, they became so numerous that the land of Canaan was called *Amurri* in the Amarna letters. The Amorites are identified in Deuteronomy as one of the seven nations in the Promised Land "greater and stronger" than Israel (Deut. 7:1). The Amorites lived in the hill country on both sides of the Jordan River (Num. 13:29; Josh. 5:1). The so-called King's Highway traversed their territory (Num. 21:21-22). They were largely nomadic shepherds, supplying sheep and goats to the Canaanite cities. Notable Amorites include Sihon and Og, two kings who were defeated by the Israelites on their way to the Promised Land (Num. 21).

At the time of the conquest, the territory of Canaan was not a unified country. The rugged topography of the land was not conducive to a strong centralized government. Rather, the geographic divisions promoted separation and isolation. As a result, the region was primarily administrated by a series of city-states with separate governments. The most powerful of these included Hebron, Jerusalem, Jericho, Megiddo, and Hazor. These city-states were generally autonomous and rarely allied except when Canaan was threatened with a foreign invasion. Such was the case with the Israelite invasion. Joshua faces two major alliances during the Conquest. In southern Canaan, he encounters the Amorite alliance consisting of the kings of Jerusalem, Hebron, Jarmuth, Lachish, and Eglon. In northern Canaan, he faces a Canaanite coalition led by the king of Hazor.

Audience and Purpose

The book of Joshua was written to give an official account of the historical fulfillment of the Lord's promise to the patriarchs to give Israel the land of Canaan.[17] The major theme of the book is the conquest of the land that had originally been promised by God to Abraham (cf. Gen. 12:7; 13:14-17; 15:18-21). This promise was repeated to Isaac (Gen. 26:3-4), to Jacob (Gen. 28:13; 35:12), and to subsequent generations (Gen. 48:4; 50:24). The rest of the Pentateuch amply reaffirms this promise (e.g., Ex. 6:3-4, 8; 13:5, 11; 33:1; Lev. 20:24; 23:10; 25:2, 38; Num. 11:12; 15:2; 20:12, 24; 27:12; Deut. 1:8, 35; 6:10, 18, 23; 7:13; 8:1; 9:5; 10:11; 26:3, 15; 28:11; 30:20; 31:7, 20). The book of Joshua itself consistently emphasizes the fact that the conquest was a direct fulfillment of the Lord's promise to the nation's ancestors (e.g., 1:6; 5:6; 21:43).

The conquest of Canaan was achieved by means of a holy war led by the divine warrior, Yahweh (cf. 5:13-15). Even in the introduction (1:1-9), it is at once apparent that the Lord is the divine force behind Joshua's human success. Throughout the book, God is routinely given credit for the Israelite victories (e.g., 10:10, 14, 30, 32, 42; 11:6, 8, 20; 21:43-45). The Lord is the one who causes the walls of Jericho to collapse. The Lord is the one who sends hailstones from heaven upon the Amorites. The Lord is the one who makes the sun stand still. The Lord is the one who actively fights for His people.

The principles for this holy war were spelled out in Deuteronomy (cf. Deut. 7:1-26; 20:16-18). First, the Israelites were instructed to "utterly destroy" the inhabitants of the land (Deut. 7:2; cf. 7:24; 20:16-17). Second, the nation was forbidden to make a covenant with them (Deut. 7:2). Intermarriage was specifically forbidden (Deut. 7:3). Third, the Israelites were forbidden from showing favor to them or even from having pity for them (Deut. 7:2, 16). Fourth, the nation was instructed to destroy everything associated with their idolatrous worship (Deut. 7:5, 25). Fifth, the possessions of the Canaanites were placed under a sacred "ban" (Heb. *herem*; Deut. 7:26). As long as the nation followed these principles, they achieved success (e.g., Jericho, Ai). When they disobeyed these principles, they experienced failure (e.g., Achan's sin, Gibeonites).

Many have questioned the Lord's command to exterminate the Canaanites. However, the Lord Himself explains why He made this command. First, the wickedness of the Canaanites had become abhorrent to the holy God (Lev. 18:24-28; Deut. 9:4-5; note that it is actually the Lord Himself who is exterminating the Canaanites – cf. Ex. 23:23). In fact, the reason given by God for delaying the return of Abraham's descendants is because "the iniquity of the Amorite is not yet complete" (Gen. 15:16). A major purpose of Israel's return to the land was God's punishment of the Canaanites for their sin. As Constable writes, "In judging the Canaanites God was performing surgery on the human race to remove a malignancy."[18] Second, the nations left alive will cause the Israelites to turn from following Yahweh to serving other gods (Ex. 34:15; Deut. 7:4). These gods included Baal, Asherah, Anat, and Mot. Third, the items associated with idolatry that are left behind will become a trap for the Israelites (Deut. 7:25). These items included altars, high places, Asherah poles, and handmade idols. Fourth, the nations left alive will teach Israel all the detestable things done in the name of their gods (Ex. 23:33; Deut. 20:18). These wicked practices included sacred prostitution of both sexes, child sacrifice, and licentious carousing.[19] A failure to abstain from the idolatrous practices of the Canaanites would result in Israel's eventual destruction (Deut. 7:4). As a result, the purity of Israelite religion needed to be preserved at all costs.

Since God was being faithful to His promises, He expected Israel to be faithful to His covenant with them.[20] In fact, the possession of the land was entirely dependant upon the nation's obedience to the Lord's commands (23:9-16; cf. Deut. 4:1; 5:33; 6:18; 8:1; 11:8-9; 30:19-20). To emphasize the importance of the nation's sacred responsibilities, the book of Joshua highlights three ceremonies dedicated to the renewal of the covenant. The first ceremony takes place at Gibeath-haaraloth (Gilgal; 5:2-11). Here Joshua circumcised the males of Israel and the nation observed the Passover. The second ceremony takes place at Mount Ebal (8:30-35). Here Joshua built an altar, wrote a copy of the Law of Moses, and read the Law to the entire nation. The third ceremony takes place at Shechem (24:1-28). Here Joshua made a covenant with the people, put the nation's commitment to follow the Lord in writing, and placed a large stone near the sanctuary to serve as a witness against the nation.

The book of Joshua was written to the generation of Jews that followed Joshua. Joshua's speech of 23:2-16 was specifically addressed to this generation. In this speech, Joshua gave three exhortations. These exhortations were based on the events recorded in the rest of the book (23:3-5). The first exhortation was to "keep and do all that is written in the book of the Law of Moses" (23:6). The commandments of Moses were designed to keep the Israelites holy; separate from the nations that surrounded them. The second exhortation was to "cling to the Lord" (23:8). The nation needed to be faithful to Yahweh and abstain from worshipping other gods. The third exhortation was to "love the Lord" (23:11). This command summarizes the first two. In other words, the nation is expected to demonstrate their love for Yahweh by being obedient and faithful to Him. Joshua concluded his speech with a sharp warning. He informed the nation that the Lord would destroy them if they "transgress the covenant of the Lord" and "go and serve other gods" (23:16). Joshua presented the nation with a choice. They could serve foreign gods or they could serve Yahweh (24:14-15). The initial conquest of the land was achieved by the obedience of Joshua's generation. To maintain possession of the land, the Israelites of subsequent generations needed to remain true to the Lord and follow His commands.

Structure and Outline

The book is naturally divided into four major sections. The first section describes the invasion of Canaan by the Children of Israel (1:1-5:12). The second section is an account of the conquest of Canaan by the Israelites (5:13-12:24). The third section details the division of the land amongst the tribes of Israel (13:1-21:45). The fourth and final section serves as a sort of appendix, concluding the book by reviewing the significant events that took place after the successful conquest of Canaan (22:1-24:33). While the first, second, and fourth sections are constructed of narrative prose, the third section is characterized by the rhetoric of listing and ordering, commonly called administrative prose.[21]

<u>Outline</u>

I. The Invasion of Canaan (1:1-5:12)
    A. The commissioning of Joshua (1:1-18)
        1. God's charge to Joshua (1:1-9)
        2. Joshua's instructions to the officers (1:10-11)
        3. Joshua's charge to the Transjordan tribes (1:12-15)
        4. The people's response (1:16-18)
    B. The spies sent to Jericho (2:1-24)
        1. Rahab hides the spies (2:1-7)
        2. The promise of protection (2:8-14)
        3. The scarlet cord (2:15-21)
        4. The escape (2:22-24)
    C. The crossing of the Jordan (3:1-17)
        1. The preparations for crossing (3:1-5)
        2. The importance of the Ark of the Covenant (3:6-13)
        3. The crossing accomplished (3:14-17)
    D. The erection of memorials (4:1-24)
    E. The consecration of the nation (5:1-12)
        1. The nation is circumcised (5:1-9)
        2. The nation celebrates Passover (5:10)
        3. The change in diet: from manna to produce (5:11-12)
II. The Conquest of Canaan (5:13-12:24)
    A. The divine Commander (5:13-15)
    B. The central campaign (6:1-8:35)
        1. The conquest of Jericho (6:1-27)
        2. The setback at Ai (7:1-26)
             a. The sin announced (7:1)
             b. The defeat at Ai (7:2-5)
             c. Joshua's prayer (7:6-9)
             d. The Lord's response (7:10-15)
             e. The offender identified (7:16-18)

f. The sin described (7:19-23)

g. The offender executed (7:24-26)

3. The victory at Ai (8:1-29)

4. Covenant renewal at Mount Ebal (8:30-35)

C. The southern campaign (9:1-10:43)

   1. The Gibeonite deception (9:1-27)

      a. Introduction (9:1-2)

      b. The covenant between Joshua and Gibeon (9:3-15)

      c. The enslavement of the Gibeonites (9:16-27)

   2. The defeat of the five kings of the Amorites (10:1-27)

      a. The Amorite coalition (10:1-5)

      b. The miraculous battle (10:6-15)

      c. The attempted escape (10:16-22)

      d. The execution of the kings (10:23-27)

   3. The defeat of the rest of the southern kings (10:28-43)

D. The northern campaign (11:1-15)

   1. The northern coalition (11:1-5)

   2. The battle (11:6-9)

   3. The destruction of Hazor (11:10-15)

E. The review of the victories (11:16-12:24)

   1. The conquered areas (11:16-23)

   2. The conquered kings (12:1-24)

      a. The Transjordan kings (12:1-6)

      b. The Canaanite kings (12:7-24)

III. The Division of Canaan (13:1-21:45)

A. The land still to be taken (13:1-7)

B. The division of the land east of the Jordan (13:8-33)

C. The division of the land west of the Jordan (14:1-5)

D. The portion for Caleb (14:6-15)

E. The portion for Judah (15:1-63)

F. The portion for Ephraim and Manasseh (16:1-17:18)

G. The portion for the remaining tribes (18:1-19:48)

   1. The survey and description of the remaining land (18:1-10)

   2. The portion for Benjamin (18:11-28)

   3. The portion for Simeon (19:1-9)

       4. The portion for Zebulun (19:10-16)
       5. The portion for Issachar (19:17-23)
       6. The portion for Asher (19:24-31)
       7. The portion for Naphtali (19:32-39)
       8. The portion for Dan (19:40-48)
    H. The portion for Joshua (19:49-51)
    I. The cities of refuge (20:1-9)
    J. The Levitical towns (21:1-45)
IV. Conclusion (22:1-24:33)
    A. The eastern tribes return home (22:1-34)
    B. Joshua's final challenge to the leaders (23:1-16)
    C. The covenant renewed at Shechem (24:1-28)
       1. The historical review (24:1-13)
       2. Joshua's plea (24:14-15)
       3. The conversation between Joshua and the nation
          (24:16-28)
    D. The appendix (24:29-33)
       1. The death and burial of Joshua (24:29-31)
       2. The burial of Joseph's bones (24:32)
       3. The death and burial of Eleazar (24:33)

Summary of Contents

The Invasion of Canaan (1:1-5:12)

    The book of Joshua begins with the traditional Hebrew formula *hayah* ("Now it came about"), a common introduction for the historical narratives of the Old Testament. The books of Judges, Ruth, 1 Samuel, 2 Samuel, and Esther all begin with the same word. This introductory formula is not limited to the historical narratives; the prophetic books of Ezekiel and Jonah also begin with the same word.

    The time frame given is "after the death of Moses" (1:1). This phrase naturally leads the reader back to the final chapter of Deuteronomy where the death of Moses is described (Deut. 34:5-7). The clear implication is that the book of Joshua continues the story of Deuteronomy. Although Moses is dead, he still figures prominently in the book of Joshua, being mentioned 57 times. Moses is identified as "the servant of the Lord" (1:1) while Joshua is initially introduced as the servant of Moses. However, by the end of the book Joshua will also be called "the servant of the Lord" (24:29).

The first nine verses of the book record the Lord's charge to Joshua. The newly appointed leader[22] is commanded to "arise!" (Heb. *qum*; 1:2), an expression that denotes a call to action (cf. Jud. 4:14; 1 Sam. 16:12; 2 Kin. 1:3; Ezra 10:4; Neh. 2:18; Jer. 1:17; Oba. 1:1; Jon. 1:2; 3:2). Joshua's mission is to lead the nation of Israel across the Jordan to possess the land of Canaan. The Lord promised that the Israelites will be given every place on which they stepped; from the wilderness to the south (Negev Desert) to the mountain range of Lebanon and the Euphrates River to the north; from the Jordan River to the east to the Mediterranean Sea to the west. Although the eastern boundary is not specifically identified in the text, it is at once apparent that Joshua is positioned on the eastern edge of the Promised Land as he stands on the banks of the Jordan (1:2).

Having promised the Israelites national success, the Lord promised Joshua individual success. The Lord informed Joshua that he would be victorious in battle; that no man would be able to stand against him as long as he was "strong" and "courageous" (1:6, 7, 9). Joshua would later utter these very same words to the men of Israel just before executing the five kings of the Amorites. The Lord further swore to Joshua that He would be with him just as He was with Moses. The words "I will be with you" (1:5) form one of the greatest promises in the Scriptures. The same words were given to Isaac (Gen. 26:3), Jacob (Gen. 31:3), Moses (Ex. 3:12), Gideon (Jud. 6:16), and the nation Israel (Isa. 43:2). The promise, however, is conditioned upon the obedience of Joshua. The leader was commanded to keep the Law of Moses and to meditate on it day and night; only then would he have success.

Having been informed of his mission by the Lord, Joshua moved to instruct the nation of their responsibilities. He first addressed the officers, instructing them to prepare the people to enter the Promised Land in three days. Joshua then addressed the Transjordan tribes, commanding the warriors to assist their fellow tribes in their effort to possess the land of Canaan. The tribes responded with a pledge to follow the instructions of Joshua. They even promised to put to death anyone who disobeyed the commands of the new leader.

Following the pattern set by the Lord at Kadesh Barnea, Joshua prepared for the invasion of Canaan by sending spies to the city of Jericho. Jericho, located about six miles from the Jordan River, was the most formidable city in central Canaan. It was also the most strategic as it controlled the various passes into the central highlands. Joshua's military strategy was to divide the land in half, then conquer the southern cities and northern cities respectively. Jericho, meaning "fragrance," was named for the abundance of palm trees that surrounded the city.[23]

When the spies entered Jericho, they immediately went to the house of Rahab, the "harlot." The word used for harlot (Heb. *zonah*)[24] indicates that Rahab was a common prostitute, not a cultic prostitute (Heb. *qadesh*; cf. Gen. 38:21; Deut. 23:17). As such, she was no doubt accustomed to receiving travelers and strange men into her house. The spies probably thought that staying with the town prostitute was the best way to remain unnoticed. Despite their ruse, the spies were quickly found out and their presence was reported to the king of the city. The king immediately ordered Rahab to surrender the spies. Rahab instead decided to hide the spies, deceitfully informing the king that they had left the city before the gates were closed on the previous evening.

While some have tried to justify Rahab's blatant lie by appealing to the rules of war or by appealing to the more noble cause (i.e., a concern for the lives of the spies), there is little doubt that Rahab here commits a sin. The Bible routinely condemns deceit (Ex. 20:16; Ps. 34:13; Jer. 9:4-9; Zech. 8:16; Eph. 4:25). Even if Rahab had informed the king that the spies were in her house, that doesn't necessarily mean that they would have been captured and executed. The Lord is able to deliver those who trust in him (cf. Dan. 3, 6). Although the New Testament commends Rahab for her faith (Heb. 11:31; Jam. 2:25), here she shows a lack of faith; a trust in human ingenuity instead of a trust in God's sovereignty. Condoning Rahab's deceitful behavior would be akin to condoning her harlotry.

Having believed the lie of Rahab, the men of Jericho searched the countryside for the spies. Meanwhile, back in Jericho, Rahab pleaded with the spies to give her and her family a promise of protection from the wrath of God; the harlot was fully aware that He had given the land of Canaan to His people. Evidently, the rest of the Canaanites were aware of this fact as well, primarily because of the miraculous deliverances provided at the Red Sea and in the battles against Sihon and Og (cf. 2:9-11). The spies agreed to Rahab's request, swearing her to secrecy. The spies then escaped from Jericho by means of a scarlet rope lowered down the walls. When they returned to the Israelite camp, the spies informed Joshua of everything that had happened to them.

When the three days of preparation were completed (cf. 1:11), the nation marched to the edge of the Jordan and prepared to cross the river. Joshua instructed the people to follow the Ark of the Covenant as it led them into the Promised Land. Following the requirements of the Law, the Ark was carried into the Jordan by Levitical priests (cf. Deut. 10:8). When the soles of the priests touched the edge of the water, the river dried up so that the tribes of Israel could cross the Jordan on dry ground. Amazingly enough, the Jordan was at flood stage when the Israelites crossed the river (3:15).

To mark the importance of the occasion, the Lord told Joshua to select twelve men; one man from each of the twelve tribes of Israel. The twelve men were instructed to pick up twelve stones from the middle of the riverbed where the Ark of the Covenant was located. The men did as they were told and carried the stones to Gilgal where they erected a memorial to the Lord. This monument was meant to be a sign of remembrance to the descendants of the Israelites of God's miraculous parting of the Jordan. The text notes that the crossing of the Jordan took place on the tenth day of the first month (i.e., Nisan; late March and early April; 4:19). This day was of special significance in the Hebrew calendar as it was the day on which the Passover lamb was to be selected (Ex. 12:3). The text also notes that the warriors of the Transjordan tribes accompanied the rest of the tribes as they crossed into the Promised Land (4:12-13).

The Ark of the Covenant plays an important role in Joshua: the Ark leads the Israelites across the Jordan River as they enter the Promised Land; the Ark leads the Hebrews as they march around Jericho; Joshua falls on his face before the Ark following the nation's defeat at Ai; and the Ark is central in the covenant renewal ceremony at Mount Ebal. In all, the Ark of the Covenant is mentioned thirty times in the book. The Ark of the Covenant was the most significant piece of furniture in the tabernacle. It was crafted by Bezalel and Oholiab out of acacia wood overlaid with gold (Ex. 25:10-11; 31:1-11). The Ark of the Covenant contained a golden pot full of manna, Aaron's rod that budded, and the tablets of the covenant (Heb. 9:4). It resided in the Holy of Holies in the tabernacle and, subsequently, the temple (Heb. 9:3-4).

There are four major views concerning the location of the Ark of the Covenant. The first view asserts that the ark was removed from the temple during the reign of Solomon by Menelik I and taken to Aksum in Ethiopia. According to tradition, Menelik I was the son of Solomon and the Queen of Sheba. The second view alleges that the ark was removed from the temple during the reign of Rehoboam by Pharaoh Shishak of Egypt. In 926 B.C., Shishak "came up against Jerusalem and he took away the treasures of the house of the Lord and the treasures of the king's house, and he took everything, even taking all the shields of gold which Solomon had made" (1 Kin. 14:25-26). This view is the basis for the movie "Raiders of the Lost Ark."

These first two views seem to be disproved by 2 Chronicles 35:3, "He [Josiah] also said to the Levites who taught all Israel and who were holy to the Lord, 'Put the holy ark in the house which Solomon the son of David king of Israel built; it will be a burden on your shoulders no longer. Now serve the Lord your God and His people Israel.'" Josiah gives this command in his eighteenth year (i.e., 622-621 B.C.; cf. 2 Chron. 35:19), hundreds of years after the reigns of Solomon and Rehoboam. In fact, the Ark of the Covenant still seems to be in Jerusalem as late as 591 B.C. In 591 B.C., the sixth year of King Jehoiachin's exile (cf. Ezek. 1:2; 8:1), Ezekiel saw the Shekinah glory of the Lord leave the temple and stop above the Mount of Olives (Ezek. 10:18; 11:23). Since the Shekinah glory of the Lord resided above the wings of the cherubim on the Ark of the Covenant, it is logical to assume that the ark is still in the temple at this point.

The third view holds that the ark was removed from the temple by the prophet Jeremiah at some point just prior to the city's destruction by Nebuchadnezzar in 586 B.C. This tradition is based on the apocryphal account of 2 Maccabees 2:4-5, "It was also contained in the same writing, that the prophet, being warned of God, commanded the tabernacle and the ark to go with him, as he went forth into the mountain, where Moses climbed up, and saw the heritage of God. And when Jeremiah came thither, he found a hollow cave, wherein he laid the tabernacle, and the ark, and the altar of incense, and so stopped the door" (NRSV). The primary difficulty with this view is that Jeremiah was viewed as a traitor by the religious leaders of his day. In fact, on one occasion Pashhur, the chief officer of the temple, had Jeremiah beaten and put in stocks (Jer. 20:1-2). On another occasion, the priests seized the prophet and called for his execution (Jer. 26:8). When Jeremiah tried to leave Jerusalem, he was arrested and accused of being a traitor (Jer. 37:12-16). In light of these passages, it is hard to believe that the prophet could have entered the temple and taken its greatest treasures.

The fourth view maintains that the ark was taken to Babylon by Nebuchadnezzar when he took the city of Jerusalem in 586 B.C. 2 Chronicles 36:18 states, "And all the articles of the house of God, great and small, and the treasures of the house of the Lord, and the treasures of the king and of his officers, he [Nebuchadnezzar] brought them all to Babylon." One must assume that if the Ark of the Covenant was in the temple at this point, and there is little reason to believe that it wasn't, then it must have been taken to Babylon by Nebuchadnezzar. Since Ezra makes no mention of its return, it can be assumed that the Ark had been destroyed in Babylon, perhaps even melted down to help create the statue of gold described in Daniel 3. Josephus makes no mention of the Ark of the Covenant in his description of Herod's temple, "But the inmost part of the temple of all was twenty cubits. This was also separated from the outer part by a veil. In this there was nothing at all. It was inaccessible and inviolable, and not to be seen by any; and was called the Holy of Holies" (*Wars of the Jews* 5.5.5). The Ark of the Covenant is likewise absent from Ezekiel's vision of the millennial temple (Ezek. 40-48).

While the nation was encamped at Gilgal, the Lord once again spoke to Joshua. This time God instructed Joshua to take flint knives and circumcise the men of Israel. This procedure was necessary because the children of those who had experienced the Exodus had not been circumcised while the nation wandered in the wilderness. The rite of circumcision was originally commanded by God as a sign of His covenant with Abraham (cf. Gen. 17). An integral component of that covenant was the promise of the land of Canaan (Gen. 17:7-8). It was only fitting that the Israelites submit to the sacrament of circumcision as they entered the land promised to them by the Lord.

The fact that the people were willing to be circumcised shows the incredible faith of this generation as opposed to the previous one. As one can imagine, those who had just been circumcised were in no position to defend their families from a Canaanite attack (cf. Gen. 34). With the imposing city of Jericho before them and the flooded Jordan River behind them, the nation was trusting solely in their God to protect them. Following their circumcision, the nation celebrated Passover on Nisan 14. The nation then partook of some of the produce of the land. The very next day, manna ceased to fall from heaven.

The Conquest of Canaan (5:13-12:24)

The conquest of Canaan began with a visit from the divine Commander. As Joshua was standing near Jericho, he lifted up his eyes and saw a man standing opposite him with a drawn sword in his hand. Joshua naturally asked the man whether he was fighting on the side of the Canaanites or on the side of the Israelites. Instead of responding to Joshua's question, the Stranger simply identified Himself. He was the "Captain of the host of the Lord" (5:14). Joshua immediately realized that he was in the presence of Yahweh and asked the Lord what He had to say to His servant. The Lord responded with a command; He instructed Joshua to remove his sandals because he was standing on holy ground. This command was reminiscent of the one given to Moses when he met the Lord at the burning bush (Ex. 3:5). As one would expect, Joshua immediately obeyed the command of Yahweh. This appearance of the

Lord is known as a "theophany," from the Greek word *theophaneia,* meaning "manifestation of God."

Following the ancient strategy of divide and conquer, the Israelites began their conquest of Canaan with an attack on the central city of Jericho. Jericho was "tightly shut" (6:1) because of the Israelite threat; its gates were closed and nobody was allowed in or out of the city. Evidently, Jericho was trusting in its superior walls for protection. After all, the Israelites had no siege equipment with which to break through the walls. However, the divine Commander did not need siege equipment.

The Lord instructed Joshua to march his army around Jericho once a day for six days. The army was to be accompanied by the Ark of the Covenant led by seven priests with seven horns. On the seventh day, the army was to march around the city seven times and the priests were commanded to blow their horns. The blowing of horns was to be followed by the shouts of the people. The Lord then promised that the walls of Jericho would crumble to the ground following the shouts of the people.

Joshua instructed the people to do just as the Lord had commanded; adding further that the nation was to keep silent until the time to shout (6:10). The Israelites followed the instructions of their leader and obediently marched around the city for seven days. When the climactic moment came, Joshua commanded the nation to shout, reminding them to remember the ban that had been placed on the plunder of Jericho. As the people shouted and the priests blew their trumpets, the walls of the city collapsed. The Israelites quickly rushed into the city, killing every human and animal in Jericho except for the household of Rahab. The chapter closes with a reminder that the Lord was with Joshua (6:27), just as He had promised (cf. 1:5).

Following the great victory at Jericho, the nation proceeded to Ai, no doubt expecting more of the same. Once again, Joshua sent spies into the city in preparation for the attack. The spies returned from Ai with confidence, instructing Joshua to send only a few thousand men to attack the city. Shockingly, the men of Israel were defeated by the men of Ai, losing thirty-six men in the assault.

Sensing something had gone terribly wrong, Joshua fell to the earth in mourning. He prayed to the Lord, inquiring of Yahweh as to the reason for the defeat. The Lord responded by commanding the leader to "rise up!" (Heb. *qum*; 7:10, 13; cf. 1:2). Yahweh informed Joshua that the nation had sinned by breaking the rules of holy war; specifically, by taking things that had been placed under the ban. God then instructed Joshua to use lots to determine the guilty party.

The following morning, Joshua did as he was commanded, identifying the offender as Achan, the son of Carmi, of the tribe of Judah. Joshua immediately questioned Achan concerning his actions at Jericho. To his credit, Achan quickly confessed his sin, admitting to having taken a beautiful mantle, two hundred shekels of silver, and a gold bar weighing fifty shekels. The shekel was the standard unit of weight in the Old Testament, weighing slightly more than four-tenths of an ounce. After sending messengers to find the plunder, Joshua took the plunder and everything else owned by Achan and proceeded to the Valley of Achor. There, Achan and his family were stoned by the Israelites to appease the wrath of God.

The Lord then commanded Joshua to once again attack the city of Ai. This time, the general decided to set up a clever ambush. Joshua instructed thirty thousand of his men to lie in hiding near the city. When the main force of Israel attacked the city, they quickly retreated, giving the impression that they were defeated. As the men of Ai pursued Joshua, the Israelites who had been placed in ambush rushed into the unguarded city and set it on fire. The men of Ai, seeing their city in flames, attempted to flee into the wilderness; however, they were quickly surrounded by the men of Israel and annihilated. The entire city of Ai and its twelve thousand inhabitants were destroyed by the Israelites.

The victory at Ai was followed by a covenant renewal ceremony at Mount Ebal. There Joshua built an altar of uncut stones on which the nation presented sacrifices and offerings to the Lord. Joshua then wrote the Law of Moses on the stones and read it to the people of Israel, taking special care to mention the blessings and curses that were to be placed upon the nation based on their obedience.

When the inhabitants of Gibeon heard what had happened to Jericho and Ai, they devised a clever plan in an attempt to save their city. They pretended that they were envoys from a distant land seeking to make a covenant with the Israelites. The ruse worked because Israel did not "ask for the counsel of the Lord" (9:14). Joshua made an unfortunate treaty with the Gibeonites and swore an oath to let them live. When the Israelites discovered that they had been tricked, they decided to abide by the terms of their agreement. However, they enslaved the inhabitants of Gibeon and forced them to serve as woodchoppers and water-carriers.

When the Amorite kings of the south heard of the Gibeonite treaty, they decided to form a coalition and attack Gibeon. The kings of Jerusalem, Hebron, Jarmuth, Lachish, and Eglon formed their armies and together marched against the city. The Gibeonites immediately sent word to Joshua, calling on their allies to help defend the city. When the army of Joshua reached Gibeon, they surprised the Amorite coalition, throwing their armies into confusion and causing a great slaughter. Yahweh Himself added to the carnage, hurling great hailstones from heaven upon the fleeing Amorites. The Lord further aided His people by causing the sun to stand still in response to the prayer of Joshua. This miracle is said to be confirmed by the "book of Jashar" (10:13; cf. 2 Sam. 1:18). The book of Jashar was probably a collection of war hymns and heroic narratives that focused on the period from Joshua through the early monarchy.[25] This miracle was especially noteworthy because "the Lord listened to the voice of a man" (10:14) as He fought for Israel. Although the defeated kings of the Amorite coalition tried to escape by hiding in a cave, they were quickly discovered and executed.

Following the defeat of the Amorite coalition, the cities of southern Canaan were quickly subdued. The armies of Joshua were able to capture Makkedah, Libnah, Lachish, Eglon, Hebron, and Debir in consecutive order. They then took possession of the Negev, the lowland, and the "slopes" (10:40). These "slopes" are either the Shephelah that led from the high country to the Mediterranean Sea or the steep slopes leading down to the Dead Sea. Having "utterly destroyed" (10:40) the inhabitants of southern Canaan, the armies of Joshua returned to their base camp at Gilgal.

When the kings of northern Canaan heard of Israel's military success, they formed a coalition and decided to attack the Hebrews. The coalition gathered at the "waters of Merom" (11:5; possibly to be identified as Lake Huleh, located a few miles north of the Sea of Galilee). The armies of Joshua marched from Gilgal to Merom, surprising the northern coalition with an immediate attack. The Israelites then marched on Hazor, the most formidable city in northern Canaan. They captured the city and burned it to the ground, taking no prisoners and leaving none of the inhabitants alive.

The defeat of the northern coalition effectively meant the end of the conquest of Canaan. Although pockets of resistance remained, the Israelites had successfully claimed the territory given them by the Lord. The areas conquered by Joshua and his armies are detailed in 11:16-23 while the roster of defeated kings is provided in 12:1-24. In all, the conquest of Canaan took seven years.

The Division of Canaan (13:1-21:45)

The third major section of the book records the division of Canaan among the tribes of Israel. The section begins with a list of those territories that were left unconquered (13:1-7). These included the territories of the Philistines and the Phoenicians. Joshua 13:8-33 is a record of the division of the land east of the Jordan. This region was divided between the tribes of Reuben, Gad, and the half-tribe of Manasseh. These tribes were primarily herdsmen anxious to graze their livestock in the rich lands across the Jordan. The other nine and a half tribes received territory in Canaan proper (14:1-5). The selection of territory was done by means of casting lots, a process that ensured that it was the Lord who gave each tribe their respective territory (cf. Prov. 16:33). The tribe of Levi was not given an inheritance of territory (cf. Gen. 49:7). For his mighty deeds of valor, Caleb was given the city of Hebron (14:6-15).

The portion for Judah (15:1-63) stretched from the brook of Egypt to the northern tip of the Dead Sea. The principle cities in this territory included Beersheba, Hebron, and Lachish. The portion for Ephraim and Manasseh (16:1-17:18) included the cities of Shiloh, Beth Shan, and Megiddo. The portion for Benjamin (18:11-28) included the cities of Jericho, Bethel, Gibeon, Ramah, and Jerusalem. The portion for Simeon (19:1-9) consisted of 17 cities and towns within the territory given to Judah (cf. Gen. 49:7). The portion for Zebulun (19:10-16) included Nazareth even though the city is not mentioned in the text. The portion for Issachar (19:17-23) included the famous Valley of Jezreel, site of many famous battles in the Old Testament. The portion for Asher (19:24-31) included the cities of Aphek, Tyre, and Sidon. The portion for Naphtali (19:32-39) included the cities of Hamath and Beth Shemesh. The portion for Dan (19:40-48) consisted of 17 towns of which none are notable except Joppa. The Danites quickly grew tired of the territory given to them by the Lord and eventually migrated north, conquering Laish and renaming it Dan (Jud. 18). For his mighty deeds of valor, Joshua was given the city of Timnath Serah (19:49-51).

The cities given to the Levites are detailed in chapters twenty and twenty-one. These forty-eight cities were scattered throughout the territories inhabited by the other tribes. The roster included the six cities of refuge appointed by the Lord to provide protection to those who kill unintentionally (20:1-9; cf. Ex. 21:13; Num. 35:6-34; Deut. 19:1-10). The cities of refuge are Kedesh (located in the territory of Naphtali), Shechem (Ephraim), Hebron (Judah), Bezer (Reuben), Ramoth (Gad), and Golan (Manasseh). Other notable cities given to the tribe of Levi include Beth Shemesh, Gibeon, Gezer, and Heshbon. It has been estimated that no one in Israel lived more than ten miles from a Levitical town.[26]

Conclusion (22:1-24:33)

Following the conquest of the land, the eastern tribes were given permission by Joshua to return to their territories. The men of Reuben, Gad, and the half-tribe of Manasseh were given a considerable amount of the spoil taken from the conquered cities. They were also provided with a parting word from their general. Joshua encouraged them to: 1) "be very careful to observe the commandment and the Law;" 2) "love the Lord your God;" 3) "walk in all His ways;" 4) "keep His commandments;" 5) "hold fast to Him;" and 6) "serve Him with all your heart and with all your soul" (22:5).

Leaving Shiloh, the eastern tribes journeyed towards the region of Gilead. When they got to the Jordan they built an altar to the Lord. The western tribes misconstrued the actions of these tribes, mistakenly believing that they were erecting an idolatrous altar. A delegation led by Phinehas (cf. Num. 25:6-13) approached the eastern tribes and warned them concerning their apostasy. The eastern tribes responded with candor, explaining that they had erected the altar as a memorial, not as a place of worship. This explanation was accepted by Phinehas and the crisis was averted.

At some point subsequent to the events of chapter twenty-two, Joshua called for the elders of Israel and gave them a final charge. In his speech, Joshua gave three exhortations. These exhortations were based on the fact that the Lord had given the nation success in their conquest of the land. God had driven out the pagan nations of Canaan just as He had promised. The first exhortation given by Joshua was to "keep and do all that is written in the book of the Law of Moses" (23:6). The commandments of Moses were designed to keep the Israelites holy; separate from the nations that surrounded them. The second exhortation was to "cling to the Lord" (23:8). The nation needed to be faithful to Yahweh and abstain from worshipping other gods. The third exhortation was to "love the Lord" (23:11). This command summarized the first two. In other words, the nation was expected to demonstrate their love for Yahweh by being obedient and faithful to Him. Joshua next cautioned the nation from having any associations with the Canaanites who remained in the land. The great leader concluded his speech with a sharp warning. He informed the nation that the Lord would destroy them if they "transgress the covenant of the Lord" and "go and serve other gods" (23:16).

The final chapter of Joshua records one last covenant renewal ceremony (cf. 5:2-11; 8:30-35). As the nation gathered at Shechem to present themselves before God, Joshua uttered his final words to the entire nation. Shechem was a perfect location for this speech. The city was situated in a valley between Mount Ebal and Mount Gerizim. This valley formed a natural ampitheater where a speaker's voice could be heard by those sitting on either hillside. The great leader began his speech with a review of the acts of Yahweh on behalf of the nation. The Lord had chosen Abraham and had led him to the land of Canaan. God further blessed Abraham by giving him Isaac. God later blessed Isaac with Jacob and Esau. The Lord then sent Moses and Aaron to deliver the Israelites from the land of Egypt, performing a number of miracles on their behalf. God even turned the attempted curse of Balaam into a blessing. Most recently, the Lord had given the nation the land of Canaan; the land that He had originally promised to Abraham.

Joshua continued his speech with a series of exhortations. The great leader commanded the nation to "fear the Lord," "serve Him in sincerity and truth," "put away the gods" of Ur and Egypt, and "serve the Lord" (24:14). Joshua concluded his speech with a final plea. The nation had an option. They could serve foreign gods or they could serve Yahweh. For Joshua's family, the choice was clear. They would serve the Lord.

The nation responded to Joshua's plea with a commitment to serve the Lord. Joshua replied with the prophetic words, "You will not be able to serve the Lord" (24:19). The nation, however, insisted that they would be able to serve the Lord. Joshua then commanded the people to put away their foreign gods and incline their hearts to the Lord. Following his conversation with the people, the great leader wrote the commitment of the nation on a large stone and erected it by the sanctuary of the Lord as a witness against the nation.

The book of Joshua concludes with an appendix describing various events that took place after the covenant renewal ceremony that took place at Shechem. The first event recorded is the death and burial of Joshua (24:29-31). The great leader lived to be 110 years old. He was buried in his hometown. The second event is the burial of Joseph's bones (24:32). Joseph's deathbed command concerning his bones is one of the greatest acts of faith recorded in Scripture (Gen. 50:25; cf. Heb. 11:22). The final event recorded in Joshua is the death and burial of Eleazar, the high priest (24:33). Eleazar was the son and successor of Aaron.

Study Questions

1. Should Joshua be placed alongside the Torah to form a hexateuch or should the book be categorized as a historical book? Be sure to explain your answer.
2. Joshua appears by name in how many biblical books?
3. Do you hold to the early or late date for the Exodus? Be sure to defend your answer.
4. Identify the three major powers in the Ancient Near East during this period of biblical history.

5. Briefly describe the Canaanites.
6. Why did God call for the extermination of the Canaanites?
7. What is the major theme of the book of Joshua?
8. List the five principles of the Canaanite "holy war."
9. List the three covenant-renewal ceremonies highlighted in the book of Joshua.
10. Do you believe that it was okay for Rahab to lie to the king of Jericho? Why or why not?
11. Why does the nation get circumcised immediately upon entering the Promised Land?
12. Why did the Israelites lose their first battle against Ai?
13. What city was given to Caleb for his mighty deeds of valor?
14. List the six cities of refuge.

CHAPTER 2

Judges

"And there arose another generation . . . who did not know the Lord, nor yet the work which He had done for Israel. Then the sons of Israel did evil in the sight of the Lord, and served the Baals, and they forsook the Lord, the God of their fathers, who had brought them out of the land of Egypt, and followed other gods from among the gods of the peoples who were around them, and bowed themselves down to them, thus they provoked the Lord to anger. In those days there was no king in Israel; everyone did what was right in his own eyes" (Jud. 2:10b-12; 21:25).

The book of Judges[1] traces the history of Israel from the death of Joshua to the birth of Samuel. It continues the story of the Conquest, yet marks a dramatic turning point from success to failure. "The landscape of near-total victory, laid out for us in Joshua, is quickly redrawn in Judges as tribe after tribe meets armed resistance that it cannot overcome."[2] As a result, the Israelites are forced to withdraw to defensive strongholds in the central highlands. The various tribes of Israel are no longer led by a national leader; instead, they are led by tribal chieftains and groups of elders. The lack of a centralized government leads to tribal schisms and even outright civil war. It is in the midst of this turmoil that the Lord raises up a series of judges to deliver His people.

The title "judge" (Heb. *shophet*) means "deliverer" or "one bringing justice." Although the title implies that judges served as arbitrators in civil and social disputes (priests served as arbitrators in religious matters), there is very little evidence in the book that they ever served in this role (Deborah is a notable exception; cf. 4:5). The judges primarily functioned as military leaders. Therefore, the deliverance provided by these judges was the relief of the oppression brought on Israel by foreign nations. In this way, the period of the judges foreshadowed the monarchy. The primary role of a king in the ancient world was to protect his subjects by leading his armies in battle. Unlike kings, however, the judges did not establish a dynasty or ruling family. Also, the judge was not selected officially by the people; he was raised up by the Lord.

The judges do not appear to have served in any sort of religious capacity (again, Deborah is a notable exception; cf. 4:4). They never appear at the tabernacle. They do not call on the people to return to the Lord. They never perform a covenant renewal ceremony. The Ark of the Covenant, which played such an important role in Joshua and will play a major role in Samuel, is mentioned only one time in Judges, and that reference is in passing (Jud. 20:27).

Although the judges do not perform any spiritual functions, they are routinely filled with the Spirit (3:10; 6:34; 11:29; 13:25; 14:6, 19; 15:14). This fact demonstrates that the Lord was the One ultimately responsible for the deliverance achieved by the judges. As a result, God is the true hero of the book. In the Old Testament, the Lord's Spirit empowered an individual to complete a specific task. This task might involve craftsmanship (e.g., Bezalel; Ex. 35:31), speech (e.g., Balaam; Num. 24:2), leadership (e.g., David; 1 Sam. 16:13), military strength (e.g., judges), or even the ability to prophesy (e.g., Saul; 1 Sam. 10:10; 19:23). This filling was not permanent (cf. 1 Sam. 16:14; Ps. 51:11), as is the indwelling of the Spirit in the New Testament (cf. 2 Cor. 1:22; Eph. 4:30).

Even though the judges are often filled with the spirit, their spiritual character is somewhat suspect. The apostate tendencies of the judges are routinely emphasized. Ehud used deceit to assassinate Eglon. Gideon led the nation into idolatry by erecting an ephod in Ophrah. Jephthah sacrificed his daughter as a burnt offering. Samson carried on illicit affairs with Philistine women, broke all three parts of his Nazirite vow, and then committed suicide. Unfortunately, the period of the judges was characterized by moral and spiritual apostasy on the part of the entire nation, not just the judges.

The total number of judges identified in this book is twelve, an apparent attempt by the final editor to correspond the number of judges to the number of tribes in Israel. An addition of all the years of oppression and rest recorded in the book yields a total of 407 years. This number is much too great to fit between the death of Joshua (ca. 1370 B.C. and the birth of Samuel (ca. 1120 B.C.). Some scholars take the figures presented in Judges as "round numbers" (e.g., 10, 20, 40, 80), however, the presence of several specific numbers (e.g., 6, 7, 8, 18, 22, 23) renders this view implausible.

It is very likely that many, if not all, of the judges exercised influence only over their local jurisdiction. This allows the years recorded in Judges to overlap. The nations that oppressed Israel were variously located on all sides of the nation. The Canaanites were located in the north, the Midianites, Moabites, and Ammonites in the east, the Amalekites in the south, and the Philistines in the southwest.

Modern scholars commonly divide the judges into two categories, "major" and "minor." These terms are used to denote their respective treatment in the book of Judges rather than to imply greater or lesser historical significance. The major judges are Othniel, Ehud, Deborah, Gideon, Jephthah, and Samson. The minor judges are Shamgar, Tola, Jair, Ibzan, Elon, and Abdon.

Author

While the Bible does not identify the author of this book, tradition has long held that the book was written by Samuel. The primary support for Samuel authorship comes from the Babylonian Talmud, which ascribes the books of Judges, Ruth, and Samuel to the prophet (*Baba Bathra* 14b). Samuel is thought by many to be the greatest Old Testament figure since Moses (cf. Jer. 15:1). He was the son of Elkanah and Hannah. Samuel was a Levite who was born in the hill country of Ephraim. He spent his youth ministering in the house of the Lord in Shiloh in fulfillment of an oath taken by his mother. The honorable young boy served as a striking contrast to Hophni and Phinehas, the disreputable sons of the high priest Eli. Samuel was the final judge of Israel. As such, he was responsible for ushering in the nation's monarchy, anointing both Saul and David as kings of Israel. Samuel was also a prophet (1 Sam. 3:20). In fact, he was the first in a succession of prophets that continued through the end of the Old Testament (Acts 3:24). At his death, "all Israel gathered together and mourned for him" (1 Sam. 25:1). Samuel was buried at his home in Ramah, a village located about five miles north of Jerusalem.

Although Samuel is probably the author of the majority of the book, the final edition was likely completed about a decade after his death (ca. 1020 B.C.), probably by one of his disciples (perhaps a member of the "company of the prophets" presided over by Samuel; cf. 1 Sam. 19:20). The book may have been written in Ramah, the home of Samuel and probable center of the school of prophets.

Date

Like the books of Psalms and Proverbs, it is at once apparent that the book of Judges was compiled over the course of several centuries. The book includes a series of narratives that were probably composed shortly after the recorded events took place. For example, the Song of Deborah recorded in chapter five dates to an early period in Israel's history; almost assuredly a pre-monarchical period.[3] These narratives were then put into a collective book by a later editor. The book has an obvious prologue (1:1-3:6) and epilogue (17:1-21:25). The epilogue was probably the final portion written. The refrain "in those days there was no king in Israel" (cf. 17:6; 18:1; 21:25; see also 19:1) points to a period after the monarchy was established (ca. 1051 B.C.). The fact that there are several differences in the elements present in the various cycles indicates that the final editor made no substantial effort to conform them to a uniform style.[4]

The reference to the Jebusites living in Jerusalem "to this day" in 1:21 indicates that the book could not have been written after ca. 1004 B.C., the date of David's conquest of Jerusalem. It has been argued that the reference to "the day of the captivity of the land" in 18:30 proves that the book was written after the Assyrian exile of the northern kingdom in 722 B.C.[5] or even after the Babylonian exile of the southern kingdom in 586 B.C.[6] However, The enigmatic phrase seems to be parallel with "as long as the house of God was at Shiloh" (18:31). As a result, it must indicate a local captivity that occurred prior to the house of God being moved to Nob (ca. 1050 B.C.; cf. 1 Sam. 21:1ff). The phrase could easily refer to a localized oppression in the region of Dan. It is also possible that the reference is to the Philistine oppression during the time when the tabernacle was at Shiloh.

The political overtones of the epilogue suggest a date early in the reign of David. In the story of the Levite and his concubine a Levite journeys from the hill country of Ephraim to the city of Bethlehem in Judah. While visiting Bethlehem, the Levite is amply provided with food, drink, and lodging. In fact, when the Levite tries to leave the city on three different occasions, his host convinces him to tarry with offers of sustenance and lodging. Finally, the Levite makes a successful departure and journeys to the territory of Benjamin. The Levite's servant suggests that they stop in the city of Jerusalem for the night. However, the priest insists on proceeding further, refusing to stay in a city inhabited by foreigners. At last, they decide to stop in Gibeah. While in Gibeah, the men of the city attempt to sodomize the priest. Instead, the Levite threw his concubine out of the house where he was staying to satisfy the sexual appetite of the men. The men of Gibeah raped the concubine through the night and in the morning left her to die. After the death of his concubine, the Levite dismembers her body and sends it throughout Israel, thus rallying the tribes to make war upon Benjamin. This polemical story would have served to encourage the men of Ephraim, the most powerful tribe in the north, to join with the tribe of Judah (Bethlehem was the home of David) against Benjamin (Gibeah was the home of Saul). When seen in this light, the most obvious occasion for the book was the period of civil war between the house of David and the house of Saul (ca. 1011-1004 B.C.).[7] The story also emphasizes the need for Israel to conquer Jerusalem; David's first order of business upon gaining the throne.

Historical Background

The events recorded in the book of Judges take place between ca. 1366 B.C. (the death of Joshua) and ca. 1084 B.C. (the death of Samson).[8] During the period of the Judges, Israel[9] was oppressed by several of its surrounding nations, including the Amalekites, Ammonites, Canaanites, Midianites, Moabites, and Philistines. The primary reason Israel experienced continual oppression at this time was because of their failure to fully conquer the land (Josh. 13:1; Jud. 1:2-36). As a result, the Lord allowed these foreign nations to remain in order "to test Israel by them" (3:1).

Unfortunately, Israel failed the test. They continually succumbed to the temptation of foreign religion, falling into idolatry with the gods of the surrounding nations (cf. 3:7). Of particular significance in Judges is the religion of the Canaanites which centered on the worship of Baal and Ashtaroth (2:13). The Canaanite religion "was based on the assumption that the forces of nature are expressions of divine presence and activity and that the only way one could survive and prosper was to identify the gods responsible for each phenomenon and by proper ritual engage them to bring to bear their respective powers."[10] This ritual commonly involved sexual activity meant to excite Baal, the storm god manifested through rainfall, thunder, and lightning. The Canaanites believed that the rainfall represented the semen of Baal which fell to the earth to fertilize the soil, thus creating life. In hopes of getting Baal to send rain (i.e., ejaculate), the Canaanites employed a number of male and female cultic prostitutes who would perform sexual acts on the "high places" (cf. Hos. 10:8) while Baal lustfully watched from heaven. Israel's apostasy was "turning from Yahweh, the real source of prosperity and fertility, to the figment of depraved imaginations which confused the result of divine blessing with its cause. It was in every way an egregious act of covenant rebellion and disloyalty best described as 'whoring after other gods' (2:17, KJV)."[11]

In terms of the major world powers, the great empires of the Hittittes, Assyrians, and Egyptians are completely ignored in Judges. These nations were exclusively preoccupied with controlling the major trade routes of the Ancient Near East. Since Israel was primarily confined to the hill country of central Canaan, they had little influence on the major trade routes passing through the region. As a result, the tiny nation existed in a sort of political vacuum, insulated from the events taking place on the international level.

During the period of the judges, Egypt was governed by the eighteenth, nineteenth, and twentieth dynasties. Although Canaan was technically an Egyptian province during the Conquest, the Egyptians took little or no interest in the territory despite the desperate appeals of their Canaanite vassals to do otherwise (e.g., Amarna Letters).[12] The Egyptians finally managed to invade Canaan during the reign of Seti I (1318-1304 B.C.); however, they marched through the coastal plains to the Valley of Jezreel, avoiding any contact with the Israelites who occupied the hill country of central Canaan.

The great Rameses II (1304-1236 B.C.) likewise led military expeditions through Canaan but also managed to avoid Israel altogether. In his fifth year, he led a noteworthy campaign against the Hittites, suffering a major defeat at Kadesh on the Orontes. Rameses would eventually make a parity treaty with the Hittites in 1284 B.C., solidifying the pact with his marriage to the daughter of Hattushilish, the Hittite monarch. The only other Egyptian pharaoh to invade Canaan during this period was Merneptah (1236-1223 B.C.). The campaign of Merneptah is of special significance because it is described on the so-called Israel Stele (Merneptah Stele). On this inscription, the pharaoh mentions the nation of Israel by name, the first known reference to Israel outside of the Scriptures.[13]

In Asia Minor, the Hittite Empire experienced a resurgence around the time of Joshua's death. This resurgence was led by Suppiluliumash (1380-1346 B.C.). Under Suppiluliumash, the Hittite Empire became the preeminent force in the eastern Mediterranean world. Following a series of battles, the Hittites were finally able to destroy the Hurrian Empire of Mitanni in ca. 1350 B.C. Suppiluliumash probably would have attempted to conquer the newly formed state of Israel if not for the rise of the Neo-Assyrian Empire to the east. It is also possible that he stayed out of Canaan because he did not want to anger the Egyptians. The Hittite resurgence was short-lived, however, as Egypt and Assyria continued to grow in strength while the Hittites declined in power. The great

Hittite Empire came to a sudden and violent end ca. 1200 B.C. with the invasion of the Sea Peoples from the west.

In Mesopotamia, the Assyrians had steadily grown in power and influence and dominated the entire region. The Assyrians had originally migrated north from Babylon and settled in the region surrounding Nineveh, the city founded by Nimrod (Gen. 10:11). The land of Assyria straddled the upper Tigris River. It was almost completely surrounded by mountains; the Zagros on the east, the Armenian on the north, the Hamrin Hills in the south, and a low-lying ridge in the west that separated the Assyrian heartland from the Jazira steppe.[14] Assyria was governed by a collection of powerful city-states, including Ashur, Calah, and Nineveh. Ashur was located on the west bank of the Tigris River, about sixty miles south of Nineveh, which was situated on the east bank of the Tigris. Calah was located about twenty miles south of Nineveh and was also on the east bank of the Tigris.

The Assyrians worshipped a pantheon of gods, including Ashur, the chief god; Sin, the moon god; Shamash, the sun god; and Ishtar, the goddess of love. These gods were often treated as humans, being fed, bathed, and carried in processionals. The temples built in the names of these gods were buildings of great splendor and wealth. The king of Assyria was recognized as the high priest of Ashur. As a result, he led the various cultic ceremonies prescribed in the religious calendar. The Assyrian religion was characterized by strict ceremony, omen divination, exorcism, incantation, and astrology.[15]

With the fall of the Hurrian Empire in ca. 1350, the Assyrian Empire filled the void and occupied the territory of Mitanni. The Assyrian emergence was led by Ashur-Uballit (1365-1330 B.C.), who came to the throne at about the same time that Joshua died. Although the Assyrians dominated Mesopotamia, they were unable to make extensive forays into Canaan. This is because they were preoccupied with the Kassites of Babylon to the south and the Hittite Empire to the west. The only other king of any real significance during this period was Tiglath-Pileser I (1115-1077 B.C.). Tiglath-Pileser was able to extend the Assyrian Empire to the Mediterranean coast, exercising considerable influence over the Phoenicians and Hittites. Even Egypt was forced to recognize the power of the

Assyrians. However, Tiglath-Pileser made no attempt to extend his empire south into Canaan.

While the Egyptians, Hittites, and Assyrians do not play a significant role in Israel's history during the period of the judges, a foreign power that does impact the nation is the Sea Peoples, specifically the Philistines.[16] The Sea Peoples left[17] their coastal homes in Greece, Asia Minor, and the Aegean Islands (including Crete) and invaded the coast along the eastern Mediterranean. They also attempted to settle on the Egyptian coast, however, Rameses III was able to repel them on both land and sea in the eighth year of his reign (ca. 1190 B.C.).[18] The Philistines[19] from Crete (Caphtor; cf. Jer. 47:4; Amos 9:7) settled in southwestern Canaan and established a firm stronghold thanks to the Philistine pentapolis of Gaza, Gath, Ekron, Ashkelon, and Ashdod. Each of these cities was governed by a "lord" (Heb. *seren*; cf. 3:3).

The Philistines were the primary adversaries of Israel from ca. 1200 to ca. 1000 B.C. They stood out from their neighbors because they did not practice circumcision, hence the derisive term "uncircumcised Philistines" (14:3). The Philistines were more technologically advanced than the Hebrews, having learned the art of working with iron tools and weapons (cf. 1 Sam. 13:19-20). Little is known of the Philistine language because no obvious examples of Philistine writing have been found. However, the pottery of the Philistines is particularly well-known, primarily because of its distinctive shapes and colors. Typical shapes include the globular pilgrim jar, the delicate high-stemmed kylix, the large pyriform jar, the squat pyxis, and the popular stirrup jar.[20] The pottery was usually decorated in red and black motifs. The religion of the Philistines is also well-known. Their chief god was Dagon, the father of Baal. Dagon was often represented as a human head with the body of a fish. Dagon was worshipped in Mesopotamia as a grain god. It is possible that the originally seafaring Philistines brought their fish god with them when they migrated to Canaan and then adapted him to the Semitic god Dagon (or Dagan, as it is known outside the Bible), because of their need to become a grain-producing people (Jud. 15:3-5).[21] Ashtoreth[22] was the Philistine goddess of love and sometime consort of Baal. Baal-zebub was the patron god of Ekron (cf. 2 Kin. 1:2-3).

His name means "lord of the flies," and is probably a derogatory emendation of Baal-zebul, meaning "lord Baal." Notable Philistines mentioned in the Old Testament include Goliath and Achish.

Audience and Purpose

The book of Judges was written to a generation of Jews that was struggling to find a national identity in the midst of yet another civil war. Under the leadership of the judges, the nation had continually fallen into a snare of moral and spiritual apostasy. The Israelites intermarried with foreigners, worshipped other gods, committed heinous acts, and even fell into outright civil wars. This pattern of covenant disobedience was followed by the discipline of the Lord. With each successive judge, the situation became more and more desperate. Those responsible for teaching and enforcing[23] the Law in Israel, the priests, had failed in their God-given role (cf. Jud. 17-21; 1 Sam. 2-4). As a result, the Law was not known by the average Israelite. This lack of knowledge created a situation where "everyone did what was right in his own eyes" (21:25). The nation had forgotten the God who had so richly blessed them with redemption from Egypt and an inheritance in Canaan.

While Israel proved faithless, Yahweh proved faithful. The covenant failures of the people were met by covenant faithfulness from their God.[24] Being moved to mercy by the cries of the nation, the Lord regularly raised up judges to bring deliverance to the Israelites. These judges provided the people with temporary rest. However, the judges were not able to bring about lasting righteousness. The nation needed a king.

Yet even the institution of the monarchy did not bring an end to the suffering of the people. Throughout the reign of Saul, the nation was oppressed by the Philistines. Eventually, Saul himself would fall at the hands of his enemies. With the death of Saul came more civil war. What the nation needed was the right king; a faithful king after God's own heart; a righteous king who would keep the people from Baal-worship; a military king who would bring peace to the beleaguered nation; a charismatic king who would unite the tribes. The nation needed David. This book serves as a call for the nation to unite under the leadership of the right king, chosen by God and anointed by Samuel.

Structure and Outline

The book of Judges is naturally divided into four sections. The first section (1:1-2:5) serves as a prologue, relating Judges back to the book of Joshua and revealing that the nation had failed to fully conquer the land. The second section (2:6-3:6) functions as an introduction to the period of the judges. The third section (3:7-16:31) recounts the exploits of the various judges called by God to deliver His people. The fourth and final section (17:1-21:25) serves as an epilogue, providing ample evidence of the tribal apostasy that existed during this chaotic period in Israel's history; a sad state of affairs that emphasized the need for a monarchy in Israel.

The second section introduces the cycle of sin that will be repeated throughout the third section. The cycle begins with the observation that "the sons of Israel did evil in the sight of the Lord" (2:11). The Lord responded to the sins of the Israelites by allowing a neighboring tribe to oppress them (2:14). When the nation could no longer endure their suffering, they cried out to the Lord for salvation (2:18). The Lord responded with pity, raising up judges to liberate the oppressed Israelites (2:18). Following their deliverance, the nation experienced a period of rest until the judge died, after which the cycle began again (2:19). These elements can be summarized with the alliteration formula Sin, Servitude, Supplication, Salvation, and Silence. Although each cycle does not contain all of these elements, the overall pattern is generally consistent.

The third section is a record of six of these cycles of sin. Each cycle is introduced by the observation that "the sons of Israel did evil in the sight of the Lord" (3:7, 12; 4:1; 6:1; 10:6; 13:1). The record of cycles is best described as a "downward spiral."[25] The cycles demonstrate a deterioration in the quality of the judges and the effect of their leadership.[26] Othniel serves as the model judge. Ehud delivers Israel, but uses deceit and treachery to accomplish his mission. Deborah reveals the failure of male leadership in the land as Barak twice loses the glory that should be his to a woman (first Deborah, then Jael). Gideon achieves a great victory but then leads Israel into idolatry. Jephthah also achieves a great victory but then sacrifices his daughter to the Lord. Samson is clearly the worst judge, seducing Philistine women, breaking all three parts of his nazirite vow, and eventually committing suicide to end his tragic life.

The final section is a unit, linked by the repeated refrain "in those days there was no king in Israel" (cf. 17:6; 18:1; 21:25; see also 19:1). The events of these chapters are out of place chronologically. The Levite of chapters seventeen and eighteen is identified as Jonathan, the son of Gershom, the son of Moses (18:30, NIV, NRSV; cf. Ex. 2:22), a fact which indicates that these chapters took place shortly after the death of Joshua. The reference to Phinehas, the son of Eleazar, the son of Aaron, in 20:28 reveals that the events of chapters 19-21 also took place shortly after the death of Joshua. Further proof that these events are out of chronological order is the fact that Bethel is identified as the residence of the Ark of the Covenant (20:26-28). During the latter years of the period of the judges the Ark was located at Shiloh (cf. 1 Sam. 4:3). These chapters are intentionally placed at the end of the book to show the failure of the priesthood and the resultant extent of Israel's moral degradation.

Outline

I. Prologue: The Failure of the Nation to Expel the Canaanites (1:1-2:5)
    A. The success of Judah and Simeon (1:1-20)
    B. The failure of Benjamin (1:21)
    C. The partial success of Ephraim and Manasseh (1:22-29)
    D. The failure of the northern tribes (1:30-36)
    E. The Angel of the Lord at Bochim (2:1-5)
II. The Introduction to the History of the Judges (2:6-3:6)
    A. The passing of Joshua (2:6-10)
    B. The pattern of the period of the Judges (2:11-19)
    C. The penalty for the broken covenant (2:20-23)
    D. The list of oppressing nations (3:1-6)
III. The Judges of Israel (3:7-16:31)
    A. Othniel the judge (3:7-11)

B. Ehud the judge (3:12-30)
C. Shamgar the judge (3:31)
D. Deborah the judge (4:1-5:31)
    1. The victory of Deborah and Barak (4:1-24)
    2. The Song of Deborah (5:1-31)
E. Gideon the judge (6:1-8:35)
    1. The oppression of the Midianites (6:1-10)
    2. The call of Gideon (6:11-24)
    3. Gideon's altar (6:25-32)
    4. Gideon's fleece (6:33-40)
    5. Gideon's army (7:1-8)
    6. Gideon's first victory (7:9-25)
    7. The response of the men of Ephraim (8:1-3)
    8. Gideon's second victory (8:4-21)
    9. Gideon's ephod (8:22-31)
    10. The death of Gideon (8:32-35)
F. Abimelech the pseudo-king (9:1-57)
G. Tola the judge (10:1-2)
H. Jair the judge (10:3-5)
I. Jephthah the judge (10:6-12:7)
    1. The oppression of the Ammonites (10:6-18)
    2. The introduction of Jephthah (11:1-3)
    3. The selection of Jephthah (11:4-11)
    4. Jephthah's message to the king of Ammon (11:12-28)
    5. Jephthah's victory (11:29-33)
    6. Jephthah's sacrifice (11:34-40)
    7. The response of the men of Ephraim (12:1-6)
    8. The death of Jephthah (12:7)
J. Ibzan the judge (12:8-10)
K. Elon the judge (12:11-12)
L. Abdon the judge (12:13-15)
M. Samson the judge (13:1-16:31)
    1. The birth of Samson (13:1-25)
    2. Samson and the woman of Timnah (14:1-15:20)
    3. Samson and the harlot of Gaza (16:1-3)
    4. Samson and Delilah (16:4-20)
    5. The death of Samson (16:21-31)

IV. Epilogue: Tribal Depravity (17:1-21:25)
   A. Religious apostasy (17:1-18:31)
      1. The idolatry of Micah (17:1-13)
      2. The migration of the Danites (18:1-31)
   B. Moral degradation (19:1-21:25)
      1. The atrocity of Gibeah (19:1-30)
      2. The war against the tribe of Benjamin (20:1-48)
      3. The provision for the tribe of Benjamin (21:1-25)

Summary of Contents

Prologue: The Failure of the Nation to Expel the Canaanites (1:1-2:5)

The book of Judges begins with the traditional Hebrew formula *hayah* ("Now it came about;" cf. Joshua, Ruth, 1 Samuel, 2 Samuel, Esther). The time frame given is "after the death of Joshua" (1:1). This phrase naturally leads the reader back to the final chapter of Joshua where the death of Israel's great general was described (Josh. 24:29). The clear implication is that the book of Judges continues the story of Joshua. Joshua is mentioned seven times in Judges; all occurring in the first two chapters.

The book opens with a question[27] to the Lord by the sons of Israel, "Who shall go up first for us against the Canaanites, to fight against them?" (1:1). While it is probable that the nation is seeking an individual replacement for Joshua, God answered by specifying which tribe should lead the war effort. Yahweh replied, "Judah shall go up; behold, I have given the land into his hand" (1:2). The Lord's selection of Judah as his instrument of military justice is fitting, since Judah is predicted in Genesis 49:8 as the tribe who will deliver the other tribes from their enemies. The men of Judah, aided by the men of Simeon, attacked the Canaanites and Perizzites at Bezek, defeating ten thousand warriors. The city of Bezek is located about three miles northeast of Gezer. Following his defeat, the commander of the Canaanite and Perizzite forces, identified as Adoni-Bezek ("lord of Bezek"), attempts to flee from the Israelites. However, the king is quickly captured and taken to Jerusalem where he eventually dies.

At this point, the reader is informed how it happened that Jerusalem came to be in Israel's possession. To do this, the author uses the literary device of a flashback to an earlier period when Joshua was still alive.[28] Although the conquest of Jerusalem was not specifically recorded in the book of Joshua, it is probable that the city fell at some point shortly after the defeat and death of Adoni-Zedek, king of Jerusalem (Josh. 10). Upon its capture, the Israelites slew the inhabitants and burned the city. Unfortunately, the tribe of Benjamin allowed the Jebusites to return to the city shortly thereafter (cf. Josh. 15:63; Jud. 1:21).

Following their great victory at Bezek, the Judahites swept through the rest of their territory, systematically overcoming the major strongholds. The cities of Hebron, Debir, Hormah, Gaza, Ashkelon, and Ekron are specifically mentioned. The city of Hebron was the inheritance of Caleb (Josh. 14:13). The conquest of Debir was accomplished by Othniel, the younger brother of Caleb and first judge. For his heroic act, he was given Achsah, the daughter of Caleb, as his wife. The city of Zephath was completely destroyed, hence the name change to Hormah (from *herem*, "the ban;" cf. Josh. 6:17). The cities of Gaza, Ashkelon, and Ekron will eventually become Philistine strongholds. Although the Judahites experienced great victories in the hill country, they were unable to drive out the inhabitants of the plains because they had iron chariots, the tanks of ancient warfare.

Like Judah, the tribes of Joseph (Ephraim and Manasseh) experienced early success followed by unfortunate failure. These tribes were able to conquer Bethel when they bribed a man to show them the entrance into the city. However, Manasseh failed to capture the cities of Beth-shean (Beth Shan), Taanach, Dor, Ibleam, and Megiddo while Ephraim failed to drive out the Canaanites in Gezer. Likewise, the tribes of Zebulun, Asher, Naphtali, and Dan failed to fully occupy their territory.

To explain the reason for the nation's failure to fully conquer to land, the Angel of the Lord appeared to the Israelites at Bochim. The Angel of the Lord was a manifestation of Yahweh Himself (cf. Josh. 5:13-15; Jud. 6:12, 14, 16, 23, 25, 27).[29] The Angel informed the people that they were unable to drive out the various nations of

Canaan because they had been unfaithful to their covenant obligations. The nation had made a covenant with the Gibeonites and had failed to tear down the altars of the Canaanite gods. Hearing the words of the Lord, the people lifted up their voices and wept, hence the name Bochim ("the weepers"). The nation then offered sacrifices to the Lord.

The Introduction to the History of the Judges (2:6-3:6)

The second major section of the book serves as an introduction to the period of the judges. The account of Joshua's death is repeated, serving to tie the material that follows to the historical record begun in the book of Joshua.[30] The passage of 2:11-19 introduces the cycle of sin that will be repeated throughout the remainder of the book. The cycle begins with the observation that "the sons of Israel did evil in the sight of the Lord" (2:11). The Lord responded to the sins of the Israelites by allowing a neighboring tribe to oppress them (2:14). When the nation could no longer endure their suffering, they cried out to the Lord for salvation (2:18). The Lord responded with pity, raising up judges to liberate the oppressed Israelites (2:18). Following their deliverance, the nation experienced a period of rest until the judge died, after which the cycle began again (2:19).

Because the nation had consistently broken the covenant given to their ancestors, the Lord allowed the heathen nations that surrounded Israel to remain in the land. These foreigners were used by God to test the faithfulness of the Israelites. These nations included the Philistines, Canaanites, Phoenicians (Sidonians), Hivites, Hittites, Amorites, Perizzites, and Jebusites. The sons of Israel failed the test, intermarrying with these foreigners and serving their gods.

The Judges of Israel (3:7-16:31)

The first judge of Israel was Othniel (3:7-11). When the Israelites forgot the Lord their God and served the Baals[31] and the Asheroth, Yahweh allowed Cushan-Rishathaim, king of Mesopotamia, to oppress the nation. Cushan-Rishathaim is unknown in extrabiblical literature. He governed a territory identified as Aram Naharayim ("Aram of the two rivers"), probably to be identified with northern Syria. The oppression of Cushan-Rishathaim lasted for eight years (ca. 1358-1350 B.C.)[32] and probably affected the entire nation. In ca. 1350 B.C., the Lord raised up Othniel to deliver the Israelites. Othniel was the son of Kenaz, Caleb's younger brother. He was from the tribe of Judah, a fact which marks him as the model judge. Othniel, being filled with the Spirit of the Lord, defeated the Arameans and brought rest to the land for forty years (ca. 1350-1310 B.C.).

The second judge of Israel was Ehud (3:12-30). The name Ehud means "strong." When the Israelites again did evil in the sight of the Lord, He strengthened Eglon, king of Moab, to oppress the nation. The Moabites were the descendants of Moab, the son of Lot through his oldest daughter. They lived on the eastern side of the Jordan River and the Dead Sea, just to the south of the Ammonites. The land of Moab was famous for its pasturage. 2 Kings 3:4 testifies to the agricultural wealth of the area, "Now Mesha king of Moab was a sheep breeder, and used to pay the king of Israel 100,000 lambs and the wool of 100,000 rams." The climate of Moab also allowed for the growing of wheat, barley, vineyards, and fruit trees. The chief god of the Moabites was Chemosh (1 Kin. 11:7, 33). The worship of Chemosh included a priesthood (Jer. 48:7) and a sacrificial system (Num. 22:40; 25:2). Solomon married Moabite women and built a sanctuary for Chemosh on the Mount of Olives (1 Kin. 11:1, 7). Notable Moabites include Balak, the king who hired Balaam to curse the Children of Israel (Num. 22-24); Ruth, the widow of Mahlon and wife of Boaz (Ruth 4:10, 13); and Mesha, the king who rebelled against King Jehoram of Israel (2 Kin. 3).

Eglon was joined by the Ammonites and Amalekites, two nations that shared a close relationship with the Moabites. The Ammonites were the descendants of Ben-Ammi, the son of Lot through his youngest daughter. They lived on the eastern side of the Jordan River. The nation's territory was essentially surrounded by the Jabbok River and its tributaries. As a result, the border of Ammonite territory was referred to simply as the Jabbok River (Deut. 3:16; Josh. 12:2). The sources of the Jabbok River are near modern Amman, Jordan. This territory had previously belonged to the Rephaim, an ancient people who were displaced by the Ammonites (Deut. 2:20-21). Notable Ammonites include Naamah, the wife of Solomon and mother of Rehoboam (1 Kin. 14:21, 31; 2 Chron. 12:13), and

Tobiah, one of the major antagonists of Nehemiah (Neh. 2:19; 4:3). Solomon built a sanctuary for Molech, the "detestable" chief god of the Ammonites, on the Mount of Olives (1 Kin. 11:7). Child sacrifice was a significant part of the Ammonite Molech cult (Lev. 18:21; 20:2-5; 2 Kin. 23:10; Jer. 32:35).

The Amalekites were a nomadic tribe that dwelt in the desert region south of Judah. They were the descendants of Amalek, the grandson of Esau. Joshua fought against the Amalekites at Rephidim. Saul was commanded to "utterly destroy" them (1 Sam. 15:3), an order he disobeyed when he captured Agag and some livestock and brought them back to Israel. This fateful decision resulted in the Lord's punishment; i.e., the kingdom being torn from him and given to a "better" man (15:28). The "better" man David later fights against the Amalekites after their raid on Ziklag (1 Sam. 30).

The oppression of Eglon lasted for eighteen years (ca. 1310-1292 B.C.) and appears to be local. The text notes that the coalition was able to occupy the "city of the palm trees" (3:13; i.e., Jericho). To liberate Israel from their oppression, the Lord raised up Ehud, the son of Gera. Ehud was from the tribe of Benjamin and is noteworthy because he is identified as being a left-handed man. As he was preparing to bring tribute to Eglon, Ehud fashioned a double-edged sword[33] that was about a cubit (eighteen inches) in length and wore it on his right thigh. The positioning of the sword on his right thigh allowed him to hide the weapon from the king's bodyguards. When the tribute had been paid, Ehud informed the king that he had a secret message for him. The king naturally sent his bodyguards out of the room, eager to receive the message.

Informing Eglon that his message came directly from God, Ehud leaned forward and plunged his sword into the belly of the fat king. Leaving his weapon behind, Ehud made his escape, deceitfully telling the king's bodyguards that their master was "relieving himself" in the cool room (3:24; lit. "covering his feet," a euphemism for bodily excretion), a ploy designed to give him extra time to make his getaway. When he arrived in Seirah (an unknown location in the hill country of Ephraim), Ehud blew a trumpet, calling the sons of Israel to battle. The Israelites were able to defeat the Moabites, massacring ten thousand enemy warriors. The land then experienced peace for eighty years (ca. 1292-1212 B.C.), the longest period of rest identified in Judges. This time of rest must refer only to the local area surrounding Benjamin.

The third judge of Israel was Shamgar (3:31). The name Shamgar is Hurrian. Shamgar is identified simply as the son of Anath.[34] He may have been from the tribe of Naphtali, since Beth Anath is a city in their territory. Shamgar is said to have killed 600 Philistines with an "oxgoad," a device used to control the movement of oxen and other animals. An oxgoad can be a formidable weapon. It had a sharp metal point and was often close to ten feet long. This event probably took place shortly after the Sea Peoples invaded southwestern Canaan, perhaps about 1230 B.C. Since 4:1 continues the story of Judges from the point of Ehud's death, it can be assumed that Shamgar's judgeship took place prior to that event. The length of Shamgar's judgeship is unknown. According to Josephus (*Antiquities of the Jews* 5.4.3), Shamgar died in the same year he became judge.

The fourth judge of Israel was Deborah (4:1-5:31). The name Deborah means "honeybee." After the death of Ehud, the nation once again fell into apostasy. This time the Lord sold His people into the hands of Jabin, king of Canaan. Jabin ruled from Hazor, the most powerful city in northern Canaan. It was located about nine miles north of the Sea of Galilee. The name Jabin was probably the hereditary title of the rulers of Hazor (cf. Josh. 11:1-13), much like Abimelech among the Philistines and Ben-Hadad among the kings of Damascus. The commander of Jabin's army is identified as Sisera of Harosheth-Hagoyim, a town on the Kishon River east of Mount Carmel. The oppression of Jabin lasted for twenty years (ca. 1250-1230 B.C.) and appears to be local. The primary reason given for Jabin's military strength was the fact that he had nine hundred iron chariots, the tanks of the ancient world.

To liberate Israel from their oppression, the Lord raised up Deborah, the wife of Lappidoth, meaning "torch." Deborah is identified as a "prophetess," a title used of five women in the Old Testament (Miriam, Ex. 15:20; Huldah, 2 Kin. 22:14; Noadiah, Neh. 6:14; and the wife of Isaiah, Isa. 8:3). Deborah functioned as a judge under her palm tree, located between Ramah and Bethel in the hill country of Ephraim. As a judge, Deborah solved disputes and rendered judgments. In this way, she served in a capacity much like modern judges. Deborah was probably from the tribe of Ephraim, though Issachar is another possibility.

At some point, Deborah summoned Barak, the son of Abinoam, from Kedesh-Naphtali. Kedesh was one of the six cities of refuge established by Joshua (Josh. 20:7). The name Barak means "lightning." Deborah, speaking as a prophetess, commanded Barak to assemble ten thousand men from the tribes of Naphtali and Zebulun and march them to Mount Tabor. This mountain was located in the northeast section of the Jezreel Valley at the junction of the territories of Issachar, Naphtali, and Zebulun. It was here that the Lord was going to "draw out" the army of Sisera and "give" him to Barak (4:7).

Even though he had already been promised victory, Barak refused to go to battle unless accompanied by Deborah. The prophetess informed Barak that she would indeed accompany him; however, the glory that went with victory would be given to a woman. When Sisera heard that Barak's army was encamped at Mount Tabor, he took his army and marched to the Kishon River, located near Megiddo in the Jezreel Valley. Deborah then commanded Barak to "Arise!" (Heb. *qum*; cf. Josh. 1:2) and attack Sisera. The Israelite coalition routed the Canaanites, aided by the Lord in the form of an unexpected flooding of the Kishon (cf. 5:21). The flood made the battlefield muddy, thus immobilizing the chariots of Sisera, making them sitting deathtraps instead of formidable instruments of warfare.

Sisera himself was the only one to escape the slaughter, having fled to the tent of Jael, the wife of Heber the Kenite. The Kenites were the descendants of Hobab, a "relative" of Moses' wife (4:11; the term can mean father-in-law or brother-in-law). Heber had previously left the territory of the Kenites in southern Judah, settling near Kedesh. The family of Heber was at peace with Jabin, so Sisera expected that they would provide him with shelter. Jael (meaning "mountain goat") initially offered Sisera hospitality, supplying him with milk and a place to lie down. As soon as the Canaanite general was asleep, Jael took a tent peg and drove it through Sisera's head with a hammer. She then informed that men of Barak that Sisera was dead in her tent. The defeat of Sisera was a crippling blow to Jabin, whose influence gradually declined until he was destroyed by the Israelites.

Chapter five contains the Song of Deborah, an ancient poem of praise to the Lord that recounted His faithfulness to the children of Israel from Mount Sinai to the victory at the Kishon River. The song is similar to that of Moses and Miriam recorded in Exodus 15. The hymn begins with a call to worship the Lord. The cause for worship is His mighty deeds on behalf of the nation. The Lord had marched His people from Mount Sinai to Canaan, by way of the land of Edom. He had delivered Israel from the oppression in the days of Shamgar by raising up Deborah, the "mother in Israel" (5:7). This title of honor refers to her role in providing refuge for her people. This deliverance is recounted in 5:13-27. The poem continues with a description of the mother of Sisera as she awaits the return of her son from battle (5:28-30). As she looked "out of the window" (5:28), the mother of Sisera wondered aloud as to the reason for the delay of her son's return. This is one of three times in the Old Testament where we read of a woman who looked out a window: Sisera's mother looked for her son to return from battle; Michal, the daughter of Saul, looked at David as he was leaping and dancing before the Lord as the Ark of the Covenant was brought into Jerusalem (2 Sam. 6:16); and Jezebel, the wife of Ahab, looked at Jehu just before she was thrown to the ground and eaten by dogs (2 Kin. 9:30). The poem ends with a curse on those who oppose the Lord and a blessing on those who love God. The chapter closes with an announcement that the land had rest for forty years (ca. 1230-1190 B.C.). Deborah is the only major judge whose death is never mentioned (cf. 3:11; 4:1; 8:32; 12:7; 16:30).

The fifth judge of Israel was Gideon (6:1-8:35). The name Gideon is from the Hebrew *gada* ("to cut down") and means "hewer." When Israel once again fell into apostasy, the Lord gave them into the hands of the Midianites for seven years (ca. the decade of 1190-1180 B.C.). The Midianites were the descendants of Midian, a son of Abraham by Keturah. They lived on both sides of the Gulf of Aqaba, located south of the land of Edom. The Midianites were primarily pastoralists, accumulating tremendous herds of livestock. Notable Midianites include Zipporah, the wife of Moses, and Jethro, her father.

The oppression of the Midianites was particularly severe. The Israelites were forced to live in dens and caves. Their fields were destroyed and their livestock taken. The devastation reached as far as Gaza. When the Israelites cried out to the Lord for mercy, He sent an unnamed prophet to the people to announce the reason for the judgment, i.e., the disobedience of the nation. This is the only time a male prophet appears in the book of Judges.

Soon after the announcement of the prophet, the Angel of the Lord appeared to Gideon as he was threshing wheat in a wine-press. Gideon's father is identified as Joash the Abiezrite, a clan of Manasseh. The Angel of the Lord informed Gideon that the Lord was with him and would allow him to defeat the Midianites. Gideon, amazed at the prediction, asked the Angel for a sign to confirm his call. The Angel responded by miraculously consuming the sacrifice brought to Him by Gideon.

Later that night, the Lord instructed Gideon to tear down the altar of Baal and the Asherah that belonged to his father. An Asherah was a wooden pole planted in the ground in honor of the Canaanite goddess Asherah, the wife of El. It is clear from the passage that Joash openly worshipped Baal, a sign of the apostasy present in the land. Gideon was further instructed to build an altar to the Lord to replace the altar to Baal. Fearful of the worshippers of Baal, Gideon took ten of his men and tore down the altar and Asherah in the middle of the night. He then erected an altar to Yahweh and sacrificed a bull on it using the wood from the Asherah pole. When the men of the city found out what Gideon had done, they approached Joash and called for him to surrender his son. Joash replied by explaining that if Baal really is a god, then he should be capable of defending himself. Joash's actions resulted in a name change for Gideon. From that moment on, his father called him Jerubbaal, meaning "Let Baal contend against him" (6:32).

When the Midianites and their allies once again invaded Israel, they set up camp in the Jezreel Valley. Gideon responded by sending messengers to rally the tribes of Manasseh, Asher, Zebulun, and

Naphtali. He then tested the Lord with a piece of fleece to confirm his mission. The Lord responded by twice performing the action Gideon requested of Him.

Gideon, no doubt empowered by the Lord's confirmation, gathered his army and camped beside the Harod Spring near the enemy. There the Lord informed Gideon that his army of 32,000 was too large. Twice Gideon was instructed to whittle down his forces until only three hundred remained. Later that night, Gideon and his servant Purah approached the Midianite camp, eavesdropping on a conversation which again confirmed that the Israelites would be victorious. Gideon, empowered once more by the Lord's confirmation, took his small force and gave each man a trumpet, a pitcher, and a torch. After surrounding the Midianites, the Israelites blew their trumpets, broke their pitchers, and lighted their torches. The Midianite army was taken by surprise and in a confused state they started killing each other. They then attempted to escape but the Israelite coalition was able to cut off their retreat by securing the fords of the Jordan. The Midianite army was almost destroyed as two of its commanders were captured and executed by the men of Ephraim. However, the rest of the army (15,000 out of the original 120,000) was able to continue their escape.

When the men of Ephraim heard of Gideon's initial victory, they angrily confronted him because he had not invited them to join the coalition. Gideon quickly calmed them by explaining that their work in killing Oreb (meaning "raven") and Zeeb ("wolf"), the commanders of the Midianites, was more significant than the initial battle fought by Gideon's men. Gideon then continued his pursuit, stopping in Succoth for nourishment. When the men of Succoth refused Gideon's request for food, he announced that his army would return and discipline the elders of the city when they were finished with the Midianites. A similar sequence then took place at Penuel. Eventually, Gideon was able to destroy the rest of the Midianite army, capturing Zebah and Zalmunna, who were both Midianite kings. On his return to Israel, he fulfilled his promise to Succoth and Penuel. Gideon then executed the kings of Midian because they had killed his brothers, a fact previously unknown.

Amazed at Gideon's military success, the men of Israel approached him and asked him to be their king. Gideon refused their request, boldly declaring that the Lord is the One who will rule over the nation. Unfortunately, Gideon then asked each of the men of Israel to bring him a gold earring from their spoil (the Midianites wore gold earrings). Gideon took the gold and made it into an ephod, a sort of idol. He set the ephod in Ophrah, his hometown. This idol eventually became a source of harlotry (idolatry) for the Israelites and a snare to Gideon's family. Still, the land experienced a period of rest for forty years (ca. 1180-1140 B.C.) until Gideon died. Soon after his death, the men of Israel again fell into apostasy, worshipping the Baals and forgetting the true God who had given them rest from their enemies.

Hoping to take advantage of the Israelites' desire for a king, Abimelech, one of the seventy sons of Gideon, approached the men of Shechem and offered to rule over them as the representative of Gideon's house. The men of Shechem accepted Abimelech's offer and gave him some silver from the temple of Baal that was in the city. With the money, Abimelech hired a band of worthless men and killed all of his brothers except Jotham, the youngest, who had managed to hide himself. Abimelech was then made king over Shechem and the surrounding region.

When Jotham heard the news, he stood on the top of Mount Gerizim and told the men of Shechem a parable. In the parable, the trees of the forest decide to anoint a king over themselves. In turn, the approach an olive tree, a fig tree, and a grapevine; all of whom turn down the request because they were too busy performing their natural tasks. Finally, the bramble (thornbush) agrees to the offer, with the condition that the other trees take refuge in its shade or else perish in a forest fire. The point of the parable is clear; if the men of Shechem wanted Abimelech to rule over them, they would end up destroying each other. When his parable was finished, Jotham fled to Beer to escape from his brother.

After a three year reign (ca. 1120-1117 B.C.), the prophetic parable came true when the men of Shechem and Abimelech started a feud between each other. The men of Shechem chose to follow Gaal, the son of Ebed, who ridiculed Abimelech and his commander,

Zebul. Upon hearing the taunts, Zebul became angry and decided to arrange a battle between Abimelech and Gaal. In the ensuing battle, the men of Abimelech were able to destroy the city of Shechem, burning the town's tower in which the leaders of the city had taken refuge. They then proceeded to Thebez and attempted to do the same thing; however, a woman threw a millstone on Abimelech's head, crushing his skull. Abimelech then asked his armor bearer to kill him lest he be killed by a woman. The armor bearer did as he was asked and the prophetic parable of Jotham was fulfilled.

The sixth judge of Israel was Tola (10:1-2). The name Tola means "worm." Tola is identified as the son of Puah and grandson of Dodo. He was from the tribe of Issachar and lived in Shamir in the hill country of Ephraim. Tola's judgeship lasted for twenty-three years (ca. 1117-1094 B.C.) and was probably local in nature. The foreign oppressor during the tenure of Tola is unknown.

The seventh judge of Israel was Jair (10:3-5). The name Jair means "one giving light." He was probably from the tribe of Manasseh since he served in the Transjordan area given to this tribe. Jair had thirty sons who each ruled over a village in Gilead. Jair's judgeship lasted for twenty-two years (ca. 1115-1093 B.C.) and was probably concurrent with the tenure of Tola. The foreign oppressor during the time of Jair is unknown.

The eighth judge of Israel was Jephthah (10:6-12:7). The name Jephthah means "Yahweh will open." When Israel once again did evil in the sight of the Lord, He strengthened the Philistines and Ammonites, the latter afflicting the nation for eighteen years (ca. 1124-1106 B.C.). In great distress, the Israelites cried out to Yahweh for deliverance. Furthermore, they put away their foreign gods and committed to serving the true God. The Lord was moved to pity by the repentant actions of His people and chose to deliver them by raising up yet another judge.

Jephthah is identified as the son of Gilead by means of a harlot. As a result, his stepbrothers drove him out of their house, refusing to share their inheritance with a bastard. Jephthah fled from his brothers and took up residence in the land of Tob (probably north of Ammon and east of Manasseh). When the Ammonite oppression continued, the elders of Gilead approached Jephthah and promised him that he would become their leader if he was able to defeat the Ammonites. To guarantee their pledge, they took an oath before the Lord.

Jephthah then sent messengers to the king of Ammon, disputing his claim to the land of Gilead. The messengers reviewed the history of events from the Exodus to the modern day, explaining that the Israelites had been in the land for three hundred years, during which time the Ammonites had made no claim to the land. The Ammonites, unconvinced by the argument, rejected the message of Jephthah. So Jephthah, filled with the Spirit of the Lord, led his armies against the Ammonites. Prior to the fight, Jephthah made a vow to Yahweh, pledging to sacrifice as a burnt offering the first thing that comes out of his house to meet him when he returns home.

In the subsequent battle, Jephthah achieved a great victory, routing the Ammonites and capturing twenty cities. However, when he arrived at his house, his only child, a daughter, came out to greet him. When Jephthah saw her, he tore his clothes in anguish, informing her of the vow that he had taken before the Lord. The daughter, agreeing that he had to fulfill his vow, requested two months reprieve in which to prepare herself for her demise. When his daughter returned home, Jephthah fulfilled his vow to Yahweh.

At this point, two questions must be addressed. First, What exactly did Jephthah intend to sacrifice?; and second, Did he fulfill his vow in the way intended (i.e., as a burnt offering)? It is clear from the passage that Jephthah did not intend for his daughter to be the first thing to come out of his house upon his return. He probably anticipated a servant or perhaps even an animal.[35] Some have translated the word in question (Heb. *asher*) with the term "whatever" (NIV, NASB, NKJ).[36] Others have translated the word with the term "whoever" (RSV, NRSV).[37] It is much more likely that Jephthah anticipated that one of his servants would greet him upon his return.[38] The gender of the form is masculine (if an animal were intended, the form should be feminine) and the phrase "to meet me" refers more appropriately to a human than to an animal (cf. 1 Sam. 18:6).[39] Also, an animal does not appear to suit the lofty nature of the vow; one would naturally have expected Jephthah to sacrifice an animal upon his victory.

It seems clear from the passage that Jephthah did indeed fulfill his vow in the way intended. First, the text explicitly states that Jephthah "did to her according to the vow which he had made" (11:39). Second, the phrase "she had no relations with a man" (11:39) is best translated as a past perfect (NRSV; "she had never slept with a man"). Third, the alternative view (i.e., that she was dedicated as a perpetual virgin) is implausible. Many children were dedicated to the service of the Lord, either to serve in the sanctuary (e.g., Samuel) or as a Nazirite (e.g., Samson). Fourth, the custom which followed Jephthah's actions, i.e., the yearly lament of the daughters of Israel, suggests the finality of the vow. While the idea of child sacrifice is abhorrent to our modern sensibilities, it should be remembered that Jephthah lived in a time of great apostasy; a time when child sacrifice was common; a time without the knowledge of the Lord; a time when "everyone did what was right in his own eyes" (21:25).

When the men of Ephraim heard of Jephthah's victory, they approached him and threatened to burn his house down. Despite the diplomatic efforts of Jephthah, the Ephraimites fought with the Gileadites. The men of Jephthah routed the men of Ephraim, achieving a great slaughter when they successfully occupied the fords of the Jordan. When the men of Ephraim tried to cross the fords, they were found out by their inability to say the word Shibboleth (meaning "channel of water"). Thus 42,000 Ephraimites were slain in the battle. After a six year tenure (ca. 1106-1100 B.C.), Jephthah died and was buried in one of the cities of Gilead.

The ninth judge of Israel was Ibzan (12:8-10). The name Ibzan means "illustrious." He was from the village of Bethlehem in the territory of Zebulun. If the author had meant the Bethlehem that was in Judah he would have specified this as he does every other time in the book (cf. 17:7, 8, 9; 19:1, 2, 18). Ibzan was probably from the tribe of Zebulun. He was noted for his especially large family of 30 sons and 30 daughters. Ibzan served as a judge for seven years (ca. 1100-1093 B.C.). The foreign oppressor during the tenure of Ibzan is unknown.

The tenth judge of Israel was Elon (12:11-12). The name Elon means "oak." Like the judge who preceded him, Elon was from the tribe of Zebulun. He served as a judge for ten years (ca. 1093-1083

B.C.). Elon was buried in Aijalon in the territory of Zebulun. The exact location of this village is unknown. The foreign oppressor during the judgeship of Elon is likewise unknown.

The eleventh judge of Israel was Abdon (12:13-15). The name Abdon means "service." He is identified as the son of Hillel the Pirathonite. The village of Pirathon was located in the territory of Ephraim, thus implying that Abdon was an Ephraimite. Abdon was noted for the fact that he had forty sons and thirty grandsons who each rode on a donkey (cf. the sons of Jair, 10:4). Abdon served as a judge for eight years (ca. 1083-1075 B.C.). The foreign oppressor during the tenure of Abdon is unknown.

The twelfth and final judge of Israel was Samson (13:1-16:31). The name Samson means "sunlike." When the Israelites once again did evil in the sight of the Lord, He gave them into the hands of the Philistines for forty years (ca. 1124-1084 B.C.). The beginning of the Philistine oppression coincided with the beginning of the Ammonite oppression that preceded the judgeship of Jephthah (cf. 10:7). In the midst of this oppression lived a man named Manoah (meaning "rest"). Manoah, a member of the tribe of Dan, lived at Zorah in the Sorek Valley. There the Angel of the Lord appeared to his barren wife and informed her that she would soon conceive and bear a son. The Lord instructed the woman to raise the child as a Nazirite (meaning "devoted"). A Nazirite was a person who was to be disciplined in his appetite (no wine or grapes), distinctive in his appearance (no haircut), and discreet in his associations (no contact with a dead body; cf. Num. 6:2-6).[40] Typically, individuals took a Nazirite vow for a limited period of time. Samson, however, was to be a Nazirite for life.

As soon as Manoah's wife informed him of the Angel's visit, he prayed and asked the Lord for another appearance. God granted the man's request, reiterating to Manoah what He had told his wife. The Lord then performed a series of wonders while Manoah offered a sacrifice in His name. When the flame of the sacrifice rose towards heaven, the Angel of the Lord ascended in the flame and appeared to Manoah no more. Shortly thereafter, the woman gave birth to a son and named him Samson. As the young child grew, the Lord blessed him greatly.

When Samson became a man, he journeyed to Timnah, a village in the Sorek Valley. There he saw a Philistine woman and immediately desired her for a wife. He asked his parents to arrange the marriage and they reluctantly agreed. On one of his journeys to Timnah, Samson was set upon by a lion. Being filled with the Spirit of the Lord, Samson tore the lion apart with his bare hands. The next time he went to visit the Philistine woman, Samson noticed a swarm of bees and some honey in the carcass of the lion. This is the only explicit reference in the Old Testament to bee honey (as opposed to date honey). Samson unwisely scooped out some of the honey to eat it, a violation of his Nazirite vow.

At the beginning of his seven-day wedding ceremony, Samson told a riddle to his guests, "Out of the eater came something to eat; and out of the strong came something sweet" (14:14). The judge promised each of his thirty guests an outfit if they could correctly answer his riddle. When the wedding guests could not figure out the riddle after three days, they threatened Samson's bride, encouraging her to find out the answer to the riddle so that she could tell them. After repeated attempts, she finally got Samson to divulge the secret. The guests then told Samson the correct answer. In a fit of rage, Samson went to the Philistine city of Ashkelon and killed thirty of the inhabitants to pay his debt to his wedding guests. The woman of Timnah was then given to one of Samson's friends.

Samson, under the impression that he was married to the woman of Timnah, approached her house with the intention of paying her a visit. Her father refused to let him in, informing Samson that he had given her to another man. The father then offered Samson his younger daughter instead. The judge, in a fit of rage, set fire to the grain fields, vineyards, and orchards using torch-bearing foxes to accomplish the task. When the Philistines retaliated by setting the woman of Timnah and her father on fire, Samson "struck them ruthlessly with a great slaughter" and escaped to the cave of Etam (15:8). Under threat of attack by the Philistines, the men of Judah bound Samson and surrendered him to his enemies. However, the judge broke free and killed a thousand Philistines with the jawbone of a donkey. The length of Samson's judgeship was twenty years (ca. 1104-1084 B.C.). However, note that Samson's tenure occurred within the period of oppression by the Philistines ("in the days of the Philistines;" 15:20). Eventually, Samuel will put an end to the Philistine oppression (cf. 1 Sam. 7).

Some time after the events of chapter fifteen, Samson journeyed to Gaza to visit a harlot. When the Philistines of Gaza were informed that the Israelite judge was in their city, they surrounded the house of the harlot and set up an ambush at the gate of the city. Instead, Samson arose at midnight and surprised the ambushers, dislodging the entire gate and carrying it to the top of a mountain. This mountain is probably to be identified as El Montar just east of Gaza and facing Hebron. It is also possible that Samson carried the gate all the way to a hill in the vicinity of Hebron. However, the great distance (37 miles) makes this unlikely.

Samson next falls in love with a woman of the Sorek Valley named Delilah. Delilah is the only woman of the four in Samson's life who is named (cf. mother, bride, harlot). Her name is Hebrew and means "dainty one."[41] Although many have assumed that Delilah is a Philistine,[42] the text never identifies her as such. One day the five lords of the Philistines approached Delilah and bribed her to entice Samson into revealing the secret of his great strength. The sum they promised her is enormous; 5500 pieces of silver, a weight of well over one hundred pounds (a shekel was the standard unit of weight, weighing slightly more than four-tenths of an ounce).

On at least four different occasions, Delilah begged Samson to divulge his secret. On each of the first three occasions, Samson told her a lie. However, on the fourth occasion, the judge told her the truth, revealing that his hair was the source of his strength. As Samson slept on her knees, Delilah called for a man to shave his head. When Samson awoke, the Philistines captured him and gouged out his eyes. They then brought him to Gaza and bound him with bronze chains. When the Philistines assembled for a great feast in honor of their god Dagon, they drunkenly called for Samson to be brought before the assembly for entertainment. They placed him in the middle of the room between two pillars. At this point Samson prayed to the Lord, asking Him to restore his strength so that he could retaliate against his enemies. He further asked God to allow him to die alongside his victims. The Lord granted Samson's request, whereupon Samson pushed against the load-bearing pillars, collapsing the house on the Philistines. Samson's family came to Gaza and took his corpse home, burying him in the tomb of his father.

Epilogue: Tribal Depravity (17:1-21:25)

The final section of the book serves as an epilogue. The two accounts recorded here take place early in the period of the judges. The Levite of chapters seventeen and eighteen is identified as Jonathan, the son of Gershom, the son of Moses (18:30, NIV, NRSV; cf. Ex. 2:22). In chapters nineteen through twenty-one, Phinehas, the son of Eleazar, the son of Aaron, plays a crucial role in determining whether or not to attack the Benjaminites. Since both of these men are grandsons of the leaders of the Exodus, the events of these chapters should be dated no later than 1330 B.C. Together with Ruth, these stories form the so-called "Bethlehem Trilogy;" named for the prominence of the city in each of the narratives.

The first account (17:1-18:31) begins with a man living in the hill country of Ephraim. The man is identified as Micah. The name Micah means "who is like Yahweh." Micah confessed to his mother that he had stolen 1100 pieces of silver from her. Coincidently, this is the same amount promised to Delilah by each of the Philistines lords in the previous chapter. Micah's mother promptly forgave him, pronouncing a blessing on her son and even giving him 200 pieces of silver with which to make an idol. When the silversmith completed the idol, it was placed in the house of Micah alongside an ephod and teraphim, two other forms of idols. Together, these formed a shrine of worship to Yahweh (cf. 17:3). Micah even appointed one of his sons to serve as the priest of his shrine.

One day a Levite stopped at the house of Micah while searching for a place to live and work. He was originally from Bethlehem in Judah. Micah immediately invited the Levite to become his own personal priest, promising him a salary, a set of clothes, and room and board. The Levite agreed; thus pleasing Micah, who anticipated the blessings of Yahweh because he now had a Levite as his priest.

At about the same time, the Danites sent out five men to spy out the region of Ephraim because they were looking for a place to which to migrate. While traveling, they happened to stop for rest at the house of Micah. Recognizing the voice of the Levite, they questioned him as to the reason why he was staying with Micah. The Levite informed the men that he was serving as Micah's personal priest. The men then asked the Levite to inquire of the Lord as to whether or not their journey would be a success. The Levite informed the Danites that their mission was "under the eye of the Lord" (18:6; i.e., the Lord was watching over them; hence, their mission was destined for success).

As the Danites continued their journey, they happened upon the city of Laish, located about 25 miles north of the Sea of Galilee. The city seemed to them to be an ideal city. It was well-protected; it had plenty of food and water; it was wealthy; and it was far-removed from the Sidonians (Phoenicians) and Arameans (Syrians). When they returned to their homes, the spies informed the rest of their tribesmen about the wonderful city they had found.

Immediately, six hundred Danite warriors set out to capture the city. As they journeyed through the hill country of Ephraim, the five spies encouraged the small army to stop at the home of Micah. While there, the Danites took the idols of Micah and convinced the Levite to serve as the priest for the whole tribe of Dan. When Micah discovered what had happened, he assembled a force of men and overtook the Danites. The Danites refused to surrender the idols or the priest and threatened Micah's force with violence. Seeing that the Danites were too numerous for him, Micah returned to his home.

When the Danites got to Laish, they massacred the inhabitants and burned the city to the ground. The Danites then rebuilt the city and named it Dan. They set up Micah's idols and installed the Levite and his family as their hereditary priest "until the land went into captivity" (18:30). This enigmatic phrase seems to be parallel with "as long as the house of God was at Shiloh" (18:31). As a result, it must indicate a local captivity that occurred prior to the house of God being moved to Nob (ca. 1050 B.C.; cf. 1 Sam. 21:1ff). It is at this point that the Levite is identified. He is Jonathan, the grandson of Moses. The name Jonathan means "Yahweh's gift."

The second account (19:1-21:25) begins with a Levite living in the hill country of Ephraim. This Levite took for himself a concubine who was from Bethlehem in Judah. At some point, the Levite's concubine became angry with him and returned to her father's house in Bethlehem. After four months, the Levite journeyed to Bethlehem to attempt to win her back. The visit of the Levite made the concubine's father happy. He was probably eager for the chance to have his daughter taken off his hands.

While visiting Bethlehem, the Levite was amply provided with food, drink, and lodging. In fact, when the Levite tried to leave the city on three different occasions, his father-in-law convinced him to tarry with offers of sustenance and lodging. Finally, the Levite made a successful departure and journeyed to the territory of Benjamin. As they approached Jerusalem, the Levite's servant suggested that they stop in the city for the night. However, the priest insisted on proceeding further, refusing to stay in a city inhabited by foreigners.

Eventually, they decided to stop in Gibeah. The Levite intended to spend the night in the town square; however, they met an old man returning from his field who was himself from the hill country of Ephraim. The old man invited the Levite and his companions to spend the night in his home, promising to take care of their needs.

Soon, the worthless men of the city heard that the old man had a guest. They approached the home and demanded that the Levite be given to them so that they could sodomize him. The old man refused their demands and instead offered his virgin daughter. The men refused the offer and continued to demand the Levite. Eventually, the Levite threw his concubine to the men, an act that evidently appeased their sexual appetite. The men of Gibeah raped the concubine through the night and in the morning left her to die.

The concubine managed to make her way to the threshold of the old man's house and laid down until dawn. When the Levite was ready to continue his journey he opened the door and found the concubine at his feet. He callously told her to get up but she was dead. He placed her corpse on his donkey and returned to his home. When he arrived, he took a knife and cut her body into twelve pieces. He then sent a piece to each of the twelve tribes of Israel, commanding each of the messengers to say, "Has such a thing ever happened since the day that the Israelites came up from the land of Egypt until this day? Consider it, take counsel, and speak out" (19:30).

When the tribes of Israel heard the news, they assembled together at Mizpah, only four miles north of Gibeah. The number of warriors gathered was 400,000. The Levite related the story of the atrocity at Gibeah, thus provoking the coalition to march against Benjamin. When they approached the city, they demanded that the tribe of Benjamin hand over the guilty parties. The Benjaminites refused, instead gathering a force of over twenty-six thousand men to do battle against the Israelite coalition.

The Israelite coalition prepared for their attack, inquiring of the Lord as to which tribe should lead them in battle. The Lord responded, "Judah shall go up first" (20:18; cf. 1:1-2). The next day, the Israelite coalition attacked the city of Gibeah. For three days, the Israelites attacked the city, each time inquiring of the Lord before commencing the assault. Finally, the Israelite coalition was able to defeat the Benjaminites, using the same retreat and ambush tactic that had worked at Ai. The Israelites destroyed Gibeah and all the other cities in Benjamin. In fact, the entire tribe of Benjamin was almost wiped out. Only six hundred men managed to escape by hiding at the Rock of Rimmon, a defensive stronghold four miles east of Bethel.

Four months later, the tribes assembled together, being moved with compassion for the remnant of the tribe of Benjamin. The Israelites wanted to provide wives for the six hundred men who remained; however, the tribes had each taken an oath to withhold their daughters from the men of Benjamin. At last, they found a solution. They discovered that the men of Jabesh-Gilead had not supported the attack on Gibeah. The town of Jabesh-Gilead is located about two miles east of the Jordan River southeast of Beth Shan. The Israelites sent twelve thousand men to "utterly destroy" (Heb. *herem*; cf. Deut. 7:26; Josh. 6:17) the inhabitants of the city except for the virgins of marriageable age. The men did as they were asked and returned with four hundred young virgins.

This number was not sufficient, however, since there were still two hundred men of Benjamin who needed wives. As a result, the tribes decided that the men could take for themselves wives from among the young virgins who danced at the yearly feast at Shiloh. Shiloh was located about thirteen miles north of Mizpah. The plan succeeded and thus every man of Benjamin was provided with a wife. They then returned to their cities and rebuilt them. The book of Judges ends by reiterating the theme of the book, "In those days there was no king in Israel; all the people did what was right in their own eyes" (21:25; cf. 17:6; 18:1; 19:1).

Study Questions

1. What is the meaning of the term "judge?"
2. List the six major judges.
3. Who is responsible for writing the majority of the book of Judges?
4. When was the book of Judges written?
5. Who were the "Sea Peoples?"
6. Briefly describe the "cycle of sin" that recurs throughout Judges.
7. Which judge was left-handed?
8. Who killed 600 Philistines with an oxgoad?
9. What was the name of the woman who killed Sisera?
10. What was the name of the son of Gideon who tried to set himself up as king?
11. Do you believe Jephthah sacrificed his daughter as a burnt offering? Why or why not?
13. What was the name of the man who hired a Levite as his personal priest?
14. Which tribe migrated to the city of Laish?
15. Which tribe was almost wiped out by the other tribes of Israel?

CHAPTER 3

Ruth

"But Ruth said, 'Do not urge me to leave you or turn back from following you; for where you go, I will go, and where you lodge, I will lodge. Your people shall be my people, and your God, my God. Where you die, I will die, and there I will be buried. Thus may the Lord do to me, and worse, if anything but death parts you and me.' Then Naomi took the child and laid him in her lap, and became his nurse. And the neighbor women gave him a name, saying, 'A son has been born to Naomi!' So they named him Obed. He is the father of Jesse, the father of David." (Ruth 1:16-17; 4:16-17).

The book of Ruth tells the story of the events surrounding the birth of Obed, the grandfather of King David. The narrative takes place during the period of the judges. However, the positive message of the book is a startling contrast to the negative message of Judges. The story of Ruth is one of hope rather than despair; a story of courage rather than cowardice; a story of loyalty rather than betrayal; a story of blessing rather than judgment; a story of an unblemished savior rather than flawed deliverers.

The title of the book comes from its main character, Ruth. Ruth is one of five women mentioned in Matthew's genealogy of Jesus (Matt. 1:1-16; i.e., Tamar, Rahab, Ruth, Bathsheba ["her who had been the wife of Uriah"], Mary). This is the only Scriptural reference to Ruth outside of the book that bears her name. Ruth and Esther are the only two books of the Bible that are named for women.

In the Hebrew Bible, the book of Ruth is placed fourth amongst the Writings (after Psalms, Job, and Proverbs).[1] However, it appears first in the Megillot ("festal scrolls"), a subcategory consisting of five books that were read during major festivals. Ruth was read at the Feast of Weeks (Pentecost), Song of Solomon at Passover, Ecclesiastes at the Feast of Tabernacles, Lamentations at the Ninth of Ab (an extrabiblical fast that commemorates the destruction of Jerusalem), and Esther at Purim. The order of books is chronological (Ruth – judges; Song of Solomon – younger Solomon; Ecclesiastes – older Solomon; Lamentations – Jeremiah; Esther – postexilic period) and generally follows the order of the holidays in the Jewish calendar; Ruth and Song of Solomon are in reverse order because Passover precedes Pentecost. Since Song of Solomon would seem to naturally follow Proverbs (both were written by Solomon), the transposition appears intentional. Ruth may have been placed after Proverbs because of the link between the acrostic poem which closes Proverbs (Prov. 31:10-31) and the book of Ruth. The poem of Proverbs extols the "excellent wife" (Prov. 31:10; Heb. *ishah hayil*) while Ruth is identified as a "woman of excellence" (Heb. *ishah hayil*) in 3:11; a living example of the Proverbial archetype.

In the English Old Testament, the book of Ruth is placed third amongst the twelve historical books (Joshua-Esther). This place-ment follows that of the Greek Septuagint and Latin Vulgate and is quite logical. The book naturally follows Judges because the narrative takes place during the period of the judges; "Now it came about in the days when the judges governed" (1:1). The story of Ruth also concludes the so-called "Bethlehem Trilogy" that includes the narrative of Micah's idols (Jud. 17-18) and the account of the Levite's concubine (Jud. 19-21). The trilogy is named for the city of Bethlehem because it is prominent in all three stories. Ruth also serves as a fitting introduction to the book of Samuel since it concludes with a genealogy of the main character of that book, David.

Author

While the Bible does not identify the author of this book, tradition has long held that the book was written by Samuel. The primary support for Samuel authorship comes from the Babylonian Talmud, which ascribes the books of Judges, Ruth, and Samuel to the prophet (*Baba Bathra* 14b). Samuel is thought by many to be the greatest Old Testament figure since Moses (cf. Jer. 15:1). He was the son of Elkanah and Hannah. Samuel was a Levite who was born in the hill country of Ephraim. He spent his youth ministering in the house of the Lord in Shiloh in fulfillment of an oath taken by his mother. The honorable young boy served as a striking contrast to Hophni and Phinehas, the disreputable sons of the high priest Eli. Samuel was the final judge of Israel. As such, he was responsible for ushering in the nation's monarchy, anointing both Saul and David as kings of Israel. Samuel was also a prophet (1 Sam. 3:20). In fact, he was the first in a succession of prophets that continued through the end of the Old Testament (Acts 3:24). At his death, "all Israel gathered together and mourned for him" (1 Sam. 25:1). Samuel was buried in Ramah, a village located about five miles north of Jerusalem.

It has been suggested that the author of Ruth was a woman.[2] In fact, some Jewish rabbis have attributed the book to Naomi. This view is based on the facts that the two main characters in the narrative are women and that the author had women's concerns in mind (e.g., widowhood, marriage, childbirth). While this suggestion is certainly intriguing, there is little evidence to suggest that any of the books of the Old Testament were written by females. In fact, the New Testament seems to infer that all of the books of the Old Testament were written by men (cf. 2 Pet. 1:20-21).

Date

The most widely espoused date for the book is the reign of Solomon (971-931 B.C.). This period has been called the golden age of Hebrew writing.[3] The books of Proverbs, Song of Solomon, and Ecclesiastes were all written at this time. Ruth, a literary masterpiece, would seem to fit well with these books. However, the absence of Solomon's name in the genealogy that concludes the book argues against a date during his reign.

There is some evidence in the book to suggest a much later date. Ruth 4:7 explains the custom of sandal-exchange as if it had fallen out of practice many years prior to the writing of the book ("Now this was the custom in former times in Israel"). Some even argue that the placement of Ruth in the Writings supports a late date (but see Proverbs, Song of Solomon, and Ecclesiastes). As a result, many modern commentators date Ruth in the fifth (or even fourth) century B.C. These scholars stress the theme of intermarriage and view the book as a polemic against the marriage reforms of Ezra and Nehemiah. The Moabitess Ruth would have served as a powerful contradiction to the xenophobic attitudes of these reformers. Proponents of this view have found Aramaic influence in the book's language, a fact they claim supports a postexilic date. They also argue that the book departs significantly from the Deuteronomistic tradition. They see the book as presenting an idealized depiction of the period of the judges, a clear departure from the portrait painted in the book of Judges.

The major problem with this view is that the overall tone of the book is positive, not negative. Boaz and Ruth are consistently praised, not vilified (cf. 2:1, 11; 3:11). Their union is seen to be the result of the Lord's blessing, not curse (cf. 2:12, 20; 3:10; 4:11, 12, 13, 14, 15). If the book is an attack on the marriage reforms of Ezra and Nehemiah, then one would expect to see praise for the closest relative that rejected the offer to redeem Ruth. Instead, the book appears to portray him in a negative, even shameful, light. Furthermore, while the presence of Aramaisms was at one time considered a powerful argument, it is no longer so. Archaeological evidence indicates that Aramaic words were in use much earlier than was previously thought.

Assuming Samuel was the author, the book of Ruth was probably written shortly after David was anointed king of Israel. David was born ca. 1040 B.C., roughly ten years after Saul began to reign. He was certainly young at the time of his anointing (cf. 1 Sam. 16:11); however, he was old enough to care for his father's flocks by himself. An age of twelve cannot be too far off the mark. Therefore, the date of his anointing was somewhere around 1028 B.C. Since Samuel's death can be dated ca. 1021 B.C., Ruth was most likely written within two or three years of 1025 B.C. The book was probably written from Ramah, the home of Samuel.

Historical Background

The events of the book of Ruth take place ca. 1100 B.C. (Boaz is David's great-grandfather; David was born ca. 1040 B.C.). This is roughly equivalent to the time of Gideon and Jephthah. The period of the Judges was a time of moral and spiritual apostasy; a time of civil war and idolatry; a time when "everyone did what was right in his own eyes" (Jud. 21:25). Even great heroes like Gideon and Jephthah were deeply flawed individuals. Although they are both called "valiant warrior" upon their introduction (Jud. 6:12; 11:1; Heb. *gibor hayil*; cf. 2:1 where the same phrase is used of Boaz at his introduction), they each commited a great sin against the Lord. Gideon, after achieving a great victory against the Midianites, fashioned a gold ephod that became a "snare" to Gideon, his household, and all Israel (Jud. 8:27). Jephthah, after achieving a great victory against the Ammonites, sacrificed his daughter to Yahweh as a burnt offering. Such was life in the period of the Judges; and such was the world that Ruth entered when she journeyed from Moab to Bethlehem.

Since Ruth is identified as a Moabite, a word must be said concerning her people. The Moabites were the descendants of Moab, the son of Lot through his oldest daughter. They lived on the eastern side of the Jordan River and the Dead Sea, just to the south of the Ammonites. The land of Moab was famous for its pasturage. 2 Kings 3:4 testifies to the agricultural wealth of the area, "Now Mesha king of Moab was a sheep breeder, and used to pay the king of Israel 100,000 lambs and the wool of 100,000 rams." The climate of Moab also allowed for the growing of wheat, barley, vineyards, and fruit trees. The chief god of the Moabites was Chemosh (1 Kin. 11:7, 33). The worship of Chemosh included a priesthood (Jer. 48:7) and a sacrificial system (Num. 22:40; 25:2). Solomon married Moabite women and built a sanctuary for Chemosh on the Mount of Olives (1 Kin. 11:1, 7). Notable Moabites mentioned in the Bible include Balak, the king who hired Balaam to curse the Children of

Israel (Num. 22-24) and Mesha, the king who rebelled against King Jehoram of Israel (2 Kin. 3).

Audience and Purpose

Ruth was written for several reasons. First, the book was written to identify the king alluded to in the first two parts of the "Bethlehem Trilogy," that is, David, the great-grandson of Ruth and Boaz. "In Joshua and Judges, the focus of revelation is on the land God promised to the descendants of Abraham. In Ruth, the focus shifts to the seed He promised."[4] This seed, the future king of Israel (cf. Gen. 49:8, 10), was to come through the line of Judah, the fourth son of Jacob and Leah. David's ancestry is traced back to Perez, the son of Judah. Judah gave birth to Perez through Tamar, his daughter-in-law who disguised herself as a harlot to seduce him. Tamar, like Ruth, was a foreigner. Salmon, the husband of Rahab, yet another foreigner, is also mentioned in David's genealogy. The presence of these foreigners makes it possible that a secondary purpose of Ruth was to give an explanation of David's foreign ancestry. As Hubbard writes, "The book has a political purpose: to win popular acceptance of David's rule by appeal to the continuity of Yahweh's guidance in the lives of Israel's ancestors and David."[5] If Samuel was indeed the author, he may have written to justify David's claim to the throne; a throne which was then occupied by Saul, a Benjaminite. This claim was certainly enhanced by noting the extraordinarily providential circumstances through which the line of royalty was preserved (Judah-Tamar, Salmon-Rahab, and Boaz-Ruth).

Second, the book was written to give an account of the covenantal loyalty by the Lord during the period of the judges. This covenantal loyalty is best expressed through the Hebrew word *hesed*. This term is translated as "kindness" in Ruth (cf. 2:20; 3:10; 1:8 uses a derivative of the word "kindness," i.e., "kindly"). The word is often translated as "lovingkindness" in the Old Testament, especially when the word is used in conjunction with the Hebrew word *berit* (meaning "covenant;" cf. Deut. 7:9, 12; 1 Kin. 8:23; 2 Chron. 6:14; Neh. 1:5; 9:32; Psa. 106:45; Dan. 9:4; note especially the poetic Psa. 89:28 and Isa. 54:10 where the two terms occur as synonymous parallels). The term *hesed* best embodies the concept of the sovereign Lord's loyal obligations to His covenantal promises and to those who live according to His standards. This idea is behind the use of the word in 1:8 and 2:20. However, the book also uses the term to describe the loyalty shown by Ruth herself. In 3:10, Boaz applies to term to Ruth's dual acts of courage, i.e., showing loyalty to Naomi and choosing him as a potential husband.

As one reads Ruth, it is at once obvious that the characters are conscious of God's sovereignty. Of the book's eighty-five verses, twenty-three mention God.[6] Eight times the characters in the book speak of God's activity (1:13, 20-21 [four times]; 2:20; 4:12, 14).[7] The Lord is regularly petitioned to answer prayers (1:8-9; 2:12; 4:11-12) and bless faithful individuals (2:4 [twice]; 19-20; 3:10). Twice, Yahweh's name is used as part of an oath (1:17; 3:13). Yet, perhaps the most explicit reference to divine sovereignty is found in 2:12 with the phrase "the Lord, the God of Israel, under whose wings you have come to seek refuge." The word translated "wings" (Heb. *kanaph*) is used throughout the psalter to describe the Lord's providential care for His faithful (Psa. 17:8; 36:7 [note the use of *hesed*]; 57:1; 61:4; 63:7; 91:4); a theme prominent in Ruth.

Third, the book was written to reveal the faithfulness of certain Israelites. "As the historical narratives move from the Judges period to the monarchy, David can be viewed with great incredulity. How could faith like this exist after four hundred years of conditions such as those described in the book of Judges? The story of Ruth, drawn from David's ancestry, offers an explanation of the survival of faith."[8] While the time period of the judges was marked by general apostasy, certain individual Israelites remained faithful (e.g., Phinehas, Othniel, Hannah, Samuel). Boaz is one of these. He is a man of impeccable character. He is aware of the commandments of God and is determined to abide by them. When he sees a young widow in need, he graciously allows her to glean in his fields, even going beyond the requirements of the Law to provide her with a bountiful harvest. When approached by Ruth in the middle of the night, he resists sexual temptation and instead treats her like a lady, sending her on her way before dawn so that her reputation would not suffer harm. When given the opportunity for marriage, he honestly confesses that another is a closer relative than himself.

When he confronts the closer relative, he does so in the presence of the town elders. When the closer relative shirks his responsibilities, Boaz offers to redeem Ruth (and Naomi). In every scene in which he appears, Boaz is a man of honor and integrity; a glorious model for the future king of Israel. One cannot help but wonder whether David's great faith was somehow influenced by the faith of his great-grandfather.

Fourth, the book was written to demonstrate God's acceptance of foreigners who choose to worship Him. Throughout the Old Testament there are accounts of foreigners who choose to worship Yahweh and are thus rewarded for their actions. Melchizedek, the king of Salem and priest of El Elyon (God Most High), received the tithes of Abraham and became the model for Christ's role as King-Priest. Tamar, the Canaanite wife of Er, exhibited greater righteousness than Judah (Gen. 38:26) and became an ancestor of David and Christ. Rahab, the Canaanite harlot of Jericho, was rescued from the condemned city and likewise became an ancestor of David and Christ. Uriah, a Hittite warrior, faithfully served David and became one of his "mighty men" (1 Chron. 11:26, 41). Naaman, the Aramean commander (and another *gibor hayil*; 2 Kin. 5:1), dipped himself seven times in the Jordan River and became cured of leprosy. The inhabitants of Nineveh repented at the preaching of Jonah and became the accusers of those who rejected the Messiah (Matt. 12:41). These all exercised faith and thus took their rightful place among the people of God. As Hubbard states, "Foreigners who adopt Yahweh and outdo the Israelites in *hesed* merit acceptance as full-fledges Israelites."[9]

Unfortunately, Ruth was not just a foreigner; she was a Moabite. The Moabites were particularly unwelcome in the covenant community. As the Law stated, "No Ammonite or Moabite shall enter the assembly of the Lord; none of their descendants, even to the tenth generation, shall ever enter the assembly of the Lord, because they did not meet you with food and water on the way when you came out of Egypt, and because they hired against you Balaam the son of Beor from Pethor of Mesopotamia, to curse you. Nevertheless, the Lord your God was not willing to listen to Balaam, but the Lord your God turned the curse into a blessing for you because the Lord your

God loves you. You shall never seek their peace or their prosperity all your days" (Deut. 23:3-6). In later years, Ezra will specifically forbid intermarriage between Israelites and Moabites (Ezra 9:1ff.).

However, Ruth is ultimately elevated to the status of Rachel and Leah, through whom the house of Israel was built (cf. 4:11). Why is she accepted? Perhaps the Law only applied to male Moabites, as the Talmud stipulates (*Yebamoth* 76b). Yet there is no evidence to support this. In fact, Ezra specifically applies the commands to both men and women (Ezra 9:12). Perhaps Boaz simply ignored the Mosaic Law. But this is entirely inconsistent with his righteous character. The fact is, Ruth had expressed her commitment to Naomi and her God (1:16). The Law's prohibition applies only to unbelievers. Genesis 17 expressly allowed for foreigners to become part of community (see also Ex. 12:48). In fact, the acceptance of foreigners was always part of God's plan. In His initial covenant with Abraham, the Lord promised that they would eventually receive His blessings; "in you all the families of the earth shall be blessed" (Gen. 12:3). Such is the case with Ruth. She chose God and became the great-grandmother of David and ancestor of Christ.

Structure and Outline

Although the book is short (eighty-five verses), it is nevertheless a literary masterpiece. Herman Gunkel, the noted form-critical scholar, has characterized the book as a "novella," by which he meant "a short, well-constructed story, with carefully developed plot and characters, extensive use of dialogue, which moves to a climax and denouement, put together by one author."[10] He concluded that the book was derived from an earlier legend and that it implied fictionality. The book's "pastoral seting, portrayal of common people, and lack of a villain qualify it as an idyll, though idylls are usually fictional."[11] Sasson prefers the classification "folktale."[12] Since the book is referring to actual events, it seems best to identify it as a "historical short story."[13]

The book has a clear sense of movement; the narrative moves from famine to feasting; from death to life; from widowhood to marriage; from bitterness to joy.[14] The story's conversations, not the narration or structure, carry the plot along. Fifty-nine of the 85 verses in the book contain dialogue.[15] These conversations provide the story with an element of suspense. The author only gives information when necessary (e.g., closer relative in 3:12; parcel of land in 4:3). "The writer cleverly dispenses information like a card player wary of tipping his hand."[16] As a result, the reader is anxious to continue the story until the climax; the marriage of Boaz and Ruth. The story ends with a description of the fruit of this union; a child born who will become the grandfather of David.

Some have seen the genealogy of David in 4:18-22 as a later addition. The following arguments are used to support this view: First, the genealogy repeats information that has already been provided (cf. 4:17b); Second, the simpleness of the genealogy is inconsistent with the intricate artistry of the narrative; Third, this is the only instance in the Old Testament of a genealogy following (rather than introducing) the narrative to which it is connected.[17] Fourth, the primary purpose of the genealogy is to connect the birth of Obed to David, a character who is of no significance in the narrative.

While these arguments are certainly compelling, a careful study of the book reveals that the genealogy is critical to a proper interpretation of the narrative. The genealogy confirms the blessing of 4:12; the genealogy identifies the king anticipated in the first two segments of the so-called "Bethlehem Trilogy" (i.e., Jud. 17-18; 19-21; Ruth); the genealogy serves as an inclusio with the family details of 1:2; and the genealogy honors the central characters Naomi, Ruth, and Boaz by revealing their relationship to the future king of Israel.

<u>Outline</u>

I. Introduction (1:1-5)
II. Naomi and Ruth Return to Bethlehem (1:6-22)
    A. The loyalty of Ruth (1:6-18)
    B. The bitterness of Naomi (1:19-22)
III. Ruth Meets Boaz (2:1-23)
    A. Ruth in the fields of Boaz (2:1-16)
        1. The introduction of Boaz (2:1)
        2. Ruth goes to the fields of Boaz (2:2-3)
        3. The conversation between Boaz and his men (2:4-7)
        4. The conversation between Boaz and Ruth (2:8-13)

Summary of Contents

Introduction (1:1-5)

The book of Ruth begins with the traditional Hebrew formula *hayah* ("Now it came about;" cf. Joshua, Judges, 1 Samuel, 2 Samuel, Esther). The time frame given is "in the days when the judges governed" (1:1). This phrase naturally leads the reader back to the book of Judges and gives the reader a sense of trepidation, knowing that the period of the judges was a time of great apostasy. As a result, the reader assumes that the story which follows will continue the downward spiral begun in the book of Judges. This sense of foreboding is enhanced as the reader is informed that there is a famine in the land, a clear sign of God's judgment upon Israel for sin. The parallels continue with the mention of Bethlehem in Judah, a city prominent in the closing chapters of Judges (Jud. 17:7, 8, 9; 19:1, 2, 18). Bethlehem is located about five miles south of Jerusalem. The name Bethlehem means "house of bread," a title inconsistent with the idea of famine.

The "certain man" (1:1) who lived in Bethlehem is identified as Elimelech (meaning "my God is King"). His wife is Naomi ("pleasantness"). Their children are named Mahlon ("sickly") and Chilion ("wasting away"). The depressing names of the children add to the anxiety, giving the impression that the "God-King" has not been "pleasant" to Elimelech and Naomi. Since Yahweh has seemingly failed them, the family left their home and moved to the land of Moab, the hated enemy of Israel.

Elimelech, the Ephrathite (Ephrathah was another name for Bethlehem; cf. 1 Sam. 17:12; Mic. 5:2), died shortly after the move to Moab, a sign of God's further judgment upon the family. Instead of returning to Bethlehem, the family remained in Moab; Mahlon and Chilion even took Moabite women as wives. At this point, the reader surely anticipates another calamity, remembering what took place the last time Israelite men hooked up with Moabite women (Num. 25). This sense of forboding is confirmed as the reader learns of the death of both Mahlon and Chilion ten years after the move to Moab.

Naomi and Ruth Return to Bethlehem (1:6-22)

When Naomi heard that the famine in Judah was over, she decided to return to Bethlehem. She encouraged both of her daughters-in-law to stay in Moab with their own families. The names of the daughters-in-law are Orpah (meaning "gazelle"), the widow of Chilion, and Ruth ("friend, companion"), the widow of Mahlon. Naomi, intending to return alone, pronounced a blessing on Orpah and Ruth, requesting that the Lord "deal kindly" (Heb. *hesed*) with them (1:8) and grant them "rest" (1:9). The concept of rest referred to here is the security that is found in marriage (cf. 3:1).[18]

Orpah and Ruth initially refused the request, expressing their desire to accompany Naomi on her return to Bethlehem. Naomi replied by informing the young widows that she was much too old to bear sons capable of taking the place of Mahlon and Chilion. Here we have an allusion to the law of levirate marriage. The rules governing levirate marriage are recorded in Deuteronomy 25:5-10. According to this law, a widow's brother-in-law is required to marry her in order to provide an heir who can carry on the family name of the deceased. If the living brother is unwilling to perform his duty, then the elders of the city are commanded to shame him, allowing the widow to spit in his face and remove his sandal and giving his family the name, "The house of him whose sandal is removed" (Deut. 25:10).

The explanation of Naomi is enough to convince Orpah. She gave Naomi a kiss goodbye and returned to her family (and her gods [cf. 1:15]). Orpah is never again mentioned in the narrative. However, Ruth "clung" to her mother-in-law (1:14). Naomi, sensing Ruth's commitment to her, again encouraged her daughter-in-law to return to her family. Ruth's reply, which appears as poetry in most Bibles, is "one of the most beautiful expressions of commitment in all the world's literature."[19] She binds her future with that of Naomi. Ruth pledges to go wherever Naomi goes; become a member of her people; worship her God; die wherever Naomi dies, and there be buried. To show the depth of her commitment, Ruth places a curse on her own head; requesting death if she fails to live up to her oath. Naomi, seeing Ruth's resolve, finally agreed to take her along on the journey to Bethlehem.[20]

When Naomi arrived in Bethlehem, the women of the city greeted her warmly, surprised at her return. Naomi, full of self-despair, requested that the women call her Mara (meaning "bitterness") instead of Naomi ("pleasantness") because the Almighty (Heb. *Shadday*) had dealt very "bitterly" towards her (1:20).[21] Naomi explained to the women that she had left full but had returned empty, a sure indication that the Lord had afflicted her. The chapter closes by informing the reader that Naomi arrived in Bethlehem at the beginning of the barley harvest (Nisan; late March-early April). Barley, a winter cereal which was planted between the end of October and mid-December, was the first crop to ripen in ancient Israel.

Ruth Meets Boaz (2:1-23)

The timing of Ruth and Naomi's arrival in Bethlehem is providential since it provides an immediate opportunity for Ruth to earn a living by gleaning in the fields. As the reapers would cut the stalks of grain, some of the grain would fall to the ground; hence, the gleanings. According to the Mosaic Law, reapers were not allowed to gather these gleanings; they were to be left for the poor (cf. Lev. 19:9-10; 23:22; Deut. 24:19-21). Evidently, Naomi herself was too old to glean in the fields alongside Ruth (cf. 1:12).

At this point, the narrative interjects a key piece of information. Naomi has a kinsman named Boaz. The name Boaz means "strength." Boaz is identified as a man of "great wealth" (2:1; Heb. *gibor hayil*; literally "valiant warrior;" cf. Jud. 6:12; 11:1). After gaining the permission of Naomi, Ruth set out to choose a field in which to glean. As fate would have it, Ruth "happened" to come to the field belonging to Boaz (2:3). Although the narrative initially credits this choice to chance, the text later reveals that the choice was not coincidental, it was providential; it was an act of *hesed* by the Lord (2:20).

While Ruth was gleaning, Boaz arrived at the field and greeted his reapers with the customary greeting, "May the Lord be with you" (2:4; cf. Josh. 1:17; 1 Sam. 17:37; 20:13; 2 Sam. 14:17; 1 Chron. 22:16). Soon Boaz took notice of the young lady in his field and questioned his foreman as to her identity. The foreman explained that she was the Moabitess who had returned with Naomi.

Boaz approached Ruth and commanded her to remain in his fields to glean alongside his maids. He then informed Ruth that he had instructed his servants not to "touch" (2:9; Heb. *naga*) her, an indication that the average Israelite in the time of the judges was not to be trusted (cf. 2:22; Jud. 19). The term used here can mean "to strike a blow" (Gen. 32:25), "to harm" (Gen. 26:11), or "to touch sexually" (Gen. 20:6). The latter meaning is probably in use here. Boaz also informed Ruth that she was welcome to drink of the water drawn by his servants.

Ruth, quickly realizing the incredible generosity of Boaz, immediately fell at his feet and questioned him as to the nature of his kindness. Boaz replied by informing Ruth that her reputation for loyalty had preceeded her. He then pronounced a blessing on her, asking the Lord to reward her labor. Ruth responded by thanking Boaz for showing "favor" (2:13; Heb. *hen*; cf. Esth. 2:15, 17) to her. Note that Ruth now calls herself the "maidservant" (2:13) of Boaz as opposed to a "foreigner" (2:10), an indication of the change in their relationship.

When it came time to eat, Boaz asked Ruth to join his party for lunch. Their meal consisted of bread dipped in vinegar and roasted grain. Roasted grain was one of the most common meals in biblical times. The grain was usually roasted on an iron or bronze plate over an open fire. After the meal, Boaz instructed his reapers to let Ruth glean among the sheaves. He further commanded them to intentionally leave behind some grain so that her task would be even easier.

In the evening, Ruth "beat out" (i.e., threshed) her gleanings. In all, she had accumulated an "ephah" of barley. An ephah was a little more than half a bushel and weighed about thirty pounds; an extraordinary amount for a day's labor. Ruth then returned to Naomi, who immediately recognized that someone had been gracious to her daughter-in-law. When she found out that Ruth's benefactor was Boaz, Naomi informed her that he was a *goel*; one of their "closest relatives" (cf. 3:9, 12, 13; 4:1, 3, 4, 6, 8, 14). This Hebrew term referred to "a relative who acted as a protector or guarantor of family rights. He could be called on to perform a number of duties: 1) to buy back property that the family had sold; 2) to provide an heir for a deceased brother by marrying that brother's wife and producing a child with her; 3) to buy back a family member who had been sold into slavery due to poverty; and 4) to avenge a relative who had been murdered by killing the murderer. The Scripture calls God the Redeemer or 'close relative' of Israel (Isa. 60:16)."[22]

Naomi next pronounced a blessing on Boaz in the name of the Lord "who has not withdrawn His kindness (Heb. *hesed*) to the living and to the dead" (2:20). This phrase is probably a reference to both Naomi and Ruth (living) as well as Elimelech and Mahlon (dead). Ruth then informed Naomi that Boaz had given her permission to glean in his fields until the end of both the barley and wheat harvest season (i.e., end of May). The chapter closes by noting that Ruth lived with her mother-in-law.

Naomi's Plan (3:1-18)

About a month after the events of chapter two, Naomi spoke to her daughter-in-law and proposed an ambitious plan. She asked Ruth to approach Boaz in hopes of securing a marriage proposal. Naomi knew that Boaz was going to be winnowing his barley harvest at the threshing floor that evening. A threshing floor was a flat hard area about 25- 40 feet in diameter on a slightly raised platform or hill. Ideally, it was situated in an open field to take full advantage of the wind. Threshing floors were often surrounded by a border of stones to keep in the grain. In threshing, the grain was beaten out from the stalks with flails or sticks or was trodden over by domesticated animals such as donkeys or oxen. Another common threshing technique involved attaching a large iron drag to a pair of oxen and running it over the stalks of grain. In winnowing, the grain was thrown in the air with shovels so that the wind could carry the chaff away. The grain was then removed from the threshing floor, sifted to remove stones and debris, and placed in piles. Eventually, it was sold or stored in granaries. Boaz had to spend the night at the threshing floor to protect his harvest from thieves.

As Naomi explained her plan, she encouraged Ruth to do eight things: 1) to wash herself; 2) to anoint herself (with perfume); 3) to put on her best clothes; 4) to go to the threshing floor (at night); 5) to wait until Boaz was drunk; 6) to watch for the spot where Boaz chose to rest for the evening; 7) to uncover his feet; and 8) to lie next to him. It appears obvious that Naomi is here advocating a sexual encounter. Her advice is filled with sexual overtones. If Naomi had been acting properly, she should have done the following.[23] First, she should have referred to Boaz as a legal *goel*; instead she uses the term "kinsman" (3:2; Heb. *modaath*). Second, she should have sent Ruth to the city gate during the day where business and legal issues were transacted in public; instead she sends her to approach a drunken man in the middle of the night. She even asks Ruth to lie next to him and "uncover his feet" (3:4). The act of uncovering one's feet was designed to awaken the sleeping party. The technique was often used by prostitutes seeking a midnight sexual encounter. If the awakened party spread his blanket over the woman, it was an indication of his willingness to proceed with sexual activities. Third, she should have insisted that Ruth remain in her mourning clothes because they identified her as a widow; instead she encourages Ruth to put on her best clothes to enhance her physical appeal.

That evening, Ruth followed the advice of Naomi and went to the threshing floor. She carefully watched Boaz as he feasted. The time of threshing and winnowing was an occasion for great celebration. Eventually, Boaz became quite drunk ("his heart was merry;" 3:7; cf. 1 Sam. 25:36; 2 Sam. 13:28; Esth. 1:10) and laid down for the night near the pile of grain. Ruth secretly laid down next to Boaz and uncovered his feet. In the middle of the night, Boaz awoke and was startled to find a woman lying at his feet. He immediately asked who she was. Ruth identified herself and asked Boaz to cover her with his blanket. The scene hints of the sexual union that is to come later.[24]

Boaz pronounced a blessing on Ruth and praised her for her *hesed*. He explained that her present act of kindness was even greater than her kindness to Naomi in Moab. Instead of running off after younger men, Ruth had chosen to follow the wishes of her mother-in-law. Boaz informed Ruth that he would do as she asked, since her reputation as a "woman of excellence" had preceded her (3:11; Heb. *ishah hayil*; cf. Prov. 31:10). Although Boaz was willing to perform the duty of a *goel*, he admitted to Ruth that there was an even closer relative than himself. He instructed Ruth to remain for the evening and promised her that he would redeem her if the closer relative was unwilling to do so.

In the morning, Boaz sent Ruth away before it was light. Obviously, he was concerned for her reputation as a "woman of excellence." The admirable actions of Boaz and Ruth throughout this passage are to be contrasted with the unfortunate advice of Naomi. Ruth identifies Boaz as a *goel* (3:9). She asks him to spread his wings over her, i.e., to fulfill the blessing he had pronounced earlier (3:9; cf. 2:12). Boaz pronounces a blessing on Ruth and affirms her act of *hesed*. He honestly admits that there is a closer relative than himself. He promises to redeem Ruth if the closer relative is unwilling to perform his duty. Boaz sends Ruth away before dawn to preserve her reputation. And later that morning, he takes the legal matter before the elders at the city gate.

Boaz didn't send Ruth away empty-handed; he provided her with six measures of barley. The "measure" was probably the seah (one-third of an ephah or about ten pounds).[25] Six measures would have weighed about sixty pounds. When Ruth returned to her mother-in-law, she informed her of all that had happened. Naomi reassured her with the knowledge that Boaz would not rest until the matter was settled.

The Marriage of Ruth and Boaz (4:1-17)

In the morning, Boaz went to the gate of the city and waited for the closer relative to pass by. Soon the man appeared and Boaz asked him to sit alongside him. The absence of the man's name appears to be an intentional omission on the part of the narrator. The term Boaz used to address the man, "friend" (4:1; Heb. *peloni*), quickly became a catchword in Israel to designate an unknown male, similar to our modern "John Doe." The word has also taken on negative connotations and is often used as a derogatory term or as part of a joke.

While at the city gate, Boaz gathered ten elders together to serve as witnesses of the conversation. Legal and business transactions were often conducted at city gates. It was also the place where the elders of the city sat. The number ten takes on great significance in later centuries; it becomes the number necessary for a Jewish marriage benediction and for a quorum for a synagogue meeting.[26]

In front of the witnesses, Boaz spoke to the man and informed him that Naomi needed to sell the portion of land that had belonged to her husband Elimelech. Elimelech is identified as the "brother" (4:3; Heb. *ah*) of Boaz and the closer relative. However, it is quite unlikely that Boaz and the closer relative were actual brothers of Elimelech. The word is better translated "kinsman" or "relative." Ancestral land was supposed to remain in the family. A family could mortgage property but a kinsman was expected to buy it back. If the land was still mortgaged when the Year of Jubilee (every fifty years) arrived, it was returned to the original owners.

Boaz next informed the man that he is the closest relative and, as such, he has the right to redeem the property if he is willing to do so. The man at this point agreed to the transaction. However, Boaz then informed him that he must also "acquire" (i.e., marry) Ruth as part of the transaction. The purpose of the marriage was to raise up an heir who would eventually inherit the property. In this way, the "name of the deceased" would not be "cut off" (4:10).

The transaction described here does not appear to be an application of the law of levirate marriage; there is no marriage between a widow and her brother-in-law. The relevant term found in Deuteronomy 25:5 (Heb. *yabam*, meaning "to perform the duty of a husband's brother") is not used in Ruth. Instead, Ruth uses the term *gaal* ("to redeem, to act as a kinsman;" cf. *goel*, "kinsman-redeemer"), a word found in Leviticus 25:24-55 to describe the laws concerning redemption. Although marriage is not specifically addressed in Leviticus 25, it is clear that Boaz assumes that it is part of the redeemer's responsibilities. These laws were designed to protect family and land, important covenant concepts.

Having been informed of this second obligation, the closer relative was now unwilling to redeem the parcel of land because it would "jeopardize" (4:6) his own inheritance. Although some have suggested that the nearest kinsman turned down the offer because he was already married, it seems far more likely that he refused the obligation because he would eventually lose the property to a rightful heir. After hearing the original offer, the man agreed, apparently believing that he was able to care for Naomi until her death because he would then inherit the property. However, now that he was faced with the obligation to care for both Naomi and Ruth (and any children born to Ruth) and the prospect of losing the property if she gave birth to an heir, he decided that the prospective gain was not worth the inherent risk. His answer was, in essence, "I do not have the resources to do this!"[27] Notice the contrast between this man and Ruth in terms of commitment. "For Ruth, loyalty [*hesed*] stands head and shoulders over anything else. For this person, loyalty is expendable, especially when it may mean sacrifice."[28]

At this point the man removed his sandal, thus signifying his unwillingness to purchase the land. The removing of one's sandal was a symbolic way of relinquishing one's right to walk on the land that was being sold. This custom had evidently fallen out of use by the time the book was written (cf. 4:7).

Boaz then spoke to the elders and all the people gathered at the city gate, announcing that he had bought the property of Elimelech and acquired Ruth as part of the transaction. Apparently, he was wealthy enough to care for Ruth and Naomi despite the fact that he would eventually lose the property. When the people heard the speech of Boaz, they pronounced a blessing on Ruth and Boaz. They called upon the Lord to bless the union with children, wealth, and fame. Of these, the most important is children. Twice the people reiterate the idea of seed, comparing the house of Ruth and Boaz to those of Jacob (Rachel and Leah were the founding mothers of Israel) and Judah.

Having redeemed Ruth (and Naomi; cf. 4:14; the child born to Boaz continued the family line of Elimelech), Boaz takes her as his wife.[29] As they consummated their marriage, the Lord allowed Ruth to conceive. She eventually gave birth to a son. The women of the city then pronounced a blessing on Naomi, requesting that the name of Boaz become famous in Israel. The women further requested that the child be a source of revitalization for Naomi in her old age. This opportunity was made possible through the love of her daughter-in-law; a woman worth more than seven sons (i.e., the epitome of a productive mother; cf. 1 Sam. 2:5). Ruth 4:15 is the only instance in the Old Testament where one woman is said to love another woman.[30] Naomi took the child, laid him in her lap, and became the child's nurse. The women of the city then gave the child a name, Obed (meaning "worshipper").

Conclusion (4:18-22)

The book closes with a genealogy tracing the lineage from Perez to David. Several names in this list are of significance. Perez was the son of Judah through Tamar, his daughter-in-law who disguised herself as a harlot to seduce him. Hezron was among those from the family of Jacob who journeyed to Egypt (cf. Gen. 46:8, 12). Amminadab (meaning "my kinsman is noble") was the father-in-law of Aaron (Ex. 6:23). Nahshon was the leader of the tribe of Judah during their wilderness wanderings (Num. 2:3). As such, he marched at the front of Israel's procession as they approached the Promised Land (Num. 10:13-14). Salmon was married to Rahab (Matt. 1:5). Although Salmon is identified as the father of Boaz, the fact that he was married to Rahab makes this designation impossible (he lived about 250 years before Boaz was born). Salmon was the ancestor of Boaz, not his actual father.

Obed became the father of Jesse, the father of David. The mention of David is a fitting conclusion to the book. Not only does it serve to announce the fulfillment of the blessings pronounced by the women of the city (4:11-12, 14), it identifies the king alluded to in the epilogue of Judges (17:6; 18:1; 19:1, 21:25); the king who will usher in Israel's golden age of peace and prosperity.

Study Questions

1. What are the Megillot?
2. What three narratives make up the "Bethlehem Trilogy?"
3. List the four purposes of the book of Ruth.
4. What is the meaning of the names Naomi and Mara?
5. What is the meaning of the name Boaz?
6. List the four duties of a *goel.*
7. Describe the acts of threshing and winnowing.
8. Why does the closer relative refuse to redeem Ruth?
9. What is the meaning of the name Obed?
10. What is the relationship between Obed and David?

CHAPTER 4

First and Second Samuel

"Thus says the Lord of hosts, 'I took you from the pasture, from following the sheep, that you should be ruler over my people Israel. And I have been with you wherever you have gone and have cut off all your enemies from before you; and I will make you a great name, like the names of the great men who are on the earth. I will also appoint a place for my people Israel and will plant them, that they may live in their own place and not be disturbed again . . . The Lord also declares to you that the Lord will make a house for you. When your days are complete and you lie down with your fathers, I will raise up your descendant after you, who will come forth from you, and I will establish his kingdom. He shall build a house for My name, and I will establish the throne of his kingdom forever. I will be a father to him and he will be a son to Me; when he commits iniquity, I will correct him with the rod of men and the strokes of the sons of men, but my lovingkindness shall not depart from him, as I took it away from Saul, whom I removed from before you. And your house and your kingdom shall endure before Me forever; your throne shall be established forever.'" (2 Samuel 7:8b-10a; 11b-16).

The books of First and Second Samuel fall together naturally as a unit and originally constituted a single book.[1] The earliest Hebrew manuscripts made no distinction between the books and the unit was simply called Samuel. The title comes from the name of the first primary character in the book. The Septuagint (ca. 200 B.C.) appears to have been the first translation to separate the books, perhaps because of the greatly increased length of the Greek version (the Greek language is written with vowels while Hebrew is written without vowels).[2] The Septuagint entitled the books the First and Second Books of Kingdoms (our books of First and Second Kings were called the Third and Fourth Books of Kingdoms respectively). This division has persisted to the present day in all translations and versions. From a literary and theological standpoint the Samuel books must be viewed as a unit. Hence, in the remainder of this chapter the two books will be regarded as a unit and will simply be called the book of Samuel.

In the Hebrew Bible, Samuel is placed amongst the "Prophets" between Judges and Kings. This sequence is chronological. The book is transitional in nature, beginning in the period of the judges and ending with the monarchy firmly in place. The book of Samuel traces the development of kingship in Israel and reveals its theological significance. The nation is transformed from a confederacy of loosely affiliated tribes to a unified monarchy with a strong central government. Three characters dominate the book. Samuel is the final judge; the man responsible for instituting the monarchy. Saul is the first king of Israel; the man who "acted foolishly" (1 Sam. 13:13) and thus was "rejected" (1 Sam. 15:26) by God. David is the second king of Israel; the "better" (1 Sam. 15:28) man after God's "own heart" (1 Sam. 13:14) who was given an unconditional covenant by the Lord (2 Sam. 7:8-16).

Author

While the Bible does not identify the author of the book, tradition has long held that it was written by Samuel, the prophet, priest, and judge. The primary support for Samuel authorship comes from the Babylonian Talmud, which ascribes the books of Judges, Ruth, and Samuel to the prophet (*Baba Bathra* 14b). Samuel was evidently a capable writer (1 Sam. 10:25) who was an eyewitness to many of the events recorded in the first part of the book. From the testimony of 1 Chronicles 29:29, it is apparent that Samuel wrote at least part of the record of David's life. However, it is likely that the prophet wrote only those sections that deal with the history of Israel prior to his death (1 Sam. 25:1; ca. 1020 B.C.). *Baba Bathra* 15a claims that the book of Samuel was completed by Gad the seer and Nathan the prophet following the death of Samuel.

The book is located in the Torah among the books known as the *Former Prophets*, a fact indicating that Samuel was most likely written by a prophet. One suggestion, an intriguing one, is that Abiathar wrote much of Samuel, especially those parts that concern the court life of David. Abiathar was intimately associated with the rise and fortunes of the great king of Israel because he spent some time with David in his exile. Also, he came from a priestly family and thus had access to the art of writing and record-keeping. Another suggestion is that one of the sons of the prophets from the school founded by Samuel carried on the history of Israel begun by his master. Most probable is that an unknown editor (this does not exclude Abiathar) with intimate knowledge of the house of David compiled most of the book of Samuel shortly before David's death utilizing the memoirs of Samuel, Nathan, and Gad (cf. 1 Chron. 29:29). From the detailed literary style (e.g., lengthy verbatim dialogues, meticulous knowledge of characters and events), it is quite clear that the author relied heavily on eyewitness testimony.

Date

There is no record of David's death in Samuel, a fact that would seem to indicate that the book was written before 971 B.C., especially since the book records the deaths of its other primary characters, Saul and Samuel. However, 1 Samuel 27:6 records that the city of Ziklag "has belonged to the kings of Judah to this day," a notation that suggests that the book was completed after the split of the kingdom in 931 B.C. There are also repeated references to Israel and Judah in the book (1 Sam. 11:8; 17:52; 18:16; 2 Sam. 5:5; 11:11; 12:8; 19:42-43; 24:1, 9). It is probably best to see the majority of the book as having been written near the end of David's reign, probably shortly after the episode of 2 Samuel 24:18-25 (ca. 975 B.C.). The book in its final form was completed sometime before 722 B.C. (there is no indication of the fall of Samaria). The book was probably written from Jerusalem, the home of King David and capital city of the kings of Judah.

Historical Background

The events recorded in the book of Samuel take place between about 1120 and 975 B.C. At this time, the great superpowers of the previous centuries (Egyptians, Hittites, and Assyrians) were all in a state of decline; a situation that allowed Israel to become a dominant political power during the period of the united monarchy. The Egyptians were governed by a very weak Dynasty 21. The pharaohs of this era showed little interest in Palestine, perhaps because they were preoccupied with internal matters and conflicts with the nations that bordered Egypt on the south. The fortunes of Egypt would soon change, however, with the founding of Dynasty 22 by Shishak in 945 B.C.

The great Hittite Empire had come to a sudden and violent end ca. 1200 B.C. with the invasion of the Sea Peoples from the west. The Assyrians experienced a precipitous decline soon after the death of Tiglath-Pileser I (1115-1077 B.C.). Early in his reign, Tiglath-Pileser was able to extend the Assyrian Empire to the Mediterranean coast, exercising considerable influence over the Phoenicians and Hittites. Even Egypt was forced to recognize the power of the Assyrians. However, Tiglath-Pileser made no attempt to extend his empire south into Canaan. This was probably due to the emergence of the Arameans. The Assyrian king was plagued by the marauding nomads. In one inscription he states, "I have crossed the Euphrates twenty-eight times, twice in one year, in pursuit of the . . . Arameans."[3]

The Arameans were either the descendants of Aram, a grandson of Abraham's brother Nahor (Gen. 22:21), or Aram, the son of Shem (Gen. 10:22). In either case, they were Semitic in origin (Nahor was the descendant of Arpachshad, the son of Shem; cf. Gen. 10:22; 11:11-26). The history of the Arameans prior to the twelfth century B.C. is completely unknown. They were evidently nomads from the

Syrian Desert who gradually infiltrated the area around Damascus.[4] By the time of Saul, the Arameans had emerged as the dominant force in the region; a potent threat to Israel's northern borders. They governed the territory from Damascus north as far as the Euphrates River. As a result, they controlled the major trade routes between Anatolia and Mesopotamia. The Aramean Empire would continue to trouble Israel until the re-emergence of the Assyrians under Tiglath Pilesar III (745-727 B.C.), at which time they were absorbed into the Assyrian Empire.

The Arameans who settled in Syria[5] were primarily pastoralists and villagers. Their religion was borrowed from the West Semitic fertility cults of Canaan. The chief deity of the Arameans was the storm god Hadad-Rimmon, i.e., Hadad the Thunderer. Two other notable Aramean deities were the moon god Sin, the patron god of Haran, and the sun god Shamash. The capital of the Aramean state was Damascus, one of the oldest cities in the world. The city was strategically located at the convergence of the two major north-south trade routes through Canaan, the Via Maris (also known as the Way of the Philistines), which led to Egypt, and the King's Highway, which led to Arabia.

The most significant contribution of the Aramean civilization was its language. The Arameans spoke a Northwest Semitic language known as Aramaic. The Northwest Semitic subgroup also includes Hebrew, Phoenician, Moabite, Ammonite, and Ugaritic.[6] Thanks to the Assyrian policy of deporting large numbers of people from their conquered homelands into Assyria, a substantial part of the Assyrian population by the eighth century B.C. was Aramean.[7] Soon, Aramaic was being used for official communication throughout the Assyrian Empire. When the Babylonians destroyed the Assyrian Empire (ca. 612-605 B.C.), they adopted Aramaic as their spoken language of choice (Akkadian was primarily a written language). The Persians, who conquered Babylon in 539 B.C., followed suit and Aramaic became the *lingua franca* of the Persian Empire. Eventually, Aramaic even replaced Hebrew as the most popular language in Israel. As a result, translations of the biblical text into Aramaic (called Targumim) were produced and read alongside the original Hebrew texts in the synagogues.[8] Aramaic was probably the primary language used by Jesus throughout his earthly ministry. Certain dialects of Aramaic are still spoken today.

The chief antagonists of Israel in the book of Samuel are the Philistines.[9] The Philistines were one of the Sea Peoples. The Sea Peoples left[10] their coastal homes in Greece, Asia Minor, and the Aegean Islands (including Crete) and invaded the coast along the eastern Mediterranean. They also attempted to settle on the Egyptian coast, however, Rameses III was able to repel them on both land and sea in the eighth year of his reign (ca. 1190 B.C.).[11] The Philistines[12] from Crete (Caphtor; cf. Jer. 47:4; Amos 9:7) settled in southwestern Canaan and established a firm stronghold thanks to the Philistine pentapolis of Gaza, Gath, Ekron, Ashkelon, and Ashdod. Each of these cities was governed by a "lord" (Heb. *seren*; cf. 3:3).

The Philistines stood out from their neighbors because they did not practice circumcision, hence the derisive term "uncircumcised Philistines" (14:3). The Philistines were more technologically advanced than the Hebrews, having learned the art of working with iron tools and weapons (cf. 1 Sam. 13:19-20). Little is known of the Philistine language because no obvious examples of Philistine writing have been found. However, the pottery of the Philistines is particularly well-known, primarily because of its distinctive shapes and colors. Typical shapes included the globular pilgrim jar, the delicate high-stemmed kylix, the large pyriform jar, the squat pyxis, and the popular stirrup jar.[13] The pottery was usually decorated in red and black motifs. The religion of the Philistines is also well-known. Their chief god was Dagon, the father of Baal. Dagon was often represented as a human head with the body of a fish. Dagon was worshipped in Mesopotamia as a grain god. It is possible that the originally seafaring Philistines brought their fish god with them when they migrated to Canaan and then adapted him to the Semitic god Dagon (or Dagan, as it is known outside the Bible), because of their need to become a grain-producing people (Jud. 15:3-5).[14] Ashtoreth[15] was the Philistine goddess of love and sometime consort of Baal. Baal-zebub was the patron god of Ekron (cf. 2 Kin. 1:2-3). His name means "lord of the flies," and is probably a derogatory emendation of Baal-zebul, meaning "lord Baal." Notable Philistines mentioned in Samuel include Goliath and Achish.

Another group that significantly impacts Israel in the book of Samuel is the Ammonites. The Ammonites were the descendants of Ben-ammi, the son of an incestuous relationship between Lot and his younger daughter. They lived on the eastern side of the Jordan River. The nation's territory was essentially surrounded by the Jabbok River and its tributaries. As a result, the border of Ammonite territory was referred to simply as the Jabbok River (Deut. 3:16; Josh. 12:2). The sources of the Jabbok River are near modern Amman, Jordan. This territory had previously belonged to the Rephaim, an ancient people who were displaced by the Ammonites (Deut. 2:20-21). The earliest documentation of hostilities between the Ammonites and the Children of Israel is the record of Judges 3:12-14, where the Ammonites join the coalition formed by Eglon, king of Moab. Jephthah later defeats an unnamed king of Ammon (Judg. 11). Notable Ammonites include Naamah, the wife of Solomon and mother of Rehoboam (1 Kin. 14:21, 31; 2 Chron. 12:13), and Tobiah, one of the major antagonists of Nehemiah (Neh. 2:19; 4:3). Solomon built a sanctuary for Molech, the "detestable" chief god of the Ammonites, on the Mount of Olives (1 Kin. 11:7). Child sacrifice was a significant part of the Ammonite Molech cult (Lev. 18:21; 20:2-5; 2 Kin. 23:10; Jer. 32:35).

Audience and Purpose

The book of Samuel was written to trace the move of the nation from a theocratic judgeship to a theocratic monarchy. The institution of a monarchy had always been a central part of God's program for Israel. Promises about kingship were given to the patriarchs. Abraham and Sarah were told that kings would be produced through their offspring (Gen. 17:6, 16). Jacob is later given the same promise (Gen. 35:11). The promise is then repeated to Judah (Gen. 49:8-12). Even Balaam prophesied concerning the future king who would come from the line of Jacob (Num. 24:17-19). The Mosaic Law contained a list of regulations for the institution of a monarchy (Deut. 17:14-20). According to this passage, the future king was to be a man of God's choosing (15), an Israelite who was not preoccupied with personal gain (15-17), and one who lived his life according to the Law of Moses (18-20).

Although Saul is anointed as the first king of Israel, it is at once apparent that he cannot be the fulfillment of these promises. The Lord had promised that the future king would come from the tribe of Judah (Gen. 49:8-12). Saul was a member of the tribe of Benjamin. Therefore, the dynasty of Saul comes to a sudden end after one king and is quickly replaced by the dynasty of David.

The text takes great care to show that it was God who rejected Saul and appointed David (cf. 1 Sam. 13:14; 15:28); the young shepherd did not usurp the throne on his own volition. In fact, the middle portion of the book amounts to an apology for David's rise to the throne. The *Nelson's New Illustrated Bible Commentary* shows the remarkable similarities between this section and the *Apology of Hattusilis*, a thirteenth-century B.C. writing. In this ancient document, a Hittite king outlined the reasons for the legitimacy of his rule. Such an apology was particularly important in the case of a king—like David—who founded a new dynasty. Hattusilis's dynastic defense included the following elements:

1) A detailed description of the disqualifications of the preceding ruler (compare 1 Sam. 15:1-35).
2) An extended history of events leading up to the new king's accession (compare 1 Sam. 16:1-2 Sam. 5:17).
3) A defense of the new king's ability to rule, as evidenced by military achievements (compare 1 Sam. 17:1-58).
4) A record of the new king's leniency on political foes, in contrast to usurpers, who typically assassinated the former king (compare 1 Sam. 24:1-10; 26:1-9).
5) A report of the new king's interest in religion (compare 2 Sam. 6:1-19; 7:1-29).
6) A conclusion that included a summary of the new king's reign, demonstrating the divine blessing on his rule as evidenced by the expansion of his kingdom and the establishment of peace with surrounding nations (compare 2 Sam. 8:1-18).[16]

The climax of the book is the Davidic Covenant recorded in 2 Samuel 7:8-16, a passage that clearly identifies David as the chosen king. In this covenant, the Lord promised David that he would be given a great name (cf. Gen. 12:2). Yahweh further promised that He would appoint a place for the people of Israel and plant them in their own land (cf. Gen. 12:1). There they will finally experience rest (i.e., peace). Finally, the Lord promised that David would be the patriarch of an everlasting dynasty (cf. Gen. 17:6), saying, "Your house and your kingdom shall endure before Me forever; your throne shall be established forever" (7:16). The Lord's lovingkindness (Heb. *hesed*) would never be taken away from the family of David as it was removed from Saul. The Davidic Covenant is an expansion of the Abrahamic Covenant (cf. Gen. 12:1-3). The ultimate fulfillment of these promises will take place in the Millennium. At that time, Israel will be safely planted in the land promised to them. There they will be governed forever by Jesus Christ, the Seed of David and promised Messiah.

The Davidic Covenant involved a parental relationship between Yahweh and Israel's king that involved discipline rather than rejection.[17] The king was now identified as the son of God while God Himself was characterized as the father of the king (2 Sam. 7:14). The future kings of Israel would be judged according to their faithfulness to God's covenant; obedience would bring the blessings of God while disobedience would result in the curses of God (cf. Deut. 28). However, the kingdom will never be taken away from the house of David.

The primary way in which God communicated with His kings is by the use of prophets. Throughout the book of Samuel, Yahweh sent His messengers to His kings both to reward (1 Sam. 9; 10; 16; 2 Sam. 7) and to reprimand (1 Sam. 13; 15; 28; 2 Sam 12; 24). Prophets who are identified by name in the book include Samuel, Nathan, and Gad. There is also an unnamed prophet simply called a "man of God" (1 Sam. 2:27).

Structure and Outline

The unity of the book of Samuel has been questioned since the time of Wellhausen. In 1871, he published a groundbreaking work[18] in which he argued that 1 Samuel 7:2-15:35 was comprised of two sources. The first source was written during the monarchical period. It was pro-kingship and included 1 Samuel 9:1-10:16 and all of chapters eleven, thirteen and fourteen. The second source was written during and after the exile. It was anti-kingship and included 1 Samuel 7:2-8:22; 10:17-27; and all of chapters twelve and fifteen.[19] The source critics who followed Wellhausen have greatly expanded his original work, identifying several other distinct blocks of material that are routinely identified as early or late depending on whether or not the text fits the Deuteronomistic theory.[20] A significant reason why many scholars now believe that the book is comprised of multiple sources is the presence of several so-called "doublets" in the text, some of which appear to provide contradictory accounts. These include the reason given for Saul's accession (1 Sam. 8:5-10 and 1 Sam. 9:15-17); the rejection of Saul as king (1 Sam. 13:13-14 and 15:10-31); the initial meeting between David and Saul (1 Sam. 16:14-23 and 1 Sam. 17:31-40, 55-58); the sparing of Saul's life by David (1 Sam. 24 and 1 Sam. 26); and the account of Goliath's death (1 Sam. 17:50-51 and 2 Sam. 21:19).[21]

While it is readily acknowledged that the author of Samuel used a variety of sources in compiling his work, the final product is much more unified than these scholars admit. The book is comprised of seven distinct sections that share a number of common themes (e.g., the journeys of the Ark of the Covenant, the emphasis on the Lord's "anointed" [Heb. *Meshiah*; 1 Sam. 2:10, 35; 12:3, 5; 16:6; 24:6, 10; 26:9, 11, 16, 23; 2 Sam. 1:14, 16; 19:21; 22:51; 23:1]) and literary features (e.g., extended dialogues, descriptive epithets, inclusios).[22] The first section (1 Samuel 1:1-4:1a) contrasts Samuel with the sons of Eli. The second section (4:1b-7:1) emphasizes the journeys of the Ark of the Covenant. The third section records the ministry of Samuel and the early years of Saul's reign (7:2-15:35). The fourth section (16:1- 2 Samuel 1:27) highlights the conflict between Saul and David. The fifth section (2:1-10:19) describes the early years of David's reign. The sixth section (11:1-20:26) focuses on the fight for the throne after David's adultery with Bathsheba and murder of Uriah. The seventh and final section serves as an appendix, stressing the greatness of David's reign (21:1-24:25).

The idea that the book is to be seen as a single unit is strengthened by the arrangement of Hannah's prayer in 1 Samuel 2:1-10 and David's psalm in 2 Samuel 22:1-51. These two passages serve as an inclusio, uniting everything in between. Both poems praise the actions and attributes of Yahweh (2:1, 2, 3, 6, 7, 10; 22:1, 2, 4, 7, etc.); speak of the author's "horn" (2:1; 22:3);[23] highlight God's actions against one's "enemies" (2:1; 22:1, 4, 38, 41, 49); emphasize "salvation" (2:1; 22:3, 36, 47); picture God as a "rock" (2:2; 22:2, 3, 32, 47); speak of being girded with "strength" (2:4; 22:40); reference "Sheol" (2:6; 22:6); portray God as thundering in the heavens (2:10; 22:14); and pay tribute to the Lord's "anointed" (2:10; 22:51). In effect, Hannah's prayer is a prophetic summary of the themes that permeate the book while David's psalm reveals that those themes have become reality.

<u>Outline</u>
I. The Eli-Samuel Exchange (1 Samuel 1:1-4:1a)
    A. Samuel's miraculous birth (1:1-28)
        1. Samuel's family (1:1-3)
        2. Hannah's barrenness (1:4-8)
        3. Hannah's prayer (1:9-18)
        4. Hannah's prayer answered (1:19-23)
        5. Hannah's gift (1:24-28)
    B. Hannah's song (2:1-10)
    C. Samuel contrasted with the sons of Eli (2:11-4:1a)
        1. Samuel's ministry under Eli (2:11)
        2. The sin of Eli's sons (2:12-17)
        3. Samuel's growth (2:18-21)
        4. Eli's failure (2:22-25)
        5. Samuel's continued growth (2:26)
        6. The prophecy against the house of Eli (2:27-36)
        7. The Lord calls Samuel (3:1-4:1a)
            a. The divine voice (3:1-10)
            b. The divine message (3:11-14)
            c. Samuel the prophet (3:15-4:1a)
II. The Journeys of the Ark (4:1b-7:1)
    A. The capture of the Ark (4:1b-22)
        1. The first defeat at Aphek (4:1b-3)
        2. The Ark brought to Aphek (4:4-9)
        3. The second defeat at Aphek (4:10-11)

4. The death of Eli (4:12-22)

B. The Ark in Philistine territory (5:1-6:12)

    1. The Ark in Ashdod (5:1-8a)

    2. The Ark in Gath (5:8b-10a)

    3. The Ark in Ekron (5:10b-12)

    4. The Philistines send the Ark to Israel (6:1-12)

C. The Ark back in Israel (6:13-7:1)

    1. The Ark in Beth-Shemesh (6:13-21)

    2. The Ark in Kiriath-Jearim (7:1)

III. The Establishment of the Monarchy (7:2-15:35)

A. The ministry of Samuel (7:2-10:27)

    1. The victory at Mizpah (7:2-17)

    2. The selection of a king (8:1-10:27)

        a. The demand for a king (8:1-9)

        b. The rejected advice of Samuel (8:10-22)

        c. The anointing of Saul by Samuel (9:1-10:8)

        d. Saul is made king (10:9-27)

B. The early reign of Saul (11:1-15:35)

    1. Saul rescues Jabesh Gilead (11:1-15)

    2. Samuel's farewell address (12:1-25)

    3. Samuel rebukes Saul (13:1-15)

    4. Saul's victory at Gibeah (13:16-14:46)

        a. The weaponless Israelites (13:16-22)

        b. Jonathan's valiant attack (13:23-14:14)

        c. Israel defeats the Philistines (14:15-23)

        d. Jonathan's narrow escape (14:24-46)

    5. The victories of Saul (14:47-48)

    6. The family of Saul (14:49-52)

    7. The Lord rejects Saul as king (15:1-35)

        a. The instruction of Samuel (15:1-3)

        b. Saul's disobedience (15:4-9)

        c. Samuel rebukes Saul (15:10-35)

IV. The Conflict between Saul and David (16:1- 2 Samuel 1:27)

A. Samuel anoints David (16:1-13)

B. David in Saul's service (16:14-23)

C. David and Goliath (17:1-58)

D. Saul feuds with David (18:1-30:30)

1. Saul's jealousy (18:1-30)
2. David's flight (19:1-24)
3. David and Jonathan (20:1-42)
4. Saul pursues David (21:1-30:30)
   a. David at Nob (21:1-9)
   b. David at Gath (21:10-15)
   c. David at Adullam (22:1-2)
   d. David at Mizpah (22:3-4)
   e. David in the forest of Hereth (22:5-23:4)
   f. David at Keilah (23:5-12)
   g. David's wanderings (23:13-29)
   h. David spares Saul's life in the desert of En Gedi (24:1-22)
   i. David in the desert of Maon (25:1-44)
   j. David spares Saul's life in the desert of Ziph (26:1-25)
   k. David among the Philistines (27:1-30:30)

E. The death of Saul (31:1-13)
F. David's response to the death of Saul (2 Samuel 1:1-27)
   1. The report of the young Amalekite (1:1-16)
   2. David laments for Saul and Jonathan (1:17-27)

V. The King David Narrative (2:1-10:19)
   A. David anointed king of Judah (2:1-7)
   B. The civil war between the houses of David and Saul (2:8-4:12)
   C. David anointed king of Israel (5:1-5)
   D. David's early reign (5:6-10:19)
      1. The conquest of Jerusalem (5:6-16)
      2. The defeat of the Philistines (5:17-25)
      3. The Ark brought to Jerusalem (6:1-23)
      4. The Davidic Covenant (7:1-29)
      5. A review of David's early reign (8:1-18)
      6. David and Mephibosheth (9:1-13)
      7. The defeat of the Ammonites (10:1-19)

VI. The Fight for the Throne (11:1-20:26)
   A. David and Bathsheba (11:1-27)
   B. Nathan rebukes David (12:1-31)

C. Amnon and Tamar (13:1-22)
D. Absalom kills Amnon (13:23-39)
E. Absalom in Jerusalem (14:1-33)
F. Absalom's attempt to take the throne (15:1-19:8a)
   1. Absalom's conspiracy (15:1-12)
   2. David's flight (15:13-37)
   3. David and Ziba (16:1-4)
   4. David and Shimei (16:5-14)
   5. The advice of Hushai and Ahithophel (16:15-17:29)
   6. The death of Absalom (18:1-18)
   7. David mourns the death of Absalom (18:19-19:8a)
G. David returns to Jerusalem (19:8b-43)
H. Sheba rebels against David (20:1-26)
VII. Six Appendices Describing David's Great Kingdom (21:1-24:25)
A. The Gibeonites avenged (21:1-14)
B. David's heroic men (21:15-22)
C. David's psalm of praise (22:1-51)
D. The last words of David (23:1-7)
E. David's mighty men (23:8-39)
F. David's sinful census (24:1-25)

Summary of Contents

The Eli-Samuel Exchange (1 Samuel 1:1-4:1a)

The book of Samuel begins with the traditional Hebrew formula *hayah* ("Now it came about;" cf. Joshua, Judges, Ruth, Esther). The first chapter is an account of the miraculous birth of Samuel. His father was a Levite (cf. 1 Chron. 6:19, 27-28) named Elkanah (meaning "God has possessed"). Elkanah lived in Ramathaim-Zophim (also known as Ramah), a town located five miles north of Jerusalem in the "hill country of Ephraim" (1:1). The reference to the hill country of Ephraim reminds the reader of the stories of Micah's idols and the Levite's concubine (cf. Jud. 17:1; 19:1). It should be remembered that the book of Judges immediately precedes Samuel in the Hebrew Bible.

Elkanah had two wives; Hannah (meaning "grace") and Peninnah ("pearl"). While Peninnah had several children, Hannah was barren. It was customary in those days for a man whose wife was infertile to take a second wife by whom he could bear children (Gen. 16:1-3; 30:3-4, 9-10; etc.).[24] Although her husband tried to console her, Hannah became distraught over her infertility. On one of their yearly visits to Shiloh,[25] Hannah prayed to the Lord, vowing that she would dedicate her son as a Nazirite[26] if God would only allow her to conceive. Hannah's praying was so fervent that the high priest Eli ("God is high") thought she was drunk. Eventually, the Lord allowed Hannah to conceive and she gave birth to a son. She named him Samuel, meaning "God has heard," because the Lord had answered her prayer. When the child was weaned (probably at the age of three),[27] she brought him to the tabernacle at Shiloh and dedicated him to the Lord.

To honor the One who had shown her grace, Hannah offered a prayer of thanksgiving to the Lord.[28] She began her prayer with a statement of exaltation; the Lord had indeed blessed her. Hannah expressed joy in her "salvation" (2:1), a reference to the deliverance (from the taunts of Peninnah) achieved by the birth of her son. She then praised God for His attributes, including His holiness, knowledge, and sovereignty over the affairs of men. Hannah closed her prayer with the prophetic announcement that the Lord "will give strength to His king, and will exalt the horn of His anointed" (2:10; Heb. *Meshiah*). The king alluded to here is David, the future ruler of Israel (cf. 2 Sam. 22:51).

As a child, Samuel proved to be a sharp contrast to Hophni (meaning "pugilist") and Phinehas ("mouth of brass"), the sons of Eli.[29] While Samuel "ministered to the Lord" (2:11), the sons of Eli "did not know the Lord" (2:12). Hophni and Phinehas made a mockery of the sacrificial system, routinely embezzling extra meat and fornicating with the young women who served at the sanctuary. This latter sin was probably an attempt to emulate the sexual rituals of the fertility cults. In effect, the sons of Eli were converting the house of Yahweh into a Canaanite shrine. The sins of Hophni and Phinehas were so terrible the Lord "desired to put them to death"

(2:25). Samuel, however, "was growing in stature and in favor both with the Lord and with men" (2:26).

One day, Eli was visited by a prophet ("man of God;" 2:27) with a message from God. The prophet informed Eli that the Lord would soon remove the high priesthood from his family because of the sins of his sons. The high priesthood was going to be given to "a faithful priest" who would faithfully serve the Lord's "anointed" (2:35). This prophecy was fulfilled during the reign of Solomon when the priesthood was taken from Abiathar, a descendant of Ithamar,[30] and given to Zadok, a descendant of Eleazar (cf. 1 Kin. 2:27, 35).[31]

Soon after the visit of the prophet, the Lord spoke to Samuel. In those days, visions were uncommon because Yahweh rarely spoke to His people. When the Lord called Samuel, the young boy thought that Eli had called him. He rushed to the high priest and asked him what he wanted. When Eli informed the boy that he was mistaken, Samuel returned to his bed. The same events happened again and again. Finally, Eli perceived that Samuel was hearing the voice of God. He told Samuel to remain at his bed and listen to what Yahweh had to say. The Lord told Samuel that the house of Eli would soon come to an end; the same message that had been delivered by the prophet. When Samuel told Eli what the Lord had said, the high priest accepted his fate. This episode confirmed Samuel as a "prophet of the Lord" (3:20) to the entire nation of Israel (Dan and Beersheba were the northernmost and southernmost cities in Israel). The Lord was with him in great strength and let none of his words "fail" (3:19; lit. "fall to the ground;" an archery term symbolizing that each of Samuel's prophecies came to pass, i.e., "hit the target").

The Journeys of the Ark (4:1b-7:1)

In ca. 1104 B.C., the Israelite army journeyed to Aphek in an attempt to halt a Philistine invasion. It is entirely possible that this invasion may have been in retaliation for Samson's early heroics against the Philistines.[32] The city of Aphek is located about twenty-five miles west of Shiloh. In the resultant battle, the Israelites suffered a humiliating defeat, losing four thousand men. Superstitiously they attributed their loss to the absence of the Ark of the Covenant from the battlefield.[33] Hoping to turn their fortunes, the Israelites sent messengers to Shiloh to bring the Ark to Aphek. The Ark of the Covenant was most important religious relic in Israel.[34] It symbolized the glory of the Lord; Yahweh's presence among His people. The Israelites probably believed that the presence of the Ark guaranteed victory; there was no way the Lord was going to allow Himself to be captured. Unfortunately, the plan failed and the Philistines achieved an overwhelming victory. The Ark was captured and the Israelites lost thirty thousand men, including Hophni and Phinehas, who had accompanied the Ark in battle. When Eli heard the tragic news, he fell backward in his chair and died. He had judged Israel forty years (ca. 1144-1104 B.C.). At about this time, the wife of Phinehas died while giving birth to a son. The child was named Ichabod (meaning "no glory") because the glory of the Lord had departed from Israel.

The Philistines took the Ark of the Covenant and placed it in the temple of Dagon in Ashdod, one of the five major Philistine cities (i.e., Gaza, Gath, Ekron, Ashkelon, and Ashdod). The capture of the Ark would have naturally led to the conclusion that Dagon was more powerful than Yahweh. However, God soon showed Himself superior to the Philistine god. When the men of Ashdod entered the temple the next morning, they found the statue of Dagon lying face down before the Ark. They returned the statue to its pedestal only to find it in the same position the following day. In addition, a great plague struck the inhabitants of the city as the Lord smote them with tumors. The Ark was sent to Gath and eventually Ekron, where similar plagues broke out in each city. Finally, the Philistines returned the Ark to Israel on a cart drawn by two cows that had never experienced a yoke. In fact, to be sure that the plague was the result of Yahweh, the Philistines took their nursing calves to their birthplace. The natural inclination of the cows would have been to return home to be with their calves.

Instead, the cart went directly to Beth-Shemesh, a village located fourteen miles west of Jerusalem on the border between Philistine and Israelite territory. Upon seeing the Ark, the men of Beth-Shemesh rejoiced and immediately offered a sacrifice of thanksgiving to Yahweh. However, several of the inhabitants of the village looked into the Ark and were struck dead by the Lord. As a result, the survivors asked the men of Kiriath-Jearim to take possession of the Ark. Kiriath-Jearim is located about ten miles northeast of Beth-Shemesh. The Ark remained in Kiriath-Jearim for about one hundred years (ca. 1104-1003 B.C.) at the home of Abinadab (meaning "father of nobleness").

The Establishment of the Monarchy (7:2-15:35)

In ca. 1084 B.C. (twenty years after the battle of Aphek; cf. 7:2), Samuel informed the nation that the Lord would deliver them from the oppression of the Philistines if they would remove the Baals (the chief god of the Canaanites) and Ashtaroth (plural of Ashtoreth, the Canaanite goddess of love and sometime consort of Baal) and faithfully worship the Lord. After the sons of Israel agreed to follow Yahweh, Samuel gathered them to Mizpah to fast and pray before the Lord. Mizpah was located about seven miles north of Jerusalem. The city was a common place of assembly for Israel. There the elders of the tribes gathered to decide Benjamin's fate after the rape and murder of the Levite's concubine (Jud. 19-21). It will also become the site of Saul's coronation (1 Sam. 10:17-24). Following the destruction of Jerusalem at the hands of the Babylonians (586 B.C.), Mizpah served as the capital of Judah (cf. 2 Kin. 25:23, 25).

When the Philistines heard that the Israelites were gathered at Mizpah, they sent an army to the city. After sacrificing a lamb to the Lord, Samuel led the Israelites to a great victory, destroying the Philistine force. To commemorate the triumphant occasion, the prophet erected a memorial stone named Ebenezer (meaning "stone of God's help") halfway between Mizpah and Shen (location unknown). The great victory at Mizpah brought an end to the forty years of Philistine oppression mentioned in Judges 13:1 (ca. 1124-1084 B.C.). Samuel continued to serve as Israel's judge until the day he died, routinely making a circuit from Ramah to Bethel to Gilgal to Mizpah and back to Ramah (about fifty miles in circumference).

When Samuel was old (about 65-70 years of age), he appointed his sons Joel (meaning "Yahweh is God") and Abijah ("My father is Yahweh") as judges in Beersheba. Unfortunately, the sons of Samuel were wicked, perverting justice and taking bribes. As such, they were reminiscent of the sons of Eli. The elders of Israel, well-aware of the behavior of Samuel's sons, approached the judge and asked him to appoint a king over Israel. The request displeased Samuel because he thought that the nation had rejected him. However, the Lord informed His prophet that the nation had instead rejected God Himself as king of Israel. Samuel then warned the people that the king would be a demanding dictator who would take their sons and daughters and appropriate their property. The nation, however, would not heed the words of their judge; instead insisting on a king who would judge them and fight their battles. They didn't want to wait for the Lord to raise up a judge; they wanted a king who would always to prepared to defend them. Their underlying desire was to be "like all the nations" (8:20). A secondary reason for the nation's longing for a king was the mounting Philistine threat, a desperate situation that resulted in the tribes finally becoming more unified.

Finally, Samuel succumbed to their wishes and anointed a king. The man chosen was Saul (meaning "asked for"). He was the son of Kish, a "mighty man of valor" (9:1; Heb. *gibor hayil*; cf. Jud. 6:12; 11:1; Ruth 2:1). Saul was a member of the tribe of Benjamin, the smallest of the tribes of Israel, who lived in Gibeah, the site of the rape and murder of the Levite's concubine (Jud. 19). He was an impressive physical specimen, standing taller than any other Israelite. As Saul was looking for some lost donkeys, his servant recommended that they inquire of the prophet Samuel. When they approached the seer, Samuel told them to attend a dinner that he had set up for the occasion, having been forewarned by God. Interestingly, Saul appears to be completely ignorant of Samuel even though his home was only five miles from the prophet's home.

Early the next morning, the prophet took a flask of oil and anointed Saul as king. In ancient times, anointing with oil symbolized the setting apart of an individual for a sacred purpose (cf. Ex. 30:23-33). To confirm the decision, Samuel told Saul that he would experience three signs: 1) he would meet two men near Rachel's tomb who would inform him that his lost donkeys had been found; 2) he would meet three men at the oak tree in Tabor who would give him two loaves of bread; and 3) he would meet a group of prophets descending from the high place at Gibeath-Elohim (Gibeon) and prophesy with them when the Spirit of the Lord came upon him. After Saul departed from the region, the prophetic signs all came to pass.

Samuel then gathered the people of Israel together at Mizpah and informed them that God had given them a king. Using lots to choose tribe, family, and then individual, the prophet chose Saul as king. In the Old Testament, only four kings are divinely chosen through a prophet: Saul (10:20-21); David (16:12); Jeroboam (1 Kin. 11:31); and Jehu (2 Kin. 9:6). Samuel presented the young man before the people who shouted "Long live the king!" (10:24). After writing the "ordinances of the kingdom" (10:25; perhaps a reference to Deut. 17:14-20) in a scroll, the prophet dismissed the people.

Saul became king in ca. 1051 B.C. and reigned for forty years (Acts 13:21).[35] The chronology of Saul's reign can be fixed by working backwards from the division of the kingdom; an event that can be quite confidently fixed at 931 B.C.[36] Part of the reason for the certainty of this date is the testimony of the Shishak inscription at the great temple at Karnak. In this inscription, Shishak (Shoshenq; 945-924 B.C.) describes an invasion of Israel that took place in his nineteenth year, a date corresponding to the fifth year of Jeroboam I (2 Chron. 12:2; i.e., 926 B.C.). Since Solomon reigned for forty years (1 Kin. 11:42), his dates can be fixed at 971-931 B.C. David likewise reigned for forty years (2 Sam. 5:5), a tenure that can be established at ca. 1011-971 B.C. Hence, the end of Saul's reign was ca. 1011 B.C.

Soon after his coronation, Saul was informed that the Ammonites had besieged Jabesh-Gilead, a city across the Jordan River about twenty-five miles south of the Sea of Galilee. The newly-appointed king immediately called for the men of Israel to assemble. With a force of 330,000, Saul destroyed the Ammonite army and rescued the city. Saul's concern for the city is probably due to the ancestral ties between Jabesh-Gilead and the tribe of Benjamin. When the tribe was on the brink of extinction because of the civil war over the rape and murder of the Levite's concubine, wives for the remnant were taken from the city and given to the survivors (Jud. 21). It is likely that one of these women was a distant ancestor of Saul (other wives were taken from Shiloh).

Knowing that the nation was now in capable hands, Samuel gathered all Israel and proceeded to give a farewell address. In his speech, Samuel defended himself against any accusation of selfishness. He had faithfully served the nation without taking any liberties. Samuel then reviewed Israel's history, emphasizing the righteous acts of the Lord on their behalf. Yahweh had appointed Moses and Aaron to bring them out of Egypt; He had rescued them from their oppressors by raising up judges like Jerubbaaal (Gideon), Bedan (another name for Barak or perhaps another judge elsewhere unknown), Jephthah, and Samuel; and He had now set a king over His people. Samuel next delivered a stern warning; if the nation and its king faithfully follow the Lord then they will achieve success; however, if the nation and its king reject the Lord then they will experience judgment. The prophet concluded his speech with a call on the Lord to send thunder and rain, a phenomenon unprecedented in early summer, the time of the wheat harvest (12:17). The people responded to Samuel's speech with a request for prayer on their behalf. Samuel agreed, promising to regularly pray for them. However, he left them with a final warning, "If you . . . do wickedly, both you and your king shall be swept away" (12:25).

Soon after hearing of Israel's new king, the Philistines gathered in force at Michmash, a town in the territory of Benjamin about seven miles north of Jerusalem. The Philistines initially routed the Israelites, forcing them to scatter across the Jordan. Saul, however, was stationed with his army at Gilgal, a town about five miles southwest of Shiloh. He waited seven days for Samuel to come to Gilgal and offer a sacrifice, just as the prophet had instructed (cf. 10:8). As the days passed, the restless king grew more and more impatient; while the Philistine force was growing stronger, the Israelite force was getting smaller. Finally, Saul could wait no more. He took the offerings and sacrificed them to the Lord (cf. 2 Sam. 6:17-18; 1 Kin. 3:15). Just as he was finished, Samuel appeared on the scene. The prophet confronted the king and informed him that the Lord had rejected him and had sought out for Himself a man "after His own heart" (13:14; i.e., a man of His own choosing).

In the ensuing battle, Saul experienced a great victory, largely due to the efforts of his valiant son Jonathan (meaning "Yahweh has provided"). Jonathan and his armor-bearer were able to breach the Philistine lines and inflict heavy casualties. Seeing the Philistines retreating, Saul attacked and routed the opposing force. However, the king unwisely commanded[37] his armies to fast until the victory was complete. Jonathan, unaware of his father's order, ate some honey, thus incurring the wrath of Saul. The king would have executed his own son but for the intervention of the troops. The battle at Gibeah is the first of three major battles with the Philistines during Saul's reign (cf. 17; 31). The Philistine victory is followed by triumphs over the Moabites, Ammonites, Edomites, Arameans ("kings of Zobah;" 14:47) and Amalekites.

One day, Samuel approached Saul and informed him that the Lord had commanded him to "utterly destroy" (15:3; Heb. *herem*; cf. Deut. 7:26; Josh. 6:17) the Amalekites. In the days of the wilderness wanderings, the desert nomads had viciously attacked the beleaguered nation, a treacherous act that the Lord had promised to avenge (Ex. 17:8-16). Saul gathered his army and ambushed the Amalekites. First, however, he warned the Kenites to abandon their brethren. The Kenites were spared because they had shown kindness to Israel in the wilderness (cf. Ex. 18:9-10; Jethro was a Kenite; Jud. 1:16). The protection of the Kenites was prophesied by Balaam (Num. 24:21). Saul achieved a great victory over the Amalekites; however, he spared Agag, the Amalekite king, and the best of the livestock. As he was returning from the battlefield, Samuel met the king and informed him that the kingdom had been taken from him and given to a "better" (15:28) man. He next took a sword and hacked Agag to pieces. Samuel then returned to his home at Ramah. For the rest of his life, the great prophet would never again see Saul.

The Conflict between Saul and David (16:1- 2 Samuel 1:27)

After a period of time during which Samuel mourned for Saul, God appeared to the prophet and told him to anoint a new king. Following the Lord's orders, Samuel went to the city of Bethlehem and invited the family of Jesse to a sacrifice. Jesse was the grandson of Boaz and Ruth. As Samuel looked at the man's eldest son Eliab (meaning "My God is Father"), the prophet thought that he was surely the Lord's "anointed" (16:6; Heb. *Meshiah*). However, the Lord told him, "Do not look at his appearance or at the height of his stature, because I have rejected him; for God sees not as man sees, for man looks at the outward appearance, but the Lord looks at the heart" (16:7). After the seven eldest sons of Jesse were rejected one by one, the prophet identified David, the youngest son, as the next king of Israel. As Samuel anointed David, the Spirit of the Lord came upon the future king.

The Spirit of the Lord had previously filled Saul (11:6), but now it was replaced with an evil spirit (cf. Jud. 9:23). It is quite likely that this evil spirit was a demon. Considering how many times demon possession is referenced in the New Testament, it is amazing that the experience is so rare in the Old Testament. This evil spirit tormented Saul; the only relief coming when David played his harp. Throughout the Old Testament, harps are commonly associated with prophesying (10:5; 2 Kin. 3:15; 1 Chron. 25:1, 3). Note the glorious introduction of David in this passage. He is identified as "a skillful musician, a mighty man of valor (Heb. *gibor hayil*; cf. Jud. 6:12; 11:1; Ruth 2:1; 1 Sam. 9:1), a warrior, one prudent in speech, and a handsome man, and the Lord is with him" (16:18).

For the second time in Saul's reign, the Philistines gathered together to battle the Israelites (cf. 13-14). This time, the opposing forces were facing each other on opposite sides of the Elah Valley, located a few miles southwest of Jerusalem. With neither side willing to attack the other, the Philistines sent out a champion to challenge the best warrior Israel could offer. The name of the Philistine champion was Goliath (meaning "great"). He was from the city of Gath and stood 9'9" tall. His armor weighed about 125 pounds and he carried a spear with a fifteen pound iron head (about the size of the shot thrown in a shot put). The Israelite champion Saul refused to face Goliath in combat. The nation had previously wanted a king who would "go out before us and fight our battles" (8:20). Now that king was afraid to go out before his people and fight their battle. For forty days the Philistine warrior taunted the men of Saul.

At about this time David was visiting the battlefield to bring food to his older brothers. When he heard the taunts of Goliath, the young shepherd offered to take up the challenge. Relying on his faith in Yahweh, David told Saul that God would grant him success. He then approached the battlefield, stopping to gather five stones from a dry creekbed. When the Philistine saw his challenger, he mocked him, saying, "Am I a dog, that you come to me with sticks?" (17:43).

David responded with the immortal words, "You come to me with a sword, a spear, and a javelin, but I come to you in the name of the Lord of hosts, the God of the armies of Israel, whom you have taunted. This day the Lord will deliver you up into my hands, and I will strike you down and remove your head from you. And I will give the dead bodies of the army of the Philistines this day to the birds of the sky and the wild beasts of the earth, that all the earth may know that there is a God in Israel, and that all this assembly may know that the Lord does not deliver by sword or by spear, for the battle is the Lord's and He will give you into our hands" (17:45-47). He then took a stone, placed it into his sling, and struck the Philistine in the head. David approached the fallen champion, took Goliath's sword, and cut off his head. Seeing their champion dead, the Philistine army fled with the Israelite army in close pursuit.

Saul immediately gave the young shepherd-warrior a position of leadership in his army. Wherever David went, he prospered greatly. His success caused the Israelites to take up a chant, singing "Saul has slain his thousands, and David his ten thousands" (18:7). In addition, Saul's eldest son Jonathan became David's closest friend, even though he was at least thirty years older than the young shepherd. On one occasion, Jonathan even took off his royal garment and gave it to David in acknowledgment of his divine election as king. The taunts were too much for Saul and he became jealous, twice trying to kill the lad as he played his harp (18:11; 19:9-10). The king even tried to get the Philistines to kill David, offering him his daughter Michal in return for a hundred Philistine foreskins. When the king hired assassins to murder the shepherd in his bed, the plot was foiled by his daughter Michal. Additional assassins were stopped by the Spirit of the Lord, who came upon them and caused them to prophesy instead.

Eventually, David fled from the presence of Saul with the help of Jonathan, who warned the young shepherd by signaling with arrows. As they parted, Jonathan and David swore lifelong loyalty to each other. At this point, David is probably about twenty years old. He will be on the run from Saul for the next few years, a turbulent period during which he will write some of his greatest psalms (e.g., Ps. 18; 34; 52; 54; 56-57).

The first stop in David's flight was Nob, a city on the Mount of Olives near Jerusalem that was home to the high priest Ahimelech (meaning "my brother is king;" also known as Ahijah, meaning "my brother is Yahweh;" cf. 1 Sam. 14:3). Hungry from his flight, David lied to Ahimelech in order to secure the holy showbread that had been recently replaced. It is unknown when or why the tabernacle was moved from Shiloh to Nob. It is possible that the city of Shiloh was destroyed by the Philistines shortly after they captured the Ark at Aphek (cf. Jer. 7:12, 14; 26:6, 9).

David next stopped in Gath, the home of the Philistine giant Goliath. There he was immediately recognized as the great warrior of Israel. David quickly feigned madness because he was "very much afraid of King Achish of Gath" (21:12; NRSV). This ruse saved his life. As Merrill explains, this is in keeping with "the practice of the ancient world to regard the insane as being in some sense an evil portent and to exempt from harm lest the gods be provoked."[38]

When David left Gath, he proceeded to a cave at Adullam, located about twenty miles southwest of Jerusalem and ten miles northeast of Gath. There, four hundred refugees, including the prophet Gad (meaning "fortune"), gathered under his leadership. He then took his family to Mizpah in the territory of Moab and asked the king of Moab to protect them. It should be remembered that David's great-grandmother Ruth was a Moabitess (Ruth 1:4). David next hid in the forest of Hereth, near Adullam. While David was in the forest of Hereth, Saul was informed of David's activities at Nob. The king immediately ordered the execution of the priests who lived there, an assignment performed by Doeg, an Edomite warrior in Saul's army. Abiathar ("father of excellence"), the son of Ahimelech, managed to escape the slaughter and join David in exile. At this point, the tabernacle seems to have been moved to Gibeon (cf. 1 Chron. 16:39; 21:29).

David continued to flee from Saul, making brief stops at the town of Keilah, the town of Horesh in the wilderness of Ziph, the wilderness of Maon, and finally, the wilderness of En Gedi, an oasis ten miles north of Masada along the shores of the Dead Sea. When Saul heard that David was staying at En Gedi, he gathered three thousand men and pursued him. Amazingly enough, Saul happened upon the very cave in which David and his men were hiding. When Saul went into the cave to relieve himself, David cut off a piece of his robe as evidence of his opportunity to assassinate the king. David refused to take his life, however, because Saul was the Lord's "anointed" (24:6; Heb. *Meshiah*).

As he was camping in the wilderness of Maon, David sent messengers to a wealthy herdsman named Nabal (meaning "fool") in hopes of getting provisions for his men. Nabal refused David's request, scoffingly asking, "Who is David?" (25:10). When David was told of Nabal's contempt, he immediately gathered his men for an attack on the foolish herdsman. The man's life was temporarily spared, however, when his wife Abigail ("father of joy") met David with several donkey loads of food. She acknowledged David as the Lord's anointed and asked him to show mercy to her family. No doubt amazed at her courage, David granted Abigail's request. When Abigail told Nabal what had happened, his heart failed him and he died ten days later. David then took Abigail as his wife.

Shortly thereafter, David encamped in the wilderness of Ziph. When Saul heard that David was staying there, he gathered three thousand men and pursued him. As Saul was sleeping one night, David took his servant Abishai and entered his camp. This time, David took Saul's spear and water jug as evidence of his opportunity to assassinate the king. David again refused to take his life, however, because Saul was the Lord's "anointed" (26:11; Heb. *Meshiah*). When Saul learned that David had again spared his life, he repented, acknowledging that he had played the part of a "fool" (26:21). The king then blessed David and returned to his palace.

David next journeyed to Gath, where he entered the service of Achish, the Philistine king. For his military exploits, David was given the city of Ziklag, located between Gath and Beersheba. The Philistine king probably intended that the city serve as a buffer between the Philistines at Gath and the Israelites at Beersheba. Finally, a day came when the Philistines gathered their forces and prepared another assault on Israel, the third such attack during the reign of Saul (cf. 13-14; 17). When Saul saw the Philistine army, he was greatly afraid. Using a medium who lived at Endor, he attempted to get the support of his former prophet Samuel, who was now dead

(25:1). Appearing from the dead, Samuel informed Saul that the kingdom would be taken from him and given to David. The dead prophet further told Saul that he would die the next day, information that made Saul fall prostrate on the ground.

The following day, the Philistines gathered at Aphek, the site of their earlier victory in the days of Eli. Fearful of betrayal, the Philistine king Achish sent David back to Ziklag. When David arrived at his home, he discovered that Amalekite raiding parties had burned the town and captured his family. After inquiring of the Lord through Abiathar, David pursued the Amalekites and rescued his family. Meanwhile, the Philistines achieved an overwhelming victory over the Israelites in the Jezreel Valley. Saul and three of his sons (all except Ish-Bosheth) died on the slopes of Mount Gilboa (in the eastern part of the Jezreel Valley) as they attempted to flee the slaughter. Saul's death was at his own hands, a relatively rare occurrence of suicide in the Old Testament (cf. Abimelech [Jud. 9:54], Samson [Jud. 16:30], Ahithophel [2 Sam. 17:23], and Zimri [1 Kin. 16:18]).

When the Philistines discovered the body of Saul, they took his armor and put it on display in the temple of Ashtoreth. They then took his body, and those of his sons Jonathan, Abinadab, and Malki-Shua, and fastened them to the wall of Beth-Shan, a prominent city overlooking the Jordan Valley. When the men of Jabesh-Gilead heard what had been done to Saul, they rescued his corpse and buried it under an oak tree near the city. This act of reverence was a fitting tribute to the king who had rescued their city some forty years before (11:1-11).

When David heard the tragic news, he fell on the ground and wept. He then had the Amalekite who brought him the news executed because he claimed to have killed the Lord's "anointed" (1:14; Heb. *Meshiah*). Evidently, the Amalekite fabricated his story in hopes of claiming a reward from the new king. When he recovered from his mourning, David wrote a lament psalm entitled "The Song of the Bow" for Saul and Jonathan and placed it in the Book of Jasher (cf. Josh. 10:13). The lament begins and ends with the immortal refrain, "How have the mighty fallen!" In the lament proper, David warned the people against telling the Philistines lest they rejoice. He next cursed the mountains of Gilboa, the scene of the tragedy. He then praised the exploits of the king and his son Jonathan, concluding the lament with a special word of tribute for his close friend, "Your love to me was more wonderful than the love of women" (2 Sam. 1:26).

The King David Narrative (2:1-10:19)

Fifteen years after he was first anointed by Samuel, David was anointed as king over Judah in ca. 1011 B.C. This official act took place at Hebron, located twenty miles south of Jerusalem in the territory of Judah. The rest of the nation, however, remained loyal to the house of Saul. The northern tribes were governed by Ish-Bosheth (meaning "man of shame;" known originally as Esh-Baal, meaning "fire of Baal;" cf. 1 Chron. 8:33), the youngest son of Saul. Ish-Bosheth ruled from Mahanaim, a city in the Transjordan near the Jabbok River. Although Ish-Bosheth was technically king, the real power behind the throne was Abner ("father of light"), Saul's cousin. Since the reign of Ish-Bosheth does not begin until five years after the death of Saul, it is likely that Abner held power in the north until he appointed the son of Saul as king. Perhaps these five years were needed to recover the territory occupied by the Philistines after their climactic victory. With Ish-bosheth installed as king, Abner took it upon himself to lead an attack on David's men at Gibeon. The men of David were under the leadership of Joab ("Yahweh is Father"), David's nephew. While the battle was a great victory for Judah, Abner was able to kill Asahel ("God has made"), Joab's younger brother.

The civil war between the house of Saul and the house of David lasted a total of seven years. Throughout this period, the house of Saul grew weaker while the house of David grew stronger. The end of the feud began with a dispute between Abner and Ish-Bosheth. Abner took Rizpah, a concubine of Saul, as his concubine, a clear indication that he had designs on the throne (cf. 16:21-22). In the Ancient Near East, the royal harem was the property of the king's successor. When he was confronted by Ish-Bosheth, Abner deserted the northern king and decided to help David gain control over all Israel. To ingratiate himself with David, Abner restored Michal to him.

The new friendship between David and Abner did not sit well with Joab. At his first opportunity, he assassinated Abner to avenge the death of his brother Asahel. Making this act all the more reprehensible was the fact that it occurred in Hebron, a city of refuge, where such vengeance was not permitted (Num. 35:22-25). David responded to this act of treachery by pronouncing a curse on the house of Joab. However, he allowed him to remain as his commander-in-chief. Sensing that the reign of Ish-Bosheth was coming to an end, two assassins from the tribe of Benjamin, Baanah and Rechab, assassinated him while he lay in his bed. When David heard the news, he quickly ordered the execution of the two assassins.

David was finally anointed king over all Israel at the age of thirty in ca. 1004 B.C., seven years after the death of Saul. His first order of business was the conquest of Jerusalem, the largest city in central Canaan. The city had been occupied by the Jebusites[39] since the time of the judges. The Israelites had made little effort to recover the city, primarily because of its status as a defensive stronghold. Merrill explains, "Jerusalem's long history of independence as an island in an Israelite sea can be attributed in no little way to her defensibility. This . . . must have made the city all the more attractive to David. But it also posed a real problem. How could he take the city without a long and costly siege? As was characteristic of all the great walled cities of Canaan, Jerusalem had a vertical water shaft connecting with a tunnel leading to an underground water supply outside the walls. As necessary as these systems were for the survival of a city under siege, they also constituted a major weakness in that they provided access into the city for anyone who could find the entrance."[40] This feat was achieved by Joab, who discovered the source of Jerusalem's tunnel and led an attack on the city through it. The water shaft of Jerusalem extended about 230 feet up from the Gihon spring to the top of the hill where the Jebusite fortress was located.[41]

David quickly made Jerusalem his capital, a wise political move since the city was strategically located on the border between Judah and the northern tribes. It was also a relatively neutral site because it had remained independent for hundreds of years. The city of Hebron was no longer a fitting capital for at least three reasons. "First, it was far to the south and almost totally inaccessible to the Galilean and Transjordanian districts. Second, it was a city so important in the history of Judah that it almost epitomized that tribe. It would be unreasonable to expect the Israelites to develop any affection for or loyalty to a city so closely associated with the alienation of the past. Third, Hebron was a Levitical city; though not a fatal liability for a national capital, this fact may have tended to erode its neutrality in religious affairs."[42] David eventually contracted Hiram, king of Tyre, to build him a palace in his capital city.[43] This palace was designed to house his numerous wives (eight are named in Scripture), concubines, and their children.

David's second order of business was the conquest of the Philistines. The decisive battles took place in the Valley of Rephaim, a few miles southwest of Jerusalem. After inquiring of the Lord on both occasions, David twice defeated the Philistines, thus ending the Philistine threat to Israel. The first victory was marked by the heroic efforts of three "mighty men" who risked their lives to get water for their king from the well at Bethlehem (23:16). The second victory was achieved when David ambushed the Philistines from the rear; a ruse devised by God (5:23-25).

David's third order of business was to build a temple to house the Ark of the Covenant. For the last hundred years (ca. 1104-1003 B.C.), the Ark had been kept at the house of Abinadab. David, along with thirty thousand men, journeyed to Kiriath-Jearim to bring the Ark to Jerusalem. The Ark was placed on a new cart led by Uzzah and Ahio, the sons of Abinadab. Meanwhile, the men of David accompanied the procession, celebrating with all kinds of musical instruments. As the cart reached an uneven stretch of ground near the threshing floor of Nacon, the oxen pulling the cart stumbled. Uzzah, in an attempt to steady the Ark, reach out and grabbed hold of it. God immediately struck him down for his irreverence. David was unwilling to move the ark any further, so it was placed in the house of Obed-Edom the Gittite (a native of Gath) for three months. Eventually, the Ark was brought to Jerusalem, accompanied by David, who wore a linen ephod[44] and danced with all his might. The spectacle offended Michal, who rebuked the king when he returned home that night. David responded by separating from her so that she never had any children to the day of her death.

As David prepared to build the temple of God, the Lord appeared to Nathan (meaning "gift") with a message for the king. Nathan had evidently replaced Samuel as David's prophet. Yahweh informed Nathan that David would not be allowed to build the house of God; instead God would build the house of David. The Lord promised David that he would be given a great name (cf. Gen. 12:2). He further promised that He would appoint a place for the people of Israel and plant them in their own land (cf. Gen. 12:1). There they will finally experience rest (i.e., peace). Finally, the Lord promised that David would be the patriarch of an everlasting dynasty (cf. Gen. 17:6), saying, "Your house and your kingdom shall endure before Me forever; your throne shall be established forever" (7:16). The Lord's lovingkindness (Heb. *hesed*) would never be taken away from the family of David as it was removed from Saul. This passage (7:8-16) has become known as the Davidic Covenant. The promises are in the form of an Ancient Near Eastern royal grant by which a sovereign graciously bestowed a blessing, usually in the form of land or a fiefdom, upon a vassal.[45] The Davidic Covenant is an expansion of the Abrahamic Covenant (cf. Gen. 12:1-3). The ultimate fulfillment of these promises will take place in the Millennium. At that time, Israel will be safely planted in the land promised to them. There they will be governed forever by Jesus Christ, the Seed of David and promised Messiah.

The next chapter is a record of the fulfillment of the Lord's promise to give David rest from all his enemies (7:11). Throughout this chapter David defeats the Philistines, Moabites, Arameans, Ammonites (see also chapter ten), Amalekites, and Edomites. These nations surrounded Israel on all sides: the Philistines to the southeast; the Arameans to the north; the Moabites and Ammonites to the west; the Amalekites to the south; and the Edomites to the southwest (the Mediterranean Sea borders Israel on the east). Yahweh truly "helped David wherever he went" (8:14).

Hoping to keep his promise of "kindness" (Heb. *hesed*) to Jonathan (9:1; cf. 1 Sam. 20:14-17), David inquired as to whether anyone remained of the house of Saul. When he was informed that Mephibosheth (meaning "exterminator of shame, i.e., of idols;" known originally as Merib-Baal, meaning "contender with Baal;" cf.

1 Chron. 8:34), the son of Jonathan, remained alive, David brought him to his palace and gave him a royal pension. Mephibosheth had been crippled at the age of five while attempting to flee following the death of Saul and Jonathan (4:4). David also restored to Mephibosheth Saul's personal estate.

The Fight for the Throne (11:1-20:26)

In the spring, after the latter rains were over, it was customary for kings to lead their troops into battle. One spring, however, David decided to remain in Jerusalem and instead sent Joab into battle. Joab led his men in a siege of Rabbah (modern Amman, Jordan), the capital city of the Ammonites, located about twenty miles east of the Jordan River. This campaign took place ca. 993 B.C. and was in response to the shameful treatment suffered by the delegation that had been sent by David to congratulate the new Ammonite king Hanun.

One evening, as David took a walk on his roof, he spied a beautiful woman bathing herself. He was soon told that the woman was Bathsheba (meaning "daughter of an oath"), the wife of Uriah ("my light is Yahweh"), one of David's mighty men (23:39). Filled with lust, David immediately sent messengers for the woman. When she came to his palace, he had sex with her and then sent her home.

Soon after their union, Bathsheba sent word to David announcing that she was pregnant. Hoping to cover his sin, the king ordered Uriah sent home from the battlefield. David twice tried to get Uriah to sleep with Bathsheba, obviously hoping that he might appear to be the father. However, Uriah was unwilling to have relations with his wife while his fellow troops were engaged in combat. Finally, David sent Uriah back to Rabbah with a message for Joab. The general was ordered to abandon Uriah at the walls of the city with a sudden retreat. David's plan was successful; Uriah was killed in battle. After an appropriate time of mourning (perhaps seven days; cf. 1 Sam. 31:13), the king sent for Bathsheba and she became his wife. The city of Rabbah eventually fell to Joab's army, a situation that resulted in the enslavement of the Ammonites.

The Lord was greatly displeased with the actions of David. He sent the prophet Nathan to David with a parable. Nathan told of a poor man who had a pet lamb who was like a child to him. One day, his rich neighbor decided to entertain a traveler. Instead of taking an animal from one of his herds, he took the poor man's pet lamb and had it slaughtered. David was outraged at the story and immediately decreed that the man who had done this injustice must make restitution for the lamb fourfold. Nathan then identified David as the man. The prophet further informed the king that "the sword shall never depart from your house" (12:10), a prophecy of the calamity that would soon confront him.

The king quickly acknowledged his sin, yet was told that the child to be born would die. Although David fasted and prayed to God for the life of the child, the Lord struck him down, the first of four sons of David who would die violent deaths. The king comforted Bathsheba by impregnating her with another son. The child was named Solomon (meaning "peaceful") by his father; however, Nathan gave the child the name Jedidiah (meaning "beloved of Yahweh") because the Lord loved him. Solomon was probably born ca. 991 B.C.

The prophecy concerning David's house (12:10) quickly came to pass. Amnon (meaning "faithful"), the son of David through Ahinoam, fell in love with his half-sister Tamar ("palm"), the daughter of David through Maacah. When he failed to win her favor, he raped her by means of a clever plot to get her alone. Although he was commanded by the Law to marry her (Deut. 22:28-29), Amnon refused to do so on the grounds that he now hated her. Soon, Tamar's brother Absalom ("father of peace") discovered what Amnon had done. Two years later, Absalom had his servants murder Amnon during a party at Baal-Hazor, located six miles south of Shiloh. He then fled to Geshur, a city east of the Sea of Galilee.

Three years later, Absalom returned to Jerusalem after David was forced to allow his return. The king, however, did not welcome him back. In fact, Absalom lived two years in Jerusalem without ever seeing his father. Finally, a full five years after the murder of Amnon, the king allowed him to come to the palace. When Absalom arrived, David kissed him after his son prostrated himself on the ground. The gesture, however, was too little, too late.

Absalom hatched a conspiracy to take the throne from his father. He ingratiated the people to himself by listening to their problems by the side of the road leading into the city. The inference was clear, the king would not listen to his people, but his son would. After four years of this, Absalom put his plan in motion. He asked his father for permission to go to Hebron to pay a vow. When he arrived at Hebron, Absalom announced his ascension to the throne (this event took place ca. 976 B.C.). Upon hearing the news, David fled from Jerusalem by way of the Mount of Olives. There he heard that his trusted adviser Ahithophel (meaning "brother of foolishness") had joined Absalom. Ahithophel was the grandfather of Bathsheba (cf. 11:3; 23:34).

As David headed east, he was met by Ziba, the servant of Mephibosheth, who informed him that his master had turned against the king. He then came across Shimei, another relative of Saul, who cursed him and threw stones at the procession. Although Abishai, the king's bodyguard, wanted to cut off his head, David would not allow him to do so. The actions of Mephibosheth and Shimei probably indicated that the house of Saul was restating its claim to the throne.

Absalom quickly took possession of the city of Jerusalem, setting himself up as king by sleeping with his father's concubines in the sight of all the people. He then sought the advice of two confidants. Ahithophel encouraged him to pursue David immediately and kill him. However, Hushai, acting as David's spy, encouraged the new king to wait until he could amass an army large enough to defeat the deposed king. Absalom, moved by the Lord, decided to follow the advice of Hushai. When Ahithophel learned that Absalom had rejected his advice, he committed suicide.

David, knowing that a confrontation with Absalom was necessary, organized his men into three goups. These he assigned to Joab, Abishai, and Ittai. David commanded each of these men to spare the life of Absalom should they meet him in battle. The confrontation between the men of Absalom and the men of David took place in the forest of Ephraim. The men of David achieved a great victory, routing the men of Absalom, who suffered great casualties. As he was retreating from the battlefield, Absalom became entangled in the branches of a large oak tree, perhaps because of his long hair (cf. 14:25-26). When Joab came upon the helpless Absalom, he thrust three spears through his heart. Upon hearing the news, David mourned greatly, crying, "Would I had died instead of you, O Absalom, my son, my son!" (18:33).

The exiled king soon returned to Jerusalem to reclaim his throne. He was greeted by Shimei, who immediately sought the king's forgiveness, and Mephibosheth, who claimed that Ziba had lied about his true loyalties. David was also met by a contingent of representatives from both Judah and Israel, who argued with each other over which one had the right to claim David as their own. This episode reveals the schism which was developing between Israel and Judah, a rift that would eventually lead to the split of the nation.

Sheba (meaning "seven"), a member of the tribe of Benjamin, convinced the northern tribes to make a break with David. The king responded to the threat by ordering Amasa ("burden"), his nephew and new commander-in-chief (cf. 17:25) to organize the army of Judah. Joab, upset at his demotion, assassinated his cousin Amasa with a dagger as he pretended to greet him. He then took command of David's men and laid siege to Abel Beth-Maacah, a city four miles west of Dan in which Sheba had taken refuge. When the inhabitants of the city threw the body of Sheba over the wall, Joab stopped the siege and returned to Jerusalem.

Six Appendices Describing David's Great Kingdom (21:1-24:25)

The book of Samuel concludes with six appendices describing David's great kingdom. The first appendix (21:1-14) is a record of the appeasement of the Gibeonites who had been wronged by Saul. Saul had broken the covenant made with the Gibeonites by Joshua (Josh. 9:15-21). The king had slain several Gibeonites during his tenure, an act of treachery not recorded in the biblical account. To appease their wrath (and that of God, cf. 21:1), David executed seven male descendants of Saul.

The second appendix (21:15-22) is a list of David's heroic men. These men had been instrumental in the king's conflicts with the Philistines. The noteworthy names include: Abishai, who saved David's life by killing the giant Ishbi-Benob; Sibbecai, who killed the giant Saph; Elhanan, who killed Lahmi, the brother of Goliath (1 Chron. 20:5); and Jonathan, who killed a giant who had six digits on each hand and foot.

The third appendix (22:1-51) is a majestic psalm of praise (cf. Ps. 18). The psalm shares remarkable similarities with the prayer of thanksgiving offered by Hannah in 1 Samuel 2:1-10. David began his psalm by acknowledging the protection of the Lord, describing His greatness with a series of figures designed to signify strength. He then reviewed the many exploits of God which reveal His sovereignty over the entire earth. David next described his faithfulness to God; faithfulness that was rewarded with the Lord's work in delivering him from his enemies. David closed his psalm with a commitment to give thanks and sing praises to Yahweh, who "shows 'lovingkindness' (Heb. *hesed*) to His 'anointed' (Heb. *Meshiah*), to David and his descendants forever" (22:51).

The fourth appendix (23:1-7) records the last words of David. He began by identifying himself as "the son of Jesse," "the anointed (Heb. *Meshiah*) of the God of Jacob," "the sweet psalmist of Israel" (23:1). David then acknowledged that God had spoken through him to the nation of Israel. The king concluded his speech by recounting the promises given him through the Davidic Covenant.

The fifth appendix (23:8-39) is a list of David's mighty men. Notable names include Abishai, Benaiah (meaning "Yahweh has built;" the future replacement of Joab, cf. 1 Kin. 2:35), Asahel, and Uriah. Striking in its absence is the name of Joab, perhaps omitted because of the treacherous murders he committed.

The sixth and final appendix (24:1-25) is an account of David's sinful census. This event probably took place just before David gave instructions to Solomon about the temple construction (cf. 1 Chron. 21; ca. 975 B.C.). David, moved by Satan (1 Chron. 21:1), decided to take a census of the men of Israel and Judah. This act greatly displeased the Lord. So He sent Gad, a prophet, to David with a list of three calamities from which he could choose one. In this way, the wrath of God would be appeased. The first calamity was three years of famine (cf. NIV). The second calamity was three months of enemy encroachment. The third calamity was three days of plague. David chose the plague, a judgment which resulted in the death of

70,000 Israelites. When the avenging angel approached Jerusalem, the Lord stopped him at the threshing floor of Araunah (meaning "strength"), the Jebusite. To atone for his sin, David purchased the threshing floor and erected an altar on it. This site will eventually become the home of the Solomonic temple.

Study Questions

1. What is the name of the three characters who dominate the book of Samuel?
2. Briefly describe the Arameans.
3. Identify the three prophets who are named in this book.
4. What are the names of Elkanah's wives?
5. What are the names of Eli's sons?
6. In what battle is the Ark of the Covenant captured by the Philistines?
7. What is the meaning of the name Ichabod?
8. Saul was a member of what tribe?
9. Briefly describe the relationship between Saul and the city of Jabesh-Gilead.
10. Saul is commanded to "utterly destroy" what group of people?
11. Where did David defeat Goliath?
12. What is the meaning of the name Nabal?
13. Where did Saul die?
14. Briefly explain why David moved his capital from Hebron to Jerusalem.
15. In which chapter is the Davidic Covenant recorded?
16. Why does Absalom kill Amnon?
17. Who are the "mighty men" in your own life?

CHAPTER 5

First and Second Kings

"But if you or your sons shall indeed turn away from following Me, and shall not keep My commandments and My statutes which I have set before you and shall go and serve other gods and worship them, then I will cut off Israel from the land which I have given them, and the house which I have consecrated for My name, I will cast out of My sight. So Israel will become a proverb and a byword among all peoples. And this house will become a heap of ruins; everyone who passes by will be astonished and hiss and say, 'Why has the Lord done thus to this land and to this house?' And they will say, 'Because they forsook the Lord their God, who brought their fathers out of the land of Egypt, and adopted other gods and worshiped them and served them, therefore the Lord has brought all this adversity on them.'" (1 Kings 9:6-9).

The books of First and Second Kings fall together naturally as a unit and originally constituted a single book. The earliest Hebrew manuscripts made no distinction between the books and the unit was simply called Kings. The title comes from the Hebrew title of the book *melakim*, meaning "Kings." The Septuagint (ca. 200 B.C.) appears to have been the first version to separate the books, perhaps because of the greatly increased length of the Greek version (the Greek language is written with vowels while Hebrew is written without vowels). The Septuagint entitled the books the Third and Fourth Books of Kingdoms (our books of First and Second Samuel were called the First and Second Books of Kingdoms respectively). This division has persisted to the present day in all translations and versions. From a literary and theological standpoint the books of Kings must be viewed as a unit. Hence, in the remainder of this chapter the two books will be regarded as a unit and will simply be called the book of Kings.

In the Hebrew Bible, Kings follows Samuel and is placed last in the section entitled "Former Prophets." The book continues the narrative from 2 Samuel 20 and traces the history of the Jews from the death of David to the exile of the southern kingdom of Judah. The book focuses on the various kings who ruled over the united nation of Israel and later over the divided kingdoms of Israel and Judah. The book also stresses the important role played by the prophets in relation to these kings.

Author

The book of Kings is anonymous and the identity of the author is unknown. The Babylonian Talmud claims that Jeremiah wrote the book (*Baba Bathra* 15a). This claim is based primarily on the fact that Jeremiah 52 and 2 Kings 24:18-25:30 are synonymous. An additional argument supporting Jeremiah as the author is the book's emphasis on the role of the prophets in Israel's history. Jeremiah would surely have been a capable writer. He was a priest and prophet; he had access to the governing authorities and their records; and he was personally involved in the circumstances surrounding the fall of Jerusalem and the immediate aftermath. While it is certainly possible that Jeremiah was the author, the fact that he was taken to Egypt after the destruction of Jerusalem makes this option improbable (cf. Jer. 43:1-8).[1] The author was more likely an exile living in Babylon. The release of Jehoiachin would have been especially significant to captive Jews. Because of this assumption, some scholars feel that the author may have been Ezekiel or Ezra. Whoever the author was, it is clear that he made extensive use of source material. He refers to three books as the sources of his information, i.e., the Book of the Acts of Solomon (1 Kin. 11:41), the Book of the Chronicles of the

Kings of Judah (cited fifteen times), and the Book of the Chronicles of the Kings of Israel (cited seventeen times). These books were probably official court histories written by royal scribes.

Date

The book of Kings closes with the release of Jehoiachin from prison, an event that took place in the thirty-seventh year of his imprisonment (562 B.C.). The book in its final form could not have been written before this date. It is almost certain that Kings was written before the return from Babylon in ca. 537 B.C. since this deeply significant event is not mentioned in the book. Therefore, the most probable date for the book is between 562 and ca. 537 B.C. The book was likely written from Babylon, the chief home of the exiled community.

Those who believe that the book is a product of the so-called Deuteronomistic School[2] argue that the book was composed in two redactions (editorial stages). According to this theory,[3] the first redaction took place at about the same time as Josiah's glorious reforms (ca. 625 B.C.). This optimistic edition portrays Josiah's reign as the culmination of the promises concerning land and blessing found in Deuteronomy. In Kings, Josiah is characterized as the faithful imitation of David, "He did what was right in the sight of the Lord, and walked in all the ways of his father David; he did not turn aside to the right or to the left" (2 Kin. 22:2; NKJV). Further, he is the embodiment of Deuteronomy's foremost command,[4] "Before him there was no king like him who turned to the Lord with all his heart and with all his soul and with all his might, according to all the law of Moses; nor did any like him arise after him" (2 Kin. 23:25; cf. Deut. 6:5; in fact, these are the only two verses in the Old Testament where the terms "heart," "soul," and "might" are linked). The second redaction coincided with the release of Jehoiachin from prison (ca. 560 B.C.). This pessimistic edition revised the first account in light of the historical reality of Judah's exile and sought to provide a theological explanation for it. Predictions of the exile were inserted into key passages to emphasize the Lord's decision to temporarily abandon His people. In this version, the reign of Josiah is pictured simply as "a brief hiatus in the nation's tragic downward spiral."[5]

There are several problems with this view. First, there is little actual evidence to support the idea of a Deuteronomistic History. Second, those who hold to the view cannot agree on the origin, content, and extent of the material. Third, an underlying belief of those who accept this theory is the denial of biblical prophecy. Fourth, the similarities between the structure of Deuteronomy and ancient Hittite suzerain-vassal treaties support an early date for Deuteronomy.

Historical Background

The events of the book of Kings take place between 971 B.C., the year of David's death and Solomon's accession to the throne of Israel, and 562 B.C., the date of the release of Jehoiachin from prison. The kingdom that Solomon inherited was a powerful union of tribes. David had effectively united the nation with a strong central government based in a formidable capital city. Even more importantly, he had subdued the nation's enemies on all sides, bringing peace and stability to the region. Under Solomon, the nation quickly became the most powerful state in the Ancient Near East. Israel's strength is evidenced by the Egyptian pharaoh's willingness to give his own daughter to Solomon as his wife. Normally, Egyptian kings took foreign princesses as wives; they did not give up their own daughters to foreign kings.[6]

The pharaoh in question is Siamun of Dynasty 21, who reigned from 978-959 B.C. At this time Egypt was in a political nadir. The pharaohs of Dynasty 21 were among the weakest in the nation's history. The fortunes of Egypt would soon change, however, with the founding of Dynasty 22 by Shishak (Shoshenq) in 945 B.C. Shishak was able to reunite Upper and Lower Egypt, thus creating a rather formidable empire. When the powerful nation of Israel split in 931 B.C., Shishak quickly took advantage of the situation. He invaded Judah and threatened the city of Jerusalem. The holy city was spared when Rehoboam paid heavy tribute to the Egyptian pharaoh. Shishak was followed by Osorkon I, who reigned from 924-889 B.C. Osorkon strengthened Egytian relations with Byblos, a powerful city-state strategically located on the major trade routes north of Israel. This gave Egypt a powerful ally against the increasing Aramean threat.

The Arameans governed the territory from Damascus north as far as the Euphrates River. As a result, they controlled the major trade routes between Anatolia and Mesopotamia. The Arameans plagued the northern kingdom of Israel throughout her entire history. The Aramean Empire had been founded by Hezion (Rezon; cf. 1 Kin. 11:23) during the reign of David. Hezion was an adversary of Israel throughout Solomon's reign (1 Kin. 11:25). His grandson Ben-Hadad (ca. 900-841 B.C.) led a coalition of thirty-three kings in an attack on Samaria in 857 B.C., probably in response to the marriage between Ahab and Jezebel, a union that solidified ties between Israel and Phoenicia. Ahab initially agreed to the ransom demands of Ben-Hadad; however, when the Aramean king increased his demands, Ahab attacked the coalition, catching them in a state of drunkenness and routing their forces. The following year, Ben-Hadad returned. Ahab again was victorious, this time forcing the Aramean king to submit to a treaty returning Israel's captured cities and guaranteeing Ahab commercial access to Damascus. Three years later, Ahab lost his life in a third battle against Ben-Hadad as he tried to recover the city of Ramoth-Gilead for Israel.

Ben-Hadad was succeeded by Hazael (841-801 B.C.), one of his servants. Hazael, encouraged by the anointing by Elisha, murdered his master by smothering him in his sleep. Hazael would prove to be a source of constant irritation to Israel. He began his reign with a successful defense of Ramoth-Gilead, a strategic outpost attacked by Joram. He then marched against the Transjordan and captured Israelite cities as far south as the Arnon River. Throughout the reigns of Jehu and Jehoahaz, Hazael continued to harass Israel (cf. 2 Kin. 13:3, 22). When Ben-Hadad II (801-773 B.C.) succeeded his father Hazael, Jehoash was able to recapture the Israelite cities in the Transjordan, three times defeating Ben-Hadad in battle (cf. 2 Kin. 13:25). Eventually, Jeroboam II would also defeat Ben-Hadad and recover the Aramean territories that had belonged to Israel during the reign of Solomon, including the significant city of Damascus. The next Aramean king is Rezin, who was able to gain the throne of Damascus in ca. 750 B.C. From 773-750 B.C., the Israelite kings ruled over Damascus. However, Rezin was able to gain indepen-dence during the reign of Menahem.

It was also during the reign of Menahem that the Assyrians emerged as the dominant power in the Ancient Near East. The Assyrian Empire is the first of five great world empires mentioned in Scripture (i.e., Assyria, Babylon, Persia, Greece, Rome). Its emergence was led by Tiglath-Pileser III (745-727 B.C.).[7] Shortly after gaining the throne, Tiglath-Pileser was able to subdue the Babylonians to the south and the Urartians to the north. He then set his sights on the west, including Syria and Israel. The Assyrian king quickly subdued Syria and forced Israel to pay tribute, a fact commemorated by both the biblical record (2 Kin. 15:19-20) and the Assyrian annals.[8]

When Pekah gained the throne of Israel in 740 B.C., he imme-diately broke the treaty with Assyria and took steps to create a coalition that would be able to resist the Assyrians. He formed an alliance with Rezin of Damascus that also included the Phoenicians, Philistines, and Edomites. This coalition soon approached Judah and attempted to persuade Jotham (and Ahaz his son and coregent) to join them against the Assyrians. Ahaz, the dominant king of the coregency, resisted their demands and chose instead to request help from the Assyrians. The resultant war was a devastating defeat for Judah as both Rezin and Pekah defeated Ahaz in battle, seizing vast tracts of land and sacking numerous cities. Even the Philistines and Edomites were able to launch attacks against settlements in the southern kingdom.

Tiglath-Pileser responded to the frantic appeal of Ahaz by launching an invasion of Syria in 734 B.C. The city of Damascus fell two years later and the Arameans were absorbed into the Assyrian Empire. Israel escaped the same fate when Pekah was assassinated and replaced by the pro-Assyrian king Hoshea (732-722 B.C.). The military failures of Ahaz left Judah in a greatly weakened state. When Tiglath-Pileser finally arrived on the scene, Ahaz was forced to plunder the temple in order to pay tribute to the king of Assyria.

When Tiglath-Pileser died, Hoshea attempted to take advantage of the situation by rebelling against Assyria. He appealed to the Egyptian king Osorkon IV (biblical So; cf. 2 Kin. 17:4) for help, evidently in hopes of forming an alliance against the Assyrians. It was a disastrous decision that resulted in an invasion of Israel by Shalmaneser V (727-722 B.C.). The city of Samaria fell in 722 B.C. after a three year siege. The inhabitants of the northern kingdom were exiled throughout the Assyrian Empire by Sargon (722-705 B.C.). The territory was repopulated with foreigners from Babylon, Cuthah, Ava, Hamath, and Sepharvaim (2 Kin. 17:24). This deportation and repopulation program was designed to destroy the national identity of the Israelites. The goal of the Assyrians was to create an ethnically and politically diverse empire resistant to internal strife and rebellion. The southern kingdom was able to survive the threat and remained independent although they paid heavy tribute to the Assyrians.

There is some question as to which Assyrian king is to be credited with the fall of Samaria. While the Assyrian annals credit Sargon with the victory,[9] Shalmaneser is credited with the victory in the Old Testament (2 Kin. 17). What is known for sure is that Shalmaneser died shortly before or after the fall of Samaria. There are three possible solutions to the dilemma. First, Sargon might have been credited with the victory in the Assyrian annals because as crown prince he was likely the commander of the armies. The biblical record credits Shalmaneser because as king he was ultimately responsible for the siege of Samaria. Second, Sargon may have laid claim to the victory in an effort to solidify the throne after the death of Shalmaneser. After all, he would have been the one to govern what was written in the official Assyrian records. Third, the biblical record is vague concerning the identity of the Assyrian king after 2 Kings 17:3. It is possible that the Assyrian king named in 17:3-5 (Shalmaneser) is not the same individual as the Assyrian king of 17:6 (Sargon). The second view is the most likely and is supported by the Babylonian Chronicle which attributes the victory to Shalmaneser.

The relationship between Judah and Assyria changed dramatically in 715 when Hezekiah severed the ties with the foreign power. In 702 B.C., Merodach-Baladan of Babylon sent emissaries to Hezekiah in an attempt to acquire his participation in a coalition against Sennacherib (705-681 B.C.). Sennacherib responded to the threat by taking the city of Babylon and reasserting Assyrian dominance. The Assyrian king then invaded Judah in 701 and destroyed forty-six Judean cities, including Lachish. When Sennacherib arrived at Jerusalem, he surrounded the city and made preparations for an extended siege, hoping to starve the city into submission. King Hezekiah responded to the threat with a prayer to the Lord, "O Lord, our God, I pray, save us from his [Sennacherib's] hand, that all the kingdoms of the earth may know that You are the Lord God" (2 Kin. 19:19). Hezekiah's prayer was answered when the angel of the Lord struck down 185,000 Assyrians in a single night (2 Kin. 19:35).

Having failed in his attempt to destroy Jerusalem, Sennacherib returned to Nineveh and established the city as his new royal residence. Nineveh was originally founded by Nimrod, the great hunter (ca. 3000 B.C.). The city was located on the east bank of the Tigris River in northeastern Mesopotamia (in modern Iraq). The city took its name from the Babylonian *Nina* meaning "fish." The name is apt as the region is famous for the abundance of fish in its waters. Nineveh was the city to which God called the reluctant prophet Jonah in the early eighth century B.C. The modern city of Mosul is located at the ruins of Nineveh.

Sennacherib tripled the size of Nineveh and made it the Assyrian capital. He constructed a magnificent palace on the southwest corner of the city that covered five acres and had 71 rooms, including two large halls almost 200 feet long and 40 feet wide. He beautified the city with parks and gardens, which were watered by a thirty-mile long aqueduct. The city also boasted a botanical garden and a zoo. The city was enclosed by eight miles of walls with fifteen gates. The population of Nineveh has been estimated to have been about 200,000. The splendor of Sennacherib's Nineveh was probably surpassed in the ancient world only by Nebuchadnezzar's Babylon.[10]

Following a rebellion by the Elamites and Babylonians, Sennacherib destroyed the city of Babylon in 689 B.C. In 681 B.C., the Assyrian king was murdered by two of his sons in Nineveh in fulfillment of Isaiah 37:7 (cf. 2 Kin. 19:37). The Babylonians viewed the assassination as divine judgment for the destruction of their city. Esarhaddon (681-669 B.C.), another son of Sennacherib, was able to seize the throne and restore order. He immediately began to rebuild Babylon, thus gaining the temporary allegiance of the Babylonians. He further solidified his empire by defeating the Scythians and Sidonians. Having quieted the home front, Esarhaddon launched a successful invasion of Egypt in 671 B.C. He defeated the Nubian pharaoh Tirhakah, forcing him to flee to Thebes. His conquest of Memphis gave him control of all of Lower Egypt. The city rebelled two years later when Tirhakah returned from Thebes. While en route to Egypt to put down the insurrection, Esarhaddon died in 669 B.C.

After a brief struggle for the throne, Ashurbanipal (668-627) succeeded his father Esarhaddon as king of Assyria. He immediately set out to reconquer Egypt. In 667 B.C., Ashurbanipal recaptured the city of Memphis. He then pressed further south, eventually taking the ancient capital Thebes. Tirhaka fled to Napata and died there three years later.

Ashurbanipal returned to Assyria and took steps to expand Nineveh. He constructed a palace on the northern side of the city marked by brilliant reliefs of royal lion hunts. He amassed a library of some 20,000 clay tablets, which contained important literary epics, religious documents, legal literature, scientific and geographic works, texts on astronomy and astrology, various letters, and royal archives. The tablets were all carefully numbered and catalogued.

The greatest threat to Ashurbanipal came in 652 B.C. when a coalition of Elamite, Arabian, Aramean and Babylonian forces attacked the army of Ashurbanipal. The Assyrian king withstood this revolt and launched retaliatory strikes against each kingdom. The latter years of Ashurbanipal's reign were largely uneventful. In 2 Chronicles 33:11, the chronicler reports that Manasseh's wickedness led to his deportation to Babylon by the king of Assyria. The Assyrian king alluded to in this verse is Ashurbanipal. Since Ashurbanipal did not bring Babylon under his control until 648 B.C., the exile of Manasseh could not have occurred prior to this date. It is unknown how long Manasseh lived in Babylon but it could not have been more than a few years since Manasseh died in 642 B.C. While in Babylon, the king repented of his sins, humbling himself greatly before the Lord and praying for mercy (2 Chron. 33:12-13).

Ashurbanipal would prove to be the last significant Assyrian king. His death was followed by a series of successful revolts throughout the empire, including those by Babylon, Media, Phoenicia, and even Judah. The final years of the Assyrians were filled with turmoil. Ashurbanipal was succeeded by his son Ashur-etil-ilani (627-623 B.C.). Sin-sum-lisir (623 B.C.) rebelled against his brother Ashur-etil-ilani and managed to briefly occupy the Assyrian throne. He was quickly overthrown by a third son of Ashurbanipal, Sin-sar-iskun (623-612 B.C.). The Assyrian Empire gradually crumbled until the city of Nineveh itself came under attack in 612 B.C. After a brief siege, the city fell to a coalition of Median, Chaldean, and Scythian forces.

The Chaldeans were a Semitic people who lived in southeastern Babylonia. They migrated from Aramea and are first attested in a document from the reign of Ashur-nasirpal II of Assyria (ca. 878 B.C.). The Chaldeans comprised three major tribes, the Bit-Yakin, the Bit-Dakkuri, and the Bit-Amukani. In 633 B.C., the Chaldean Nabopolassar rose to prominence in southeastern Mesopotamia, thereby establishing the roots of the great Babylonian Empire. He revolted against the Assyrians shortly after the reign of Ashurbanipal, decisively defeating the Assyrian general Sin-sar-iskun in the battle of Uruk. Nabopolassar declared his independence and formally ascended to the throne of Babylon on November 23, 626 B.C. In 623 B.C., he again defeated Sin-sar-iskun, now king of Assyria, and expelled the Assyrians from Babylonia.

Not content with ruling Babylon, Nabopolassar invaded Assyria and took the sacred city of Asshur in 614 B.C. He then made an alliance with the Medes and Scythians and surrounded Nineveh in 612 B.C. Shortly thereafter, thanks to a fortuitous flood of the Tigris River which opened a breach in the city walls, the allies captured the Assyrian capital. The Assyrians moved their capital to Haran and sought the help of the Egyptians under Pharaoh Neco (Necho). In 609 B.C., Josiah attempted to intercept the Egyptians at Megiddo, losing his life in the resultant battle. Later that year, the Babylonians under the command of general Nebuchadnezzar defeated the combined Assyrian and Egyptian armies at Haran, pushing the Assyrians across the Euphrates River. The final battle between these same groups took place at Carchemish in 605 B.C. The Assyrian Empire was effectively destroyed and the Egyptians were forced to return to Egypt. The Babylonians then proceeded south to Jerusalem, forcing the city to pay tribute and surrender prisoners, including Daniel and his three friends.

The king of the Jews when Nebuchadnezzar took Jerusalem in 605 B.C. was Jehoiakim (608-598 B.C.), the son of Josiah. Although the Jews had made his younger brother Jehoahaz the king following Josiah's death in 609 B.C., the Egyptians had deposed Jehoahaz after a three-month reign. Nebuchadnezzar forced Jehoiakim to swear allegiance and allowed him to remain as king. Shortly after taking Jerusalem, Nebuchadnezzar learned of his father Nabopolassar's death in Babylon. The Babylonian general quickly rushed back to Babylon to solidify his claim to the throne.

Jehoiakim remained loyal to Nebuchadnezzar for three years. However, in 602 B.C., rejecting the advice of Jeremiah, Jehoiakim rebelled against the Babylonians. Nebuchadnezzar responded by invading Judah with the help of the Arameans, Moabites, and Ammonites. As the Babylonians approached the city, Jehoiakim was killed by his own court and dragged through the streets of Jerusalem. Jehoiakim was succeeded by his son, Jehoiachin (598-597 B.C.). After a brief three-month reign, Jehoiachin was captured by the Babylonians when Jerusalem fell. He was taken to Babylon and lived the remainder of his days in exile.

Nebuchadnezzar appointed Zedekiah (597-586 B.C.), yet another son of Josiah, to rule over Judah. Following the example of his brother, Zedekiah also rejected the advice of Jeremiah and rebelled against the Babylonians. Nebuchadnezzar returned to Jerusalem and laid siege to the city in 588 B.C. After a horrific two-year siege, the city fell in July of 586 B.C. Zedekiah was captured by the Babylonians after initially fleeing to Jericho. He was brought before Nebuchadnezzar at his headquarters in Riblah. There he was forced to witness the execution of his sons before being blinded and taken to Babylon with an ox ring through his nose.

Audience and Purpose

Simply put, the book of Kings was written to the exiles in Babylon to show them why they were in exile. As a result, the book should be viewed as a theodicy. Theodicy is "literature that seeks to justify the way God has dealt with people; it vindicates divine nature in the face of evil."[11] Perhaps the best example of theodicy is the book of Job. Whereas Job was written to justify the way God dealt with an individual, Kings was written to justify the Lord's actions towards a nation. Nowhere is this more clear than in God's use of His servants, the prophets. More than ten prophets are identified in Kings, with Elijah and Elisha actually serving as the chief characters in the central portion of the book. Routinely, these prophets warn the people of their apostasy, pleading with them to turn from their wicked ways and follow the Lord. One cannot escape the conclusion that God did everything He could to prevent the exile. Essentially, the nation forced Him to take away their land. The Lord was innocent of their blood.

Kings traces the history of the kingdom period from the time of Solomon to the release of Jehoiachin. Yet, the book is not simply a historical record. The author analyzes each reign and evaluates it according to the standards set forth in the book of Deuteronomy. Each king is identified as good or evil. There is no attempt to conceal the sins of the kings, even the good ones. Rather, their sins are routinely emphasized, quite often being described in great detail. The king's political success is directly tied to his spiritual faithfulness.

The climax of the book is found in the very first section; the building of the temple of Yahweh by Solomon. The good kings are those who show regard for the temple. In this respect, Deuteronomy 12:5 reveals the test of a Godly monarch, "But you shall seek the Lord at the place which the Lord your God shall choose from all your tribes, to establish His name there for His dwelling, and there you shall come."

The ungodly kings are those who show contempt for the temple. This is painfully obvious in the history of the kings of the northern kingdom. These kings routinely walked in the "sins of Jeroboam" (1 Kin. 14:16; 15:30; 16:31; 2 Kin. 3:3; 10:29, 31; 13:2, 6, 11; 14:24; 15:9, 18, 24, 28), a reference to the idolatrous calf-worship set up by

Israel's first king. In fact, these sins are identified as the chief reason for the nation's exile, "And the Lord rejected all the descendants of Israel, and afflicted them and gave them into the hand of plunderers, until He had cast them out of His sight. When He had torn Israel from the house of David, they made Jeroboam the son of Nebat king. Then Jeroboam drove Israel away from following the Lord, and made them commit a great sin. And the sons of Israel walked in all the sins of Jeroboam which he did; they did not depart from them, until the Lord removed Israel from His sight, as He spoke through all His servants the prophets. So Israel was carried away into exile from their own land to Assyria until this day" (2 Kin. 17:20-23).

The kings themselves serve as representatives of the nation. In fact, on several occasions, the entire nation is judged for the actions of a single king. This is not meant to excuse the sins of the people, for they are held responsible for their own actions. However, they routinely follow the example of their monarch; as the king goes, so goes the people. Rarely do we see the nation acting on its own behalf. When the king sets up a foreign idol, the people bow down and worship it. When the king tears down the high places and restores the temple, the people experience revival and make a commitment to serve the Lord.

In spite of its pessimistic outlook, the book ends on a hopeful note. The release of Jehoiachin from prison shows that the Lord has not forgotten his covenant with David, a commitment referred to often in Kings (1 Kin. 2:24, 45; 3:6; 5:5; 6:12; 8:15-26; 9:5; 11:38; 15:4; 2 Kin. 8:19). "The God who had brought the Babylonians against Jerusalem could also cause them to show favor to a son of David. God has not forgotten His promise, even in a distant land and difficult circumstances. The book ends in the exile, but with a muted note of hope—that God would continue to remember His promises to David."[12]

Structure and Outline

The book of Kings is naturally divided into three sections. The first section (1 Kings 1:1-11:43) is an account of the reign of Solomon. The second section (1 Kings 12:1-2 Kings 17:41) is a history of the kings of Israel and Judah from the split of the kingdom to the fall of

Samaria. The third section (2 Kings 18:1-25:30) is a record of the kings of Judah from the reign of Hezekiah to the fall of Jerusalem.

The division of Kings occurs at a most unfortunate place. The account of the reign of King Ahaziah over Israel begins in 1 Kings 22:51 and ends in 2 Kings 1:18. Further, the account of the ministry of the prophet Elijah begins in 1 Kings 17:1 and ends in 2 Kings 2:14. A much more natural division of the book would be between 2 Kings 1:18 and 2:1 (2:1 begins by announcing the end of Elijah's ministry and anticipating the succession of Elisha).

Following the division of the kingdom, the author uses a predictable structure to organize his material.[13] The framework begins with an accession notice and ends with a death notice. The accession notice typically includes: 1) a synchronistic reference to the king of the other kingdom (until the reign of Hoshea); 2) the king's age at accession (Judah only); 3) the length of the king's reign; 4) a reference to the capital city; 5) the king's ancestry (for the kings of Judah, the name of the king's mother is provided, a fact reflecting the continuity of the Davidic succession in Judah;[14] for the kings of Israel, the name of the king's father is ordinarily given); and 6) the theological verdict. The death notice typically includes: 1) a source citation; 2) a record of the king's death and burial; and 3) a notice of succession.

This framework can be seen in the record of King Azariah of Judah, "In the twenty-seventh year of Jeroboam king of Israel, Azariah son of Amaziah king of Judah became king. He was sixteen years old when he became king, and he reigned fifty-two years in Jerusalem; and his mother's name was Jecoliah of Jerusalem. And he did right in the sight of the Lord, according to all that his father Amaziah had done" (2 Kin. 15:1-3; accession notice). "Now the rest of the acts of Azariah and all that he did, are they not written in the Book of the Chronicles of the Kings of Judah? And Azariah slept with his fathers, and they buried him with his fathers in the city of David, and Jotham his son became king in his place" (2 Kin. 15:6-7; death notice).

In the northern kingdom of Israel, not one king (out of nineteen total kings) was judged to have done what was right in the sight of Yahweh. The closest the northern kingdom comes to having a good king is Jehu. He is anointed by a representative of the prophet Elisha at the command of the Lord, he destroys the wicked house of Ahab, he massacres the prophets of Baal, and he is rewarded by the Lord for his deeds, "And the Lord said to Jehu, 'Because you have done well in executing what is right in My eyes, and have done to the house of Ahab according to all that was in My heart, your sons of the fourth generation shall sit on the throne of Israel'" (2 Kin. 10:30). This promise allowed Jehu to be the patriarch of the longest-lasting dynasty in Israel (841-753 B.C.). However, the very next verse announces the overall verdict of God, "But Jehu was not careful to walk in the law of the Lord, the God of Israel, with all his heart, he did not depart from the sins of Jeroboam, which he made Israel sin" (2 Kin. 10:31). In the southern kingdom of Judah, eight kings (out of twenty total kings) are identified as having done right in the sight of the Lord. These kings are Asa, Jehoshaphat, Joash, Amaziah, Azariah, Jotham, Hezekiah, and Josiah. Unfortunately, the first six of these kings failed to completely remove the idolatrous places of worship from the land. Only Hezekiah and Josiah received unqualified praise.

Concerning the framework's overall pattern, Howard identifies four significant implications. First, the close attention to such precise records indicates the author's desire to write an accurate, comprehensive history. Second, however, this was not a dispassionate, "balanced" history; it was a theological history. Third, the author intended his work to be part of the larger history of Israel's experience as a nation. Fourth, the careful synchronisms for each king's reign with the dates of the sister nation's king indicates the author's desire to represent the histories of Israel and Judah as the history of one people, not two.[15]

Outline
I. The Reign of Solomon (1 Kings 1:1-11:43)
    A. Solomon's ascension to the throne (1:1-2:46)
        1. The plot of Adonijah (1:1-53)
        2. David's final charge to Solomon and his death (2:1-12)
        3. Solomon solidifies his throne (2:13-46)

        a. Adonijah (2:13-25)
        b. Abiathar (2:26-27)
        c. Joab (2:28-34)
        d. Benaiah and Zadok (2:35)
        e. Shimei (2:36-46)
    B. Solomon's wise request (3:1-28)
    C. Solomon's political administration (4:1-34)
    D. Solomon's building activity (5:1-9:28)
        1. Preparation for building (5:1-18)
        2. Construction of the temple (6:1-38)
        3. The palace built and the temple furnished (7:1-51)
        4. Dedication of the temple (8:1-66)
        5. Confirmation of the Davidic covenant (9:1-9)
        6. More building projects (9:10-28)
    E. Solomon's glory (10:1-29)
    F. Solomon's shame (11:1-43)
        1. Solomon's sin (11:1-8)
        2. Solomon's punishment (11:9-40)
        3. Solomon's death (11:41-43)
II. The Divided Kingdom to the Fall of Israel (12:1-2 Kings 17:41)
    A. The division of the kingdom (12:1-24)
    B. Jeroboam's evil reign in Israel (12:25-14:20)
    C. Rehoboam's evil reign in Judah (14:21-31)
    D. Abijah's evil reign in Judah (15:1-8)
    E. Asa's good reign in Judah (15:9-24)
    F. Nadab's evil reign in Israel (15:25-32)
    G. Baasha's evil reign in Israel (15:33-16:7)
    H. Elah's evil reign in Israel (16:8-14)
    I. Zimri's evil reign in Israel (16:15-20)
    J. Omri's evil reign in Israel (16:21-28)
    K. Ahab's evil reign in Israel (16:29-22:40)
        1. Ahab becomes king and marries Jezebel (16:29-34)
        2. Elijah's ministry (17:1-19:21)
            a. Elijah fed by Ravens (17:1-6)
            b. The widow at Zarephath (17:7-24)
            c. Elijah and Obadiah (18:1-15)

   d. Elijah on Mount Carmel (18:16-46)
   e. Elijah flees to Mount Horeb (19:1-18)
   f. The call of Elisha (19:19-21)
  3. Ahab and Ben-Hadad (20:1-43)
  4. Naboth's vineyard (21:1-29)
  5. Ahab's defeat and death (22:1-40)
L. Jehoshaphat's good reign in Judah (22:41-50)
M. Ahaziah's evil reign in Israel (22:51-2 Kings 1:18)
N. Elisha succeeds Elijah (2:1-25)
O. Joram's evil reign in Israel (3:1-8:15)
  1. Joram's rise to the throne (3:1-8)
  2. Elisha's ministry (3:9-8:15)
   a. The three kings (3:9-27)
   b. The widow's oil (4:1-7)
   c. The Shunammite's son restored (4:8-37)
   d. The poisoned pot (4:38-41)
   e. The feeding of a hundred (4:42-44)
   f. Naaman healed of leprosy (5:1-27)
   g. The floating axe head (6:1-7)
   h. The blinded Arameans (6:8-23)
   i. Famine in besieged Samaria (6:24-7:20)
   j. The Shunammite's land restored (8:1-6)
   h. Hazael murders Ben-Hadad (8:7-15)
P. Jehoram's evil reign in Judah (8:16-24)
Q. Ahaziah's evil reign in Judah (8:25-9:29)
R. Jehu's evil reign in Israel (9:30-10:36)
S. Athaliah's evil reign in Judah (11:1-20)
T. Joash's good reign in Judah (11:21-12:21)
U. Jehoahaz's evil reign in Israel (13:1-9)
V. Jehoash's evil reign in Israel (13:10-25)
W. Amaziah's good reign in Judah (14:1-22)
X. Jeroboam II's evil reign in Israel (14:23-29)
Y. Azariah's good reign in Judah (15:1-7)
Z. Zechariah's evil reign in Israel (15:8-12)
AA. Shallum's evil reign in Israel (15:13-16)
BB. Menahem's evil reign in Israel (15:17-22)
CC. Pekahiah's evil reign in Israel (15:23-26)

DD. Pekah's evil reign in Israel (15:27-31)

EE. Jotham's good reign in Judah (15:32-38)

FF. Ahaz's evil reign in Judah (16:1-20)

GG. Hoshea's evil reign in Israel (17:1-6)

HH. Israel's fall and captivity (17:7-41)

III. The Kingdom of Judah to the Babylonian Captivity (18:1-25:30)

A. Hezekiah's good reign (18:1-20:21)

B. Manasseh's evil reign (21:1-18)

C. Amon's evil reign (21:19-26)

D. Josiah's good reign (22:1-23:30)

E. Jehoahaz's evil reign (23:31-33)

F. Jehoiakim's evil reign (23:34-24:7)

G. Jehoiachin's evil reign (24:8-17)

H. Zedekiah's evil reign (24:18-20)

I. The fall of Jerusalem (25:1-21)

J. The rule of Gedaliah (25:22-26)

K. Jehoiachin released from prison (25:27-30)

Summary of Contents

The Reign of Solomon (1 Kings 1:1-11:43)

The book of Kings begins in the final days of the reign of David. The great king of Israel was an old man; so weak that he could not keep himself warm. To remedy the situation, his servants recruited a beautiful young woman to lie in his bed and keep him warm. This practice was evidently a popular custom. It is refered to by Josephus (A.D. 37-ca. 100), a Jewish historian, and Galen (ca. A.D. 130-200), a Greek physician. The name of the young maiden was Abishag (meaning "father of wandering"). She was from the village of Shunem, located seven miles northwest of Nazareth in the tribal territory of Issachar. The text notes that David did not have sexual relations with the "very beautiful" Abishag (1:4). This fact may have been recorded to highlight the weakness of David, thus explaining why he was powerless to personally stop the plot of Adonijah. It is also possible that the fact is recorded to highlight the virginity of Abishag, especially if she is the Shulammite woman of Song of Solomon (Shulammite is an alternative spelling of Shunammite).

While David lay on his bed, his son Adonijah (meaning "my Lord is Yahweh") decided to make a play for the throne. Adonijah is identified as the son of Haggith. Adonijah was the fourth son of David. He was probably the oldest living son, thus making him the apparent heir to the throne. Amnon, the eldest son, was killed by Absalom; Chileab, the second son, apparently died at an early age; and Absalom, the third son, was killed by Joab. To help him gain the throne, Adonijah recruited Joab, the commander of Israel's armies, and Abiathar, the high priest. Together, the conspirators went to the spring of En-Rogel to offer sacrifices in preparation for the anointing of Adonijah. The spring of En-Rogel was located near the intersection of the Hinnom and Kidron valleys.

When the prophet Nathan discovered the plot, he approached Bathsheba, the mother of Solomon, and commanded her to inform David. The queen instantly realized that her life (and that of her son Solomon) was in grave danger (cf. 1:12). In the Ancient Near East, a new king routinely eliminated his political enemies. Bathsheba quickly approached the king and informed him of the plot, reminding him that he had promised the throne to Solomon. David immediately gathered the prophet Nathan, the priest Zadok (meaning "righteous), and the commander of the king's bodyguard Benaiah, and instructed them to take Solomon and anoint him at the Gihon spring. The Gihon spring was the principal water supply for Jerusalem. It was situated in the Kidron Valley north of the En-Rogel spring (and closer to the city).

The men did as they were instructed and soon returned. They then paraded Solomon through the city on the royal mule, accompanied by blaring trumpets and shouts of "long live King Solomon!" The conspirators heard the tumult and were quickly informed that Solomon had been anointed king of Israel. Adonijah, fearing for his life, ran to the altar and placed his hands on the horns of the altar, an apparent plea for mercy (cf. Ex. 21:12-14). Solomon decided to spare his brother's life, promising him that he would not be harmed if he proved to be a "worthy" (Heb. *hayil*; cf. Jud. 6:12; 11:1; Ruth 2:1; 1 Sam. 9:1; 16:18) man.

As David's death grew near, he gave a final charge to his son Solomon. The king instructed his son to "Be strong!" (2:2; cf. Deut. 31:7, 23; Josh. 1:6, 7, 9, 18) and follow the standards of righteousness detailed in the Mosaic Law so that he could experience personal success and an everlasting dynasty. David also warned his son about Joab and Shimei, two men who had personally offended the king. Shortly after his final charge to Solomon, the great king of Israel died, having reigned just over forty years (ca. 1011-971 B.C.).

Having gained the throne, Solomon immediately took steps to solidify his position. First, he ordered Benaiah to execute his chief rival to the throne, his brother Adonijah. Adonijah betrayed his continued lust for the crown by asking for the hand of Abishag in marriage. This request was surely a subversive plot to usurp the throne. The harem of the previous king was ordinarily the possession of his successor. Second, he dismissed Abiathar from his duties as high priest. However, since Abiathar had faithfully served his father for many years, the king spared his life. Solomon replaced Abiathar with Zadok, an act that fulfilled the curse placed on the house of Eli (1 Sam. 2:31-36). Third, he ordered Benaiah to execute Joab. Joab had fled to the horns of the altar, probably believing that Solomon would spare his life just as he had initially spared the life of Adonijah. However, Joab was guilty of the murders of Abner and Amasa (2 Sam. 3:27; 20:10; cf. 2:5), treacherous acts that invalidated his right to mercy (cf. Ex. 21:14). Solomon replaced Joab with Benaiah. Fourth, he ordered Benaiah to execute Shimei. Initially, Shimei was placed under house arrest in Jerusalem. However, he disobeyed the command of Solomon three years later when he went to Gath in pursuit of two runaway slaves.

Solomon's early reign was one of considerable success. Shortly after offering a sacrifice to the Lord at Gibeon, the home of the tabernacle (cf. 1 Chron. 16:39), God appeared to him in a dream and offered to grant him whatever he requested. Solomon asked Yahweh for an "understanding heart" (3:9), i.e., the ability to effectively govern the nation. The king's request pleased the Lord, who further promised him wealth and prestige. Solomon's wisdom was quickly evidenced when he resolved a dispute between two harlots who each claimed a child as their own. Solomon ordered the child divided in two, a decision that revealed the identity of the true mother when she offered to let the other harlot take the child.

Solomon's wisdom was also demonstrated through the administration of his empire. He appointed twelve governors who were each responsible for an administrative district. These governors were under the authority of Azariah (meaning "Yahweh helps"), the son of Nathan. The king also appointed secretaries, priests, and various other leadership positions. The empire of Solomon stretched from the border of Egypt in the south to the Euphrates River in the north, a distance of more than two hundred miles. The king was also a prolific writer, authoring three thousand proverbs and composing more than a thousand songs, including the Song of Solomon and Psalm 72.

However, Solomon's greatest achievement was the building of the temple in Jerusalem. An important collaborator in the building of the temple was Hiram, the king of Tyre (980-947 B.C.). Hiram provided Solomon with wood and skilled laborers. Since Israel did not have native forests, the Israelites did not have any workmen who were capable of building with timber. The magnificent cedar and cypress trees of Phoenicia covered the western slopes of the Lebanon Mountains east of Tyre. To reimburse Hiram for his service, Solomon provided the king of Tyre with wheat, barley, olive oil, and wine. It was difficult to grow these staples in the mountainous terrain of Tyre.

Work on the temple was begun in 966 B.C. 1 Kings 6:1 is one of the most important chronological markers in the Old Testament. It identifies the fourth year of Solomon's reign as the "four hundred and eightieth year after the sons of Israel came out of the land of Egypt." This notation fixes the Exodus at 1446 B.C., a date from which numerous other dates can be calculated.

The temple was approximately ninety feet long, thirty feet wide, and forty-five feet high. It was constructed on Mount Moriah (cf. Gen. 22:2) at the threshing floor of Araunah. Mount Moriah was located just north of the City of David. Like the tabernacle, the temple was divided into the most holy place, the holy place, and an outer courtyard. The most holy place was thirty feet long and the holy place was sixty feet long. The Ark of the Covenant, the most important piece of furniture in the temple, was placed in the most holy place. The temple was completed in 959 B.C., seven years after the start of construction.

Shortly after the completion of the temple, Solomon arranged to have the Ark of the Covenant brought from the City of David to its new dwelling place. The Ark was transported by the priests and Levites during the Feast of Tabernacles. The Feast of Tabernacles commemorated the years of Israel's wandering in the wilderness. The duration of the feast was extended from one week to two weeks due to the significance of the occasion.

When the Ark was placed in the most holy place, the glory of the Lord filled the temple. Solomon responded with a lengthy prayer to Yahweh. He began his prayer by stressing God's "lovingkindness" (8:23; Heb. *hesed*) and faithfulness to His covenants. The king then made several requests. First, he asked that the Lord listen to the prayers offered towards the temple (8:25-30). Second, he asked for righteous judgment (8:31-32). Third, he asked for forgiveness of sins that caused defeat in battle (8:33-34). Fourth, he asked for forgiveness of sins that resulted in drought (8:35-36). Fifth, he asked for forgiveness of sins that had brought on other calamities, including famine, pestilence, blight, locusts, enemies, disaster, and disease (8:37-40). Sixth, he asked that the Lord answer the prayers of foreigners who come to Jerusalem (8:41-43). Seventh, he asked for victory in battle (8:44-45). Eighth, he asked for restoration after captivity (8:46-51). Ninth, he asked that the Lord answer the prayers of His people, the Israelites (8:52-53). When Solomon finished his prayer, he stood and pronounced a benediction on the people. He then sacrificed 22,000 oxen and 120,000 sheep to Yahweh.

The Lord responded to Solomon's dedication by appearing to him for a second time (cf. 3:5). God assured Solomon that He had heard his prayer and had consecrated the temple. The Lord then promised the king an everlasting dynasty if he would faithfully follow the Mosaic Law. However, if Solomon failed to keep the Law and committed idolatry, then Israel would experience the loss of their land and the abandonment of their God.

The rest of Solomon's achievements are described in 9:10-10:29. The great king had already built a beautiful temple and a magnificent palace. Now, he built storage cities and heavily fortified key cities as defensive strongholds. He also enslaved the foreigners who remained in Canaan. He was even able to assemble a navy based in Ezion-Geber (modern Eilat), located on the northern shore of the Red Sea. Solomon's fame was so great that foreigners came from great distances to hear his wisdom. One of these was the queen of Sheba. Sheba is located in southwestern Arabia (modern Yemen), about 1,200 miles from Jerusalem. The region was home to the Sabeans, a tribe of merchants whose commercial trade routes stretched from Africa to India. The queen of Sheba asked Solomon a series of "difficult questions" (Heb. *hidot*; cf. Prov. 1:6) to test the extent of his wisdom. Her curiosity satisfied, she gave the king an incredible amount of gold, spices, and precious stones. Perhaps the greatest indicator of Solomon's success was his wealth. The king acquired vast amounts of gold, largely due to his control of all of the major trade routes that passed between Africa and Asia. He made silver "as common as stones" (10:27) in Jerusalem. The king also developed an imposing army built on the strength of 1400 chariots and 4000 horses.

Unfortunately, Solomon also accumulated a large number of wives and concubines. The king had an incredible 700 wives and 300 concubines. The actions of Solomon were in violation of the Mosaic Law. Kings were specifically prohibited from multiplying horses, women, and silver and gold (Deut. 17:16-17). Israelites in general were commanded not to marry foreign women (Deut. 7:1-3). Many of Solomon's wives were foreigners. These wives turned Solomon's heart away from the Lord. He accommodated their pagan worship by building temples to their gods on the Mount of Olives. He began to worship Chemosh, Molech, and Ashtoreth, the detestable gods of the nations that surrounded Israel.

As a result, God sent a series of judgments on the unfaithful king. First, the Lord announced that most of the kingdom would be torn from him and given to his servant; a prediction of the split of the kingdom at the hands of Jeroboam. Second, the Lord raised up a foreign adversary named Hadad. Hadad was an Edomite prince who had escaped the slaughter of Joab by fleeing to Egypt where he was protected by Amenemope, the Egyptian pharaoh. The exiled prince had returned after the death of David to wreak havoc on Solomon's southern trade route, the King's Highway. Third, the Lord raised up another foreign adversary named Rezon. Rezon was an Aramean who became the king of Damascus, an important city on the major trade routes between Israel and Mesopotamia. Rezon led raids against the caravans of Solomon, his bitter enemy.

Finally, the Lord raised up Jeroboam (meaning "the people contend") who led an internal rebellion against the king. Jeroboam was an Ephraimite from the city of Zeredah. He is identified as a "valiant warrior" (11:28; Heb. *gibor hayil*; cf. Jud. 6:12; 11:1; Ruth 2:1; 1 Sam. 9:1; 16:18). Jeroboam was the commander of Solomon's labor force.

One day, Jeroboam was approached by the prophet Ahijah (meaning "my brother is Yahweh"). The prophet took off his new cloak and tore it into twelve pieces. He gave Jeroboam ten pieces, signifying that he would be given ten of the tribes of Israel to rule over (all except Judah and Benjamin). The prophet then promised Jeroboam an "enduring house" (11:38; i.e., extended dynasty; cf. 1 Sam. 2:35; 25:28) if he would faithfully follow the Mosaic Law. When Solomon heard the news, he tried to put Jeroboam to death. However, Jeroboam fled to Egypt where he was provided asylum by Shishak, the Egyptian pharaoh. Eventually, Solomon died after a forty year reign (971-931 B.C.). The great king of Israel was buried alongside his father in the City of David.

The Divided Kingdom to the Fall of Israel (12:1-2 Kings 17:41)

Solomon was succeeded by his son Rehoboam (meaning "he enlarges the people") through Naamah, the Ammonitess. Interestingly enough, Rehoboam is the only son of Solomon identified in Scripture. He was born the year before his father's accession to the throne and was now forty-one years old. Rehoboam reigned from 931-913 B.C. At his coronation ceremony in Shechem, the new king was approached by Jeroboam, the representative of the northern tribes of Israel. Jeroboam asked Rehoboam to lighten the load that had been placed on them by Solomon, a reference to the heavy taxes imposed by the previous king. To his credit, Rehoboam sought the advice of his counselors before giving a response to Jeroboam. The elders agreed with the request of the northern tribes and advised Rehoboam to lighten their load. However, the younger men who had grown up with Rehoboam recommended that the new king impose an even greater burden on the northern tribes. Unfortunately, Rehoboam decided to follow the advice of his young counselors. He replied to Jeroboam with the famous line, "My father disciplined you with whips, but I will discipline you with scorpions" (12:14), an indication that Jeroboam intended to be even more harsh than his father Solomon. "Scorpions" were whips with sharp pieces of metal and glass in the strands.

As one can imagine, the northern tribes were incensed at the response of Jeroboam. They stoned Adoram, the commander of forced labor and rebelled against the rule of Jeroboam. Rehoboam attempted to restore order by raising an army to march against the northern tribes; however, he was stopped by the prophet Shemaiah (meaning "Yahweh hears"). Although this initial attack did not come to pass, the strife between the northern and southern kingdoms would last throughout the reign of Rehoboam.

In the fifth year of Rehoboam (i.e., 926 B.C.), Pharaoh Shishak of Egypt mounted an invasion of Judah (from this point on, the northern kingdom will be referred to as Israel and the southern kingdom will be referred to as Judah). The Egyptian ruler managed to capture 156 cities and even threatened to destroy Jerusalem. The holy city was spared when Rehoboam paid heavy tribute to Shishak, including the five hundred gold shields that Solomon had made after the visit of the queen of Sheba (cf. 10:16-17). The record of Shishak's invasion is immortalized with an inscription on the south wall of the temple of Amon at Karnak (modern Luxor).

Jeroboam was appointed as king of Israel. He reigned from 931-910 B.C. The king chose to rule from Shechem, making it the capital of the northern kingdom. Soon, he would move his capital to Tirzah (cf. 14:17). Jeroboam's first order of business was the creation of an alternative religion. He realized that the nation would quickly reunite if the men of Israel continued to pilgrammage to Jerusalem for the sacred festivals. He set up golden calves at Bethel and Dan, the southernmost and northernmost cities in the northern kingdom. The golden calf statues were erected to serve as aids in the worship of Yahweh (cf. 12:28 and Ex. 32:4). It was common practice in the Ancient Near East to picture one's god as riding on the back of a young bull.[16] This image promoted the idea that the god was powerful since young bulls were almost impossible to ride. Jeroboam also instituted a new festival designed to compete with the Day of Atonement. He even instituted a new priesthood, allowing men from any tribe to become priests. As a result, many of the priests and Levites who lived among the northern tribes deserted their homes and took up residence in Judah (2 Chron. 11:13-14).

The actions of Jeroboam were quickly condemned by the Lord. He sent an unnamed prophet ("man of God;" 13:1; cf. 1 Sam. 2:27) from Judah to Bethel to announce the judgment of Yahweh. The prophet informed Jeroboam that the Lord would raise up a powerful king named Josiah who would destroy the altar of Bethel and massacre its priests. This prophecy is one of the most remarkable in Scripture. Josiah is identified by name almost three hundred years before his birth. The sign provided to authenticate the prophecy was the splitting of the altar. When Jeroboam tried to order the prophet's arrest, his hand immediately withered. The prophet graciously healed the king's hand, refusing to accept any reward for his services.

As the prophet began the journey back to Judah, he was over-taken by an old prophet from Bethel. The older prophet tricked the younger prophet into returning to Bethel for a parting meal by claiming that he had received a revelation from God. Having disobeyed the commandment of the Lord to neither eat nor drink in Bethel, the young prophet was killed by a lion when he left the city. Constable explains the harsh judgment of God, "All Israel would have heard about his prophecy of God's judgment on Jeroboam for his disobedience to the word of the Lord through Moses. If God had not judged His own prophet for his disobedience to the word given him by God and which he had announced publicly, doubt would have been cast on his prophecy and on God's credibility."[17]

Shortly thereafter, the Lord "sent" (14:6; although it appears that Jeroboam initiated the contact, God sovereignly moved his heart to do so) another prophet to Jeroboam. Ahijah, who had earlier given Jeroboam ten pieces of his cloak, now announced that the dynasty of Jeroboam would quickly end because he had forsaken the Law of Moses. The sign provided to authenticate the prophecy was the death of Abijah, the son of Jeroboam.

Rehoboam was succeeded in Judah by his son Abijam (meaning "father of the sea;" also known as Abijah) through Maacah, the daughter of Absalom[18] (Abishalom is an alternate spelling). Abijam reigned from 913-911 B.C. He was an evil king who continued to support the idolatrous practices put in place by his father (cf. 14:22-24). However, the Lord allowed him to rule because of the faithfulness of his ancestor David. Yahweh even fought against Israel on behalf of Abijam. Soon after his accession, the armies of Abijam faced the armies of Jeroboam on Mount Zemaraim, located less than two miles from Bethel. Outnumbered two to one and surrounded by the men of Jeroboam, the forces of Abijam were victorious because "they trusted in the Lord, the God of their fathers" (2 Chron. 13:18).

Abijam was succeeded in Judah by his son Asa (meaning "healer"). His mother is identified as Maacah (15:10); however, Maacah was actually Asa's grandmother. The reason for the reference to Maacah is because Asa deposed her as queen mother and cut down the Asherah pole that she had erected. Asa reigned from 911-870 B.C. He was a good king who sought to remove the idolatrous practices put in place by his father and grandfather. In 897 B.C.,[19] Asa fought against Zerah, a Cushite (Ethiopian) king, in the Valley of Zephathah at Mareshah, a town in the western foothills of Judah. The army of Asa was victorious when Yahweh, personally fighting on behalf of His faithful king, routed the Ethiopians (2 Chron. 14:12).

The following year, Asa went to war with Baasha, king of Israel. The conflict began when Baasha started to fortify the border city of Ramah to prevent the Israelites from journeying to the southern kingdom. Asa, evidently viewing the actions of Baasha as a threat to Judah, enlisted the support of Ben-Hadad, king of Damascus. When Ben-Hadad invaded Israel from the north, Baasha was forced to abandon Ramah and retreat to Tirzah. Asa then appropriated the building materials left by Baasha and erected his own fortifications at Geba and Mizpah, Judahite cities that bordered Ramah on both sides. When Asa grew old, he was struck with a foot disease, an affliction that necessitated the appointment of his son Jehoshaphat as coregent, a tradition that will be followed by several Hebrew kings.[20]

Jeroboam was succeeded in Israel by his son Nadab (meaning "generous"). Nadab reigned from 910-909 B.C. Nadab repeated the idolatrous sins of his father Jeroboam, a situation that will become all too familiar among the northern kings. Not one of the nineteen kings will be characterized as having done "right in the sight of the Lord" (cf. 15:11). While laying siege to the Philistine fortress of Gibbethon (just west of Gezer), Nadab was murdered by Baasha, one of his commanders. The assassin then proceeded to exterminate the entire royal family, an act that fulfilled the prophecy of Ahijah (14:10).

Baasha (meaning "boldness"), the founder of Israel's second dynasty, reigned from 909-886 B.C. He too "walked in the way of Jeroboam" (15:34), a reference to the golden calf cult instituted by the northern kingdom's first king. As a result, the Lord sent the prophet Jehu ("Yahweh is he") to pronounce on Baasha the very same judgment that had been given to Jeroboam; the dynasty of Baasha will soon be cut off (16:3).

Baasha was succeeded in Israel by his son Elah (meaning "oak"). Elah reigned from 886-885 B.C. Like Nadab, the son of Jeroboam, Elah was assassinated by a trusted lieutenant after a brief two year reign. This time, the culprit was Zimri, the commander of half of the king's chariot corps. Zimri immediately massacred the entire royal family, an act that fulfilled the prophecy of Jehu (16:3).

Zimri (meaning "wild goat"), the founder of Israel's third dynasty, reigned only seven days. When news of the assassination of Elah reached the Israelite warriors who were once again laying siege to Gibbethon, they appointed their general, Omri, as king of Israel. The army then marched to Tirzah to dethrone Zimri. When Zimri realized that the city was about to fall, he set fire to the palace, allowing himself to be consumed in the flames.

Omri (meaning "servant of Yahweh"), the founder of Israel's fourth dynasty, reigned from 885-874 B.C. His accession was opposed by Tibni, who had the support of half of Israel. The bitter struggle lasted for four years until finally the forces of Omri prevailed and Tibni was killed. Two years later, Omri bought a hill from a man named Shemer for two talents (ca. 150 pounds) of silver. The hill was located twelve miles west of Tirzah in the heart of the northern kingdom. Omri fortified the hill with an imposing wall filled with defensive fortifications and built a beautiful palace on the summit. He named his new capital Samaria after Shemer, the previous owner.

Omri was succeeded in Israel by his son Ahab (meaning "father [perhaps a reference to God] is brother"). Ahab reigned from 874-853 B.C. He was the most wicked king to rule over the northern kingdom, primarily because he married Jezebel, the daughter of Ethbaal, the Sidonian king. Together, Ahab and Jezebel attempted to make Baal-worship the official religion of Israel. The king built a temple for Baal in Samaria. He then adorned the temple with an altar and an Asherah pole. The queen ordered the execution of all of the prophets of Yahweh.

The Lord responded to the threat by raising up a powerful prophet named Elijah (meaning "my God is Yahweh"). Elijah hailed from the city of Tishbe, located west of the Jordan River in the region of Gilead. The prophet approached Ahab and announced that the nation would endure three years of drought, a direct attack on Baal, the storm god. Elijah then hid from the king, first at the brook Cherith, where he was fed by ravens, and then in Zeraphath, a city in Phoenicia that belonged to Sidon. In Zeraphath, the prophet stayed at the home of a widow. There he continually restored her supply of flour and oil. The prophet even restored her son when he died.

Three years after his initial prophecy, Elijah returned to Israel. His presence was announced to Ahab by Obadiah (meaning "servant of Yahweh"), a man who "feared the Lord greatly" (18:3). Obadiah demonstrated his faithfulness to God by protecting a hundred prophets who had escaped the slaughter of Jezebel. Elijah instructed Ahab to meet him on Mount Carmel, the site of a major Baal shrine. There the prophet confronted the prophets of Baal and Asherah. In the classic contest that followed, the Lord showed that He was the only true God; He was the One who could bring fire and rain from heaven, acts normally attributed to the storm god Baal. After the contest was over, Elijah killed the prophets of Baal.

When Jezebel heard what had happened on Mount Carmel, she sent a messenger to Elijah with a promise to kill him. Fearing for his life, the prophet fled to Mount Horeb (Sinai). There, he asked God to take his life, believing that he was the only true prophet who remained in Israel. The Lord appeared to Elijah and gave him a threefold mission: first, the prophet was to anoint Hazael as king of Aramea; second, he was to anoint Jehu as king of Israel; and third, he was to anoint Elisha as his replacement. Together, these three would eradicate Baal worship from the land.

The first to be anointed was Elisha (meaning "my God is salvation"). Elisha lived in Abel-Meholah, located about four miles south of Beth Shan. As Elisha was plowing in the fields one day, Elijah approached him and threw his mantle on him. This act symbolized the passing of Elijah's power and authority to Elisha. Elisha immediately left his home and began to serve as Elijah's assistant.

In 857 B.C., Ben-Hadad of Aramea led a coalition of thirty-three kings in an attack on Samaria, probably in response to the marriage between Ahab and Jezebel, a union that solidified ties between Israel and Phoenicia. Ahab initially agreed to the ransom demands of Ben-Hadad; however, when the Aramean king increased his demands, Ahab attacked the coalition, catching them in a state of drunkenness and routing their forces. The following year, Ben-Hadad returned. Ahab again was victorious, this time forcing Ben-Hadad to submit to a treaty returning Israel's captured cities and guaranteeing Ahab commercial access to Damascus.

Shortly after his victories over the Arameans, Ahab became enamored with a vineyard that bordered his palace. He approached Naboth (meaning "fruits"), the owner of the vineyard, and offered to buy it from him. Naboth refused, arguing that the Lord would not want him to sell his family's inheritance. The matter troubled Ahab so deeply that he refused to eat. When Jezebel heard what had happened, she formulated a plot designed to get Naboth stoned. Her plan succeeded and Ahab gained possession of the vineyard. The Lord then sent Elijah to Ahab with a message of judgment. The prophet informed the king that his dynasty would soon come to an end and that his wife would be eaten by dogs.

Three years after the establishment of the treaty between Ahab and Ben-Hadad, Ahad decided to break the treaty and attack Ramoth-Gilead. This city had originally belonged to Israel. Evidently, it had been captured by the Arameans, perhaps during the reign of Baasha. In the resultant battle, Ahab was killed when an arrow pierced a gap in his armor. The king's body was taken to Samaria and buried. The death of Ahab fulfilled two prophecies. First, Micaiah (meaning "who is like Yahweh?") had prophecied that the army of Israel would be like scattered sheep without a master (22:17), a reference to the defeat of the Israelites and death of Ahab. Second, Elijah had prophecied that dogs would lick up the blood of Ahab (21:19), a prophecy fulfilled when the blood of Ahab was drained out of his chariot at the pool of Samaria.

Asa was succeeded in Judah by his son Jehoshaphat (meaning "Yahweh judges") through Azubah, the daughter of Shilhi. Jehoshaphat reigned from 873-848 B.C. Like his father, Jehoshaphat did "right in the sight of the Lord" (22:43); however, he failed to fully rid the land of idolatry. While the record of Jehoshaphat's reign in the book of Kings is only ten verses long (22:41-50), the book of Chronicles devotes four chapters to the great king (2 Chron. 17-20). In the third year of his reign, Jehoshaphat sent missionaries throughout the land to teach the Law of Moses to the people. He also appointed judges in each of the fortress cities of Judah, commanding them to render righteous judgments in the "fear of the Lord" (2 Chron. 19:9). These judges were presided over by Amariah ("Yahweh has spoken"), the chief priest, and Zebadiah ("Yahweh has given"), the prime minister. Because of his faithfulness, the Lord richly blessed Jehoshaphat. He was able to subdue the Philistines and Arabs, who both brought tribute to Judah. He built fortresses and storage cities throughout Judah. And in what is probably his most remarkable achievement, he built an army that numbered over three quarters of a million men.

Ahab was succeeded in Israel by his son Ahaziah (meaning "Yahweh holds"). Ahaziah reigned from 853-852 B.C. Ahaziah served Baal, just as his parents had done. When Ahaziah injured himself in a fall, he sent messengers to inquire of Baal-Zebub, the god of Ekron, whether he would recover from his illness. Elijah intercepted the messengers and informed them that the king would die from his illness. Ahaziah twice sent a captain with fifty men to bring Elijah to him and both times the prophet called fire down from heaven to consume the troops. Finally, Elijah agreed to visit the king. When the prophet arrived at the king's palace, he repeated his earlier prophecy. The king never left his bed, eventually dying without an heir.

One day, Elijah and Elisha travelled from Gilgal to Bethel, a distance of about seven miles. When they arrived in Bethel, some prophets came out of the city to inform Elisha that this would be Elijah's last day on earth; however, the younger prophet replied that he already knew this fact. The two prophets then continued on to Jericho. Once again, the prophets of the city came out to tell Elisha what he already knew. Finally, the two prophets reached the Jordan, where Elijah parted the river so that they could cross on dry ground. Elijah then asked Elisha what he wanted from him. Elisha asked for a double portion of his spirit. As they continued on their journey, a fiery chariot appeared in the sky and Elijah was swept up to heaven in a whirlwind. Elisha then put on the robe of Elijah that had fallen from the prophet and proceeded to prove his power with a series of miracles. These included the following: 1) parting the Jordan River (2:14); 2) purifying the spring of Jericho (2:19-22); 3) calling out two bears to punish the young boys who mocked him (2:23-24); 4) providing the widow with oil (4:1-7); 5) restoring the son of the Shunammite woman (4:8-37); 6) purifying the poisoned pot (4:38-41); 7) feeding a hundred men with twenty loaves of barley and some grain (4:42-44); 8) healing Naaman of leprosy (5:1-27); 9) floating an axe head (6:1-7); 10) blinding an army of Arameans (6:8-23); 11) relieving the siege of Samaria (6:24-7:20); and 12) announcing a seven-year famine on the land (8:1-6). Elisha's amazing power continued even after his death; when a dead man's body was thrown onto his corpse, the man was revived and went on his way (13:21).

Since Ahaziah died without an heir, he was succeeded in Israel by his brother Joram (Jehoram; meaning "Yahweh is exalted"). Joram reigned from 852-841 B.C. The new king immediately tore down the image of Baal that his father had erected; however, he followed in the "sins of Jeroboam" (3:3), a reference to the golden calf cult established by the first king of the northern kingdom. Shortly after his accession, Joram attempted to recover the territory of Moab that had rebelled after his father's death (1:1; 3:5). The Moabites were led by Mesha, a sheep breeder who had previously paid an annual tribute of lambs and wool to the king of Israel. There is extra-biblical documentation of the famous shepherd; the exploits of Mesha are immortalized on the so-called Moabite Stone.[21] The Israelite attack was abandoned when the Moabite king sacrificed his own son as a burnt offering, an act that repulsed the Hebrew warriors.

In 841 B.C., Elisha travelled to Damascus. When Ben-Hadad heard that the great prophet was in the city, he sent his servant Hazael to inquire of him as to whether or not he would recover from an illness. Moved to tears by the knowledge of the future atrocities that he would inflict upon Israel, Elisha reluctantly informed Hazael that Ben-Hadad would soon die and that he would become the next king of Aramea. Emboldened by the prophet's message, Hazael murdered his master by smothering him in his sleep.

Jehoshaphat was succeeded in Judah by his son Jehoram. Jehoram reigned from 848-841 B.C. Jehoram was an evil king who "walked in the way of the kings of Israel" (8:18). The primary reason for Jehoram's wickedness was the fact that he married Athaliah, the daughter of Ahab, king of Israel. Shortly after gaining the throne, Jehoram killed all his brothers and many other members of the royal family in an attempt to solidify his position. Despite his reputation as a cruel and bloodthirsty king, the nation of Edom revolted against Jehoram and set up its own king. Soon thereafter, Jehoram sent an army to subdue them. This attempt was unsuccessful and Edom remained free of Judean control.

During Jehoram's reign, the Philistines and Arabs launched an attack on Jerusalem. This attack resulted in the looting of the king's palace and the enslavement of his entire family with the exception of his youngest son Jehoahaz (Ahaziah). This judgment was predicted in a letter to the king by Elijah (2 Chron. 21:12-15). Elijah also foretold the painful death that Jehoram would endure. This prophecy came to pass in 841 B.C. when Jehoram succumbed to an intestinal disease. The sack of Jerusalem at the hands of the Philistines and Arabs serves as the occasion for Obadiah, a book that condemns Edom for its role in the attack. Despite Jehoram's wickedness, the Lord was not willing to destroy Judah because of the Davidic Covenant.

Jehoram was succeeded in Judah by his son Ahaziah through Athaliah, the granddaughter of Omri, king of Israel. Ahaziah reigned in 841 B.C. Ahaziah repeated the sins of his father, largely due to his close family connections to the house of Joram, his uncle. Together, Ahaziah and Joram mounted an attack on Hazael at Ramoth-Gilead. In the resultant battle, Ahaziah was wounded, necessitating his retreat to Jezreel.

In the meantime, Elisha sent one of his disciples to anoint Jehu, the son of Jehoshaphat, the son of Nimshi, as king over Israel. This act completed the threefold mission originally given to Elijah (19:15-16). Jehu was a commander in the army of Israel. When he informed his officers of his anointing, they blew a trumpet and hailed him as king. Jehu immediately went to the region of Jezreel, where he met and killed Joram in Naboth's vineyard, just as Elijah had predicted (21:19, 29). He then ordered the execution of Ahaziah, who was shot as he attempted to flee. Ahaziah eventually died in Megiddo. When Jehu arrived in Jezreel, he was sarcastically greeted by Jezebel, whom he ordered thrown out a window. The wicked queen was then eaten by dogs in fulfillment of the prophecy of Elijah (21:23).

Jehu, the founder of Israel's fifth dynasty, reigned from 841-814 B.C. His reign was marked by violence. Shortly after gaining the throne, he sent letters to the elders of Samaria, commanding them to kill the sons of Ahab. He then executed the family and friends of Ahab who lived in Jezreel and departed for the capital city. On his journey, Jehu slaughtered the relatives of Ahaziah who had come to visit the house of Ahab. When the king reached Samaria, he exterminated the remnant of Ahab's family until there was nobody left of royal blood. Finally, he gathered together all the prophets and priests of Baal at the temple of Baal in Samaria, whereupon he had them put to death. He then destroyed the temple and turned it into a public latrine.

Jehu was the closest the northern kingdom came to having a good king. In fact, the Lord rewarded him for his deeds, "And the Lord said to Jehu, 'Because you have done well in executing what is right in My eyes, and have done to the house of Ahab according to all that was in My heart, your sons of the fourth generation shall sit on the throne of Israel'" (10:30). This promise allowed Jehu to be the patriarch of the longest-lasting dynasty in Israel (841-753 B.C.). However, the next verse announces the overall verdict of God, "But Jehu was not careful to walk in the law of the Lord, the God of Israel, with all his heart, he did not depart from the sins of Jeroboam, which he made Israel sin" (10:31). As a result, the Lord allowed Shalmaneser III, king of Assyria, to encroach upon Israel's borders, a threat relieved only after Jehu paid an enormous tribute to the Assyrians. The submission of Jehu to Shalmaneser is immortalized on the so-called Black Obelisk, where the king (or his representative) is pictured bowing at the feet of the Assyrian king.

Ahaziah was succeeded in Judah by his mother Athaliah, the daughter of Ahab, king of Israel. Athaliah reigned from 841-835 B.C. Following the deaths of Ahaziah and many members of his family in Jehu's bloody purge, Athaliah seized the throne. Once in power, she slaughtered her own children and grandchildren, hoping to reunite the kingdoms of Judah and Israel under the Omride dynasty. Fortunately, Jehoram's daughter Jehosheba (meaning "Yahweh is an Oath") was able to rescue her infant nephew Joash, the son of Ahaziah. For the length of Athaliah's reign, the child was hidden in the temple under the protection of the high priest Jehoiada ("Yahweh knows").

Finally, the time came to reveal the child to Judah. Jehoiada recruited the military officers and stationed them with their men to guard the temple, giving them orders to kill anyone who approached the area. The high priest then brought out the young boy and placed a crown on his head. All those around immediately rejoiced, shouting "Long live the king!" (11:12). The officers took Athaliah and executed her outside the palace. Jehoiada then led the people in making a covenant to faithfully follow the Lord; a commitment evidenced by their execution of Mattan, the priest of Baal, and the destruction of his temple.

Athaliah was succeeded in Judah by Joash (meaning "Yahweh is strong"), the son of Ahaziah through Zibiah. Joash became king at the age of seven and reigned from 835-796 B.C. Since Joash gained the throne at such a young age, he was under the tutelage of Jehoiada for the early part of his reign. The high priest even chose wives for the young ruler (2 Chron. 24:3). Perhaps because of the events of his childhood, Joash developed a love for the temple. He commanded the Levites to repair and restore the temple using the tithes of the people.

Unfortunately, the faithfulness of Joash lasted only as long as the high priest lived. Shortly after the death of Jehoiada, the king abandoned the house of God and worshipped Asherah, the goddess of his grandmother Athaliah. When confronted of his sin by Zechariah, the priestly son of Jehoiada, Joash had him executed, evidently forgetting the kindness that had been shown him by Zechariah's father. The Lord then brought Hazael, the king of Damascus, against Jerusalem. The city was spared only when Joash paid an enormous tribute to the Aramean king. Eventually, Joash was assassinated by his servants Jozacar and Jehozabad. In spite of the apostasy that characterized the last years of his life, Joash is still identified as a king who did "right in the sight of the Lord" (12:2).

Jehu was succeeded in Israel by his son Jehoahaz (meaning "he who Yahweh holds"). Jehoahaz reigned from 814-798 B.C. Jehoahaz was an evil king who repeated the "sins of Jeroboam" (13:2). He even allowed an Asherah pole to remain standing in Samaria. As a result, the Lord allowed Hazael to be a source of constant irritation to Israel. Eventually, Jehoahaz called on the Lord for mercy and God raised up a "deliverer" for the nation (13:5). This "deliverer" is probably the Assyrian King Adad-Nirari III, who launched an effective campaign against Aram which resulted in the subjugation of Hazael and thus the deliverance of Israel.[22]

Jehoahaz was succeeded in Israel by his son Jehoash (meaning "Yahweh is strong"). Jehoash reigned from 798-782 B.C. Like his father and grandfather, he walked in the "sins of Jeroboam" (13:11). Nevertheless, the Lord was gracious to him because of an act of kindness towards Elisha. As the prophet was dying, Jehoash wept over him, lamenting "My father, my father, the chariots of Israel and its horsemen!" (13:14), a reference to the important role played by Elisha in protecting the nation. In response, the great prophet informed Jehoash that he would successfully defeat the Arameans on three different occasions. These victories allowed the northern kingdom to recapture several Israelite cities in the Transjordan.

Joash was succeeded in Judah by his son Amaziah (meaning "Yahweh is mighty"), through Jehoaddin. Amaziah reigned from 796-767 B.C. Amaziah was a good king who "did right in the sight of the Lord" (14:3), although not to the same degree as his ancestor David. The new king's first order of business was the execution of Jozacar and Jehozabad, the wicked servants who had assassinated his father. His second order of business was the resubjugation of Edom. He attacked and destroyed the Edomite army in the Valley of Salt, located between Beersheba and Arad, massacring a total of twenty thousand Edomites in the battle and its aftermath. Amaziah then brought the Edomite idols that he had captured to Jerusalem, where he worshipped them. When the king ignored the prophet who had been sent to warn him of his sins, the man of God announced that he would be destroyed by the Lord. Amaziah's third order of business was an attack on Jehoash, king of Israel. The two kings clashed at Beth Shemesh. The battle was a resounding victory for Israel. Amaziah was captured and taken to Jerusalem, where he was forced to watch as the temple was looted. Amazingly enough, Jehoash allowed Amaziah to remain alive, taking him to Samaria, where he was eventually freed when the Israelite king died. The prophecy of the man of God was eventually fulfilled when Amaziah's own people conspired against him, killing him in Lachish, a border city located southwest of Jerusalem.

Jehoash was succeeded in Israel by his son Jeroboam II. Jeroboam reigned from 793-753 B.C. Even though he too committed the "sins of Jeroboam" (14:24), the Lord, moved to pity by the great affliction of Israel, graciously allowed Jeroboam to experience great success. The king was able to recapture the territories of Israel in Aramea and the Transjordan that had fallen to the Arameans, even including the city of Damascus itself. Yet, perhaps the most significant thing about Jeroboam is the fact that all three writing prophets to Israel ministered during his reign (i.e., Jonah, Amos, and Hosea).

Amaziah was succeeded in Judah by his son Azariah (also known as Uzziah, meaning "Yahweh is my strength"), through Jecoliah. Azariah reigned from 792-740 B.C. Azariah was a king who "did right in the sight of the Lord" (15:3). As a result, God blessed him with a long and prosperous reign. Under Azariah, the kingdom of Judah experienced its greatest success since Solomon. In fact, the territory controlled by Jeroboam II and Azariah, whose reigns overlap for thirty-nine years, almost equaled that of the great king of Israel. Amazingly enough, for a king who reigned for fifty-two years, the book of Kings only gives him seven verses.

Amaziah was appointed as king by the people of Judah rather than by his own father (2 Chron. 26:1), who was hated by his subjects. Amaziah enlarged and equipped the army of Judah and engaged in a string of military successes against the Philistines, Arabs, Meunites, and Ammonites. The king rebuilt Elath and restored it to Judah. He constructed a series of defensive fortifications around Jerusalem and placed settlements in the desert south of the city. He even built a series of cisterns to collect water for irrigation, thus greatly expanding the amount of productive land. The exploits of Amaziah earned him a far-reaching reputation as a great leader (cf. 2 Chron. 26:8, 15). Unfortunately, these successes also led to his downfall. The pride of Amaziah was revealed when he entered the temple of the Lord to burn incense on the altar of incense. When confronted by Azariah the priest, the king became furious and refused to leave the temple. As a result, the Lord struck him with leprosy until the day of his death. The king was forced to hand over the reins of the kingdom to his son Jotham and spent the remainder of his life in isolation.

Jeroboam was succeeded in Israel by his son Zechariah (meaning "Yahweh has remembered"). Zechariah reigned for only six months in 753 B.C. His assassination brought the dynasty of Jehu to an end after five generations, just as the Lord had promised (10:30). Zechariah's assassin was Shallum ("retribution"), the son of Jabesh, who reigned less than a month before being assassinated himself.

Shallum's assassin was Menahem (meaning "comforter"), the son of Gadi and founder of Israel's seventh dynasty. Menahem reigned from 752-742 B.C. Menahem was from the city of Tirzah, the previous capital of the northern kingdom. It is likely that bad blood remained from the citizens of Tirzah over the rejection of their city, thus explaining the actions of Menahem. As Merrill states, "One can be sure that the move from Tirzah was not universally popular and that a residue of resentment and even partisanship remained at Tirzah."[23] During the reign of Menahem, the Assyrian King Tiglath-Pileser III emerged as a potent threat to Israel, forcing the northern kingdom to agree to a treaty and pay a heavy tribute.

Menahem was succeeded in Israel by his son Pekahiah (meaning "Yahweh has opened" [his eyes]). Pekahiah reigned from 742-740 B.C. Like most of his predecessors, Pekahiah "did not depart from the sins of Jeroboam" (15:24). As a result, he was assassinated after a brief two-year reign, perhaps because of his pro-Assyrian stance.

Pekahiah's assassin was Pekah (meaning "open-eyed"), the son of Remaliah and founder of Israel's eighth dynasty. Pekah reigned from 752-732 B.C.[24] Pekah had previously been an army officer under Menahem. He was supported in his quest for the throne by a Gileadite element that was fiercely anti-Assyrian. When Pekah gained sole possession of Israel in 740 B.C., he immediately broke the treaty with Assyria and took steps to create a coalition that would be able to resist the Assyrians. He formed an alliance with Rezin of Damascus that also included the Phoenicians, Philistines, and Edomites. This coalition soon approached Judah and attempted to persuade Jotham (and Ahaz his son and coregent) to join them against the Assyrians. Ahaz, the dominant king of the coregency, resisted their demands and chose instead to request help from the Assyrians. The resultant war was a devastating defeat for Judah as both Rezin and Pekah defeated Ahaz in battle, seizing vast tracts of land and sacking numerous cities. Tiglath-Pileser responded to the frantic appeal of Ahaz by launching an invasion of Syria in 734 B.C. The city of Damascus fell two years later and Syria was annexed into the Assyrian Empire. Israel escaped the same fate when Pekah was assassinated and replaced by the pro-Assyrian king Hoshea.

Azariah was succeeded in Judah by his son Jotham (meaning "Yahweh is perfect"), through Jerusha. Jotham reigned from 750-731 B.C. Like his father, Jotham "did what was right in the sight of the Lord" (15:34), the fourth Davidic king in a row to be characterized as good. In total, this era of godly leadership lasted over one hundred years (835-731 B.C.). Jotham continued the building projects started by his father and launched a successful attack against Ammon, subjugating the Ammonites for three years.

Jotham was succeeded in Judah by his son Ahaz (meaning "possessor"). Ahaz reigned from 735-715 B.C. Ahaz is characterized as an evil king who "walked in the way of the kings of Israel" (16:3), thus bringing to an end Judah's streak of godly kings. The military failures of Ahaz described above left Judah in a greatly weakened state. Even the Philistines and Edomites were able to launch attacks against settlements in the southern kingdom during his reign. When Tiglath-Pileser finally arrived on the scene, Ahaz was forced to plunder the temple in order to pay tribute to the king of Assyria. Committing an even greater offense against the Lord, the king engaged in idolatrous acts, even sacrificing his son to another god.

Pekahiah was succeeded in Israel by Hoshea (meaning "salvation"), the son of Elah and founder of Israel's ninth, and final, dynasty. Hoshea reigned from 732-722 B.C. Originally, Hoshea served as a puppet king for the Assyrians; however, he attempted to take advantage of the turmoil surrounding the death of Tiglath-Pileser in 727 B.C. by rebelling against Assyria. Hoshea appealed to the Egyptian King So for help, evidently in hopes of forming an alliance against the Assyrians. It was a disastrous decision that resulted in an invasion of Israel by Shalmaneser. The city of Samaria fell in 722 B.C. after a three year siege. The inhabitants of the northern kingdom were exiled throughout the Assyrian Empire and the territory was repopulated with foreigners from Babylon, Cuthah, Ava, Hamath, and Sepharvaim. This deportation and repopulation program was designed to destroy the national identity of the Israelites. The goal of the Assyrians was to create an ethnically and politically diverse empire resistant to internal strife and rebellion.

The Kingdom of Judah to the Babylonian Captivity (18:1-25:30)

Ahaz was succeeded in Judah by his son Hezekiah (meaning "Yahweh has strengthened") through Abi. Hezekiah reigned from 729-686 B.C. He was a king who "did right in the sight of the Lord" (18:3). It was during the reign of Hezekiah that the Assyrians conquered Israel and exiled the inhabitants of the northern kingdom throughout their empire. The southern kingdom survived, though it remained a vassal state of Assyria and continued to pay tribute to the Assyrian king.

The situation changed dramatically in 715 when Hezekiah became sole regent and severed the ties with Assyria. The king demonstrated his loyalty to Yahweh by restoring the temple and reestablishing the sacrificial system. The purification of the temple took sixteen days, after which Hezekiah called a solemn assembly and commanded the priests to offer sacrifices on behalf of the people. The king reorganized the priests and meticulously outlined their responsibilities. Hezekiah tore down the high places and altars dedicated to pagan idolatry and even destroyed the bronze serpent which Moses had fashioned in the Sinai desert. Incredibly, the people were burning incense to it, transforming the symbol of their salvation into an idolatrous object of worship.

The Assyrian king Sennacherib invaded Judah in 701, destroying forty-six Judean cities, including Lachish. The events of this campaign are immortalized on the "Taylor Prism," a hexagonal baked-clay inscription of the annals of Sennacherib. When Sennacherib arrived at Jerusalem, he surrounded the city and made preparations for an extended siege, hoping to starve the city into submission. King Hezekiah responded to the threat with a prayer to the Lord, "And now, O Lord, our God, I pray, deliver us from his [Sennacherib's] hand, that all the kingdoms of the earth may know that Thou alone, O Lord, art God" (19:19). Hezekiah's prayer was answered when the angel of the Lord struck down 185,000 Assyrians in a single night. While the Taylor Prism predictably makes no mention of the loss of 185,000 warriors, it does provide indirect verification of the biblical account. "As to Hezekiah, the Jew, he did not submit to my yoke . . . Himself I made a prisoner in Jerusalem, his royal residence, like a bird in a cage. I surrounded him with earthwork in order to molest those who were leaving his city's gate. . . . Hezekiah himself, whom the terror-inspiring splendor of my lordship had overwhelmed . . . did send me, later, to Nineveh, my lordly city [tribute]."[25] One unfamiliar with the biblical account must wonder why Sennacherib went to the trouble of destroying forty-six cities and besieging Jerusalem simply to leave and return to Nineveh prior to its fall. The silence of

Sennacherib on this point speaks volumes, a mute testimony to the accuracy of Scripture.

In the year prior to Sennacherib's invasion, Hezekiah became deathly ill. The prophet Isaiah visited the king and instructed him to get his house in order because he was about to die. Hezekiah responded to the devastating news in his customary way, he offered a prayer to the Lord. He reminded the Lord that he had walked before Him in truth and with a loyal heart. The Lord answered the prayer of his faithful king and promised to grant him fifteen more years of life. To confirm his promise, the Lord gave Hezekiah a sign. The Lord caused the shadow of the sun to move backward ten degrees. Ironically, this sign was displayed on the "sundial of Ahaz" (Isa. 38:8, NKJV), named for the king who had previously rejected a sign from the Lord (cf. Isa. 7:11-12).

Shortly after this event, Merodach-Baladan of Babylon sent emissaries to Hezekiah in an attempt to acquire his participation in a coalition against Sennacherib. Having heard of Hezekiah's illness, the Babylonian king also sent letters of congratulation and a present. Hezekiah greeted the emissaries warmly, proudly taking them on a tour of his treasures to show off his power and might. When Isaiah heard what Hezekiah had done, he informed the king that the Babylonians would soon take everything they had seen to Babylon as the spoils of war. The prophet also informed the king that many of his descendants would be taken as well. The king's response to the prophet's message is chilling. The king viewed the message of the Lord in a positive way, noting that the fulfillment would not come in his lifetime.

Hezekiah was succeeded in Judah by his son Manasseh (meaning "causing to forget") through Hephzibah. Manasseh reigned from 696-642 B.C., spending more time on the throne than any other ruler of Israel or Judah. Manasseh was perhaps the most wicked king to ever reign on Judah's throne. He "did evil in the sight of the Lord, according to the abominations of the nations whom the Lord dispossessed before the sons of Israel" (21:2). Manasseh rebuilt the high places that Hezekiah had torn down. He then constructed altars for Baal and made Asherah poles, even erecting them in the holy temple. The wicked king sacrificed his own son to a god and practiced witchcraft and divination. The nation followed the king's example, as "Manasseh seduced them to do evil more than the nations whom the Lord destroyed before the sons of Israel" (21:9). Judah's wickedness was so great that Yahweh promised to destroy Jerusalem and abandon the remnant of His inheritance.

In 2 Chronicles 33:11, the chronicler reports that Manasseh's wickedness led to his deportation to Babylon by the king of Assyria. The Assyrian king alluded to in this verse is Ashurbanipal (668-627 B.C.). Since Ashurbanipal did not bring Babylon under his control until 648 B.C., the exile of Manasseh could not have occurred prior to this date. It is unknown how long Manasseh lived in Babylon but it could not have been more than a few years since Manasseh died in 642 B.C. While in Babylon, the king repented of his sins, humbling himself greatly before the Lord and praying for mercy (2 Chron. 33:12-13). The Lord responded favorably to Manasseh's prayer and allowed him to return to Jerusalem. When he returned to Jerusalem, Manasseh removed the foreign gods from the holy city and destroyed the idolatrous altars. He restored the temple and offered sacrifices to the Lord. He fortified the city and commanded the people to worship the Lord.

Manasseh was succeeded in Judah by his son Amon (meaning "builder") through Meshullemeth, the daughter of Haruz. Amon reigned from 642-640 B.C. Amon did not learn from the example of his father; he also worshipped foreign gods. As a result, he was assassinated by his servants in his palace.

Amon was succeeded in Judah by his son Josiah (meaning "Yahweh supports") through Jedidah, the daughter of Adaiah. Josiah reigned from 640-609 B.C. Josiah was installed as king at only eight years of age. The major reforms that marked his administration did not occur until the second half of his reign. It is probable that the nation's spiritual condition during the first half of Josiah's reign was similar to that of Manasseh and Amon's reigns. This can be inferred from the statement in 2 Chronicles 34:3, "in the twelfth year he began to purge Judah and Jerusalem of the high places, the Asherim, the carved images, and the molten images." One assumes that before the twelfth year of Josiah's reign the atrocities of Manasseh and Amon's reigns were still occuring in Judah.

In 628 B.C., Josiah resolved to worship the Lord alone and began a systematic purge of the land. From Galilee to Judea he removed the places of idolatrous worship. Most notably, he destroyed the altar and high places at Bethel, burning the bones of the priests who had officiated there during the reign of Jeroboam I, thus fulfilling the prophecy of the "man of God" (cf. 1 Kin. 13:1-2). A few years later, Josiah restored the temple in Jerusalem and reinstituted proper Yahweh-worship according to the regulations of Moses. The reinstitution of proper Yahweh-worship was made possible by the fortuitous discovery of a copy of the "Book of the Law of the Lord given by Moses" (2 Chron. 34:14) by Hilkiah (meaning "Yahweh is my portion"), the high priest. It is probable that all other copies of this scroll had been destroyed during the reign of Manasseh. When the book was read to the inhabitants of Jerusalem, the people made a commitment to abide by the commands of the covenant. The ceremony of covenant renewal was followed by a glorious celebration of Passover. The reforms of Josiah would continue until his death.

In 609 B.C., Pharaoh Neco (Necho) of Egypt marched north through Palestine to assist the fledgling Assyrian army based at Haran. The Assyrians were in the last stages of their magnificent empire, Nineveh having fallen in 612 B.C. at the hands of the Medo-Babylonian coalition led by Nebuchadnezzar. Josiah, having learned of Neco's plans, attempted to intercept the Egyptian forces at Megiddo. It should be remembered that Judah had been an ally of Babylon since the days of Hezekiah. Although warned by God to turn away, Josiah insisted upon meeting the Egyptians. In the resultant battle, Josiah was mortally wounded. He lived long enough to return to Jerusalem and die in the city of his fathers. Josiah would prove to be the last good king in Judah.

Josiah was succeeded in Judah by his son Jehoahaz (meaning "Yahweh has grasped") through Hamutal, the daughter of Jeremiah of Libnah. Jehoahaz reigned for three months in 609 B.C. He did "evil in the sight of the Lord" (23:32), beginning a run of four straight ungodly kings in Judah, the longest such streak in the nation's history. As Neco retreated from the Medo-Babylonian forces following his defeat at Haran, he deposed Jehoahaz and replaced him with Jehoiakim (Eliakim, meaning "God raises up"), his older brother. Jehoahaz was taken to Riblah, a city north of Damascus, and imprisoned there. Eventually, Jehoahaz was exiled to Egypt where he spent the rest of his life.

Jehoahaz was succeeded in Judah by his brother Jehoiakim (meaning "Yahweh raises up"), the son of Josiah through Zebidah, the daughter of Pedaiah. Jehoiakim reigned from 608-598 B.C. In 605 B.C., Nebuchadnezzar entered the city of Jerusalem. The Babylonian king forced Jehoiakim to swear allegiance, unwisely allowing him to remain as king. Shortly after taking Jerusalem, Nebuchadnezzar heard of his father Nabopolassar's death in Babylon. Nebuchadnezzar immediately rushed back to Babylon to solidify his claim to the throne. He took with him the best and brightest of Judah, including Daniel and his three friends, Hananiah, Mishael, and Azariah (i.e., Shadrach, Meshach, and Abednego).

Jehoiakim remained loyal to Nebuchadnezzar for three years. However, in 602 B.C., rejecting the advice of Jeremiah, Jehoiakim rebelled against the Babylonians. Nebuchadnezzar responded by invading Judah with the help of the Arameans, Moabites, and Ammonites. As the Babylonians approached the city, Jehoiakim was killed by his own court and dragged through the streets of Jerusalem.

Jehoiakim was succeeded in Judah by his son Jehoiachin (meaning "Yahweh appoints") through Nehushta, the daughter of Elnathan. Jehoiachin reigned for only three months before being deposed by Nebuchadnezzar and replaced by Zedekiah (Mattaniah, meaning "gift of Yahweh"), his uncle. Jehoiachin was taken to Babylon where he spent the remainder of his days. He was accompanied by the temple treasures and the entire population of Judah that were of use to the Babylonians, including soldiers and craftsmen. The prophet Ezekiel was also take to Babylon at this time. Only the poor remained in Jerusalem.

Jehoiachin was succeeded in Judah by his uncle Zedekiah (meaning "Yahweh is righteous"), the son of Josiah through Hamutal. Zedekiah reigned from 597-586 B.C. Following the example of his older brother Jehoiakim, Zedekiah rejected the advice of Jeremiah and rebelled against the Babylonians. Nebuchadnezzar returned to Jerusalem and laid siege to the city in 588 B.C. After a horrific two-year siege, the city fell on July 16, 586 B.C. Zedekiah was captured by the Babylonians after initially fleeing to Jericho. He was brought before Nebuchadnezzar at his headquarters in Riblah. There he was forced to witness the execution of his sons before being blinded and taken to Babylon with an ox ring through his nose.

Nebuchadnezzar appointed Gedaliah ("Yahweh is great"), the son of Ahikam, as governor over the province of Judea. The new governor immediately made Mizpah the new capital. Although Gedaliah encouraged the people to remain faithful to the Babylonians, a contingent rebelled and killed him two months after the fall of Jerusalem. The assassins were led by Ishmael, the son of Nethaniah and a member of the royal family. Fearing Babylonian reprisal, the remnant fled to Egypt, taking Jeremiah the prophet with them.

Despite the overall pessimism of the book, Kings ends on a positive note. In 562 B.C., the exiled King Jehoiachin was released from prison when Evil-Merodach, the son of Nebuchadnezzar, came to the throne in Babylon. Evil-Merodach gave Jehoiachin a place of honor at his table and a regular allowance for his needs until the day of his death. This postscript reveals that God was still watching over His people, even though He had sent them into exile.

Study Questions

1. Who is identified as the author of Kings in the Babylonian Talmud?
2. Do you believe in the two redaction theory? Why or why not?
3. What is the name of the pharaoh who gave his daughter to Solomon in marriage?
4. Who was the last significant Assyrian king?
5. Which empire defeated the Assyrians, thus replacing them as a world power?
6. List the eight good kings of the southern kingdom.
7. Of these eight kings, which two received unqualified praise?
8. Identify Adonijah's two co-conspirators.
9. What was Solomon's greatest achievement?
10. Identify the three adversaries of Solomon who were raised up by the Lord to punish him for his sins.
11. Describe the "sins of Jeroboam."

12. What was the name of Ahab's wife?
13. What was the threefold mission given to Elijah by the Lord?
14. In your opinion, what was the greatest miracle performed by Elisha?
15. Who was the best king of the northern kingdom?
16. Which king was hidden from the slaughter of Athaliah as an infant?
17. Who was the final king of the northern kingdom?
18. Who was granted fifteen extra years of life by the Lord?
19. Which king is released from prison at the end of the book of Kings?

CHAPTER 6

First and Second Chronicles

"Then the Lord appeared to Solomon at night and said to him, 'I have heard your prayer, and have chosen this place for Myself as a house of sacrifice. If I shut up the heavens so that there is no rain, or if I command the locust to devour the land, or if I send pestilence upon My people, and My people who are called by My name humble themselves and pray, and seek My face and turn from their wicked ways, then I will hear from heaven, will forgive their sin, and will heal their land. Now My eyes shall be open and My ears attentive to the prayer offered in this place. For now I have chosen and consecrated this house that My name may be there forever, and My eyes and My heart will be there perpetually.'" (2 Chronicles 7:12-16).

The books of First and Second Chronicles fall together naturally and originally constituted a single book. The earliest Hebrew manuscripts made no distinction between the books and the unit was simply called "the words of the days" (Heb. *dibre hayyamim*; i.e., the events of past time). While the Hebrew title is usually taken from the first verse, here the expression is found in 1 Chronicles 27:24. The Targums (translations of the biblical text into Aramaic) offer a fuller title; "This is the book of genealogies, the chronicles from days of antiquity." This idea was followed by Jerome, the author of the Latin Vulgate, who suggested that the books be called "the chronicles (Gr. *chronikon*) of the whole of sacred history." The fact that Jerome used a Greek word to signify the books indicates that he used the word as a title. Jerome's suggestion was quickly adopted and the word "Chronicles" has become the most widely-used title for these books in the modern day.

The Greek Septuagint (ca. 200 B.C.) entitled the books "things omitted" (Gr. *paralipomenon*), probably because of their supplementary nature to the books of Samuel and Kings. The Septuagint appears to have been the first translation to separate the books, perhaps because of the greatly increased length of the Greek version (the Greek language is written with vowels while Hebrew is written without vowels). The division of Chronicles has persisted to the present day in all translations and versions. From a literary and theological standpoint the books of Chronicles must be viewed as a unit. Hence, in the remainder of this chapter the two books will be regarded as a unit and will simply be called the book of Chronicles.

Chronicles is the final book of the Hebrew Bible. The accuracy of this placement seems to be suggested by the Lord Himself. In Matthew 23:35 he refers to past events with the phrase "from the blood of righteous Abel to the blood of Zechariah, the son of Berechiah." According to the structure of the Hebrew Bible, Abel is the first person murdered in the first book (Genesis) and Zechariah is the final person murdered in the final book (Chronicles).

It has been suggested that the placement of Chronicles is due to its late acceptance into the Old Testament canon, because the book was viewed as an appendix to the Writings since it supplemented the histories found in Samuel and Kings, or so that the Hebrew Scriptures might end on a positive note. A much more likely possibility, however, is that the book closes the Hebrew Bible for a more theological reason. The book of Chronicles ends with the decree of Cyrus allowing the Jews to return to their homeland. However, the decree of Cyrus is intentionally abbreviated (cf. 2 Chron. 36:23 with Ezra 1:2-4). The abridged version found in Chronicles is designed to encourage the remnant and returnees to remain in the land and to urge those who remained in exile to return to the land.[1] In effect, the final words an Israelite would read in his Bible (i.e., "and let him go up [to Jerusalem]!") would be an exhortation to remain in or return to the land. The proper worship of Yahweh was of primary importance to the Chronicler. That worship could only take place in the land; more specifically, in Jerusalem, "But you shall seek the Lord at the place which the Lord your God shall choose from all your tribes, to establish His name there for His dwelling, and there you shall come" (Deut. 12:5). The English version follows the Septuagint in placing Chronicles after Kings and before Ezra. This arrangement is chronological in nature.

The book of Chronicles is closely related to the books of Samuel and Kings, from which it draws much of its material. However, even though the two accounts are parallel, there is a significant difference in the theological outlook of the books. Here is where Chronicles finds its uniqueness. The book portrays the Davidic monarchy as "a theocratic expression of God's sovereign elective and redemptive purposes for His people and ultimately for all nations."[2] The book has even been called a "biography of God."[3]

Author

Jewish tradition holds that Ezra the scribe wrote the book of Chronicles (*Baba Bathra* 15a; the genealogies that continue past the time of Ezra are said to have been completed by Nehemiah). The book bears a remarkable resemblance to the book of Ezra: both were written about 450 B.C.; both record extensive genealogies; both place emphasis on temple practices and worship; and both express devotion to the Law of Moses. Ezra is also the historical counterpart to Chronicles since it picks up Jewish history where Chronicles leaves off, that is, with the decree of Cyrus. These facts seem to indicate that Ezra and Chronicles were originally composed by the same author, i.e., Ezra. Furthermore, if Ezra the scribe was the writer of Chronicles, this would account for the detailed acknowledgments of historical sources in the book. These sources can be divided into the following categories: 1) genealogical records (e.g., 1 Chron. 4:33; 5:17; 7:40); 2) letters and official documents (e.g., 2 Chron. 32:17; 36:22-23); 3) poems, prayers, speeches, and songs (e.g., 1 Chron. 16:8-36; 29:10-19); 4) other histories (e.g., "The Book of the Kings of Israel," 1 Chron. 9:1; "The Book of the Annals of King David," 1

Chron. 27:24; "The Book of the Kings of Judah and Israel," 2 Chron. 16:11); and 5) prophetic writings (e.g., "The Records of Samuel the Seer," 1 Chron. 29:29; "The Records of Nathan the Prophet," 2 Chron. 9:29; "The Visions of Iddo the Seer," 2 Chron. 9:29).[4]

However, there are also notable differences between the books of Ezra and Chronicles. For a list and discussion of these differences, please see Appendix One. Whoever the author was, it seems obvious that he was a priest. He highlighted the tribe of Levi in the genealogies. He emphasized the significant role played by the temple and its personnel in Israel's history. He had access to a variety of documents and records. He apparently lived in or near Jerusalem. And he wrote from the perspective of a preacher; in fact, the book is characterized by the same sort of preaching common among teaching Levites (i.e., instruction and exhortation). Because the identity of this man is unknown, from this point on he will be referred to simply as the Chronicler.

With the onset of higher criticism and its attacks on the Bible, the character of the Chronicler fell under considerable attack. Torrey wrote over one hundred years ago, "No fact of Old Testament criticism is more firmly established than this; that the Chronicler, as a historian, is thoroughly untrustworthy. He distorts facts deliberately and habitually; invents chapter after chapter with the greatest freedom; and, what is most dangerous of all, his history is not written for its own sake, but in the interest of an extremely one-sided theory."[5] This attack has continued in the modern age. In fact, the accuracy of the book of Chronicles has been called into question more than any other book of the Old Testament except Genesis.[6] The main reason for the attack is the fact that several numbers in Chronicles conflict with those in Samuel and Kings. However, out of 213 parallel numbers, there are only nineteen disagreements. Eleven times Chronicles has a higher number and seven times it is lower. On one occasion, the number is the same when the different method of calculation is taken into account.[7] Other reasons cited against the validity of the Chronicler include the tendency to ignore the major sins committed by the Davidic kings and the addition of material not found in Samuel and Kings. However, these omissions and additions are intentional on the part of the Chronicler. His purpose is different from the authors of Samuel and Kings; therefore, his choice of material is going to be different. Just as the authors of the Gospels selectively chose to include or ignore material from the life of Christ to fit their purpose in writing, so too do the authors of Samuel, Kings, and Chronicles.

Date

The book of Chronicles does not explicitly state when it was written. As a result, conjecture as to a probable date must be made on the basis of internal evidence. The book records events down to Cyrus' decree of 538 B.C.; however, the genealogies indicate that the book was written well after this time. Eight generations of Jeconiah (Jehoiachin) are traced (Pedaiah, Zerubbabel, Hananiah, Shecaniah, Shemaiah, Neariah, Elioenai, and Anani; cf. 1 Chron. 3:17-24). Jeconiah was taken captive in 597 B.C. and it can be assumed that Pedaiah was born at or near this time (2 Kin. 24:15 indicates that Jeconiah's wives were taken captive with him so he was at least old enough to have had children). Therefore, the book was probably written seven generations after 597 B.C. or about 425 B.C. allowing roughly 25 years per generation. If the book was written after this date, it can be assumed that the genealogy of Jeconiah would have been extended because the posterity of David was of extreme importance to the Chronicler. The book may have been the final book written in the Old Testament. The other candidates are Nehemiah and Malachi. The book was almost assuredly written from Jerusalem, the chief city of the returned remnant.

Historical Background

The events of the book of Chronicles take place between about 1011 and 539 B.C. Since the historical background of this period is identical to that of Samuel, Kings, and Ezra, the reader is referred to the appropriate sections of chapters 4, 5, and 7.

Audience and Purpose

The purpose of the book of Chronicles was to restore the national and spiritual pride of the people of Israel in an attempt to reinstitute proper Yahweh-worship under the leadership of the Levites. This purpose is comprised of essentially two main points which must be defended. First, the book was written to restore the national and spiritual pride of the people of Israel. The national and spiritual pride of the people of Israel had been severely damaged as a result of the fall of both the northern and southern kingdoms of Israel and the resultant exiles. The Chronicler sought to restore that pride by writing a history of Israel's greatest period and by portraying that period in the best light possible. The Davidic dynasty is viewed as the ultimate experience God wanted for His people. The greatest kings of the Davidic dynasty are emphasized and their greatest deeds magnified. It was also through this dynasty that Israel received its greatest hope, that is, the fulfillment of the Davidic covenant. According to Chronicles, the Davidic covenant is that element which most clearly expresses the meaning of Israel's continuing life as the people of God.

This emphasis of the Chronicler on the people of Israel as the children of God must not be overlooked. The line of God's election is traced directly from Adam to Israel in the first chapter of the book. The genealogy then continues in an unbroken line all the way to the post-exilic Jerusalem community in chapter nine. Throughout the book the children of Israel are seen to have a direct relationship with God, whether through the king or the Levites. Chronicles demonstrates that the exile did not break this union between God and Israel; the book closes with the initial fulfillment of one of God's promises to the patriarchs, namely, the restoration to the land after repentance (cf. Deut. 30:1-10). In effect, "the rehearsal of Israel's past became a guarantee of God's continued intervention to accomplish His covenant purposes for the Hebrews as His special possession (e.g., 1 Chron. 17:16-27)."[8]

Second, the book was written to reinstitute proper Yahweh-worship under the leadership of the Levites. Even a brief scan of Chronicles reveals that there is a significant emphasis on worship in the book. In fact, Chronicles is often characterized as a manual for worship. The instances of worshipful acts in the book (including sacrifices, feast, offerings, songs, and prayers) are told in such an explicit manner that they could easily be copied by the readers of the text. Throughout the book, the activity of worship is directed by the king (cf. 1 Chron. 15-17; 2 Chron. 5-7). However, with the fall of the monarchy, the mantle of leadership is placed squarely upon the Levites. Chronicles prepares for this transition by highlighting the important role played by the Levites as religious representatives of the king.

Structure and Outline

The book is naturally divided into four major sections. The first section consists of a series of genealogies (1 Chron. 1:1-9:44). The second section is an account of the reign of David (10:1-29:30). The third section is a record of the reign of Solomon (2 Chron. 1:1-9:31). The fourth and final section details the major events in the reigns of the kings of the Davidic dynasty (10:1-36:23).

The collective similarities between the books of Ezra and Nehemiah and the book of Chronicles have led many scholars to incorporate all three books into a single unified work attributed to a "Chronicler." For a full discussion of the relationship between the books of Chronicles, Ezra, and Nehemiah, see Appendix One.

According to Hill, the "Chronicle" as a literary form is a prose composition consisting of a series of reports or selected events in third-person style, arranged and dated in chronological order.[9] The book of Chronicles certainly fits this description. The book is characterized by a variety of literary types including genealogies, lists, letters, prayers, speeches and sermons, prophetic revelations, and songs.[10] Despite the presence of so many different features, the book shows remarkable unity; a testimony to the skillfulness of the author in weaving together his "Chronicle."

Outline

I. Genealogies (1 Chron. 1:1-9:44)
    A. Patriarchal genealogies (1:1-54)
        1. Genealogy of Adam (1:1-4)
        2. Genealogy of Japheth (1:5-7)
        3. Genealogy of Ham (1:8-16)
        4. Genealogy of Shem (1:17-27)
        5. Genealogy of Abraham (1:28-34)
        6. Genealogy of Esau (1:35-54)

B. Genealogy of Judah (2:1-55)
    1. Sons of Judah (2:1-4)
    2. Genealogies of Perez and Zerah (2:5-8)
    3. Genealogy of Hezron (2:9-41)
    4. Genealogy of Caleb (2:42-55)
C. Genealogy of David (3:1-24)
    1. Sons of David (3:1-9)
    2. Descendants of Solomon (3:10-24)
D. Genealogies of the tribes of Israel (4:1-8:40)
    1. Genealogy of Judah (4:1-23)
    2. Genealogy of Simeon (4:24-43)
    3. Genealogy of Reuben (5:1-10)
    4. Genealogy of Gad (5:11-17)
    5. Exploits of the transjordan tribes (5:18-22)
    6. Genealogy of the transjordan half-tribe of Manasseh (5:23-26)
    7. Genealogy of Levi (6:1-81)
    8. Genealogy of Issachar (7:1-5)
    9. Genealogy of Benjamin (7:6-12)
    10. Genealogy of Naphtali (7:13)
    11. Genealogy of the other half-tribe of Manasseh (7:14-19)
    12. Genealogy of Ephraim (7:20-29)
    13. Genealogy of Asher (7:30-40)
    14. Genealogy of Benjamin (8:1-40)
E. The record of the returned remnant (9:1-34)
    1. Political leaders (9:1-9)
    2. Priests (9:10-13)
    3. Levites (9:14-16)
    4. Gatekeepers and others (9:17-34)
F. Genealogy of Saul (9:35-44)
II. The Reign of David (10:1-29:30)
A. The fall of Saul (10:1-14)
    1. The death of Saul and his sons (10:1-6)
    2. The rescue of Saul's body (10:7-12)
    3. The transfer of the kingdom to David (10:13-14)

B. David secures the throne (11:1-12:40)
    1. The coronation at Hebron (11:1-3)
    2. The capture of Jerusalem (11:4-9)
    3. The unification of the kingdom (11:10-12:40)
C. David brings the Ark to Jerusalem (13:1-16:43)
    1. The Ark at the house of Obed-edom (13:1-14)
    2. The fame of David (14:1-17)
    3. The preparation in Jerusalem for the Ark (15:1-24)
    4. The Ark is brought to Jerusalem (15:25-16:43)
D. David's preparation for the Temple (17:1-22:19)
    1. David's desire for a temple (17:1-27)
    2. David's foreign affairs (18:1-20:8)
        a. The Philistines and Moabites (18:1-2)
        b. The Arameans (18:3-11)
        c. The Edomites (18:12-13)
        d. The royal administration (18:14-17)
        e. The Ammonites (19:1-20:3)
        f. The Philistines (20:4-8)
    3. David's census and punishment (21:1-22:1)
    4. The plans for the Temple (22:2-19)
E. David's organization (23:1-27:34)
    1. The successor (23:1)
    2. The Levites (23:2-32)
    3. The priests (24:1-31)
    4. The singers (25:1-31)
    5. The Temple servants (26:1-32)
    6. The army (27:1-34)
F. David's farewell address (28:1-29:22a)
    1. Instructions concerning the covenant (28:1-8)
    2. Instructions concerning the Temple (28:9-21)
    3. The appeal for offerings (29:1-9)
    4. Thanksgiving and sacrifices (29:10-22a)
G. David's successor to the throne (29:22b-30)
III. The Reign of Solomon (2 Chron. 1:1-9:31)
A. Solomon's wisdom and wealth (1:1-17)
B. Solomon builds the Temple (2:1-5:1)
    1. The preparations for building (2:1-18)

2. The Temple proper (3:1-17)
3. The Temple furnishings (4:1-5:1)
C. Solomon dedicates the Temple (5:2-7:10)
   1. The arrival of the Ark (5:1-10)
   2. The glory of the Lord fills the Temple (5:11-14)
   3. Solomon's prayer (6:1-42)
   4. The consumption of the offering (7:1-3)
   5. The dedicatory feast (7:4-10)
D. God's blessings and curses (7:11-22)
E. Solomon's successes (8:1-9:31)
   1. Solomon's building programs (8:1-16)
   2. Solomon's fame (8:17-9:12)
   3. Solomon's wealth (9:13-28)
   4. Solomon's long and prosperous reign (9:29-31)
IV. The Reign of the Davidic Dynasty (10:1-36:23)
  A. The reign of Rehoboam (10:1-12:16)
     1. Israel's rebellion (10:1-11:4)
     2. Rehoboam's fortifications (11:5-23)
     3. The attack on Judah by Egypt (12:1-16)
  B. The reign of Abijah (13:1-22)
  C. The reign of Asa (14:1-16:14)
     1. Asa's obedience (14:1-15)
     2. Asa's reforms (15:1-19)
     3. Asa's treaty with Aram (16:1-14)
  D. The reign of Jehoshaphat (17:1-20:37)
     1. Jehoshaphat's power (17:1-19)
     2. Jehoshaphat's unwise alliance with the northern kingdom (18:1-34)
     3. Jehoshaphat's reforms (19:1-20:37)
  E. The reign of Jehoram (21:1-20)
  F. The reign of Ahaziah (22:1-9)
  G. The reign of Athaliah (22:10-23:21)
  H. The reign of Joash (24:1-27)
     1. Joash's early reforms (24:1-16)
     2. Joash's later apostasy (24:17-27)
  I. The reign of Amaziah (25:1-28)
  J. The reign of Uzziah (26:1-23)

K. The reign of Jotham (27:1-9)

L. The reign of Ahaz (28:1-27)

M. The reign of Hezekiah (29:1-32:33)
  1. Hezekiah's reforms (29:1-31:21)
    a. The cleansing of the Temple (29:1-36)
    b. The reinstating of the Passover (30:1-27)
    c. The re-establishment of proper worship (31:1-21)
  2. The defeat of Sennacherib (32:1-33)

N. The reign of Manasseh (33:1-20)

O. The reign of Amon (33:21-25)

P. The reign of Josiah (34:1-35:27)
  1. Josiah's reforms (34:1-35:19)
  2. Josiah's death (35:20-27)

Q. The reign of Jehoahaz (36:1-4)

R. The reign of Jehoiakim (36:5-8)

S. The reign of Jehoiachin (36:9-10)

T. The reign of Zedekiah (36:11-16)

U. The Babylonian conquest and exile (36:17-21)

V. The decree of Cyrus (36:22-23)

Summary of Contents

Because the vast majority of the events recorded in Chronicles have already been surveyed in the Summary sections of Samuel and Kings, a review of the material will not be provided here. Instead, this section will focus on the major themes of Chronicles; themes that the Chronicler weaves throughout his book to present a different portrait of the monarchical period from that of Samuel and Kings. In this way, Chronicles can be reviewed with minimal overlap with other sections of this book.

Davidic Dynasty

The dominant theme of Chronicles is the rise and success of the Davidic dynasty. While Saul's dynasty occupies a large section of the book of Samuel (1 Sam. 9-31), the Chronicler affords him only fourteen verses (1 Chron. 10). Moreover, these verses portray him in a wholly negative light. The Chronicler begins his biography with a description of Saul's death. While at first glance it might appear as if the Philistines killed Saul, the Chronicler reveals that Yahweh killed Israel's first king, "So Saul died for his trespass which he committed against the Lord, because of the word of the Lord which he did not keep; and also because he asked counsel of a medium, making inquiry of it, and did not inquire of the Lord. Therefore He killed him, and turned the kingdom to David, the son of Jesse" (1 Chron. 10:13-14).

The rest of the book is preoccupied with the Davidic dynasty, especially David and Solomon. Fully one-third of Chronicles (1 Chron. 11-2 Chron. 9) is devoted to these two kings. North notes that "the person and dynasty of David forms the heartbeat of all the Chronicler's theology."[11] Clines goes into even more detail, "Already in the genealogies of 1 Chron. 1-9 it is plain that for him the whole movement of the history of salvation has been towards the election of the Davidic state: Judah takes first place among the sons of Jacob (1 Chron. 2:3; cf. 5:1f.) and little attention is paid to Ephraim and Manasseh (7:14-27). The story proper starts, not with Patriarchs, Exodus, Sinai, or Conquest, but with the establishment of the Davidic dynasty at Jerusalem and the organisation [sic] of the whole structure of Israelite society and worship by David."[12]

David himself is the central figure in Chronicles. The king is idealized throughout Chronicles, receiving credit for many of the important successes in the history of Israel, including the building of the temple. It is David's devotion to the cult which becomes the standard by which his successors are evaluated (e.g., 2 Chron. 28:1; 29:2).[13] For the Chronicler, "David becomes the prototype of Israel's Messiah, the anointed king who will ultimately restore Israel, fulfilling all the divine promises."[14] Overlooked are the various blemishes which serve to tarnish his reputation throughout the books of Samuel and Kings. For example, there is no mention of his adultery with Bathsheba and murder of Uriah, pivotal events in Samuel, nor of the murder of his son Amnon and the subsequent rebellions of his sons Absalom and Adonijah. The transition from Saul to David is portrayed as a smooth one; there is no mention of the seven-year civil war that plagued the nation. There is really only one major sin named on the part of David; his census of the nation. However, this sin is named simply to show how the land for the temple was acquired. Furthermore, the Chronicler claims that Satan moved David to number the people; a fact that seems to lessen David's responsibility.

The portrait of Solomon is likewise optimistic. The Chronicler presents a smooth transition from David to Solomon. "Instead of an aged, bedridden David who only saves the kingdom for Solomon at the last minute due to the promptings of Bathsheba and Nathan (1 Kings 1), the Chronicler shows a smooth transition of power without a ripple of dissent. David himself publicly announces Solomon's appointment as his successor, an announcement greeted with enthusiastic and total support on the part of the people (1 Chron. 28:1-29:25), including the other sons of David, the officers of the army and others who had supported Adonijah's attempted coup."[15] When the subject of Solomon's foreign wife is addressed in 2 Chronicles 8:11, Solomon is seen as attempting to preserve the purity of the cult in Israel, removing his Egyptian wife from Jerusalem to her own palace because his wife "shall not dwell in the house of David king of Israel, because the places are holy where the ark of the Lord has entered." As this verse implies, the emphasis throughout the account of Solomon's reign is on the building of the temple and the worship performed there. "Whereas in Kings, Solomon's wisdom is wisdom for ruling (1 Kings 3:7-15; cf. 3:16-4:34), in Chronicles it is wisdom for building (cf. 2 Chron. 2:12 and its parallel at 1 Kings 5:7)."[16]

The rest of the Davidic dynasty is also presented in a positive way. Largely overlooked by the Chronicler are the great sins of Jehoshaphat and Hezekiah. Further proof of the Chronicler's attempt to portray this dynasty in a favorable light is found in 2 Chronicles 33. This passage records the repentance of Manasseh. If one were to base an opinion of Manasseh solely upon the book of Kings, one would surely regard him as the most evil king ever to sit on David's throne. Yet the Chronicler portrays him in a much more favorable light. Although his many sins are mentioned, they are done so only in an attempt to magnify the significance of his repentance. The five great kings of the Davidic dynasty (David, Solomon, Jehoshaphat, Hezekiah, and Josiah) dominate 38 of the last 55 chapters. The other 17 chapters are devoted to 16 other kings plus Athaliah. Contrary to the book of Kings, there is no mention of the kings of Israel except where they play an incidental and antagonistic role in the history of Judah.

Genealogies

The book of Chronicles opens with an extensive genealogical record surveying the entire Old Testament period. The genealogies begin with Adam, the first man who lived upon the earth, and continue well into the postexilic period. The genealogies cover an incredible nine chapters; a section that is regarded by many modern readers to be one of the most boring and tedious portions of the entire Bible. However, these chapters were probably regarded by most of the original readers as one of the most exciting sections of the Hebrew Scriptures. For it was in precisely this section that their name and heritage would be identified and preserved for all eternity. The modern reader should realize that the Jews were a tribal people who made such fundamental and life-changing decisions as where to live, who to marry, and what job to do based on their lineage. Thus, the importance the Hebrews placed on their genealogies and tribal heritage is often overlooked by those today who cannot see the value and importance in being able to trace one's family line.

M. D. Johnson identifies nine purposes for Old Testament genealogies: 1) to demonstrate existing relationships between Israel and neighboring tribes; 2) to bring together previously isolated elements; 3) to bridge gaps in the narrative records; 4) to perform a limited chronological function; 5) to perform the military function of numbering warriors; 6) to legitimate individuals; 7) to establish and preserve the homogeneity of the Jewish community; 8) to demonstrate the continuity of the people of God; and 9) to express a priestly concern for order and arrangement, and the conviction that the course of history is governed and ordered according to a prearranged plan.[17]

The genealogies of Chronicles relate specifically to numbers six, eight, and nine above. The genealogies legitimate those members of Judah and Levi, the tribes of kingship and priesthood in Israel (purpose six). The genealogies confirm God's election of "all Israel" (1 Chron. 9:1; cf. 1 Chron. 11:1, 4, 10; 13:5-6; etc.) by showing the relationship between the preexilic and postexilic communities, thus demonstrating that the promises given to the patriarchs can be appropriated by the restored remnant (purpose eight). And the genealogies reveal that the whole of human history has been ordered by God to fit His sovereign plan (purpose nine).

Worship

As mentioned above, a major purpose of the book of Chronicles was to reinstitute proper Yahweh-worship in the land. During the period of the monarchy, this worship was led by the Davidic rulers, who served in a priestly role (1 Chron. 15:25-28; cf. 2 Sam. 6:12-15; Ps. 2, 110). The king guided the procession of the Ark of the Covenant as it is moved to Jerusalem (1 Chron. 15); the king built the temple (2 Chron. 3-7); the king led the people in worship (cf. 2 Chron. 6; 7; 34); the king assigned the Levites their temple duties (cf. 1 Chron. 23-26; 2 Chron. 19:8-11); the king brought revival to the land (cf. 2 Chron. 15; 34); and the king read the Law to the people (cf. 2 Chron. 34:30). The king was ably assisted by the Levites (cf. 2 Chron. 20; 35), who served as the religious representatives of the king. They were responsible for service as singers, musicians, gatekeepers, teachers of the law, and judges (cf. 1 Chron. 24-26; 2 Chron. 17:7-9; 19:11).

The place of worship is of utmost importance in the mind of the Chronicler. He spends several chapters describing the planning for and construction of the temple. The temple was to be built according to the pattern of the tabernacle; both were intended to house the Ark of the Covenant, the dwelling place of God. The temple is closely linked with the city of Jerusalem; both are identified as the only legitimate place of worship (2 Chron. 6:5-6; 33:7). In effect, the temple served as the heartbeat of the nation; as the temple went, so went the nation. Those kings who promoted the temple are routinely praised by the Chronicler while those who ignored the temple are vilified. Unfortunately, the kings who rejected the temple outnumbered those who embraced it. In fact, one of the chief reasons for the exile is the royal failure to enforce correct worship at the temple.[18]

The act of worship is also emphasized by the Chronicler. In fact, Chronicles is often characterized as a manual for worship. Both corporate and individual worship are highlighted. The Chronicler valued worship as an attitude; a condition of the human heart and mind (cf. 1 Chron. 16:10-11; 28:9; 2 Chron. 15:12, 15). For the Chronicler, the act of worship was active, not passive. In the book, the Israelites present sacrifices, bow down, burn incense, present offerings, pray, fast, perform ritual washing and cleansing, dance, tear their clothes in repentance, feast, and observe religious festivals.[19]

Study Questions
1. Why is Chronicles placed at the end of the Hebrew Bible?
2. Do you believe that the Chronicler is a trustworthy historian? Why or why not?
3. When was Chronicles written?
4. What is the purpose of the book?
5. Why is the legacy of the Davidic dynasty of such importance to the Chronicler?
6. Explain the importance of genealogies in the Old Testament.
7. In what ways can we make modern worship more active?

CHAPTER 7

Ezra

"The good hand of his God was upon him. For Ezra had set his heart to study the law of the Lord, and to practice it, and to teach His statutes and ordinances in Israel" (Ezra 7:9b-10).

The book of Ezra is one of the most significant books in the Hebrew Bible. It describes the fulfillment of the Lord's promise to return His people to their land after seventy years of exile in Babylon. Throughout the book the Lord is seen as completely sovereign, stirring up the hearts of the key characters to act as He wants them to act. The Lord is pictured as sovereign even over the most powerful nations on earth as He raises up the Persians to reverse the wrongs committed by the Babylonians.

The book of Ezra also describes the efforts of the Jewish remnant to restore their cultic worship of Yahweh. The remnant is sincere in their efforts to please God; however, their devotion is affected by the apostasy of their age. When the rebuilding efforts do not go smoothly, they abandon the work. When they are attracted to foreign women, they abandon their Jewish wives and marry foreigners. In each case, the Lord raises up spiritual leaders to inform the remnant of their apostasy. Haggai and Zechariah are instrumental in getting the nation to finish the temple while Ezra is used to purify the land of the ungodly marriages. In both cases the nation responds with immediate repentance.

While this repentance was genuine and immediate, it was not long-lasting. The nation began the task of rebuilding the walls of Jerusalem only to halt the work when opposition arose. The nation's resolve to separate from foreigners lasted but a few years as Nehemiah reveals that the remnant's practice of intermingling with their foreign neighbors continued in his day. Thus, the story of Ezra is one of finished business (temple) and unfinished business (complete restoration with spiritual and physical purity). The unfinished business of Ezra is completed in Nehemiah, a fact that explains why the books were originally joined in the Hebrew Bible.

Author

The author of the book is the scribe Ezra. As a scribe, Ezra was well qualified to write this book. He had probably been educated in the Persian courts, perhaps even serving as one of the royal scribes of King Artaxerxes. If he was a scribe in the court of Artaxerxes it would account for his apparent relationship with the king (cf. 7:6, 21). Ezra's position as scribe allowed him the time needed to effectively study the law of the Lord.

Prior to the second temple period, scribes usually served as little more than secretaries, writing down the king's decrees and keeping a record of the events that occurred during each reign (cf. 2 Kin. 22:10; 1 Chron. 24:6; see also Ezra 4:8). Their access to the monarch also meant that they often served as the king's confidants, messengers, treasurers, or even military commanders (cf. 2 Kin. 18:17-19:7; 25:19; 2 Chron. 24:11; 26:11). Beginning with Ezra, the position of scribe takes on far more importance. Scribes were now primarily students of the law who were responsible for copying, writing, and teaching. By the time of the New Testament, scribes wielded significant power throughout Israel.

The primary duties of a scribe were threefold. First, they served as the copyists of the law. This duty also involved the interpretation of the law. When the law did not speak to a specific case then the scribes created precedent. As a result, they in effect became legislators creating new law. Second, they served as the teachers of the law.

It was their duty to make sure that every Israelite was acquainted with the rules and regulations of the law. Third, they served in a judicial capacity, passing sentence in the court of justice. Their knowledge of and skill in interpreting the law made them ideal candidates for the position of judge. Scribes were routinely found among the ranks of the Sanhedrin.

Ezra was also a priest. This fact explains his interest in the temple, the house of God, as well as the sacrificial system. Additionally, this fact provided Ezra with the God-given authority to teach the statutes and ordinances of the Lord to Israel. As a priest, Ezra could take the necessary steps to correct the spiritual condition of the remnant, including commanding those in mixed marriages to separate from their wives.

The name Ezra means "help" and may be a shortened form of the name Azariah, meaning "the Lord has helped." Ezra was probably somewhere in his forties when he returned to the land in 458 B.C. This would have allowed enough time for his remarkable skills as a scribe to have become noticeable (cf. 7:6, 11). Ezra could not have been much older than this since he was still living fourteen years later when Nehemiah returned to the land in 444 B.C. (cf. Neh. 8:1). It is likely that he died before Nehemiah returned to Babylon in 432 B.C. One would assume that if Ezra was still alive, the reforms of Nehemiah recorded in Nehemiah 13 would have been dealt with by the scribe during Nehemiah's absence.

Date

The last historical event referred to in the book is the reading of the copy of the decree of King Artaxerxes in 4:23. The exact date of this decree cannot be ascertained, though it must have been written between 458 B.C. (the date of Ezra's return to Jerusalem referred to in 4:12) and 444 B.C. (the date of Nehemiah's return to Jerusalem and subsequent rebuilding of the walls of the city). One would assume that Ezra would have wanted to begin work on the walls of the city immediately upon his return so a date closer to 458 B.C. is to be preferred. As a result, the book could have been written as early as 455 B.C.

Historical Background

The events of the book of Ezra take place between 538 B.C. and roughly 455 B.C. Throughout this entire period, the Persians dominated world events as the Persian Empire was at its peak. The Persians were an Indo-European tribe who entered the Iranian plateau about 1400 B.C. They systematically grew in size and power over the next eight hundred years. The various kings of this vast empire were known as Achaemenians, after an eponymous ancestor, Achaemenes (c. 700 B.C.).[1] From the reign of Cyrus until the time of Alexander the Great, the Achaemenians were able to build one of the largest and most successful of all ancient empires. At its peak, the empire stretched from the Hellespont in the northwest and the Nile in the southwest to the Indus in the east.[2] Economically speaking, the Persian Empire was largely made up of nomadic pastoralists.[3]

The region of Judea was simply part of Trans-Euphrates, one of the satrapies in the Persian Empire. The Jews were not autonomous but were governed by the official representatives of the Persian kings. The fortunes of the Jews were dictated by the decisions of foreign kings living more than a thousand miles from the Promised Land. In light of this, it becomes necessary to briefly review the Persian kings of this period.

The founder of the Persian Empire was Cyrus the Great. Cyrus was the son of Cambyses I, a Persian, and Mandane, the daughter of Astyages, king of the Medes. Cyrus became king of the Persians in 559 B.C. and was originally a vassal of King Astyages. Cyrus led a successful revolt against Astyages in 550 B.C. The final battle between the Medes and the Persians took place in the plain of Pasargadae. Cyrus' victory was assured when he was aided by the defection of Astyages' own men. To commemorate his victory, Cyrus built the city of Pasargadae which was soon to become his capital.

Having defeated the Medes, Cyrus embarked on a mission to conquer the known world. His first goal was to solidify his empire, which he accomplished by subduing Lydia and India. His next goal was to defeat the Babylonians. The Babylonians were at this time in a state of turmoil due to the fact that their king Nabonidus was in exile at Teima in Arabia because of his allegiance to the moon god Sin. His son Belshazzar served as ruler in Babylon. Cyrus, who had earlier allied himself with the Babylonians against the Medes, took advantage of the turmoil in Babylon and marched against the city. In 539 B.C., the Persians, under the command of Gubaru,[4] laid siege to the great city of Babylon. Herodotus records that the Persians gained entrance into the city by diverting the Euphrates River (*Histories* 1.191). The city fell on October 12, 539 B.C. with nominal resistance. Belshazzar was killed during or shortly after the battle while Nabonidus was eventually captured and sent into exile to Carmania.

Two and a half weeks later, on October 29, Cyrus himself triumphantly marched into the great city of Babylon, appearing more like a liberator than a conqueror. He forbade destruction and immediately issued an edict allowing all captive peoples to return to their respective homelands. This benevolent foreign policy allowed the Jews to return to Jerusalem under the leadership of Sheshbazzar with the blessing of the king. Cyrus continued to build and solidify his empire until his death in 530 B.C. at the hands of the Massagetae, at which time his son Cambyses II inherited the throne.

Cambyses II was able to secure his control over the throne of Persia by killing his brother Smerdis. The most significant event of the relatively brief reign of Cambyses was his conquest of Egypt in 525 B.C. The Persian armies invaded Egypt and routed the Egyptians at Pelusium. With the Egyptian army defeated, the Persians immediately moved to capture Memphis, the key city in Lower Egypt. Following the fall of Memphis, the rest of Egypt quickly yielded to the Persian armies. Cambyses remained in Egypt for three years, during which time he invaded Ethiopia and was repelled. Cambyses died in the spring of 522 B.C. in the region of Syria. He was on his way home to Persia after learning of a coup d'etat when he accidentally stabbed himself in the thigh while mounting his horse. The wound developed gangrene and Cambyses died three weeks later without leaving an heir.

Following the death of Cambyses, a man named Gaumata usurped the throne and attempted to pass himself off as Smerdis, the murdered brother of Cambyses. In an effort to win over the populace, Gaumata pronounced exemption from taxes and obligatory military service for three years. The ruse was exposed by Phaedyme, the daughter of Otanes, when she discovered that Gaumata's ears had been cut off, a punishment that never would have been committed on the real Smerdis. Darius, a distant cousin of Cambyses, and six nobles formed a coalition to overthrow Gaumata. The coalition managed to assassinate Gaumata in Media on September 29, 522 B.C.

Darius the Great gained the Persian throne in 522 B.C. following the assassination of Gaumata. The father of Darius was Hystaspes, the satrap of Parthia. Darius served at the side of Cambyses as an officer in the ranks of the Immortals, an elite force of ten thousand royal soldiers. Since Darius was not an obvious heir, revolts erupted throughout the Persian Empire. It took nineteen different battles and a little more than a year, but Darius finally succeeded in solidifying his throne.[5] It was during the reign of Darius that the Jews were able to finish building the temple thanks to the motivation of the prophets Haggai and Zechariah. Darius proved to be an extraordinary administrator, implementing far-reaching reforms. Perhaps chief among these was the standardization of coinage, weights, and measures, thus facilitating trade and commerce. He also instituted a system of taxation and reorganized the government of the Persian Empire. Another significant measure taken by Darius was to move the capital of the Persians to Susa where he erected a magnificent palace, referred to in Nehemiah as the "citadel of Susa" (1:1).

Unfortunately, Darius proved a less than stellar military commander. He had some early successes in his military endeavors (e.g., northwestern India, the coastland between the Bosporus and the Grecian state of Thessaly, Thrace, Macedonia), but that would change with his ill-fated decisions to invade Greece. His initial invasion against the Greeks occurred in 493 B.C. This invasion force never even made it to the Grecian mainland because its fleet was destroyed by a storm off Mount Athos in northern Greece. Darius' second, more famous, invasion of Greece took place in 490 B.C. The Persian fleet attacked the coast of Greece, taking the city of Eretria after a week-long siege. The Persians then sailed to the Bay of Marathon where they disembarked and prepared to attack Athens. In one of the most significant battles in history, the Persians were defeated at Marathon by the Athenians. The remaining Persian army refused to give up and attempted to surprise the city of Athens by boarding their ships and sailing around the southern tip of Attica. Thanks to a 26-mile race by a messenger and an all-night march by the weary Athenian army, the city of Athens was protected. The Persians, seeing the Athenian army in battle formation at the harbor of Athens, finally admitted defeat and sailed away. Technically, Darius did not accompany his troops in either invasion. The armies were led by his generals. Although Darius made plans to personally lead his men in a third invasion of Greece, he was never able to quench the rebellions he faced in Egypt. After a long and prosperous reign, Darius died at Persepolis in November of 486 B.C. at the age of sixty-four.

Xerxes, the son of Darius, ascended to the throne at the age of thirty-two. His mother was Atossa, the daughter of Cyrus. The name Xerxes means "he who rules over men." Xerxes is well known in biblical history as the king who chose Esther to be his queen. He is mentioned only in passing in the book of Ezra (4:6). Xerxes, like his father Darius, is notorious in secular history primarily for an ill-fated invasion of Greece. In 481 B.C., he took an army of 200,000 men and hundreds of warships to Greece to avenge his father's defeat at Marathon in 490 B.C. Without a doubt, the troops of Xerxes comprised the largest army and navy ever assembled in antiquity. Initially, Xerxes enjoyed considerable success when the badly divided Greek city-states were unable to achieve an effective coalition.[6] The tide began to turn when the Spartans met this massive invasion force with fierce resistance at the battle of Thermopylae, fighting to the last man. The ill fortune continued for the Persians as their vast navy was destroyed in the battle of Salamis. Xerxes blamed the defeat on his Phoenician and Egyptian mercenaries, accusing them of cowardice. As a result, these mercenaries abandoned him and returned to their homelands. Xerxes himself left for Persia, leaving his armies under the command of Mardonius. Mardonius suffered a series of setbacks until losing his life in the battle of Plataea. The Persians finally admitted defeat with their loss at Mycale in 479 B.C. After a twenty-one year reign, Xerxes was assassinated by Artabanus, a powerful courtier and captain of the royal bodyguard, in 465 B.C.

The empire soon fell into the hands of Artaxerxes. Artaxerxes, whose name means "having a kingdom of justice," was the third son of Xerxes and Amestris, the Ahasueras and Vashti of the book of Esther. Artaxerxes managed to kill Artabanus and murder his older brother Darius, the rightful heir to the Persian throne. He then defeated his other brother Hystaspes in battle in the region of Bactria. Artaxerxes, whose first reignal year is reckoned from April 13, 464 B.C.,[7] enjoyed a rather lengthy reign, eventually dying of natural causes in 424 B.C. The returns of both Ezra and Nehemiah took place during his reign.

Audience and Purpose

The book of Ezra was written to the Jews of the postexilic community living in the region of Judea in the mid fifth century B.C. The ancestors of these Jews had returned with Sheshbazzar in 538 B.C. It was now almost a hundred years since that original return. It was well over fifty years since the temple had been rebuilt in 515 B.C. Little had been accomplished since the rebuilding of the temple. A good portion of the recipients had returned with Ezra in 458 B.C. Both the new returnees and the descendants of the original returnees were in need of hope.

The only hope for the nation lay in the fact that God had promised to bless them if they were obedient to the covenant He had given them. The formula had been provided in Deuteronomy 30:1-10. In that passage, the Lord had promised to restore His people from captivity, have compassion on them, and gather them from all the peoples where He had scattered them (Deut. 30:3). The Lord further promised to bring them into the land that their fathers had possessed and prosper them abundantly in all the work of their hands, in the offspring of their cattle, and in the produce of their ground (Deut. 30:5, 9). However, these promises were conditional upon the obedience of the nation. The Lord would do all these things if the nation would obey the Lord to keep His commandments and statutes which are written in the book of the law and turn to the Lord with all their heart and soul (Deut. 30:10).

The book of Ezra is a record of the initial fulfillment of this covenant. The Lord had fulfilled His promise to restore His people from captivity and gather them from the lands to which they had been scattered. He had fulfilled His promise to bring them into the land which their fathers had possessed. However, the Lord had not prospered them abundantly. This was due to the disobedience of the nation. Even though the Lord had given them the ability and resources to rebuild His temple, the exiles had stopped working on the project because of the opposition of their neighbors. As a result, the Lord raised up the prophets Haggai and Zechariah to encourage the remnant to complete the project.

The remnant had further disobeyed the Lord by failing to follow His commandments concerning intermarriage with foreigners. As a result, the Lord brought them Ezra the scribe and priest. Ezra showed the remnant the error of their ways and took steps to eliminate the sin from the nation, calling on the guilty parties to divorce their ungodly wives. The key verse of the book is Ezra 9:12, "So now do not give your daughters to their sons nor take their daughters to your sons, and never seek their peace or their prosperity, that you may be strong and eat the good things of the land and leave it as an inheritance to your sons forever." The sin mentioned in this verse is the one specifically addressed by Ezra but it could really have been any sin. The point of the verse is this. Be obedient so that you can receive the blessings promised to you by the Lord forever. The book of Ezra is essentially a call to the postexilic community to be obedient to the Lord so that they can experience the blessings promised to them.

Structure and Outline

There is considerable debate concerning the original boundaries of the book of Ezra. Ezra's extensive similarities to Nehemiah have called into question its independence from that book, thus leading many scholars to regard the two books as one unified work. The problem is exacerbated by the fact that the two books are preserved in the Masoretic Text as a single book (for a full discussion of the relationship between the books of Ezra and Nehemiah, see Appendix Two). Furthermore, the collective similarities between the books of Ezra and Nehemiah and the book of Chronicles have led many scholars to incorporate all three books into a single unified work attributed to the "Chronicler" (for a full discussion of the relationship between the books of Chronicles, Ezra, and Nehemiah, see Appendix One). However, an examination of the evidence leads to the conclusion that Ezra was originally an independent work and will be treated as such in this analysis.

The book of Ezra is naturally divided into three sections. The first section records the return of the Jewish remnant to Jerusalem (1:1-2:70). The second section describes the rebuilding of the temple in Jerusalem (3:1-6:22). The third section details the return of Ezra and his ministry of restoring the remnant (7:1-10:44) The events of the first six chapters take place between 538 and 515 B.C. The events of chapters 7-10 take place in 458 B.C.

The book of Ezra is noted for its extensive use of lists. The more noteworthy lists include the following: 1:9-11 is an enumeration of the temple treasures that were returned to the Jews by Cyrus; 2:1-70 is a roster of those who returned to Jerusalem following the decree of Cyrus in 538 B.C.; 8:1-14 is a record of those who returned to Jerusalem with Ezra in 458 B.C.; and 10:18-44 is a list of those who were guilty of intermarriage with foreigners.

The book of Ezra is also renowned for its use of Aramaic. Ezra 4:8-6:18 is written in Aramaic. So too is 7:12-26. Daniel 2:4-7:28 is the only other section of the Old Testament written in Aramaic. Aramaic is a Northwest Semitic dialect. The Northwest Semitic subgroup also includes Hebrew, Phoenician, Moabite, Ammonite, and Ugaritic. Thanks to the Assyrian policy of deporting large numbers of people from their conquered homelands into Assyria, a substantial part of the Assyrian population by the eighth century B.C. was Aramean. Soon, Aramaic was being used for official communication throughout the Assyrian Empire. When the Babylonians destroyed the Assyrian Empire (ca. 612-605 B.C.), they adopted Aramaic as their spoken language of choice (Akkadian was primarily a written language). The Persians, who conquered Babylon in 539 B.C., followed suit and Aramaic became the *lingua franca* of the Persian Empire. The Jews who resisted the exile and settled at Elephantine in Upper Egypt spoke and wrote in Aramaic. Eventually, Aramaic even replaced Hebrew as the most popular language in Israel. As a result, translations of the biblical text into Aramaic (called Targumim) were produced and read alongside the original Hebrew texts in the synagogues. Aramaic was probably the primary language used by Jesus throughout his earthly ministry. Certain dialects of Aramaic are still spoken today.

There is an obvious reason for most of the Aramaic in Ezra. It is mainly comprised of copies of official correspondence, for which Aramaic was the customary language. 52 of the 67 verses fall into this category. The other 15 verses serve as connecting passages. There are two main views as to the reason for this occurrence. First, the Aramaic material may be extracted from an Aramaic history of the period. In this case, the entire section would have been copied from a single source document. Second, since the original readers of Ezra obviously knew Aramaic, the author simply keeps the connecting passages in Aramaic to avoid transitioning from one language to another. Either view is equally plausible.

Outline

I. The Jews Return to Jerusalem (1:1-2:70)
  A. The Opportunity to Return (1:1-11)
    1. The Decree of Cyrus (1:1-4)
    2. The Support of the Neighbors (1:5-6)
    3. The Support of Cyrus (1:7-11)
  B. The Roster of Returnees (2:1-70)
    1. The Leaders of the Return (2:1-2a)
    2. The List of Those with Proof of Ancestry (2:2b-58)
    3. The List of Those without Proof of Ancestry (2:59-63)
    4. The Sum Total of Returnees (2:64-67)
    5. The People Return to Their Cities (2:68-70)
II. The Jews Rebuild Their Temple (3:1-6:22)
  A. The Building of the Altar (3:1-6)
    1. The Nation Gathers in Jerusalem (3:1)
    2. The Altar Rebuilt (3:2-3)
    3. The Nation Celebrates the Feast of Booths (3:4)
    4. The Reinstitution of the Sacrificial System (3:5-6)

B. The Building of the Foundation (3:7-13)
   1. The Preparations for the Project (3:7)
   2. The Overseers of the Project (3:8-9)
   3. The Completion of the Project (3:10-11)
   4. The Twofold Response of the People (3:12-13)
C. The Response of the Enemies (4:1-5)
   1. The Request of the Enemies (4:1-2)
   2. The Reply of the Remnant (4:3)
   3. The Result of the Rejection (4:4-5)
D. Further Attempts to Stop the Project (4:6-24)
   1. The Attempt in the Days of Xerxes (4:6)
   2. The First Attempt in the Days of Artaxerxes (4:7)
   3. The Second Attempt in the Days of Artaxerxes (4:8-23)
   4. The Project is Halted (4:24)
E. The Project is Restarted (5:1-5)
   1. The Ministry of Haggai and Zechariah (5:1-2)
   2. The Response of Tattenai (5:3)
   3. The Resolve of the Jews (5:4-5)
F. The Letter of Tattenai (5:6-17)
   1. The Actions of Tattenai (5:6-10)
   2. The Answer of the Jews (5:11-16)
   3. The Request of Tattenai (5:17)
G. The Actions of Darius (6:1-12)
   1. The Discovery of the Decree of Cyrus (6:1-5)
   2. The Instructions to Tattenai (6:6-7)
   3. The Decree of Darius (6:8-12)
H. The Completion of the Temple (6:13-22)
   1. The Impact of the Decree of Darius (6:13-15)
   2. The Dedication of the Temple (6:16-18)
   3. The Celebration of Passover (6:19-22)
III. The Ministry of Ezra (7:1-10:44)
  A. The Introduction of Ezra the Scribe (7:1-10)
    1. Ezra's Genealogy (7:1-5)
    2. Ezra's Return to Jerusalem (7:6-9)
    3. Ezra's Ministry (7:10)
  B. Ezra's Commission from King Artaxerxes (7:11-28)
    1. The Introduction to the Letter (7:11)

2. The King's Permission (7:12-14)
3. The King's Provision (7:15-20)
4. The King's Orders for the Treasurers (7:21-24)
5. The King's Orders for Ezra (7:25-26)
6. The Thanksgiving of Ezra (7:27-28)
C. Ezra's Journey to Jerusalem (8:1-36)
  1. The Roster of Returnees (8:1-14)
  2. The Search for Levites (8:15-20)
  3. The Spiritual Preparation (8:21-23)
  4. The Treasure Bearers (8:24-30)
  5. Ezra's Arrival in Jerusalem (8:31-36)
D. The Problem of Mixed Marriages (9:1-10:44)
  1. Ezra Learns of the Apostasy (9:1-4)
  2. Ezra's Prayer (9:5-15)
    a. The Time of the Prayer (9:5)
    b. The Sins of the Nation (9:6-7)
    c. The Faithfulness of God (9:8-9)
    d. The Words of the Prophets (9:10-12)
    e. The Future of the Remnant (9:13-15)
  3. The Solution to the Problem (10:1-8)
    a. The Approach of the People (10:1)
    b. The Recommendation of Shecaniah (10:2-4)
    c. The Proclamation to Assemble in Jerusalem (10:5-8)
  4. The Assembly in Jerusalem (10:9-44)
    a. Ezra's Call for Repentance (10:9-11)
    b. The Response of the Assembly (10:12-15)
    c. The Investigation Hearings (10:16-17)
    d. The List of Those Guilty of Intermarriage (10:18-44)

Summary of Contents

The Jews Return to Jerusalem (1:1-2:70)

The book of Ezra begins with the phrase "Now in the first year of Cyrus king of Persia." The first year of Cyrus king of Persia is 539/538 B.C. This date is a reference to the first year in which he was king over all of Mesopotamia, including Babylon. Cyrus the Great was the founder of the Persian Empire. The rise of Cyrus is one of the most amazing fulfillments of biblical prophecy. Identifying him by name, Isaiah had prophesied the coming of Cyrus almost 200 years before he came to power, revealing that Cyrus will be used by the Lord to initiate the rebuilding of the city of Jerusalem, including the temple (Isa. 44:28; 45:1).

In his first year, Cyrus issued a proclamation allowing the Jews to return to their homeland to rebuild the temple in Jerusalem. This event is said to "fulfill" the words spoken by Jeremiah. The reference here is to Jeremiah 25:11-12 and 29:10 where Jeremiah predicts seventy years of captivity for the Jews. It is to these same passages that Daniel appeals while praying for the Lord's mercy in Daniel 9:2.

A question arises at this point as to the exact nature of the fulfillment of Jeremiah's prophecy. There are two alternatives for the reckoning of Jeremiah's seventy years. First, the time can be seen as referring to the initial deportation of the Jews in 605 B.C. to the first return of the Jews in roughly 538 B.C. Second, the time can be reckoned from the destruction of the city, and consequently the temple, in 586 B.C. until the temple is completely rebuilt in 515 B.C.

While both alternatives are possible, the first view makes better sense for the following reasons. First, the emphasis of the prophecy is on the exile of the nation, not on the state of the temple. Jeremiah 25:11 says "these nations shall serve the king of Babylon seventy years." The nation first begins to serve Nebuchadnezzar in 605 B.C. It is difficult to see the nation serving the king of Babylon from 538 until 515 B.C. unless Cyrus is to be identified as the current king of Babylon. Second, Daniel obviously anticipates in 9:2 that the end of the seventy years is about to take place. That is why he prays to the Lord and asks Him to restore His people. Daniel was taken captive in 605 B.C. and realizes that he has now been in Babylon almost 70 years.[8]

The events of the book of Ezra are seen as having been arranged by divine decision. The text notes that the Lord "stirred up the spirit" of King Cyrus. Even though Cyrus is the most powerful man on the face of the earth, he is still just a pawn in God's hands, easily manipulated into fulfilling the desires of Yahweh. This phrase reveals one of the major themes of the postexilic historical books, that is, the sovereignty of God.[9]

The proclamation of Cyrus was put in writing[10] and sent[11] throughout the entire kingdom of Persia.

Cyrus' decree authorized all the Jews living in exile to return to the land of Judah and rebuild the temple of Yahweh. The phrase "house of the Lord" in 1:3 is a reference to the temple built for Yahweh by Solomon in 966 B.C. This temple had been burned by the armies of Nebuchadnezzar when they destroyed the city of Jerusalem in 586 B.C. (cf. 2 Kin. 25:9; 2 Chron. 36:19). The final portion of Cyrus' decree concerns the support necessary to carry out this decree. The Jewish remnant that remained in Babylon supported their brethren with monetary wealth as well as material goods and cattle. They also contributed a "freewill offering"[12] to be taken to the temple.

In accordance with his attempt to gain the favor of Yahweh, Cyrus returned the articles which had been taken from the house of the Lord in Jerusalem. These articles had been taken by Nebuchadnezzar during his campaigns against Judah in 605, 597, and 586 B.C. These articles had been treated as trophies and otherwise misused by the Babylonian kings (cf. Dan. 5:1-4).

Cyrus ordered his royal treasurer Mithredath to distribute the temple articles to Sheshbazzar, the "prince" of the Jews. Sheshbazzar was the original leader of the Jews who decided to return to Judah. The Hebrew word translated "prince" (*nasi'*) simply means "leader" or "chief." It does not have the inherent meaning of "son of a king" as the English usage might imply. Sheshbazzar was appointed by Cyrus to be the governor of Judah when the initial returnees reached Jerusalem. How long he held this position is unclear. What is clear is that Zerubbabel has succeeded Sheshbazzar as the governor of Judah by 520 B.C. (cf. Hag. 1:1).

Chapter two is a list of those Jews who returned to Jerusalem from Babylon. The section is set apart from the narrative by means of an inclusio (note the use of the word "city" in verses one and seventy). An inclusio occurs when similar or identical phrases, motifs, or episodes begin and end a literary unit. A nearly identical list is found in Nehemiah seven. The phrase "each to his city" in 2:1 shows that the Jews were the rightful owners of the territory of Judah. The region had been divided up and given to individual families during the time of Joshua (Josh. 13-20). That is why the list that follows is divided according to genealogical lineage. Each family was expected to return to the property originally given to their ancestors.

The first half of verse two lists the major leaders who led the return to Jerusalem. There are eleven names listed here. Nehemiah adds one more, that of Nahamani (Neh. 7:7). Zerubbabel and Jeshua are named first. These two individuals are clearly the major leaders in Ezra 1-6. They are routinely mentioned together (cf. 3:2, 8; 4:3; 5:2). With the exception of 3:2, Zerubbabel is always mentioned first. Zerubbabel served as the governor of Judah while Jeshua served as the high priest. Together they represented the political and religious leadership of the nation. They work together to return to the land (2:2), to lay the foundation of the temple (3:8-10), to respond to the enemies of Judah (4:1-3), and to resume the rebuilding of the temple (5:2). So significant is their partnership that the prophet Zechariah uses it to describe the coming "Branch" (Zech. 6:12). From Jeremiah 23:5 it is clear that the "Branch" is going to come from the line of David and will "reign as king." Zechariah uses Jeshua to illustrate that this "Branch" will also "build the temple of the Lord" and "be a priest on His throne" (Zech. 6:12-13). The "Branch" is an obvious prophetic reference to Jesus Christ who unites the offices of both King and Priest (cf. Psalm 110; Heb. 7).

The name Zerubbabel means "the seed of Babel" or "born in Babel." He is not to be identified with the Sheshbazzar of chapter one. Zerubbabel is one of the most popular figures in the Bible. He is mentioned in 1 Chronicles, Ezra, Nehemiah, Haggai, Zechariah, Matthew, and Luke. The name Jeshua means "salvation." It is the Old Testament equivalent of the name Jesus. Jeshua was the first high priest of the returned remnant.

Verses 2b-35 identify the family leaders who returned with Zerubbabel. The designations "sons of" (Hebrew *bene*) and "men of" (Hebrew *'aneshe*) in these verses indicate the two ways by which the exiles could validate their Jewish ancestry, either by family name or by location in Judah. Verses 36-39 identify the priests who returned. The priests were the descendants of Aaron, a subset of the Levites.

Verses 40-42 identify the Levites who returned. The Levites served as assistants to the sons of Aaron in the service of the Tabernacle (cf. Num. 18:4). They would have been responsible for cleaning the various pieces of furniture, baking the show-bread, inspecting animals for sacrifices, and generally making sure that everything involved in the cultic process was done according to the Mosaic Law. Within the larger group of Levites two guilds are identified; the temple singers and the gatekeepers. The temple singers were often associated with the Levites (cf. Neh. 11-12) and were primarily responsible for leading the music during worship. The gatekeepers were responsible for guarding the gates leading into the temple as well as locking and unlocking the doors of the temple. They also watched over the temple chambers and treasuries (1 Chron. 9:17-29).

Verses 43-54 identify the temple servants who returned. The temple servants were an order of Israelites who assisted the Levites. David was responsible for their creation (cf. 8:20). They are referred to as the Nethinim ("dedicated ones") in 7:24. The presence of several foreign names shows that this guild was primarily made up of foreigners. The temple servants were the lowest class of temple personnel. Verses 55-58 identify the descendants of Solomon's servants who returned. They were likely foreigners who were enslaved by Solomon and appointed to serve in the temple. The total in verse 58 includes both the temple servants and the descendants of Solomon's servants, a fact which signifies the close relationship between these two groups.

Verses 59-63 identify those individuals who could not prove their ancestry. Evidently, the rest of the individuals named in this list could provide proof of their citizenship. Although the individuals named here could not prove their ancestry, they were still allowed to return with the rest of the exiles. It is probable that they lost proof of their heritage during the chaos that surely existed during the Babylonian invasion and subsequent exile. They were probably given the same rights as circumcised foreigners.

Verses 61-63 reveal that even some priests were unable to prove their ancestry. These men were not allowed to serve as priests until the high priest could determine whether they were legitimate. He did this by using the Urim and Thummim. The exact nature of the Urim and Thummim is one of the great mysteries of the Old Testament. It has been suggested that they were two small objects which were used to signify the will of God, much like the casting of lots. Josephus contends that the answer was given by a miraculous shining of the jewels on the high priest's garments (*Antiquities of the Jews* 3.8.9).

The total number of those who returned with Zerubbabel was 49,897 (Nehemiah records 49,942; cf. Neh. 7:66-67). This number does not correspond with the sum of the various groups mentioned in the chapter (i.e., 29,818). It is possible that women and children were not included in the initial numbers but were included in the final tally. However, this seems to be a very low number of women and children when compared to the number of men. Perhaps the difficulties of the journey and the uncertainty of what awaited them in Judah caused many women and children to remain in Babylon. It is also reasonable to assume that not all families are listed in the individual tabulations. A final possibility is scribal error, which is much more common in numerical lists.

The returnees contributed to the rebuilding of the temple by donating money to the effort. The remnant was probably inspired to take up this collection by the example of their forefathers at the building of the Tabernacle (Ex. 25:1-8). This collection added to the assistance provided by Cyrus and by the Jewish neighbors mentioned in 1:6. Although the remnant returned initially to Jerusalem, many continued on to their ancestral properties throughout Judah.

The Jews Rebuild Their Temple (3:1-6:22)

While chapter two described the return of the Jews from exile, chapter three describes the nation's activities when they first enter the land. The first order of business for the returned remnant is the reestablishment of proper Yahweh-worship in the land. The foundational element in Yahweh-worship was the sacrificial system.

The restored remnant naturally begins with the building of an altar. Without an altar it is impossible to offer sacrifices.

The activity of chapter three begins in the month Tishri (late September and early October) according to the Jewish calendar. The holy days in the month of Tishri included the Feast of Trumpets (Tishri 1), the Day of Atonement (Tishri 10), and the Feast of Booths, also named Tabernacles (Tishri 15-21). This fact helps us to narrow the time of year when the exiles returned to the land of Israel. One would assume that if the nation had been in the land during the month of Nisan then they would assuredly have celebrated the great holidays in that month, especially the Feast of Unleavened Bread, one of the three required holidays for all male Jews (along with the Passover and Feast of Booths; cf. Deut. 16:16). Hence the remnant had not yet returned by the month of Nisan.

It is likely that the returning exiles would have traveled during the spring, probably leaving Babylon early in the month of Iyyar (also called Ziv; late April and early May) and arriving in Jerusalem in the month of Tammuz (late June and early July). In this scenario, the nation would have avoided travel during the most difficult times of the year, that is, the cold winter, the early spring, which included the latter rains and the flood season, and the hot summer. The only major holiday from Nisan to Tishri is the Day of Pentecost, also called the Feast of Weeks, occurring fifty days after Passover on Sivan 7. Since all male Jews had to journey to Jerusalem for the Passover it can be assumed that the remnant had not yet returned to Israel by this date. It is likely that Passover occurred while the nation was traveling. So the first holidays that occurred after the nation entered the land are those in Tishri. The year is probably 537 B.C., although a year before or after is entirely possible.

Jeshua and Zerubbabel work together to rebuild the altar. This is the only passage in the Bible where the name of Jeshua precedes Zerubbabel. This phenomenon is almost certainly because this section deals with the reinstitution of worship, the responsibility of the priests. This new altar was built on the foundation of the previous one, that of Solomon's temple.

The phrase "for they were terrified because of the peoples of the lands" (3:3) is somewhat enigmatic. Perhaps in order to build the new altar the remnant was forced to destroy the previous one that had been utilized by those Jews and Samaritans who lived in Jerusalem during the exile. The destruction of their altar would surely have infuriated these groups. This may account for the rift between those who returned from Babylon and those who remained in the land (cf. 4:1-5). A more likely possibility, however, is that the phrase provides the reason why the remnant was so eager to reinstitute the sacrificial system, that is, because they were afraid of their enemies. They needed the help of their God. At this point, this is a healthy sort of fear. It is a fear that drives the one who is afraid to be obedient to the will of God regardless of the circumstances, trusting in the Lord for help and protection. Unfortunately, this fear of their enemies will continue to grow, eventually causing the remnant to stop the rebuilding project (cf. 4:4). After the completion of the altar the nation once again begins the ritual of offering morning and evening sacrifices, being sure to follow the ordinances contained in the Law of Moses. They also begin to celebrate the various holidays prescribed by the Lord.

The nation congregates in Jerusalem to celebrate the Feast of Booths. The Feast of Booths was one of the most significant days in the Jewish calendar. It was celebrated from Tishri 15 to Tishri 21. During this week the Jews were required to live in booths (i.e., tents) set up around Jerusalem. This was done to commemorate the wilderness wanderings of the Exodus generation. The text states that the remnant offered the sacrifices according to the daily requirements. A special sacrifice was offered each of the seven days of this feast (see Numbers 29:12-38 for the details on what was to be offered on each day). The first day of the feast was to be a day of rest as well as the day after the feast ended.

The Jews prepare for the building of the temple's foundation by hiring masons and carpenters, two groups of artisans whose skills were essential to the project. The word "masons" refers specifically to stonecutters. Following the example of Solomon (cf. 2 Chron. 2:16), the remnant contracted the Phoenicians to bring timber from the region of Lebanon to the port city of Joppa. The Phoenicians are referred to by their principal cities Tyre and Sidon. The cedar logs purchased from the Phoenicians were taken by boat to the port city of Joppa. Joppa (Hebrew *yapo*; meaning "beauty") was located about thirty miles northwest of Jerusalem on the shores of the Mediterranean Sea. Its harbor made it the port city for Jerusalem. Permission for the acquisition of cedar logs from the Phoenicians had been granted by King Cyrus himself. It is likely that Cyrus needed to approve this transaction because it involved multiple provinces in the Persian Empire.

The remnant begins to rebuild the foundation of the temple in the second month of the second year following their return from Babylon. The second month in the Jewish calendar was the month Iyyar (late April and early May). The year is probably 536 B.C., nearly 70 years after the first exiles were taken to Babylon (605 B.C.). The second month was the perfect time of the year to start a building project. It is the beginning of the dry season and the great holidays of Nisan have been completed. This was also the month in which Solomon began building the first temple (cf. 1 Kin. 6:1).

The leaders of the project are Zerubbabel and Jeshua. Although Sheshbazzar is not named here, he evidently had a hand in the project since he is credited with it in Ezra 5:16. The priesthood assumes the role of overseeing the project. This is to make sure that the project was ritually correct.

Chapter three closes with a description of the celebration of the people following the completion of the work. This celebration is led by the religious leaders, the priests and the Levites. Although the majority of the people viewed this day as a time of celebration, many in the audience viewed it as a time of mourning. The mourning was done by those who had seen the original temple before it had been destroyed by Nebuchadnezzar in 586 B.C. These men could see that this second temple would never compare to the glorious temple of Solomon. The weeping of these old men is drowned out by the rejoicing of the youth. As a result, those who witnessed this event could not distinguish between the two.

With the progress of the rebuilding project comes the antagonism of those who had previously controlled the land of Israel (4:1-24). This section builds on the previous chapter by detailing the response of the neighbors to the efforts of the Jews. One might anticipate that the foreigners of the land would be hostile to the growing Jewish influence in the province. By this time, they had lived in the province of Judah for decades, many perhaps being born in the land of Israel. Now, a group they currently regarded as "foreigners" was taking their land and influence away.

Upon learning of the early success of the Jews in their rebuilding project the neighbors of the remnant approach the workers and ask if they can help in the effort. These neighbors of the Jews are identified as "enemies" with their very first appearance in the narrative. As a result, their subsequent request should be seen as a veiled attempt to hinder the work of the remnant rather than as a sincere request to join the project. The neighbors of the returned remnant had been brought to the land of Israel by Assyrian kings. Originally, Sargon brought in the colonists from a number of Mesopotamian towns when the city of Samaria fell in 722 B.C. (cf. 2 Kin. 17:24). Additional colonists were later brought in during the reigns of Esarhaddon (680-669 B.C.) and Ashurbanipal (669–626 B.C.).

Since the worship of the foreigners was not genuine, the remnant did not allow them to help in the project. The remnant, led by Zerubbabel and Jeshua, quickly reject the request of the foreigners. There is a bit of diplomacy, however, in their rejection as they appeal to the original decree of Cyrus which only granted the right of rebuilding the temple to those who returned from exile.

The rejection of the foreigners on the part of the remnant served to inspire them to try to stop the project. Their initial actions were threefold. First, they discouraged the remnant. This technique would have consisted of the mocking, heckling, and otherwise taunting of the workers. This was also the first method employed in future years by Sanballat and Tobiah when they were trying to discourage the rebuilding efforts of Nehemiah's men (Neh. 4:1-3). Second, they frightened the remnant. This approach would have involved threats to the remnant, perhaps endangering their lives. There was little the Jews could do to protect themselves. The supply lines from Tyre and Sidon were long and unguarded. The small remnant was surrounded on all sides by their enemies. They were completely vulnerable. This method was likewise used by Sanballat and Tobiah in Nehemiah's day (Neh. 4:7-11). Third, the foreigners hired counselors to frustrate the men of Israel. The exact nature of this course of action is unknown. It is probable that the "counselors" are in fact Persian officials. The resultant meaning would thus indicate that the foreigners bribed the Persian authorities to frustrate the rebuilding project. Bribery was a frequent practice in ancient times among the Persians (Josephus, *Antiquities of the Jews* 11.2.1).

The subversive tactics of the foreigners persisted until the reign of the Persian King Darius. This king is to be identified as Darius I Hystaspes (522-486 B.C.). Therefore, the opposition continued throughout the rest of the reign of Cyrus (until 530 B.C.), and during the entire reigns of Cambyses (530-522 B.C.) and Pseudo-Smerdis (522 B.C.). As verse 24 notes, the plan of the enemies was a rousing success. The remnant eventually stopped working on the temple, a condition that would continue for sixteen years.

4:6-23 is a parenthesis in the flow of the narrative. Ezra, in an attempt to illustrate some of the measures used by the enemies of the Jews, interjects into the story three events that occur more than fifty years after the events of 4:1-5. These events evidently reminded him of the lengths to which the opposition was willing to go in their repeated efforts to stop the Jews from achieving success.

The first attempt was made in the days of Ahasuerus (4:6). Ahasuerus is better known by his Greek name Xerxes. Ahasuerus was his Hebrew name, a translation of the Persian name Khshayarsha. Xerxes reigned over the Persian Empire from 486 to 465 B.C. Esther married Xerxes and became the queen of Persia after he deposed Vashti, also known as Amestris. During his reign the enemies of the Jews wrote a letter to the king containing accusations against the Jews who lived in Judah and Jerusalem. The accusations contained in this letter were probably the same ones mentioned in 4:13-16. Evidently, nothing happened as a result of this attempt.

The second attempt was made in the days of Artaxerxes (4:7). Artaxerxes, whose name means "having a kingdom of justice," was the third son of Xerxes and Amestris. He reigned over the Persian Empire from 464-424 B.C. Ezra led a return to Israel during his reign and Nehemiah served as his cupbearer. During his reign the enemies of the Jews again tried writing a letter to the Persian king in an attempt to stop the Jews from rebuilding their city. Again, it seems as if nothing happened as a result of this attempt.

The third attempt was also made in the days of Artaxerxes (4:8-23). At some point subsequent to the writing of the letter mentioned in 4:7, Rehum writes a second letter to King Artaxerxes on behalf of the enemies of the Jews. The exact date of this letter cannot be ascertained, though it must have been written between 458 (the date of Ezra's return to Jerusalem referred to in verse 12) and 444 B.C. (the date of Nehemiah's return to Jerusalem and subsequent rebuilding of the walls of the city). One would assume that Ezra would have wanted to begin work on the walls of the city immediately upon his return so a date closer to 458 is to be preferred. Although other names are given, Rehum should be viewed as the primary author. Shimshai served as his amanuensis.

The Osnappar referred to in verse ten is Ashurbanipal, king of the Assyrian Empire from 669-626 B.C. His father was Esarhaddon, the Assyrian king referred to in 4:2. Around 645 B.C., Ashurbanipal invaded the territory that included Erech and Susa, evidently exiling some of the inhabitants to the region of Samaria (cf. 4:9). The "River" (4:10) is to be identified as the Euphrates River. The entire phrase "beyond the River" refers to the Persian province named Trans-Euphrates.[13] This province stretched from the Euphrates River to the border of Egypt, thereby encompassing the whole of Syria and Palestine.

The actual letter written by Rehum is supplied in 4:11-16. The letter contained two accusations against the Jews. First, Rehum informs Artaxerxes that the Jews will stop paying tribute if the walls are successfully rebuilt. Second, Rehum warns Artaxerxes that he will lose the entire province of Trans-Euphrates if the walls of Jerusalem are successfully rebuilt. This assertion is based on Jerusalem's long history of rebelling against foreign nations (cf. 4:15, 19).[14]

Artaxerxes' reply is given in 4:17-22. Artaxerxes addresses his reply to Rehum, Shimshai, and the rest of their colleagues. Artaxerxes begins his letter by informing Rehum that the letter sent by him was "translated and read" to the king. Evidently, Artaxerxes did not understand Aramaic and needed to have the letter interpreted. Artaxerxes next details the steps he took upon hearing the interpretation of the letter. To his credit, Artaxerxes carefully researched the claims of Rehum (4:19-20). After a thorough search of the

Assyrian and Babylonian annals, the king discovered that Jerusalem did indeed have a long history of rebelling against their Suzerains. He also discovered that some of Jerusalem's kings had been quite powerful. This seems to be a reference to David and Solomon (and perhaps even to Uzziah and Hezekiah). If Jerusalem had been that powerful in the past, it could certainly rise to prominence again in the future, thereby posing a threat to the Persian Empire and Artaxerxes himself. As a result, the king issues a decree calling for the Jews to halt their rebuilding efforts.

The wording of the decree, however, supplies the king with an out. He writes, "until a decree is issued by me" (4:21). King Artaxerxes wisely leaves the door open for a change of mind since the decrees of the Persians could not be repealed once they became official (cf. Esth. 1:19; 8:8; Dan. 6:8). In fact, the decree contained in 4:17-22 represented a sort of change of his earlier decree giving Ezra virtually unlimited freedom to do as he wished (cf. 7:21). Artaxerxes would subsequently change his mind one last time, allowing Nehemiah to return in 444 B.C. to complete the walls of Jerusalem. The leaders of the opposition, no doubt thrilled at the king's reply, hurry to stop the rebuilding efforts of the Jews.

In 4:24, the narrative picks up where 4:5 left off. The repetition of the phrase "the reign of Darius King of Persia" unites the two verses. The plan of the enemies was a rousing success. This verse supplies two pieces of information which were lacking in verse five: First, the fact that the remnant stopped working on the temple (536 B.C.); And second, the fact that this condition continued until the second year of the reign of Darius (520 B.C.), a total of sixteen years.

Chapters five and six record the resumption and completion of the temple project. The time frame for these verses is supplied in 4:24. It is now the second year of the reign of Darius I (520 B.C.). The Lord who had "stirred up" the spirit of Cyrus (1:1) and the spirit of those who originally returned to the land (1:5) now speaks to the remnant through His prophets Haggai and Zechariah. Both prophets claim that their words came directly from the Lord (cf. Hag. 1:1; Zech. 1:1). The name Haggai means "festival" and the name Zechariah means "Yahweh remembers."

In his book, Haggai sharply criticizes the remnant for living in "paneled" houses while the temple was still in ruins (Hag. 1:4). The Jews had not simply stopped work to put up their own homes. The use of this word implies that improvements had been made to their dwellings. He further reveals that the remnant was engaged in extensive agricultural endeavors and economic pursuits (Hag. 1:6). Each of these demonstrates the skewed priorities of the remnant. Essentially, the message of the prophet is to give God's interests the priority over their own interests. Even the great leaders of the remnant were not above blame. Haggai specifically addresses his message to Zerubbabel and Jeshua (Hag. 1:1). The prophets Haggai and Zechariah support the Jews in their rebuilding efforts for almost five years until the temple is finally completed.

Immediately upon hearing the news that the Jews have resumed work on the temple, Tattenai, the governor of the province of Trans-Euphrates approaches the remnant and questions them regarding the project. His chief concern was assuredly whether or not these actions involved subversion. The Persian Empire had been teeming with revolts since the death of Cyrus and especially since Darius took the throne. These revolts were common in ancient times. There was always a period of uncertainty whenever a change in the monarchy occurred. Vassal nations frequently used this opportunity to rebel against their Suzerain.

It was the provincial governor's duty to question the activity of the Jews. From his point of view, it was entirely possible that the Jews were rebuilding portions of their city as part of a subversive plot to rebel against the Persians. As detailed in the previous section, the Jews had a history of rebelling against their Suzerains. While Tattenai himself should not be regarded as an enemy of the Jews, he was likely informed of their efforts by those who were. Tattenai demands the credentials of the remnant. He wants to know by what authority they are rebuilding the temple.

Evidently the Jews could not produce the credentials necessary to prove their right to rebuild the temple. The returning exiles must have had some original documents when they first returned to the land, possibly including a copy of the decree of Cyrus. It can be assumed that they would have needed to show these documents to the officials in Trans-Euphrates upon arriving in the province. Apparently, these credentials had been lost. Perhaps they had been destroyed by the enemies of the Jews. Whatever the reason, the remnant could not prove their right to rebuild the temple.

Since the Jews could not prove their right to rebuild the temple Tattenai takes pen in hand to write to the king requesting him to research the official records. Ezra provides the reader with a copy of the letter sent by Tattenai to King Darius of Assyria (5:7-17). Tattenai begins the letter by announcing that he had discovered that the Jews were rebuilding the temple of their God. The governor notes that this temple was being built with considerable strength and with great care. Special emphasis is given to the size of the boulders being used; obviously, the larger the stones the greater their strength. The phrase "huge stones" (5:8) literally means "rolling stones" and indicates boulders too large to move by any other means. The mention of timber reveals that this temple was being built following the same techniques employed by Solomon. In fact, Ezra 6:4 prescribes the same ratio of stone to timber (three to one) as that utilized by Solomon (1 Kin. 6:36). This technique of laying timber between layers of stone or brick was common in the Ancient Near East and was probably used as a means of strengthening buildings against earthquakes.[15] The overall quality of the building likely added to Tattenai's concern that this project could be part of a subversive plot against the king.

Tattenai is careful to record his own actions in questioning the remnant concerning the legal means by which they had undertaken this project. He further adds that he questioned the remnant concerning the identities of the leaders. The names ascertained by Tattenai are not supplied in the letter. This is a glaring omission since the text notes that Tattenai requested the names so that he might relay them to the king (5:10). While it is possible that Ezra intentionally deleted the names, it seems more likely that Tattenai was withholding the names until he heard from the king concerning the validity of the claims. One would expect that Zerubbabel and Jeshua were at the top of the list.

Tattenai next informs the king of the remnant's response. The response of the Jews demonstrates that they are well aware of the reason for their exile. They fully acknowledge that their ancestors had provoked the Lord to wrath by worshipping other gods (cf. Ezek. 23; Hos. 2:1-13). As a result the Lord punished their disobedience by scattering them among the nations (cf. Lev. 26:33; Deut. 28:64) and allowing their temple to be destroyed (cf. 2 Chron. 7:20-22). Although Nebuchadnezzar was the human agent who systematically deported the Jews to Babylon (605, 597, 586 B.C.) and destroyed Solomon's temple (586 B.C.), the Jews realize that it was really God who allowed it to happen ("He [God] gave them into the hand of Nebuchadnezzar;" 5:12).

The Lord still granted favor to His chosen people, however, as He "stirred up the spirit" of Cyrus (1:1) to issue a decree allowing the Jews to return to their land and rebuild their temple (1:2-4). The Jews also noted the fact that Cyrus returned the articles of the temple which had been taken by Nebuchadnezzar, further proof that he had authorized the rebuilding project.

The letter closes with a request that the claims of the Jews be verified. Tattenai expects that the matter will be resolved with a search of the king's records in Babylon (cf. 5:17). Time will show that the supporting documents will actually be found at a remote fortress in Media called Ecbatana (6:2). The final line of the letter is a request for the king's instructions concerning the entire matter. Tattenai wanted to know if the claims of the Jews were accurate and if so, whether or not Darius wanted to allow the project to continue.

Having received the letter of Tattenai, King Darius issued a decree calling for a search of the official Persian records to verify the claims of the Jews. The search began in the city of Babylon. Evidently, Darius assumed that since the returned remnant had originated in Babylon, then that was where the decree must have been made. Darius was no doubt aware that Cyrus had stayed in Babylon for a period of time following his conquest of the city. However, a record of the decree was not found in Babylon.

As it turns out, a scroll containing the original decree of Cyrus was found at the fortress of Ecbatana, the summer capital of the Persian kings during the reign of Cyrus. Xenophon informs us that Cyrus lived in Babylon during the winter, in Susa during the spring, and in Ecbatana during the summer (*Cyropaedia* 8.6.22). Ecbatana (modern Hamadan) was located in the province of Media and was the capital of the Medes until they fell under the control of Cyrus. Cyrus had stayed in Ecbatana in the summer of his first year as king of Babylon, the same year he originally made the decree allowing the Jews to return to Jerusalem and rebuild their temple.

The decree of this passage is similar to that of the first chapter; however, there are some notable differences. These differences do not necessarily mean that there were two different decrees.[16] However, they probably do indicate two different sources. The edict of 1:2-4 was probably a portion of the decree that heralds would have proclaimed in each city as they journeyed throughout the empire. This would have been a shortened form of the official decree suitable for posting. The decree of 6:3-5 was likely taken from the official records of the Persian king. The official records would have contained the full text of the original decree, thus detailing all of the particulars. Obviously, this document would have been much longer than the one quoted in 1:2-4. Only those portions that deal with the specifics of the temple are copied by Ezra. For example, there would have been no need to repeat the portions dealing with Cyrus' decree allowing the Jews to return to Jerusalem since they are already there.

The decree of this passage provides a few additional details concerning the actual building of the temple. First, the decree provides the exact dimensions of the temple, 60 cubits high and 60 cubits wide. A cubit is about eighteen inches in length. These dimensions called for the rebuilt temple to be twice as high and three times as wide as Solomon's temple (cf. 1 Kin. 6:2). Perhaps Cyrus wanted the glory of this temple to surpass that of Solomon's. Evidently, the Jews did not take advantage of this opportunity (cf. 3:12-13; Hag. 2:3). Second, the decree authorizes the use of "huge stones." The sight of these stones likely concerned Tattenai when he first inspected the building project since he specifically mentioned the "huge stones" being used in the construction (5:8). Third, the decree allows for the expenses incurred in the construction to be taken from the royal treasury. The offer to cover the expenses of this project fits well with what is known of Cyrus' policies regarding foreign religions. Fourth, the decree called for the return of the gold and silver temple utensils that had been taken by King Nebuchadnezzar. While the fulfillment of this portion of the decree was recorded in 1:7-11, it was not recorded in the decree itself (1:2-4).

Having found the original decree of Cyrus, Darius now relays his instructions to Tattenai (cf. 5:17). The original decree of Cyrus is allowed to stand. Darius instructs Tattenai and his colleagues to refrain from interfering with the remnant's rebuilding project, in essence allowing the Jews to continue working on the temple, the "house of God."

Darius also offers a decree of his own. The king's decree calls for five things. First, Darius orders the funds for the temple to be drawn from the royal treasury and paid to the Jews. Second, Darius provides for the sacrificial system of the Jews to be restored. Third, Darius instructs the remnant to pray for him and his family. Fourth, Darius reveals the punishment that is to be given to anyone who violates his decree. This punishment takes the form of poetic justice. If anyone harms the house of God, then his own house will be destroyed. The offender was also to be impaled on a timber from his own house. Fifth, Darius calls on the Lord to invoke divine judgment on all who attempt to destroy the rebuilt temple. Immediately upon receiving the instructions of Darius, Tattenai rushes to make sure the wishes of the king are carried out.

Having now received the permission of the Persian king, the Jews are able to successfully rebuild their temple. The project was completed on Adar 3 (February 19), 515 B.C., four and a half years after the remnant restarted the project and twenty-one years after they had laid the foundation. The temple was rebuilt seventy years after it had been destroyed (i.e., 586 B.C.). Solomon's temple stood for almost 400 years. This temple will stand for almost 600 years (until Titus destroys it in A.D. 70).

The Jews celebrate the completion of the temple by having a ceremony of "dedication" (6:16). The Aramaic word used here is *hanukah*. This word will eventually lend its name to an annual festival commemorating the re-consecration of the temple after its defamation at the hands of Antiochus Epiphanes (Chislev 25, 167 B.C.). As part of the celebration, the Jews offer 100 bulls, 200 rams, 400 lambs, and 12 male goats. This was certainly a significant sacrifice for the impoverished remnant; however, it pales in comparison to the 22,000 oxen and 120,000 sheep offered in dedication to Solomon's temple (1 Kin. 8:63).

The Passover was the first Jewish feast day to be celebrated in the completed temple, occurring five weeks after the dedication of the temple. Passover was celebrated on Nisan 14, the "fourteenth of the first month." Each household sacrificed a one-year-old unblemished lamb at twilight on this special day (Ex. 12:6). The lamb is then eaten with unleavened bread and bitter herbs (Num. 9:11). The Passover holiday commemorated the Lord's redemption of the nation of Israel from bondage in Egypt. The Feast of Unleavened Bread began on the day following Passover and lasted seven days (Lev. 23:6-8). During this week, the Jews were forbidden from eating leavened bread (Deut. 16:3). The first and seventh days were to be days of rest (Ex. 12:16). This festival commemorated the hasty departure of the Jews from Egypt.

These verses are the climax of the first half of the book. The nation is now resettled in the land and proper worship of Yahweh has been restored. The hero of the story is God. The narrative of the first half of the book begins when the Lord "stirred up the spirit" of the Persian king (1:1) to allow the Jews to return to the land of Israel and ends when the Lord "turned the heart" of the Persian king (6:22) to encourage the Jews to finish the temple.

The Ministry of Ezra (7:1-10:44)

The phrase "now after these things" (7:1) introduces a significant shift in the narrative, effectively separating the events of chapters 7-10 from those of 1-6. The events of these chapters take place during the reign of Artaxerxes, almost 58 years after the events of chapter six. In the meantime, the events of the book of Esther took place in Susa. The name Artaxerxes means "having a kingdom of justice." Artaxerxes I was the third son of Xerxes and Amestris and reigned from 464-424 B.C. Nehemiah was his cupbearer.

The section begins by introducing the main character of the second half of the book, that is, Ezra the priest and scribe (7:1-10). The text supplies an extensive genealogy for Ezra, thus revealing the considerable importance of this man. Since the scribe's lineage is traced to Aaron the chief priest, the primary reason for the gene-alogy seems to be to identify Ezra as a priest, thereby giving him the authority to institute various reforms.

Ezra is identified as "skilled in the law of Moses" (7:6) a phrase which denotes his wisdom and efficiency in the use of the biblical text. In a classic example of foreshadowing, the text informs the reader that the king granted Ezra everything he requested. The fact that Ezra requested something of the king is never supplied in the narrative. It can be assumed that he requested the items granted to him in Artaxerxes' letter (7:12-26).

Ezra and his party journeyed from Babylon to Jerusalem in the seventh year of King Artaxerxes (458 B.C.). The trip from Babylon to Jerusalem took four months and covered roughly 900 miles. The company left Babylon in Nisan (late March, early April) of 458 B.C. They planned to leave on the first day of the month, however, the need to recruit Levites delayed their start until the twelfth day (cf. 8:31), just two days before Passover. The group arrives on the first day of Ab (late August, early September) in 458 B.C.

Ezra 7:10 is one of the most amazing verses in the entire Bible. The conjunctive "for" connects this verse to the preceding phrase "the good hand of his God was upon him." In other words, the reason the good hand of God was upon Ezra was because of the things described in this verse. As a result, this verse can be perceived as detailing a four-step formula for gaining the favor of the Lord. First, Ezra "set his heart." The scribe determined within his heart that he would faithfully and resolutely commit himself to the habits detailed in the rest of the verse. Second, Ezra studied the law of the Lord. The scribe devoted his life to the reading and analysis of God's Word. Third, Ezra practiced the law of the Lord. The scribe's examination of the scriptures was not simply a growth of knowledge. He applied that knowledge to his life. Fourth, Ezra taught the law throughout Israel. The scribe did not keep the things he learned to himself. He taught them to others.

The text next records the commission of Ezra by Artaxerxes (7:11-28). The letter of Artaxerxes is provided in Aramaic, the language of official correspondence in the Persian Empire. The decree gives Ezra, and whoever among the Israelites who wishes to join him, the opportunity to journey to Jerusalem. The decree also entrusts Ezra with the responsibility to enforce the law of Yahweh.

The letter begins with a typical salutation. The author of the letter, Artaxerxes, is identified followed by the recipient of the letter, Ezra. The first item of business addressed in the letter is the permission of the king allowing the Israelites to return to Jerusalem. This return was not forced, only those who were "willing to go" had permission to return. The second item of business addressed in the letter is the provision of the king for the temple of Yahweh, the God of Israel. The king offers silver and gold to Ezra dedicated to the purchase of animals and other offerings. He also allows the people to make free-will donations to the collection. These offerings were to be presented at the temple in Jerusalem. Any excess money was to be used at the discretion of Ezra, probably earmarked for the daily service of the temple. The third item of business addressed in the letter is a decree given specifically to the king's treasurers. The treasurers of Trans-Euphrates are instructed to provide Ezra with whatever he requests. Ezra's rights of requisition were considerable but not unlimited, the king having provided a ceiling on each item. The fourth and final item of business addressed in the letter is a decree given specifically to Ezra. The scribe is instructed to appoint "magistrates and judges" throughout the province of Trans-Euphrates.

The letter concludes by granting Ezra (and his appointed judges) the authority to execute judgment on all Jews who refuse to obey the commandments of God and the "law of the king." This latter phrase is probably a reference to the specific decree of 7:12-26 as opposed to a general reference to the laws of the Persians. Ezra and his judges are given permission to punish lawbreakers in four ways. First, they can confiscate the offender's possessions. Second, the judges are able to imprison wrongdoers. Third, they can banish the evildoers from the province. Fourth, the judges can execute those who refuse to follow the law.

The section closes with a tribute to the Lord by Ezra. This tribute takes the form of a doxology (declarative praise) similar to those found elsewhere throughout the Scriptures (cf. 1 Sam. 25:39; 2 Chron. 2:12; Ps. 144:1; Dan. 3:28; 2 Cor. 1:3; Eph. 1:3; 1 Pet. 1:3).

Ezra also reveals that he had gathered some of the leading men of Israel to return with him to Jerusalem.

The details of Ezra's journey from Babylon to Jerusalem are supplied in 8:1-36. The passage begins with a roster of the returnees (8:1-14). Ezra assembled the company on the banks of the river that ran to Ahava. While encamped, Ezra realizes that there are no Levites in the assembly and immediately takes steps to rectify this situation. After briefing them on their mission, Ezra sends a delegation of the leading men and two "teachers" to Casiphia to talk to Iddo, himself one of the elders of the Jews. Fortunately, Iddo is able to provide the company with a small number of Levites. Iddo is also able to supply a large group of temple servants. The number of those who returned with Ezra was about 1700 men plus women and children, perhaps a total of close to 5000 individuals.

Prior to leaving their encampment, Ezra calls on the assembly to fast. The motivation for the fast was to seek the Lord's protection for the journey. The fasting of the assembly was accompanied by prayer (cf. 2 Chron. 20:3-12). The text notes that Ezra refused to ask the king for an armed escort to protect the pilgrims on their dangerous journey. In those days the roads were teeming with gangs of bandits. Ezra's reason for not making a request is admirable. He refused to request a military escort because he had told the Persian king about the power of His God. Surely Ezra could not ask for the king's help when he had already told him that he was following the Lord's will. If it really was the Lord's will, then He would protect His people.

Ezra set apart twelve priests and twelve Levites and placed the responsibility for the gold and silver in their hands. The amount of treasure is staggering. A Babylonian talent weighed close to 70 pounds. Therefore, the 650 silver and 100 gold talents together weighed almost 30 tons! Equally impressive are the various gold, silver, and bronze utensils.

The company leaves the Ahava waterway on the twelfth of Nisan (late March, early April) of 458 B.C. The exiles have a safe journey and arrive in Jerusalem on the first day of Ab (late August, early September). Upon arrival in Jerusalem, the text notes that the exiles waited three days. Perhaps this was a time of rest following their rigorous journey. It is also possible that they arrived late in the week and waited until the Sabbath was over before weighing out the valuables, an activity that would have been considered work. On the fourth day, to celebrate their safe arrival in Jerusalem, the exiles offered the treasure to the priests and burnt offerings to the Lord. The valuables are weighed out to Meremoth son of Uriah (cf. Neh. 3:4, 21). The burnt offerings expressed thanksgiving to the Lord and involved the wholehearted consecration of the worshippers. The exiles also offered sin offerings. The sin offerings provided atonement for the sins of the worshippers. After celebrating their arrival, the exiles deliver the king's edicts to his official representatives.

The final chapters of the book address the issue of mixed marriages and detail the steps Ezra took to alleviate the problem (9:1-10:44). At some point within a few months of the events of 8:33-36 (cf. 7:9; 10:9), the leaders of the remnant approach Ezra with news that many of the Jews were involved in mixed marriages with the foreigners[1] living in the land of Israel. The list of foreigners in 9:1 is reminiscent of several similar lists in the Pentateuch (cf. Gen. 15:19-21; Ex. 23:23; 33:2; Deut. 20:17). The groups mentioned include the Canaanites,[17] Hittites,[18] Perizzites, Jebusites,[19] Ammonites,[20] Moabites,[21] Egyptians,[22] and Amorites.[23] The Canaanites were the descendants of Canaan, the son of Ham. The Hittites were the descendants of Heth, the son of Canaan (Gen. 10:15). The origin of the Perizzites is unknown. They first appear in Genesis 13:7 where they are simply identified as dwelling in the land of Canaan with the Canaanites at the time of Abraham (cf. Gen. 34:10). The Jebusites were the descendants of Canaan, the son of Ham (Gen. 10:16). The Ammonites were the descendants of Ben-ammi, the son of an incestuous relationship between Lot and his younger daughter. The Moabites were the descendants of Moab, the son of an incestuous relationship between Lot and his older daughter. The Egyptians may be the descendants of Ham, the son of Noah. The land of Egypt is sometimes identified as the land of Ham in the Old Testament (Ps. 78:51; 105:23, 27; 106:22). The Amorites were the descendants of Canaan, the son of Ham (Gen. 10:16).

Deuteronomy 7:1-4 is a passage which relates directly to Ezra 9:1-2. The various people groups mentioned in both passages are the Hittites, Amorites, Canaanites, Perizzites, and Jebusites. The command of Deuteronomy 7:1 is specifically addressed against the nations which at that time occupied the land of Israel. Since the current situation involved other foreign groups living in the land of Israel, Ezra is correct in broadening the scope of the original command to include these other nations as well. Deuteronomy 7:2-3 explicitly forbids any relationship with these nations, "you shall make no covenant with them and show no favor to them. Furthermore, you shall not intermarry with them; you shall not give your daughters to their sons, nor shall you take their daughters for your sons." The reason given by the Lord; "For they will turn your sons away from following Me to serve other gods; then the anger of the Lord will be kindled against you, and He will quickly destroy you" (Deut. 7:4). The nation had originally been sent into exile for precisely this reason. They could be removed from their land yet again.

Ezra is understandably appalled by the tragic news. He tears his clothes, pulls out some of his hair, and collapses on the ground. Ezra then sits down in a public place where the nation could see his grief. Ezra is quickly joined by those who realized that the remnant was in danger of suffering the judgment of God. Ezra remains in a state of mourning until the time of the evening sacrifices (about 3:00 pm).

At about 3:00 pm, Ezra rose from his sitting state and fell on his knees, stretching out his hands to the Lord in prayer. The scribe begins his prayer with a statement of humiliation. Ezra is humiliated because of the sins of his people. Confession of sin is the major theme of this prayer. Ezra's feelings of solidarity with his people come through in his use of the first person throughout this prayer. Even though he had not personally committed the specific sin he is praying about, he still identifies himself with the remnant as a whole (e.g., "our iniquities," "our guilt").

Even though the nation had proved unfaithful to Him, the Lord still proved faithful to His covenants. He had chosen to show mercy to His people for a "brief moment" by leaving an "escaped remnant" (9:8). The "brief moment" spoken of by Ezra is a reference to the eighty years since the decree of Cyrus allowing the Jews to return to their land (538-458 B.C.). The Jews who returned are the "escaped remnant." They had escaped from their exile. Ezra illustrates the phrase "escaped remnant" by calling them a "peg in His holy place"

(9:8). The phrase "holy place" is a reference to the land of Judah as a whole, and perhaps Jerusalem in particular. The word "peg" literally means "tent peg" or "stake." The word has its roots in nomadic life and refers to a place reached after a long journey where a tent is pitched.[24] The word is used figuratively in this passage and refers to the foothold achieved with the initial returns on the part of the remnant. Just as the erecting of a tent begins with a stake driven into the ground, so the rebuilding of the nation of Israel is seen to begin with the "escaped remnant" serving as the initial foothold.

Ezra next goes into more detail concerning his reference to the nation's bondage. He maintains that the Jews are still in slavery, that is, subservient to another nation. Instead of requesting the Lord's mercy, Ezra admits the failure of his people. He acknowledges that they have forsaken the commandments of the Lord that had been revealed through His prophets.

Even though God had severely punished the Jews, He had not completely destroyed them. Ezra acknowledges that the Lord had every right to destroy His people and credits Him with showing mercy. The Lord had left a remnant, a group of Jews who were able to escape the judgment of the Lord by returning from exile. Now this remnant was in danger of repeating the sins of their ancestors. Ezra realizes that the repetition of this great sin would endanger the very life of the nation. God might completely destroy His people this time just as He had threatened to do with the generation that bowed before the golden calf (Ex. 32:10). Ezra closes his prayer with another statement of confession before the Lord.

While Ezra was praying the prayer of 9:6-15, a sizable portion of the Jewish remnant gathered to him. The crowd was made up of men, women, and children. These people were not curious onlookers; they were convicted by Ezra's spiritual mourning and wept bitterly. A man named Shecaniah speaks on behalf of the remnant. The length of Shecaniah's genealogy provided in the text indicates that he was a person of some importance, certainly to be identified among the leading men of the remnant (cf. 9:1).

Shecaniah begins his speech to Ezra by confessing the sins of the people. He admits to the fact that the remnant was being unfaithful to Yahweh by marrying foreign women. Even though the nation has sinned against God, hope is not lost. The nation can repent of their behavior and take steps to remove their offense. Shecaniah realizes that God might refrain from judging the nation if they repent and change their ways (cf. Joel 2:12-14; Jon. 3:9-10).

Shecaniah recommends that the remnant make a covenant with God to "put away" (10:3) all the foreign wives and their children. Shecaniah's recommendation advocates divorce, not separation. The word translated "put away" is the same word used in Deuteronomy 24:2 ("leaves") in the context of divorce. In the Ancient Near East mothers received custody of the children when they were divorced (cf. Gen. 21:14). In effect, the Jewish men were divorcing both their foreign wives and the offspring created by their unholy union. These marriages were viewed as sinful in the eyes of God. Nehemiah writes, "You have committed all this great evil by acting unfaithfully against our God by marrying foreign women" (Neh. 13:27).

Shecaniah ends his speech by informing Ezra that the spiritual condition of the nation is his responsibility. He calls on Ezra to take steps to rectify the problem, promising the scribe that the people will be behind him. The urgency of Shecaniah's plea is reflected in the force of the imperatives. He calls on Ezra to "arise!," "be courageous!," and "act!" (10:4).

Upon hearing the words of Shecaniah, Ezra rose from his knees. He made the elders of the Jews take an oath that they would follow the advice of Shecaniah. Oath taking was customary in the Ancient Near East (cf. Josh. 6:26; Jud. 21:5; Neh. 6:18). Ezra next goes to the chamber of Jehohanan. This chamber would have been one of the many rooms in the temple (cf. 8:29). It is unknown why Ezra went to this chamber. Perhaps he wanted to enlist the support of Jehohanan. It is also possible that he wanted to confer with one of the religious leaders of the remnant before progressing with his plan.

While at the chamber of Jehohanan, Ezra continues mourning over the sins of his people. Together, Ezra, Jehohanan, and the leaders of the remnant make a proclamation calling on the exiles to assemble in Jerusalem. The proclamation allowed the exiles three days to make their way to Jerusalem. Judah was a very small territory at this time and Jerusalem could easily be reached within three days from any city in the region. The proclamation included a promise of harsh judgment on all those who were unwilling to come; their property will be confiscated and they will be excluded from the community. The authority given to Ezra by King Artaxerxes allowed him the opportunity to make this threat (cf. 7:26). The warning had the full backing of the Persian government.

The exiles respond positively to the decree of the Jewish leaders and assemble in Jerusalem three days after the proclamation was delivered. The assembly took place on the twentieth day of the ninth month (i.e., Chislev; late November and early December), 458 B.C. The exiles congregate in the open square in front of the temple. This square could accommodate thousands of people[25] and was probably the only place in the city large enough to hold this gathering. It should be remembered that most of the city still lay in ruins (cf. Neh. 1:3).

The text notes that the exiles sitting in the open square of the temple were trembling (10:9). Two reasons for this phenomenon are provided. First, the exiles were trembling because of the sheer magnitude of this matter. Clearly, they understood the significance of the occasion. Many of their lives were about to be forever changed. Many were going to lose wives and children. Perhaps even many feared for their lives, knowing that Ezra had the authority to put them to death (cf. 7:26). Second, the remnant was trembling because of the heavy rains. These rains would not only have been extremely heavy, but also bitterly cold. The crowd was thus experiencing both an internal emotional anxiety and an external physical distress.

As the masses huddle under the driving rain, Ezra rose to speak to the assembly. His speech was short but powerful. It is comprised of four key elements. First, the scribe accused the exiles of being unfaithful to the Lord by marrying foreign women. Second, Ezra explained that their personal sin had communal implications, it added to the guilt of the nation. The entire nation could be exiled as a result of the sins of a few. Third, the scribe called on the people to make confession to the Lord. Fourth and finally, Ezra commanded the remnant to do the will of God, namely, to separate from foreigners, especially the foreign wives.

The assembly responds favorably to the speech of Ezra. They cry out their approval with a loud voice. They recognize that it is their duty to follow the commands of God. The words of the congregation as a whole end with the close of verse twelve. It is likely that the words of verses thirteen and fourteen were spoken by a few representatives who realized the enormous challenges in undertaking this endeavor.

The representatives supply two reasons why the congregation cannot immediately follow the command of Ezra. First, the sheer volume of people involved in this sin meant that a certain amount of time was required to organize and investigate their cases. Second, the weather prevented immediate action. It was the middle of the winter rainy season and the exiles were forces to stand in the open. These conditions made a thorough investigation impractical at the present time. The reasons provided by the representatives should not be viewed as a way of circumventing the problem since they offer a solution in the very next verse.

The representatives suggest that the leaders represent the congregation. These leaders would be responsible for identifying the men in their community who had committed the sin of intermarriage. At appointed times these leaders would come to Jerusalem with the guilty parties for an investigative hearing. The presence of local leaders helped to ensure that the hearings were fair and balanced.

The congregation was almost unanimous in its agreement. Only Jonathan and Jahzeiah, supported by Meshullam and Shabbethai (Neh. 8:7; 11:16) are in opposition to the agreement. The question is, to what were they opposed; the decision to divorce the foreign women or the decision to take some time to carry out the decree? It would be unusual, though certainly not impossible, for the modifying exception clause "only . . . opposed this" (10:15) to occur so far after the original statement "all the assembly" (10:12). As a result, the second option is to be preferred. These four individuals should be seen as wanting to resolve the matter as quickly as possible. They evidently regarded the delay to be unnecessary.

Ezra selected leaders from each family who were responsible for identifying those members of their families who had participated in the sin of intermarriage. The list of these leaders is not provided, a somewhat peculiar oversight in a book noted for its fondness for lists. These leaders and the guilty parties would travel to Jerusalem to have their situation investigated by the national leadership who would then offer their decision. It can be assumed that there were probably some occasions where the accused were found to be innocent. The proceedings took three months, thus revealing how deeply this sin permeated the community. Assuming the list is complete, a total of 113 Jews had married foreign women.

The book closes with a list of those guilty of intermarriage (10:18-44). The list begins with a roster of religious leaders. The roster includes 16 priests and 10 Levites, together comprising almost one-fourth of the total. The priests are listed first, revealing that the sin reached even to the highest ranks of the spiritual leaders. In fact, the family of the high priest begins the list. The priests guilty of the sin of intermarriage made a pledge to put away their wives. The list continues with a roster of the laity who were guilty of intermarriage. There are no women included in this list. It is possible that no Jewish woman married a foreigner. However, the command of Nehemiah "you shall not give your daughters to their sons" (Neh. 13:25) given less than twenty years later indicates that the practice seems to have been at least known, if not common, in his day. It is more likely that the command did not apply to Jewish women since they were not permitted to divorce their husbands.

Nothing is said concerning what was done for the victims of these divorces. They would almost certainly have returned to the homes of their father. Perhaps they would remarry. Perhaps they would have lived as widows. Clearly, this would have been a traumatic situation for them and especially for their children. Although the actions of the Jews in this chapter might seem harsh to the modern reader, they were done to ensure the stability of the remnant. The book ends rather abruptly. As Brown notes, "The narrator seems to walk off stage with the last of the women and children, leaving the reader contemplating the significance of the final scene."[26]

Ezra's reforms did not last long. Nehemiah 13:23-28 reveals that the sin of intermarriage was present when Nehemiah returned from his trip to Babylon somewhere around 430 B.C., roughly thirty years after the reforms of Ezra. The practice seems to have been uncommon in New Testament times, perhaps due to the separatistic teachings of the Pharisees.

Study Questions

1. What does the name Ezra mean?
2. What are the two occupations of Ezra?
3. What were the primary duties of a scribe?
4. Which two prophets are instrumental in getting the remnant to rebuild the temple?
5. What empire is in control during the entire historical period described in the book of Ezra?
6. The return of Ezra took place during the reign of what king?
7. When was the book of Ezra written?
8. Why does Ezra use Aramaic instead of Hebrew in various portions of his book?
9. Which prophet predicted the rise of Cyrus by name?
10. What are the two options for reckoning Jeremiah's prediction of seventy years?
11. Why is the partnership between Jeshua and Zerubbabel so important?
12. On what day is the temple completed?
13. What is the Aramaic word meaning "dedication?"

CHAPTER 8

Nehemiah

"Then I said to them, 'You see the bad situation we are in, that Jerusalem is desolate and its gates burned by fire. Come; let us rebuild the wall of Jerusalem that we may no longer be a reproach.' And I told them how the hand of my God had been favorable to me, and also about the king's words which he had spoken to me. Then they said, 'Let us arise and build.' So they put their hands to the good work" (Neh. 2:17-18).

The book of Nehemiah records the final events, chronologically speaking, of the Old Testament. The walls of Jerusalem have lain in ruins for almost a century and a half (586-444 B.C.). The failure of the Jews to rebuild the city of Jerusalem became a source of great distress and reproach to the returned remnant. The situation caused great distress because the Jews who had returned to the city were vulnerable to attack from their enemies. The situation caused great reproach because it showed that the remnant lacked faith in their God. Perilous times call for great leaders. Nehemiah rose from among his countrymen to answer the need. He was not afraid of the power of mere mortals because he recognized the power of an omnipotent God.

Author

This book, like many others in the Old Testament (e.g., Jeremiah, Daniel, Habakkuk, etc.), receives its title from its author. The name Nehemiah means "Yahweh comforts" or "My comfort is Yahweh." He is identified as the son of Hacaliah. The origin and meaning of Hacaliah are unknown. It is probable that Nehemiah came from a prominent family as he alludes to his family's sepulchers in Jerusalem (2:3, 5). Nehemiah is a popular figure in extrabiblical literature. 2 Maccabees 1:18-36 records that Nehemiah was instrumental in the offering of a sacrifice of dedication during the Feast of Tabernacles. Sirach 49:13 also preserves his legacy, "The memory of Nehemiah also is lasting; he raised our fallen walls, and set up gates and bars, and rebuilt our ruined houses" (NRSV).

Although Nehemiah is never called a prophet nor is his work placed among the prophetic writings, his ministry nevertheless resembles that of the prophets. He declares to the people what God has revealed to him. He intercedes for his people and calls on them to return in faithfulness to the Mosaic covenant. He calls down imprecations on his enemies. He addresses social issues with the same vigor as the great eighth-century prophets. He even illustrates his message with a symbolic act (5:13). Finally, like many Old Testament prophets he was harassed by the deceitful message of a false prophet (6:10-14).

Nehemiah served as the official cupbearer of the Persian King Artaxerxes. The occupation of cupbearer in the Ancient Near Eastern court was of supreme importance. The cupbearer was often the single most trusted person in the empire as he was the individual with the most direct access to the king (apart from the king's family). As a result, he was the person most capable of carrying out a successful assassination. Xenophon writes, "It is a well known fact that the cupbearers, when they proffer the cup, draw off some of it with the ladle, pour it into their left hand, and swallow it down—so that, if they should put poison in, they may not profit by it" (*Cyropaedia* 1.3.9).

The cupbearer could also be quite influential in the king's decision making process. The cupbearer would serve as a sort of confidant to the king and therefore possessed great influence. Ancient documents clearly demonstrate the importance of the position of cupbearer. In Tobit, it is recorded that Sennacherib and Esarhaddon's cupbearer Ahikar had considerable influence in the Assyrian Empire, responsible for keeping the king's signet and in charge of various administrations (Tob. 1:22). Herodotus records that Cambyses did one of his friends a favor by appointing his son as cupbearer (*Histories* 3. 34). The fact that Nehemiah occupied this position in the Persian Empire demonstrates that he was already a person of impeccable character and consummate administrative skill. Yamauchi supplies the following list of traits which Nehemiah as a royal cupbearer would likely have possessed:

1. He would have been well trained in court etiquette (cf. Dan. 1:4-5).
2. He was probably a handsome individual (cf. Dan. 1:4, 13, 15).
3. He would certainly know how to select wines to set before the king. A proverb in the Babylonian Talmud (*Baba Qamma* 92b) states, "The wine belongs to the master but credit for it is due to his cupbearer."
4. He would have to be a convival companion to the king with a willingness to lend an ear at all times. Saki, the companion of Omar Khayyam, served wine to him and listened to his discourses.
5. He would be a man of great influence as one with the closest access to the king, and one who could well determine who could see the king.
6. Above all, Nehemiah had to be an individual who enjoyed the unreserved confidence of the king. The great need for trustworthy attendants is underscored by the intrigues which were endemic to the Achaemenid court.[1]

It is speculated by some scholars that Nehemiah was a eunuch.[2] Men in the king's service who came into contact with the king's harem were often eunuchs and Nehemiah certainly had frequent contact with the queen (cf. 2:6). Perhaps the strongest extra-biblical evidence that Nehemiah may have been a eunuch is the assertion of Ctesias that cupbearers were eunuchs in his day. Ctesias was a Greek physician at the court of Artaxerxes II (404–359 B.C.).[3] However, the biblical record does not explicitly identify Nehemiah as a eunuch, nor does it even allude to him as such. While it is possible that Nehemiah may have been a eunuch, any categorical statement that he was a eunuch is untenable.

Since the narrative is written in the first person, few direct statements about Nehemiah are recorded. Instead, Nehemiah's attributes are revealed through his words and actions. Many have observed the leadership skills possessed by Nehemiah. He is the consummate servant-leader.[4] Throughout the book, he is the faithful servant of not only Yahweh and King Artaxerxes, but also of the people he leads. Reynolds writes, "Nehemiah is a vastly different kind of leader. Unlike his predecessors before and after the exile, Nehemiah puts the welfare and benefit of the people before his own interests. Instead of taxing the people, he underwrites the government from his own resources. Nehemiah reverses the trend of spiritual depravity in government. He acknowledges his sinful state and recognizes the need for God's forgiveness. . . . There are limitations on what leadership alone can accomplish, but Nehemiah ends up being the difference between victory and defeat."[5] The following list of attributes reflects expository analysis of Nehemiah.[6]

1. He was a man of *service*, demonstrated by his exalted position as the king's cupbearer.
2. He was a man of *responsibility*, demonstrated by his appointment to the position of governor of Judah.
3. He was a man of *faith*, demonstrated by his wholehearted devotion to and utter trust in his God.
4. He was a man of *preparation*, demonstrated by his practice of planning, then acting.
5. He was a man of *prayer*, demonstrated by his consistent prayer life.
6. He was a man of *action*, demonstrated by his realization of what needed to be done and his willingness to do whatever it takes to see the mission accomplished.

7. He was a man of *cooperation*, demonstrated by his willingness to work with others.
8. He was a man of *discretion*, demonstrated by his inspection of the walls of the city at night.
9. He was a man of *delegation*, demonstrated by his willingness to delegate authority to those under him.
10. He was a man of *determination*, demonstrated by his unwillingness to let opposition deter him from fulfilling his objectives.
11. He was a man of *confidence*, demonstrated by his conviction that he was doing God's will.
12. He was a man of *compassion*, demonstrated by his heart for his people.
13. He was a man of *unselfishness*, demonstrated by his refusal to accept the governor's portion.
14. He was a man of *triumph*, demonstrated by his success over both physical adversaries (the opposition group) and material adversaries (walls of Jerusalem).
15. He was a man of *confrontation*, demonstrated by his earnestness in confronting sin and wrong-doing.
16. He was a man of *motivation*, demonstrated by his desire to serve God.
17. He was a man of *convictions*, demonstrated by his unwillingness to tolerate evil around him.
18. He was a man of *inspiration*, demonstrated by his ability to motivate others to serve God.
19. He was a man of *vision*, demonstrated by his focus on God's expectations rather than on man's limitations.
20. He was a man of *perseverance*, demonstrated by his ability to finish the task at hand.

The portrait of Nehemiah in this book is further developed through his relationship to his people and his God. Nehemiah's relationship with his people can be characterized as one of attachment.[7] Even though he is in a position of authority over the people by virtue of his appointment as governor; he consistently places himself among the people, feeling solidarity with the nation (cf. 2:17; 9:32,

36). He is driven to tears when he hears that the remnant is in trouble (1:4). He includes himself when he asks God to forgive the sins of the nation (1:6-7). He is quick to admit guilt when he views his own actions as adding to the suffering of the remnant (5:10). He includes himself when he lists the individuals who made the binding agreement in chapters 9 and 10. He intercedes on behalf of the nation before both God (1:6) and king (2:5). He rejects the food allotted to him as governor so as to not be a burden to the people (5:14-18). He views his labor as being performed on behalf of the people (5:19). And, perhaps most importantly, he consistently shows how the people aided him in the successful accomplishment of his mission (3:1-32; 9:38-10:29). In fact, Nehemiah takes excessive measures to show that the entire community was intimately involved in the projects for which he is given credit, providing extensive lists detailing many of these individuals by name. He even singles out with special commendation many minor characters that influence the outcome of the narrative in some manner (e.g., Hanani, Baruch, Shallum, Hananiah).

Nehemiah's relationship with his God can be characterized as one of servitude. Nehemiah clearly recognizes that he is God's servant (cf. 1:6, 11).[8] He willingly submits to God's authority in both the religious (e.g., confession of sin) and physical (e.g., request for success) realms. It is apparent that Nehemiah views himself as attempting to carry out the will of his God. By consistently asking God to assist him in the fulfillment of his missions, Nehemiah demonstrates that he believes that God desires for him to accomplish his goals. He is likewise exhibiting an attitude of humility and dependence upon God. He recognizes that he is not able to complete the mission by himself. He needs God's help. Nehemiah is, above all, a man of prayer. The text records twelve instances of prayers offered by Nehemiah (1:4, 5-11; 2:4; 4:4-5, 9; 5:19; 6:9, 14; 13:14, 22, 29, 31). When he is opposed in his efforts, he prays.[9] When he is successful in his accomplishments, he prays. With each step he takes, Nehemiah either requests the aid of God or thanks Him for aid already provided.

Ultimately, as with all biblical books, God is to be seen as the true author of the narrative. At this point, a word must be said about the portrait of God in this book. While many scholars have refrained from considering God as a main character in the book,[10] it is quite apparent that he deserves to be regarded as such.[11] Prayers are spoken to God twelve times in the book; descriptions about God are presented by several characters, including Nehemiah; God Himself speaks through the reading of His Law; and God's actions on behalf of His people are recorded (cf. 2:8). In the narrative, the primary function of God as a character is to aid the achievements of Nehemiah.

Because of God's sovereignty, it can be assumed that He is the one who governs all of the action that takes place in the narrative. It is God who chose Nehemiah to be the agent through whom He will restore the remnant. It is God who has elevated Nehemiah to be in a position to govern His people. It is God who has placed King Artaxerxes on the Persian throne and has granted him a heart sympathetic to the plight of the Jews. And it is God who will work to overcome those who oppose His will. In short, it is God who is the true hero of the story. The book of Nehemiah is essentially the story of how God uses Nehemiah to accomplish His sovereign plan for the people of Israel.

Date

The last historical event referred to in the book is the return of Nehemiah to Jerusalem following a period of time in the service of King Artaxerxes. The exact date of this return is unknown, although it must have been sometime after 432 B.C. (the date of Nehemiah's return to Persia referred to in 13:6, i.e., "the thirty-second year of Artaxerxes"). The wording of 13:6 ("during all this time I was not in Jerusalem") gives the impression that Nehemiah was in the service of King Artaxerxes for several years. The earliest possible date for Nehemiah's return to Jerusalem is 430 B.C. As a result, the book could not have been written prior to this date. A date around 425 B.C. cannot be too far off the mark.

Historical Background

The events of the book of Nehemiah take place between 445 B.C. and roughly 430 B.C. At this time, the Persians dominated world events as the Persian Empire was at its peak. The region of Judea was simply part of Trans-Euphrates, one of the satrapies in the Persian Empire. The Jews were not autonomous but were governed by the official representatives of the Persian kings. The fortunes of the Jews were dictated by the decisions of a foreign king living more than a thousand miles from Judah.

The Persian monarch throughout this entire period is Artaxerxes. Artaxerxes, whose name means "having a kingdom of justice," was the third son of Xerxes and Amestris, the Ahasueras and Vashti of the book of Esther. The reign of Xerxes ended when Artabanus, the captain of the royal bodyguard, assassinated him in early August 465 B.C. Artaxerxes managed to kill Artabanus and murder his older brother Darius, the rightful heir to the Persian throne. He then defeated his other brother Hystaspes in battle in the region of Bactria. Artaxerxes, whose first reignal year is reckoned from April 13, 464 B.C.,[12] enjoyed a rather lengthy reign, eventually dying of natural causes in 424 B.C.

As king of Persia, Artaxerxes ruled over the Persians. The Persians were an Indo-European tribe who entered the Iranian plateau about 1400 B.C. They systematically grew in size and power over the next eight hundred years. Cyrus is regarded as the founder of the Persian Empire in power during the time of Nehemiah. The various kings of this vast empire were known as Achaemenians, after an eponymous ancestor, Achaemenes (c. 700 B.C.).[13] From the reign of Cyrus until the time of Alexander the Great, the Achaemenians were able to build one of the largest and most successful of all ancient empires. At its peak, the empire stretched from the Hellespont in the northwest and the Nile in the southwest to the Indus in the east.[14] Economically speaking, the Persian Empire was largely made up of nomadic pastoralists.[15]

The events of the narrative take place in two significant cities, Susa and Jerusalem. The city of Susa (Hebrew *shushan*, meaning "lily") took its name from the abundance of lilies which grew in its neighborhood. It was located on the Karkheh about 150 miles north of the Persian Gulf. It became a part of the Achaemenid Empire when Cyrus took Babylon and its provinces. It quickly became the winter capital of the Persian Empire, the summer capital being located at Persepolis. Nehemiah served in the royal palace in Susa as the king's cupbearer and the city is the setting for the events of Nehemiah 1:1-2:8. One should be sure to note that the king of Persia lived a considerable distance from the setting of the events of the rest of the book. When Nehemiah journeys to Jerusalem, he is somewhat separated from his benefactor. The governing authorities in the regions surrounding Jerusalem were the primary adversaries of Nehemiah. Because of the distance between them, Nehemiah never has the chance to appeal to King Artaxerxes for further aid.

The city of Jerusalem ("city of peace") is located fourteen miles west of the Dead Sea and thirty-three miles east of the Mediterranean Sea. The city is situated on a rocky plateau 2,550 feet above sea level. It was centrally located in Israel and made an ideal capital. The city of Jerusalem had been conquered by the Israelites by the time of the Judges (c. 1350 B.C.); however, it does not seem to have been occupied by the Hebrews (cf. Judg. 1:8). It is not until King David (1011-971 B.C.) conquers the city and builds himself a palace there that Jerusalem is made the political capital of the nation (2 Sam. 5:6-12). It shortly became the religious capital of the nation as well with the building of the majestic Solomonic temple in 966 B.C. From this point forward, the city of Jerusalem occupied a place of prominence in the political and religious life of the nation.

The city of Jerusalem occupies a central role in Nehemiah's narrative as it is the city around which the walls were being built.[16] Whoever was able to secure control of this central strategic city in essence controlled the land of Israel (and some of the surrounding regions as well). At the time of Nehemiah the size of the Judean province was less than nine hundred square miles,[17] an area easily controlled by a formidable central city. That is why there was such opposition to the rebuilding of the walls of the city on the part of the foreigners living in the land. If the Jews were able to secure this central fortress by raising its walls, then the Jews would once again dominate the land of Israel. If the Jews were not able to restore the walls around the city they would be relatively powerless to resist an enemy's attack against them. Fensham elaborates, "the temple of Jerusalem could be destroyed easily by the enemies, because no proper stand could be made against enemies without a defense wall. After a hundred and forty years Jerusalem and its inhabitants, the Jews, were still easy prey for any enemy who wanted to attack them."[18]

Audience and Purpose

The book was written to the Jews of the postexilic community living in the region of Judea in the mid fifth century B.C. The ancestors of these Jews had returned with Sheshbazzar in 538 B.C. It was now more than a hundred years since that original return. Even though the temple had been rebuilt in 515 B.C., little had been accomplished since that time. A good portion of the recipients had returned with Ezra in 458 B.C. While Ezra was instrumental in the effort to restore the proper worship of Yahweh, the story of Ezra is one of unfinished business. The Jewish remnant had begun the task of rebuilding the walls of the city only to halt the work when opposition arose. The nation's resolve to separate from their ungodly neighbors quickly faded. Nehemiah reveals that the remnant's practice of intermingling with foreigners continued in his day. Both the new returnees and the descendants of the original returnees were in need of restoration.

The only hope for the nation lay in the fact that God had promised to bless them if they were obedient to His commands. The formula had been provided in Deuteronomy 30:1-10. This passage promises the restoration of the nation following their exile. However, these promises were conditional upon the obedience of the nation. The Lord would cause them to prosper only if the nation obeyed His commandments and statutes and turned to the Lord with all their heart and soul (Deut. 30:10). The clear implication of the passage is that the nation would not be blessed if they were disobedient. In fact, they were in danger of being cursed yet again (cf. Ezra 9:14). The doctrine of retribution that was originally announced in Leviticus 26 and Deuteronomy 28 was still in effect.

The portrait of Yahweh as a God of retribution is developed in Nehemiah largely through the prayers recorded throughout the narrative. Nehemiah assumes that he will be rewarded by God as a result of his good works (cf. 5:19; 13:14, 22) while those who oppose him will be punished by God for their evil works (cf. 4:4-5; 6:14; 13:29).

This portrait of God is further developed through an analysis of His own words. In 1:8-9, God speaks of Himself as a God of retribution, declaring that He will scatter the people among the nations if they are unfaithful. God further promises, however, to restore the people to the land of their ancestors if they repent. God also indicates His love for the city of Jerusalem in verse 9 by describing it as the place He has chosen as a dwelling for His name.

The task for the remnant is obvious; they must be obedient to the commands of the Lord to achieve full restoration. As is His custom (e.g., Moses, David, Josiah, Ezra, etc.), the Lord raises up a significant leader to motivate the reluctant nation. Even though the people aid Nehemiah throughout the narrative, it is often only at the rebuke or encouragement of their leader (cf. 2:17; 5:1-13; 13:1-29). They do not seem to have been able to make any progress, physically or spiritually, before the arrival of Nehemiah in the land. They are characterized from the very first scene as in "great trouble" and "disgrace." The leadership of Nehemiah is instrumental in motivating the nation to rebuild the walls of their city, thereby achieving a sort of political restoration for the Jews. However, the task of Nehemiah is not yet complete. To achieve full restoration, the nation needs to institute reforms necessary to achieve spiritual restoration.

Recognizing the holiness of God through the preaching of Ezra and the forceful leadership of Nehemiah, the nation takes steps to purify themselves from the pollution of foreigners (cf. 10:29ff.; 13:1-3, 23-27). The nation's intermarriage with foreign women had already resulted in the exile from which they had recently returned. One of the conditions necessary to avoid future punishment was the separation of themselves from the nations which surrounded them. By the end of the book, the people have taken these steps and are seen as worshipping God and celebrating their spiritual restoration. However, the final chapter of the book clearly shows that this spiritual restoration was not without occasional apostasy. Therefore, the open-ended conclusion of the book serves as a reminder to each subsequent generation to take the same measures of purification in an attempt to maintain spiritual holiness[19] and to gain the favor and blessing of God.

Structure and Outline

There is considerable debate concerning the original boundaries of the book of Nehemiah. Nehemiah's extensive similarities to Ezra have called into question its independence from that book, thus leading many scholars to regard the two books as one unified work. The problem is exacerbated by the fact that the two books are preserved in the Masoretic Text as a single book (for a full discussion of the relationship between the books of Ezra and Nehemiah, see Appendix Two). Furthermore, the collective similarities between the books of Ezra and Nehemiah and the book of Chronicles have led many scholars to incorporate all three books into a single unified work attributed to the "Chronicler" (for a full discussion of the relationship between the books of Chronicles, Ezra, and Nehemiah, see Appendix One). However, an examination of the evidence leads to the conclusion that Nehemiah was originally an independent work and will be treated as such in this analysis.

The book of Nehemiah is naturally divided into four sections. The first section announces the mission of Nehemiah (1:1-2:20). The second section describes the rebuilding of the walls of Jerusalem (3:1-7:3). The third section details the efforts of Nehemiah to restore the remnant spiritually (7:4-13:3). The fourth section is an account of the final reforms of Nehemiah (13:4-31). The events of 1:1-13:3 take place between 445-444 B.C. The events described in the final section of the book take place within a few years of 430 B.C.

The book of Nehemiah is noted for its extensive use of lists. The more noteworthy lists include the following: 3:1-32 is a record of those who helped Nehemiah rebuild the walls of Jerusalem; 7:4-73a is a roster of those who returned to Jerusalem following the decree of Cyrus in 538 B.C.; 10:1-27 is a list of those who signed the document of commitment; 11:3-24 is a register of those families who lived in Jerusalem; 11:25-36 is a record of those families who lived on their ancestral properties; and 12:1-26 is a roster of those families responsible for the spiritual leadership of the nation from the time of Zerubbabel's return until the time of Nehemiah.

<u>Outline</u>
I. The Mission of Nehemiah (1:1-2:20)
    A. The Report of Hanani (1:1-3)
        1. Nehemiah's Introduction (1:1)
        2. Nehemiah's Question (1:2)
        3. Hanani's Response (1:3)
    B. The Response of Nehemiah (1:4-11)
        1. Nehemiah Mourns (1:4)
        2. Nehemiah Prays (1:5-11)
    C. The Request of Nehemiah (2:1-8)
        1. Nehemiah Serves the King (2:1)
        2. The Initial Question of Artaxerxes (2:2)
        3. The Response of Nehemiah (2:3)
        4. The Continued Conversation (2:4-8)
    D. Nehemiah Arrives in Jerusalem (2:9-20)
        1. The Journey to Jerusalem (2:9-11)
        2. Nehemiah's Secret Inspection of the Walls (2:12-16)
        3. The Jews Agree to Rebuild the Walls (2:17-20)
II. The Rebuilding of the Walls (3:1-7:3)
    A. The Roster of the Rebuilders (3:1-32)
    B. The Opposition Group Mocks the Rebuilders (4:1-6)
        1. The Taunts of Sanballat and Tobiah (4:1-3)
        2. The Response of Nehemiah (4:4-6)
    C. The Opposition Group Threatens the Rebuilders (4:7-23)
        1. The Plan of the Opposition Group (4:7-8)
        2. The Response of Nehemiah (4:9-14)
        3. The Plan of Nehemiah (4:15-23)
    D. An Internal Problem (5:1-19)
        1. A Conflict Among the Rebuilders (5:1-5)
        2. Nehemiah's Response to the Conflict (5:6-13)
        3. Nehemiah's Example (5:14-19)
    E. The Completion of the Project (6:1-7:3)
        1. The Conspiracy Against Nehemiah (6:1-14)
        2. The Completion of the Walls (6:15-19)
        3. The Watch Over Jerusalem (7:1-3)
III. The Rebuilding of the People (7:4-13:3)
    A. The Roster of the Returnees (7:4-73a)

1. The Introduction to the List (7:4-5)
2. The Contents of the List (7:6)
3. The Leaders of the Return (7:7a)
4. The List of Those with Proof of Ancestry (7:7b-60)
5. The List of Those without Proof of Ancestry (7:61-65)
6. The Sum Total of Returnees (7:66-69)
7. The People Return to Their Cities (7:70-73a)

B. The Public Reading of the Law (7:73b-8:18)
1. The Ministry of Ezra (7:73b-8:8)
2. The Holiness of the Day (8:9-12)
3. The Remnant Celebrates the Feast of Tabernacles (8:13-18)

C. The Nation's Response (9:1-37)
1. The Nation's Repentance (9:1-4)
2. The Penitential Psalm (9:5-37)

D. The Nation's Commitment (9:38-10:39)
1. The List of Signatures (9:38-10:27)
2. The Nation Takes an Oath (10:28-29)
3. The Stipulations of the Covenant (10:30-39)

E. The Nation's Resettlement (11:1-12:26)
1. The Repopulation of Jerusalem (11:1-2)
2. The List of Those Living in Jerusalem (11:3-24)
3. The Cities Inhabited by the Remnant (11:25-36)
4. The Religious Leaders (12:1-26)

F. The Dedication of the Walls (12:27-13:3)
1. The Preparations (12:27-30)
2. The Twin Processions (12:31-39)
3. The Celebration at the Temple (12:40-43)
4. The Provisions for the Religious Leaders (12:44-47)
5. The Exclusion of Foreigners (13:1-3)

IV. Nehemiah's Final Reforms (13:4-31)
A. The Reform of the Temple (13:4-14)
B. The Reform of the Sabbath (13:15-22)
C. The Reform of Marriage (13:23-31)

Summary of Contents

The Mission of Nehemiah (1:1-2:20)

The book of Nehemiah begins with "The words of Nehemiah." While this assertion of authorship is quite unique in Hebrew narrative literature, it is common in Hebrew prophetic literature (cf. "The words of Jeremiah" and "The words of Amos").[20] Since what follows in the book is identified as the very words of Nehemiah, the reader immediately understands that this is a first person account told from the point of view of an eye-witness. While the use of the first person is common in Hebrew prophetic literature (cf. Jeremiah, Ezekiel, Habakkuk), it is quite peculiar in Old Testament historical narrative. In fact, Nehemiah is the only historical book written primarily in the first person (there are some portions of Ezra written in the first person).

The historical setting of the events contained in the book is also supplied in the first verse. The time frame mentioned is "in the month Chislev in the twentieth year." It is not until 2:1 that the reader is informed that the twentieth year refers to the reign of King Artaxerxes. King Artaxerxes was a Persian king who reigned from 464 to 424 B.C. Therefore, the twentieth year of his reign was early 445 – early 444 B.C.

The month of Chislev (late November and early December, 445 B.C.) was the beginning of winter according to the Jewish calendar. Nehemiah was living in the king's palace in Susa, the winter capital of the Persian Empire. The summer capital of King Artaxerxes was located at Persepolis. Xenophon records that the Persian kings routinely shifted their dwelling places with the change of seasons (*Cyropaedia* 8.6.22). Susa was brutally oppressive during the summer months with temperatures commonly reaching 140 degrees Fahrenheit. Strabo notes that snakes and lizards crossing the street at noon in the summer heat were roasted to death (15.3.10).

Nehemiah is approached in Susa by Hanani, one of his brothers,[21] who had just returned from a trip to Judah.[22] Nehemiah immediately questions his brother concerning the welfare of the Jewish remnant residing in Judah and the condition of the city of Jerusalem. These questions reveal the main interests of Nehemiah, and consequently, the main interests of his book. The rest of the narrative centers around the steps Nehemiah takes to resolve the problems brought to light in Hanani's response to Nehemiah's inquiries.

Hanani's response is that the Jewish remnant which remained in the land of Judah is presently in "great distress" and "reproach" (1:3). The reference to the remnant being in "great distress" most likely refers to the remnant's social and economic situation while the use of the term "reproach" announces the spiritual condition of the people. The nation's social situation is in distress because of the continual oppression of the foreign neighbors (cf. Ezra 4:7-23). The nation's economic situation is in distress because of the heavy tax burden placed upon the remnant by the Persians (cf. 5:1-5). The nation's spiritual condition was in reproach because of their failure to fully separate from the foreign nations (cf. Ezra 9:10-14).

Hanani goes on to add that the wall which surrounded the city of Jerusalem is broken down and its gates are burned with fire. With the walls of Jerusalem in a state of ruin, its inhabitants were completely defenseless. Any significant attack by the enemies of the Jews would surely be successful. The temple rebuilt by Zerubbabel could be destroyed at any time. Nehemiah's task is immediately apparent. He must take steps to restore the remnant, both politically and spiritually, and rebuild the walls of Jerusalem.

Nehemiah is utterly devastated by the report of Hanani. He immediately sits down and begins to pray. Sitting down seems to have been a customary posture during mourning and fasting (cf. Job 2:8, 13). For several days Nehemiah mourns, fasts, and prays to his God. It is probable that Nehemiah's mourning went on for four months until the events of chapter two take place. This intense and emotional reaction betrays the compassionate feelings Nehemiah holds for his disgraced people and his beleaguered homeland.

In 1:5-11a Nehemiah supplies a sample of one of the prayers he offered to God. This is the first of twelve prayers recorded in the book and introduces a major theme of the book, that is, the need for God's help in the restoration project. Nehemiah realizes that the people cannot accomplish the task on their own; they need God's help. Note the use of the Hebrew word *gadol* ("great") in this scene. The "great" affliction announced in verse three can only be overcome by a "great" God (1:5) with "great" strength (1:10). Nehemiah realizes that he and the other faithful Jews are only acting as God's servants (the word "servant" appears eight times in this prayer, either in reference to Nehemiah himself, Moses, or the people of Israel in general) as God uses them to accomplish His task. In fact, the project is even portrayed as accomplishing the very will of God. Essentially, it is God who is rebuilding the city and the remnant by means of His agent Nehemiah.

The prayer begins with words of adoration extolling the greatness of God. Nehemiah identifies God with His proper name Yahweh ("LORD"). The Lord is described as "great" and "awesome" (1:5). Nehemiah uses these same words to describe God in 4:14 and 9:32. They were originally used to describe the Lord in Deuteronomy 7:21. God is characterized as one "who preserves the covenant and lovingkindness for those who love Him and keep His commandments" (1:5). This is an obvious reference back to Exodus 20:6, a verse which serves as the introduction to the Ten Commandments.

Confession of the sins of the people is next offered to God. If Nehemiah expects God to restore the political and spiritual condition of the remnant, he knows that the people need to be repentant (cf. 2 Chron. 7:14). Nehemiah takes care to include himself among those who have sinned against the Lord (note the use of the first person throughout the prayer). He maintains a strong feeling of solidarity with his people even though he is living in a foreign land. The result of these sins was evident, the people of Israel had been scattered among the nations, just as the Lord had predicted (cf. Deut. 28).

Having offered words of adoration to God and confession of the sins of the nation, Nehemiah now moves to remind the Lord of His previous acts of kindness for His chosen people. The Lord demonstrated His continued love of the nation by His redemption of them from the land of Babylon. The phrases "great power" and "strong hand" in 1:10 are a quotation of Exodus 32:11 in reference to the Lord's redemption of the nation from Egypt. Just as the Lord demonstrated His love for the generation of Moses through His redemption of them from out of bondage in Egypt, so He had demonstrated His love for the current generation through His redemption of them from out of bondage in Babylon.

Nehemiah closes his prayer by asking the Lord to grant one more request. He asks that he might be granted a favorable response from "this man" (1:11) as he approaches him with a request. The scene closes with a brief statement of Nehemiah's occupation. The statement is placed here to explain the final sentence of Nehemiah's prayer. The phrase not only explains the identity of the man referred to in the verse, the king, but also the means by which Nehemiah has access to that man, that is, by virtue of his duties as the king's cupbearer.

The events of 2:1-8 take place in the month of Nisan (late March and early April, 444 B.C.), four months after the events of chapter one. The month of Nisan is the time of early spring, a good time to travel. The winter is now over and the king is likely preparing to return to Persepolis, the summer capital of the Persian Empire. The name of the king alluded to at the end of chapter one is now revealed; it is Artaxerxes. Artaxerxes, whose name means "having a kingdom of justice," was the third son of Xerxes and Amestris, the Ahasuerus and Vashti of the book of Esther.

Artaxerxes noticed[23] a change in Nehemiah as he was being served by his cupbearer. Evidently the spiritual activities undertaken by Nehemiah over the past few months (mourning, fasting, and praying) had begun to take their toll on Nehemiah physically. The king, perceiving that Nehemiah's physical condition is not due to illness, comes to the realization that something is weighing heavily on Nehemiah's mind and questions him concerning his appearance.

Nehemiah responds to the king's question by explaining that his sad countenance results from his knowledge of the ruined state of the city of Jerusalem. Although Nehemiah does not identify the city he is referring to, it seems apparent that Artaxerxes is aware that the city is Jerusalem. One of the reasons Jerusalem is so important to Nehemiah is because it is the place where his ancestors are buried. Nehemiah mentions this fact in verse three and again in verse five.

King Artaxerxes immediately questions Nehemiah as to what he wishes to do concerning the situation. Nehemiah responds, after a brief prayer to his God, by asking for time away from his duties so that he can journey to Jerusalem and rebuild its walls. The king then asks how long he will be gone. Artaxerxes, being fond of his cupbearer, did not want to lose him for too long. Nehemiah responds by setting an exact time for his return. Since Nehemiah returns to Susa after twelve years in Jerusalem it can be assumed that Nehemiah requested a twelve year leave of absence (cf. 5:14; 13:6).

Nehemiah further asks King Artaxerxes for political aid. He requests letters from King Artaxerxes to give to the governors of the territories through which he is going to pass so that they will provide him with security throughout his journey. Some of these governors are the very same individuals who will attempt to thwart him when he reaches Jerusalem. It is likely that Nehemiah anticipates their resistance and takes steps to hinder their efforts even before they know he is coming.

Nehemiah also asks for timber to be supplied for the rebuilding project. The name of the keeper of the forest is Asaph. The forest alluded to here is probably Solomon's Garden at Etham, about six miles south of Jerusalem, though some have placed it in Lebanon, a region famed for its forests of cedars. King Cyrus had previously allowed for the import of cedars from Lebanon to rebuild the temple (Ezra 3:7). However, the relative cost of importing the cedars from Lebanon, especially for the task of building city walls, makes this alternative unlikely.

Nehemiah plans to use this timber for three projects. First, the gates of the fortress needed to be made of timber to allow easy access into the city. Stone gates would be much too heavy to open and close on a regular basis. Second, the wall of the city needed to be reinforced with timber. While it is likely that most of the city wall was made of stone and brick, wood was needed for placement and support. Third, Nehemiah's own house, the governor's mansion, was to be made of wood.

The king, moved by God, responds favorably to Nehemiah's solicitation and agrees to grant him his requests. Having requested God's help in the opening chapter of the narrative, Nehemiah immediately gives God the credit for the favorable response on the part of King Artaxerxes. The date of Artaxerxes' decree allowing Nehemiah to return to Jerusalem to rebuild the city takes on great eschatological significance when Daniel uses this event to begin his prophetic timetable of seventy "weeks" in Daniel 9:24-27.[24]

The scene of 2:9-20 begins rather abruptly with Nehemiah approaching the governors of the Trans-Euphrates to show them the king's letters. These letters greatly disturbed the governors because they essentially gave Nehemiah a certain amount of authority in an area over which they presently governed. It is apparent that quite some time had passed between verses eight and nine, at least enough for Nehemiah to gather supplies and make the long journey from Susa to Jerusalem. Nehemiah mentions that the king had sent army officers and cavalry with him. This military escort assured Nehemiah a safe journey to his homeland. It is likely that the military escort provided by Artaxerxes returned to Susa immediately after bringing Nehemiah to Jerusalem.

The governors named here are the leaders of a force that will cause great opposition to Nehemiah in his quest to rebuild Jerusalem. This opposition force rarely appears as single individuals in the narrative; instead they are routinely referenced in pairs or groups. Two of these governors are introduced in 2:10 while another is introduced in 2:19. Those identified are Sanballat the Samaritan,[25] Tobiah the Ammonite,[26] and Geshem the Arab.[27] Each of these individuals is evidently the governor of their respective region (cf. 2:9-10). Together, these three governors represent the nations surrounding Jerusalem and the territory of Judah on all three sides (Samaria to the north, Ammon to the east, and Arabia to the south; the Mediterranean Sea borders Judah to the west).

After spending three days in Jerusalem, Nehemiah decides to inspect the walls of the city. During the middle of the night, Nehemiah and a few others secretly went out the Valley gate and began to circumnavigate the city, inspecting the walls and gates. The animal on which Nehemiah is riding is either a horse or a donkey. A donkey is more probable since it is quieter than a horse. Those who accompany him were likely residents of Jerusalem who knew the way around the city. They may also have been guards responsible for Nehemiah's safety. Eventually, the route became impassable and Nehemiah is forced to turn around and reenter the city.

At some point subsequent to his return from the night inspection of the city's defenses, Nehemiah gathered the Jews around him and urged them to help him rebuild the fallen walls. The time of this event is probably the morning after the inspection. The people had evidently become complacent toward their defenseless position, having lived among the ruins since they arrived in Jerusalem. It took an outsider to assess the situation and rally the people.

For the first time, Nehemiah informs the people of the purpose of his visit. His goal is to rebuild the walls of Jerusalem. This is not simply the goal of Nehemiah. He has already informed the reader in 2:12 that God had put it into his mind to rebuild the city. This key verse announces the initial stage of Nehemiah's mission, that is, the physical restoration of the nation.

Nehemiah is able to translate this vision to the remnant. Nehemiah inspires the people by informing them of the assistance he has received from God and Artaxerxes. There was now no good reason, spiritually or politically, that the people could use to resist participating in the rebuilding effort. As a result, the people catch Nehemiah's vision and respond favorably to his request, promptly beginning to work on the walls of the city. The governors of the region are not quite so helpful, responding to the nation's efforts by hurling insults and questioning the legitimacy of the project. This is the first confrontation between Nehemiah and members of the opposition group. It certainly won't be the last.

It is interesting to note that the leaders of the opposition group question whether Nehemiah is guilty of treason against the king when in fact they themselves are guilty of treason by blocking Nehemiah's efforts to rebuild the wall. The leaders of the opposition are fully aware that Nehemiah is acting with the king's authority (cf. 2:9). Instead of using the power granted him by appealing to the authority of King Artaxerxes, Nehemiah answers the antagonists by stating his confidence that God will give them success. Nehemiah realizes that ultimately it is God who has authority over the city of Jerusalem. Recognizing that God has promised the city to the Jews, he confidently informs the opposition force that they have "no portion, right, or memorial in Jerusalem." This move continued the policy instituted by Zerubbabel (Ezra 4:3) of not allowing foreigners to help rebuild Jerusalem. Throughout the prophets, the Lord consistently promised that Jerusalem will be inhabited by the Jews, not by foreigners (cf. Joel 3:17; Zech. 14:16-21).

The Rebuilding of the Walls (3:1-7:3)

The second major section of the book begins with a list of those individuals responsible for helping him rebuild the walls of the city (3:1-32). Each family in the city who volunteered to help with the restoration project is mentioned by name as well as the section they were responsible for repairing. The list is a parenthesis in the narrative and, as such, seems to be of some significance to the narrator. This list demonstrates the joyful willingness of the people in helping Nehemiah in his task. Nehemiah is clearly emphasizing the work of the remnant since he is never once mentioned in the chapter.

The description of the rebuilding begins at the northeast corner of the wall and moves around the city in a counter-clockwise direction. Verses 1-5 describe the work performed on the north wall. Verses 6-13 describe the work performed on the west wall. Verses 14-15 describe the work performed on the south wall. Verses 16-31 describe the work performed on the east wall. Verse 32 closes the section by describing the work performed on the eastern stretch of the north wall.

The description centers on the ten gates allowing entrance into the city. The ten gates surrounding the city were the Sheep Gate, the Fish Gate, the Old Gate (Jeshanah Gate), the Valley Gate, the Refuse Gate (Dung Gate), the Fountain Gate, the Water Gate, the Horse Gate, the East Gate and the Inspection Gate. These would have been the most important segments of the project since the gates were routinely the most vulnerable sections of ancient walls.

The Hebrew word *banah* ("build") occurs seven times in this scene while the Hebrew word *hazaq* ("repair") occurs thirty-four times. In places the wall needed to be built from the ground up while in other places repairs needed to be made to the existing wall. The people were making good on their promise to rebuild the walls referenced in the previous scene (2:18). According to recent excavations, Nehemiah's wall was roughly eight feet thick.

There is some question as to the exact location and extent of the wall that Nehemiah built. While the location of some of the towers and gates is clear, others are not so obvious. The question largely revolves around whether or not the wall enclosed the southwest hill commonly called "Mount Zion." Those who hold that the hill was located within the walls are called "maximalists"[28] while those who hold that the hill was outside the walls are called "minimalists."[29] According to the maximalist position, the walls would have been two and one-half miles long and enclosed about 220 acres. According to the minimalist position, the walls would have been close to two miles long and enclosed about 90 acres. Because the various gates mentioned by Nehemiah seem to incorporate Zion, it seems better to take the maximalist position. Regardless of the position held, this chapter is widely recognized as crucial for determining the topography of Jerusalem in the Old Testament.

When Sanballat hears that the Jews have begun rebuilding the wall he becomes "furious" and "very angry." Sanballat's emotions have escalated from displeasure in 2:10 to infuriation in 4:1. Sanballat appears every time the opposition group plays a role in the story and is always identified first when they are listed by name. He is thus to be seen as the leader of those opposed to the project.

The opposition group, headed by Sanballat and Tobiah, again resorts to hurling insults and mocking the work of the Jews (cf. 2:19). Sanballat and Tobiah ask a total of five rhetorical questions in 4:2, each designed to ridicule the efforts of the Jews. The first question is designed to ridicule the worth of the Jews themselves, "What are these feeble Jews doing?" The adjective used here is commonly used in the Old Testament to indicate the withering and decaying of a plant (cf. Isa. 16:8; 24:7). It is sometimes used of people as is the case in this verse (cf. Isa. 19:8; Hos. 4:3). The sense here then is that the Jews are described as a dying people group, one that is languishing or in the last days of its existence. The second question, "Are they going to restore it for themselves?" is better rendered "Will they fortify themselves?" (cf. NKJV). This question parallels the first question and again demeans the Jews as a group. The sense would be to mock the ability of the Jewish remnant to defend themselves; the implication being that others would be needed to protect them.

The third question, "Can they offer sacrifices?" is somewhat enigmatic. The temple has been rebuilt and the sacrifices have been restored so the reference cannot be to sacrifices in general. It is possible that the consecration of 3:1 involved a sacrifice. It is also possible that the remnant offered a sacrifice when the foundation was restored. The most likely explanation is to see the phrase as referring to the sacrifices of thanksgiving and dedication which would accompany the completion of the project (cf. 12:43). Hence the taunt would question whether or not the remnant would be able to complete the walls. In that sense, the third question parallels the fourth question, "Can they finish in a day?," another taunt concerning the ability of the Jews to finish the project. In the fourth question, however, the focus is on the amount of time it would take the remnant to complete the walls. Sanballat ridicules the remnant's ability to complete the venture in a short time.

The fifth question, "Can they revive the stones from the dusty rubble even the burned ones?," refers to the present state of the defenses. The original walls had been burned and the rocks previously used had crumbled to dust. Nebuchadnezzar had thoroughly destroyed the walls of Jerusalem when he took the city in 586 B.C. (cf. 2 Kin 25:9-10). Sanballat questions the ability of the Jews to restore these ruins and make them into a secure wall.

The sixth and final statement is the most disheartening. Tobiah exclaims that if even a fox jumped on the wall it would produce a breach in the wall (4:3). It should be remembered that breaches in city walls at that time were only secured after painstaking military endeavors. The fox is one of nature's lightest predators, not too much larger than a squirrel. If a wall crumbled when a fox jumped on it, then it was flimsy indeed. Tobiah's statement reveals the utter contempt with which these foreigners viewed the efforts of the Jews.

Instead of addressing the opponent's jeers personally, Nehemiah responds to the insults by praying to God and asking for poetic justice. He regards the attacks of the enemies as an attack against God Himself. After all, the restoration project was His will and His work. Nehemiah bases his imprecatory prayer on the promises of God contained in the Abrahamic Covenant, namely, the promise to bless those who blessed Abraham's descendants and curse those who cursed them (Gen. 12:1-3). God had already pronounced judgment on Israel's enemies (cf. Joel 3, Jer. 46-49). Nehemiah is simply praying that God would act as He has already covenanted.

Nehemiah's imprecations are reminiscent of those found in the Prophets (cf. Obad. 15-21; Hab. 2:6-17) and the Psalter (cf. Ps. 35; 58; 59; 69; 109; 137). Nehemiah uses the reversal of fortune motif commonly found in imprecations. He asks that the insulters become the insulted, that the persecutors become the persecuted, and that the slavemasters become the slaves. Nehemiah further requests that the evil deeds of the opposition group would not be forgiven by God.

Nehemiah takes care to mention that the insults of the opposition group had no lasting effect on the morale of the remnant or the progress of the work. Initially, the taunts of the opposition demoralized the workers. However, the heckling was simply words with no real bite. The workers respond to the mocking by working more vigorously. The wall is raised to half its height.

As the confidence of the remnant grows, the opposition group intensifies its efforts to halt the project (4:7-23). Realizing that their insults are not achieving the desired effect, the opposition group plots to physically attack the Jews. This strategy had worked in the days of Ezra (cf. Ezra 4:23) and, it was supposed, would likely work a second time. The fact that the Jews were making considerable progress in their efforts infuriated the alliance. They plotted together to halt the effort by attacking the workers. Evidently, they had the forces necessary to overpower the Jewish remnant.

Nehemiah meets the challenge by praying to God for guidance and protection. He then takes steps to prepare the Jews for the expected military attack. Nehemiah strategically places the families to fortify the most vulnerable sections of the wall and posts a guard around the clock to announce an attack. Seeing that some of the people are questioning their ability to withstand the threat, Nehemiah rises to give an impassioned speech. Nehemiah encourages them by appealing to their relationship with their God and their families. Nehemiah's speech is brief but powerful. He appeals to the greatness of God and His ability to protect them. Nehemiah realizes that the true strength of Israel lies in their "great and awesome" God (cf. Deut. 7:21). He also appeals to their sense of comradeship. They must defend their families, their wives and their children. They must defend their brethren, their countrymen. All Jews were related in some fashion since all had come from Jacob. Nehemiah motivates his audience by appealing to their two great loves, their God and their nation.

Nehemiah's strategy works as the opposition group loses their confidence. They realize that the working Jews are unified, alert, and prepared to fight if necessary. It is easy to attack a victim when they are unaware of the danger. It is quite another task to attack when the target fully expects it. Once again, Nehemiah takes care to credit God for the success. He states that it was God who "frustrated their plan" (4:15).

When the workers became aware that their attackers had lost confidence they returned to the work, but not without taking precautions. Nehemiah divides the men into workers and guards. Half of the men were to continue working on the walls while the other half were to stand guard with weapons. The military leaders stood behind the workers, obviously watching for an ambush and prepared to give orders for the defense of the city.

As they worked, the men who labored on the walls remained prepared for action. Those who carried loads did so with one arm while carrying a weapon in the other arm. This weapon may be a sword, a spear, or even a rock which could be used as a missile. Those who actually built the wall wore a sword fastened to their side. Evidently, these artisans needed both hands free to work on the wall. A trumpeter stood next to Nehemiah, prepared to sound the alarm at the slightest hint of attack.

Nehemiah again gives a speech to the workers as they prepare to return to the work. He informs them that the project is far from complete. There is still a considerable amount of work to be done. Perhaps the laborers, seeing the enemy shrink back in fear, thought that their defenses were now sufficient. Nehemiah corrects this misconception. He adds a warning lest the workers become confident that an ambush is no longer imminent. Nehemiah warns his listeners that their ranks are now going to be spread thin. They were dispersed throughout the entire length of the wall. Evidently, the workers had congregated for the events of 4:7-14 in order to best defend against the possible ambush. Nehemiah further instructs the men to rally to the place where they hear the trumpet sound, an inventive plan to defend the city despite the fact that the people were separated. He finishes his speech by confidently assuring the laborers that God will be fighting alongside them on their behalf. Nehemiah is supremely confident that the rebuilding project is the will of God.

Nehemiah closes the section by summarizing the attitude of preparedness on the part of the laborers. He reveals that they worked from dawn to dusk. He further reveals that they remained in the city of Jerusalem instead of returning home at night. This was done for two reasons. First, if the men ventured outside the city they left themselves vulnerable to attack on the open roads. Second, if a large portion of the defenders left for the evening the remnant would be in danger of an evening assault. Nehemiah informs the reader that he was accompanied by a group of bodyguards wherever he went. Evidently, he already realizes that the opposition will try to eliminate him (cf. 6:1-14).

Chapter five records an internal problem among the Jews that threatened the successful completion of the project. The passage begins with a "great outcry" (5:1) from some of the Jews against some of their fellow Jews. The reference here is to a cry of distress. The same root word is used in Exodus 14:10 when the Children of Israel saw Pharaoh and the Egyptian troops approaching their encampment and cried out to God. The Israelites anticipated dying at the hands of the Egyptians (cf. Ex. 14:11). The situation in Nehemiah's day was equally stressful. The people again feared for their very lives (cf. 5:2).

The remnant's complaint was fourfold. Each complaint resulted from the state of poverty in which the nation found itself. The bulk of the population of Jews living in the land when Nehemiah returned belonged to the agrarian class. It is probable that the effects of the extensive destruction of the city of Jerusalem and the deportation of the skilled artisans contributed heavily to this situation. It should also be inferred that the population suffered a severe economic setback as a result of the deportation. There was a decrease in productivity throughout the region due to a decrease in manpower. There would also have been a damaging impact on normal foreign trade practices with the destruction of the major cities in the region. It is probable that the current situation developed because commercial ties were severed between Judah and its neighbors due to the rebuilding project. The work on the walls of the city was also taking men away from their usual jobs. From 4:16, it can be assumed that many farmers were staying in Jerusalem instead of returning to their fields. It is also likely that the heavy burden of taxation imposed on the community by the Persians contributed to the plight of the farmers. The heavy burden of taxation placed upon the returned remnant by the Achaemenids would have had a severe impact on the economic situation.

Regardless of how the situation developed, this state of affairs was causing strife and bitterness among the workers. The situation was so perilous that it was regarded as life-threatening (5:2). However, the people do not seem to blame Nehemiah. Their complaint is levied against their fellow Jews. They did not ask that the rebuilding project be stopped. They evidently realized that it was necessary for their long-term survival.

The first complaint raised by the remnant was that they had large families and were not able to produce enough grain to feed everyone. Second, in order to secure enough grain to feed their families, they had to mortgage their fields, vineyards, and houses. Third, the farmers had to borrow money to pay the king's taxes on their estates. Fourth, some families had to resort to selling their sons and daughters into slavery in order to get enough money to survive. Obviously, the situation was dire.

Nehemiah immediately recognizes the gravity of the situation. This conflict posed a threat not only to the building project, but to the unity of the returned remnant. Societal mistreatment is what originally tore the nation apart when Jeroboam led the ten northern tribes to secede from the rule of Rehoboam (cf. 1 Kin. 12). Nehemiah responds to the current emergency by confronting those guilty of abuse and explaining the error of their practice.

The unfaithful Jews responded in repentance and promised to give back what they had taken. Nehemiah himself even admits to having personally loaned money and grain to those in need (5:10), though this technically would not have been against the law if he had not charged them interest. In 5:12, those guilty of mistreating their fellow Jews take an oath to follow the commands of Nehemiah.

Nehemiah performs a symbolic act in 5:13, shaking out the front of his garments. In those days people often carried some of their personal belongings in the folds of their clothing. These folds essentially served as the pockets of the garments. This is probably the point of reference in the proverb, "A gift in secret subdues anger, and a bribe in the bosom, strong wrath" (Prov. 21:14). Nehemiah's symbolic act served to show the nation that if they disobeyed God then He will shake them out just like this garment. They would have nothing left after the Lord finished with them. The assembly responds to the actions of Nehemiah by shouting, "Amen!" The Hebrew word *amen* literally means "Let it be so." They were accepting the consequences of their binding oath.

Crucial background information is provided in 5:14. Nehemiah reveals that he had been appointed governor and that he served as governor for twelve years. The dates of Nehemiah's tenure as governor are 444-432 B.C. As governor, Nehemiah had the ability to raise taxes not only on behalf of King Artaxerxes, but also for himself. He had the right to be supported by the people he governed. However, Nehemiah explains that he had taken great care to be above reproach politically by not using the portions due him as governor of the region. Previous governors had chosen to accept these payments. Once again, Nehemiah is able to overcome opposition with the help of God. Recognizing this fact, he takes care to close the chapter by offering a brief prayer to the Lord.

The first half of the book reaches its climax in 6:1-7:3 as the remnant feverishly works to finish the walls of the city. The section begins with the opposition group receiving word that Nehemiah's efforts in rebuilding the wall were nearing their completion. As a result, the leaders of the opposition group decide to assassinate Nehemiah. They invite the governor to Chephirim on the plain of Ono in order to meet with them. Nehemiah sees through the plot and declines the invitation. Five times the opposition group attempts to induce Nehemiah into meeting with them and five times he rejects their proposal. The text notes that the fifth message was an "open letter." Anybody was capable of reading the letter and spreading the rumors contained in the message. This letter consisted of a report that the Jews were planning to rebel immediately following the completion of the walls of the city. It further stated that Nehemiah was going to attempt to set himself up as king over the Jews. One of the techniques that Nehemiah was supposed to use was to appoint prophets who would announce him as the king of Judah. The opposition group, feigning concern lest these rumors reach the ears of the king (i.e., Artaxerxes), request the presence of Nehemiah so that they can take counsel together. Nehemiah responds by sending a message asserting that the opposition leaders are inventing fables designed to frighten the remnant in hopes of getting them to halt the project. Nehemiah again offers a quick prayer to God for the strengthening of his hands, an appeal for the endurance needed to complete the project.

Having failed in their previous attempts, the opposition group hired an unfaithful Jew, Shemaiah, in an effort to betray and entrap Nehemiah. Shemaiah invited Nehemiah to meet together with him at the temple in Jerusalem in the evening with the doors closed. Nehemiah once again sees through the sinister plot and rejects the deceitful invitation. Again, Nehemiah gives God the credit for helping him to see through the various plots and escape bodily harm. The scene closes with an imprecatory prayer offered by Nehemiah requesting that God enact justice against the leaders of the opposition group.

6:15-19 describes the successful completion of Nehemiah's initial mission, the rebuilding of the walls of Jerusalem. The entire rebuilding project was completed in only fifty-two days. The wall is said to have been completed on the twenty-fifth day of the month Elul (late September and early October) in 444 B.C.[30] This is the end of the hot season. Therefore, the people have been rebuilding the wall throughout the oppressive summer months. With the close of the month Elul came the time for plowing fields and sowing crops. It is quite likely that Nehemiah deliberately attempted to finish the walls of the city before the populace had to return to their own homesteads. Within a year of hearing the report of Hanani concerning the perilous state of Jerusalem, Nehemiah had returned to the city and rebuilt its walls. Nehemiah is again quick to give credit both to God and the Jews in helping him complete his mission.

When the leaders of the opposition group saw that the project had been completed they were demoralized and discontinued their attempts on Nehemiah's life. They still continued to oppose Nehemiah through a letter-writing campaign; however, by now the suspense is gone. The desired task has been accomplished. The city is now fortified. The section closes by detailing Nehemiah's vigilance in posting guards throughout the city and closing the gates during certain parts of the day.

The Rebuilding of the People (7:4-13:3)

Nehemiah begins his rebuilding of the people by appealing to the faithfulness of their ancestors who had taken a leap of faith by returning to the land during the days of Zerubbabel (7:4-73a). This list was originally utilized in Ezra 2:1-70 where Ezra uses it to describe those who had returned with Zerubbabel.[31] Here, Nehemiah uses the same list to motivate the descendants of these individuals to move to Jerusalem. The repopulation of the land, especially the city of Jerusalem, was one of the primary goals of the original return. In light of 7:73b, it is also possible that the extensive list was utilized for genealogical reasons.[32] Nehemiah wanted pure-blooded Jews to inhabit the city (cf. 10:28-30; 13:23-28).

7:4-5 serves as an introduction to the list. Nehemiah announces that the city of Jerusalem was large and spacious; however, its inhabitants were few in number. Obviously, this posed a significant problem for the remnant. The walls of the city had just been rebuilt in an effort to protect the city, and, consequently, the entire Jewish population in Judah. This protection was certainly imperative in light of the actions of the opposition force described in the previous chapters. The walls of the city were of little value without a population capable of manning and defending those walls. Evidently, the number of people residing in the city was insufficient to adequately defend the city. Steps needed to be taken to repopulate the city.

In an effort to solve this crisis, Nehemiah decides to assemble the leadership of the land. This gathering is not simply according to the will of Nehemiah. He asserts that God had put it into his heart to call the assembly. The use of this phrase parallels the use of the same phrase in 2:12. Just as 2:12 had announced the first stage of Nehemiah's mission, the physical restoration of the nation, this verse announces the second stage of Nehemiah's mission, the spiritual restoration of the nation. When the remnant congregates in Jerusalem, they will read the law, celebrate the Feast of Tabernacles, confess their sin, and make a commitment to obey the commands of the Lord. It is not until 11:1 that the remnant finally gets around to repopulating the city of Jerusalem, the supposed primary objective of the meeting. Nehemiah realizes that the nation cannot go about the business of settling the holy city until they first take care of their relationship with their God.

7:6 reveals the contents of the list. The roster that follows is a record of those who returned to the region of Judah from Babylon subsequent to the decree of Cyrus. The first half of verse seven lists the major leaders who led the return to Jerusalem. There are twelve names listed here. Ezra's list only has eleven names, omitting that of Nahamani (Ezra 2:2). Nehemiah's list is probably original as the number twelve would be used to represent the twelve tribes of Israel. Zerubbabel and Jeshua are named first (for a full discussion of these two important men see the discussion of Ezra 2 in the previous chapter entitled "Ezra").

Verses 2b-38 identify the family leaders who returned with Zerubbabel. The designations "sons of" (Hebrew *bene*) and "men of" (Hebrew *'aneshe*) in these verses indicate the two ways by which the exiles could validate their Jewish ancestry, either by family name or by location in Judah. Verses 39-42 identify the priests who returned. The priests were the descendants of Aaron, a subset of the Levites. Verses 43-45 identify the Levites who returned. Within the larger group of Levites two guilds are identified; the temple singers and the gatekeepers. The temple singers were often associated with the Levites (cf. Neh. 11-12) and were primarily responsible for leading the music during worship. The gatekeepers were responsible for guarding the gates leading into the temple as well as locking and unlocking the doors of the temple. They also watched over the temple chambers and treasuries (1 Chron. 9:17-29). Verses 46-56 identify the temple servants who returned. The temple servants were an order of Israelites who assisted the Levites. Verses 57-60 identify the descendants of Solomon's servants who returned. They were likely foreigners who were enslaved by Solomon and appointed to serve in the temple. The total in verse 60 includes both the temple servants and the descendants of Solomon's servants, a fact which signifies the close relationship between these two groups.

7:61-65 identifies those individuals who could not prove their ancestry. Evidently, the rest of the individuals named in this list could provide proof of their citizenship. This proof would likely have consisted of a genealogy tracing one's heritage to one of the sons of Israel. These genealogies were also used to exclude those with foreign blood. Although the individuals named here could not prove their ancestry, they were still allowed to return with the rest of the exiles. Verses 63-65 reveal that even some priests were unable to prove their ancestry. These men were not allowed to serve as priests until the high priest could determine whether they were legitimate. He did this by using the Urim and Thummim. The exact nature of the Urim and Thummim is one of the great mysteries of the Old Testament. It has been suggested that they were two small objects which were used to signify the will of God, much like the casting of lots. Josephus contends that the answer was given by a miraculous shining of the jewels on the high priest's garments (*Antiquities of the Jews* 3.8.9). Evidently, at least one of these families, the sons of Hakkoz, had their claim upheld since Meremoth the son of Uriah is identified as a priest in Ezra 8:33 and as the grandson of Hakkoz in Nehemiah 3:4.

The total number of those who returned with Zerubbabel was 49,942 (Ezra records 49,897; cf. Ezra 2:64-65). This number does not correspond with the sum of the various groups mentioned in the chapter (i.e., 31,089). It is possible that women and children were not included in the initial numbers but were included in the final tally. However, this seems to be a very low number of women and children when compared to the number of men. Perhaps the difficulties of the journey and the uncertainty of what awaited them in Judah caused many women and children to remain in Babylon. It is also reasonable to assume that not all families are listed in the individual tabulations. A final possibility is scribal error, which is much more common in numerical lists.

The chronological narrative of Nehemiah begins again in the second half of 7:73. The time frame indicated is the first day of the seventh month (Tishri). The year is still 444 B.C. While the character of Ezra does not appear in Nehemiah's narrative until chapter eight, it seems evident from 12:26 that he had been present throughout the rebuilding project. Ezra is introduced in chapter eight as both a scribe and a priest. As a scribe, Ezra would have been intimately involved in the transmission of God's word. This position gave him the authority to read and interpret God's word to the people. As a priest, Ezra was fully qualified to lead the nation in their spiritual worship. Each time the reader encounters Ezra, he is faithfully pursuing righteousness. This is in distinct contrast to the remnant, who only responds faithfully after the rebuke or encouragement of their spiritual leaders (cf. 2:17; 5:1-13; 8:1-10:39; 13:1-29).

The first day of the seventh month was the day on which the Jews were to celebrate the Feast of Trumpets. The descendants of those individuals detailed in the previous chapter are assembled in Jerusalem at the plaza in front of the Water Gate so Nehemiah can begin his task of restoring the spiritual commitment of the nation. The fact that Nehemiah had not returned to Babylon after the completion of the walls of the city reveals that his mission had not yet been accomplished. Although the walls of the city had been restored, the spirituality of the inhabitants was still in need of restoration. Until the people take steps to restore their relationship with God, the walls of the city will offer little protection (cf. Ps. 127:1).

The process outlined in this passage reflects the form of Israelite worship that developed while the nation was in captivity. Virtually the same elements that characterized the synagogue services which had begun during the exile occur here in this chapter. The people assemble, there is a request for the reading of the Law, the scroll is opened, the people stand, praise is offered to Yahweh, the audience answers, instruction is offered, the Law is read, an explanation follows, and the people depart for a fellowship meal.[33]

The scene begins with the congregation of godly Jews requesting Ezra to bring out the Law of Moses and read it to the assembly. Ezra reads from the book while standing at a wooden podium that was made especially for this purpose. The scribe reads for several hours, from "early morning until midday" (8:3), perhaps from 7:00 am until noon. As he reads, he is surrounded by some of the most notable leaders in the nation. Six of these leaders stand on his right side while seven of them stand on his left, making a total of thirteen. When Ezra finished reading, several Levites instructed the people as to the meaning of the text. As the meaning of the text was given to them, the people began to weep. Evidently, they realized the degree to which they had failed to keep the commands of the Lord.

Nehemiah, Ezra, and the Levites strongly encourage the assembly to stop weeping and rejoice instead. The reading of the law was not producing the desired effect. Although the law certainly should have convicted the nation of their trespasses, thus resulting in their mournful repentance; this was not the primary purpose for which Ezra read. He wanted them to celebrate the completion of the rebuilding project. This celebration would cause the remnant to be strengthened (cf. 8:10).[34] The congregation responded to the words of their religious leaders by rejoicing with a celebration of food and drink.

The next day Ezra again reads from the Law of Moses, this time detailing the regulations concerning the Feast of Booths (also known as Tabernacles, Lev. 23:34-36). The Feast of Booths was one of the most significant days in the Jewish calendar. It was celebrated from Tishri 15 to Tishri 21. It was one of the three Feasts during which every male Jew was required to be in Jerusalem (Deut. 16:16). During this week the Jews were required to live in booths (i.e., tents) set up around Jerusalem. This was done to commemorate the wilderness wanderings of the Exodus generation. A special sacrifice was offered each of the seven days of this feast (see Numbers 29:12-38 for the details on what as to be offered on each day). The first day of the feast was to be a day of rest as well as the day after the feast ended.

This feast seems to have taken on special significance for the restored remnant (cf. Ezra 3; Nehemiah 8). Since they had grown up outside of the land of Israel they probably identified with the Exodus generation. In fact, they had gone through a sort of Exodus themselves.[35] Surely they and their ancestors had lived in temporary shelters as they made the long journey from Babylon (or Susa) to

Jerusalem. The remnant had also depended on the sovereign providence of their Lord as they journeyed to the Promised Land (cf. Ezra 8:21-22).

The emphasis of the passage is on the procedures to be followed while celebrating the Feast of Booths. The nation is particularly interested in how to make the booths and where to put them. Each day of the feast Ezra read from the Law and the congregation celebrated. On the eighth day, the nation rested and observed a solemn assembly. This was in keeping with the prescription provided in Leviticus 23:39.

The events of chapter nine take place on the twenty-fourth day of the seventh month. This scene details the success of Ezra's ministry as the people separate themselves from foreigners and offer up a majestic psalm of praise to God.[36] On Tishri 24, the nation once again assembles in Jerusalem. This time the congregation meets for repentance. As noted earlier, the reading of the book of the law by Ezra served to convict the nation of their trespasses. While the nation was forbidden to mourn in 8:9-11 because the occasion called for celebration, here the leaders seem to encourage the repentant mourning. The people demonstrate their repentance by fasting in sackcloth with dirt upon their heads.

The nation listens to the reading of the law for three hours. This reading assuredly followed the process described in chapter 8 where translation followed each passage. The remnant responds to the reading of the law by worshipping God and confessing their sin for three hours. The nation is led in its worship by the Levites.

Following their repentance, the congregation offers up a majestic psalm of praise to God.[37] The psalm details the past works of God as He protected and guided the nation's forefathers. This pattern was common in psalm writing (cf. Ps 78, 105, 106, 135, 136) and was used for the purpose of instructing the people. The implication of the psalm is obvious. The remnant expects the Lord to protect and guide their generation as He had protected and guided their forefathers. The assembly admitted the sins of their ancestors and acknowledged the faithfulness of God. In spite of their rebellion, the Lord still took care of His chosen people. The emphasis is clearly on God's compassion as the Hebrew word *raham* ("compassion") occurs six times. There is also an emphasis on the Promised Land as the Hebrew word *'eretz* ("land") occurs twelve times in this psalm in reference to the land of Canaan.

The psalm begins with words of adoration extolling the name of Yahweh. Yahweh is identified as the only God, the creator of the world. Verses seven and eight refer to the Lord's relationship with Abraham. The Lord chose Abraham, brought him from Ur of the Chaldees to the Promised Land, and gave him a new name. Most significantly, the Lord made a covenant with Abraham when he demonstrated his faithfulness. Verses 9-11 recount the Lord's providence for His people while they were in Egypt. The Lord responded to the groanings of His people by delivering them from out of the hands of those who "acted arrogantly toward them," a description of the actions of the Egyptians towards the children of Israel. Yahweh accomplished this redemption by sending a series of plagues against the Pharaoh and by dividing the Red Sea so that the nation could pass through it on dry ground. Verses 12-21 provide an account of the Lord's providence for His people throughout their wilderness wanderings. The Lord led them daily with a pillar of cloud by day and a pillar of fire by night. He brought them to Mount Sinai where He gave them the regulations of the Mosaic Law. Verses 22-25 describe the conquest of the land by the generation of Joshua. The nation was initially able to defeat Sihon and Og, the kings of the Amorites. These kings are routinely used in the Old Testament to describe the Lord's providential deliverance of His people (cf. Deut. 31:4; Josh. 2:10; 9:10; Ps. 135:11; 136:19-20). The nation was next able to defeat the inhabitants of the land, the Canaanites, despite the fact that many of them lived in fortified cities. Verses 26-31 recount the numerous acts of disobedience committed by the children of Israel. The nation killed the prophets who had been sent by the Lord (cf. 1 Kin. 18:4, 13; 19:10, 14; 2 Chron. 24:21). They committed great blasphemies (e.g., Ezek. 23; Hos. 2; Mic. 3). The nation did evil, acted arrogantly, did not listen to the commandments, and sinned. In each case, the Lord sent words of warning designed to gain the repentance of the people. And in each case, the nation proved faithless.

Verses 32-37 conclude the psalm with a confession of the sins of the nation, past and present. In 9:32, the appeal is made to the great, mighty, and awesome God who keeps his "covenant" (Hebrew *berit*) and "lovingkindness" (Hebrew *hesed*). Nehemiah has already used the words *berit* and *hesed* in his prayer of 1:5-11. Just as Nehemiah prayed in the first chapter that the Lord would show *hesed* by keeping His *berit*, here the psalmist appeals for the Lord to show *hesed* by keeping His *berit*. The appeal is for the deliverance of the people. They have been subservient to foreigners from the days of the kings of Assyria to the present day. The Assyrians forces Israel and Judah to pay heavy tribute, eventually taking the Northern Kingdom into exile in 722 B.C. The Babylonians then oppressed the Southern Kingdom, eventually taking them into captivity in a series of exiles culminating in 586 B.C. The people acknowledge that the Lord was just in sending their ancestors into exile. Even though the nation had been delivered by the Persians (cf. Ezra 1:2-4), the final verses reveal that the nation is still subservient to the Persian kings. The psalm closes with a petition by the nation for deliverance from the hardships they are presently suffering.

The cultic activities performed by the nation in chapter nine manifest themselves in chapter ten as the people make a pledge to change their sinful lifestyle. The nation puts their commitment to repentance in writing, composing a document which was sealed by the nation's leaders. Nehemiah 10:1-27 provides a record of those who signed this document. Nehemiah puts his name at the top of the list. Verses 2-8 detail the heads of 21 priestly families. Verses 9-13 record the leaders of 17 Levitical families. Verses 14-27 identify the heads of 44 other notable families.

The nation as a whole joins with the elders in this commitment. The remnant took an oath to fulfill the obligations of the covenant. The covenant itself is basically a list of stipulations that the nation feels obligated to fulfill. The first stipulation is the obligation to abstain from mixed marriages, a prevalent theme throughout Ezra and Nehemiah (cf. Ezra 9-10; Neh. 13:23-28). The second stipulation is the obligation to keep the Sabbath as a day of rest. This obligation was particularly difficult to maintain because of the abundance of foreigners in the land. These foreigners did not follow the

Jewish Sabbath regulations; instead they routinely worked on the Sabbath (cf. Neh. 13:16). The third stipulation is the obligation to contribute to the service of the temple. The nation pledges to give a third of a shekel each year for the service of the house of God. The nation further commits to providing the priests and the temple with wood, crops, livestock, and manpower. The document closes with a statement announcing the nation's resolution to take care of the temple.

Chapter eleven continues to show the positive response on the part of the Jews by detailing their commitment to have one-tenth of the people live in the city of Jerusalem.[38] This effort to repopulate Jerusalem naturally began with the leaders as they decide to live in the city. The rest of the people cast lots for the responsibility of living in Jerusalem. This problem was first introduced in 7:4 where Nehemiah states that not enough people were living within the city. Those who volunteered to live in the city were commended by the rest of the people. From this statement it can be deduced that circumstances were such that some were forced to reside in Jerusalem. It can be assumed that living in the city was not an attractive option because the city lay in ruins. One out of every ten families living outside the city was chosen to move into the city. The rest of the people remained in the rural parts of the province.

Verses 3-24 provide a list of those who resided in Jerusalem. Estimates of Jerusalem's population at this time range from 4,800[39] to 8,000.[40] The list begins by identifying the laity living in Jerusalem. The city was primarily populated with members of the tribes of Judah and Benjamin. There were almost twice as many men from Benjamin (928) living in Jerusalem as there were men from the tribe of Judah (468). It should be remembered that Jerusalem was among those cities originally given to the tribe of Benjamin (cf. Josh. 18:28). Joel the son of Zichri was placed in charge of Jerusalem as the overseer while Judah the son of Hassenuah was his second in command. Among those men who lived in Jerusalem were priests (11:10-14), Levites (11:15-18), and gatekeepers (11:19).

11:25-36 details those Israelites who settled on their ancestral properties. Those cities south of Jerusalem were located in the territory of Judah. Nehemiah lists 17 prominent villages in this region.

Those cities north of Jerusalem were located in the territory of Benjamin. Nehemiah identifies 15 prominent towns in this region. Together, these two regions made up the Persian province of Judah. God was fulfilling his promises to restore the nation to the land after the Babylonian captivity.

The first half of chapter twelve is a record of those families responsible for the spiritual leadership of the nation from the time of Zerubbabel's return until the present (12:1-26).[41] The list is divided into four parts. The first part of the list is a record of those priests and Levites who ministered during the time of Zerubbabel and Jeshua (12:1-9). The second part of the list is a genealogical record of the high priest from Jeshua to Jaddua (12:10-11). The third part of the list is a record of the priests in the time of Joiakim the high priest (12:12-21). The final part of the list identifies the current leadership in the land (12:22-26).

12:27 picks up where 11:2 left off and once again reverts to narrative prose. The entire section between 11:2 and 12:27 (i.e., 11:3-12:26) was comprised of a group of extensive lists. This passage (12:27-13:3) contains the climax of the second half of the book as the nation responds favorably to the spiritual leadership of the religious leaders. The section begins with a description of the preparations for the dedication of the walls of Jerusalem. It is impossible to tell how much time has elapsed since the completion of the walls described in 6:15 and the events of this section. Likely, only a month or two has passed. One would assume that the dedication of the walls would be a priority for those who built them.

The preparations begin with a gathering of Levites from various villages surrounding Jerusalem. These Levites were primarily responsible for leading the musical activities which were planned for the dedication ceremony. They brought along several types of instruments, including cymbals, harps, and lyres. The emphasis of the passage is clearly on the worshipful activities of the remnant. Singing is mentioned eight times in this chapter, thanksgiving six times, rejoicing seven times, and musical instruments three times.[42] An integral part of the preparation was the purification of the priest, Levites, laity, gates, and walls.

Nehemiah appoints two choirs to march around the city. The first choir mounted the city walls, probably at the Valley Gate, and walked around Jerusalem in a counterclockwise direction. This choir marched atop the southern and eastern walls and was led by Ezra, who walked in front of the procession. The second choir mounted the city walls and marched around the city in a clockwise direction. This choir marched atop the western and northern walls and was led by Nehemiah himself.

The two choirs meet at the temple, having together circumnavigated the city by walking atop the wall. This was the same wall that Tobiah had earlier claimed a fox would destroy if it walked upon it! The religious leaders of Judah celebrate the occasion by leading the congregation in acts of spiritual worship, including singing and offering sacrifices. The shouts of the people could be heard from a far distance.

12:44-47 describe the actions taken to restore the service of the temple. Trustworthy men were appointed to care for the chambers in the temple. Their duties included the gathering of the first fruits and tithes from the surrounding communities. These individuals, along with the singers and gatekeepers, performed their duties in accordance with the prescriptions laid out by David and Solomon (cf. 1 Chron. 23-26). The passage closes by noting the faithfulness of the laity in supporting these guilds during the governorships of both Zerubbabel and Nehemiah.

13:1-3 can be seen as an introduction to 13:4-31 or as a conclusion to 12:27-47. It seems best to see them as a conclusion to 12:27-47 because of the repetition of the phrase "on that day" (cf. 12:43, 44; 13:1). In these verses, the people once again hear the law as it was read to them by their spiritual leaders. The passage alluded to in these verses is Deuteronomy 23:3-5, "No Ammonite or Moabite shall enter the assembly of the Lord; none of their descendants, even to the tenth generation, shall ever enter the assembly of the Lord, because they did not meet you with food and water on the way when you came out of Egypt, and because they hired against you Balaam the son of Beor from Pethor of Mesopotamia, to curse you. Nevertheless, the Lord your God was not willing to listen to

Balaam, but the Lord your God turned the curse into a blessing for you because the Lord your God loves you."

It is at this point that Nehemiah has gained the victory in his second mission, that is, the rebuilding of the people. The city has now been rebuilt, the law has been reestablished, and the spiritual condition of the remnant has been restored. These verses serve as a model for revival. The nation reads Scripture, prays, commits to give to the service of the Lord, and commits to personal purity. The conviction of sin in chapter eight led to the nation's confession of sin in chapter nine which resulted in the nation's commitment to God in chapters ten through twelve.

Nehemiah's Final Reforms (13:4-31)

The final three scenes form an appendix to the book. The events of these scenes take place sometime after the thirty-second year of Artaxerxes (432 B.C.). Nehemiah had journeyed to Persia in the thirty-second year of Artaxerxes to return to the service of the king. After an unknown period of time, Nehemiah once again asks the king for permission to return to Jerusalem. Upon arriving in Jerusalem, he encounters a variety of spiritual problems which arose among the people over the intervening years. Each of these problems involved unfaithfulness to the commitment made by the remnant in chapter ten.

The first scene describes the misuse of the temple's storage room by Eliashib, an unfaithful Jew. Eliashib was related to Tobiah the Ammonite (the reader will remember Tobiah as one of the main opponents of Nehemiah in the first half of this book; cf. 2:19; 4:3; 6:12, 19). Tobiah was evidently well connected with many important Jewish families (cf. 6:18). The close relationship between Eliashib and Tobiah led to the pollution of the temple. Eliashib was responsible for the management of the storerooms in the temple area. He agreed to allow Tobiah to live in one of these storerooms. It can be assumed that many of the temple storerooms were empty due to the fact that the nation had been unfaithful in supporting the priests (cf. 13:10).

Tobiah wanted to live in the temple area to gain control of the temple system. The temple system economy became a lucrative source of income and power for the priesthood. As a result, there was a continual struggle for dominance of the temple system among the highest levels of the priesthood, including the high-priestly family and the Levites. The high-priestly family sought to gain complete control over the material and monetary resources of the temple. They made several alliances with the Judean aristocracy and the ruling families in neighboring lands designed to further their own interests. The marriages of Sanballat and Tobiah reflect this reality. Nehemiah's reforms brought him into direct conflict with these groups as he sought to limit their control of the temple. Nehemiah wanted to restore control of the temple to the Levites.

When Nehemiah returned from Persia, he discovered the evil thing that Eliashib had done. Nehemiah immediately kicked Tobiah out of the storeroom where he had been staying and restored order in the temple. Following the expulsion of Tobiah, Nehemiah cleansed the rooms and returned the utensils and offerings that had previously been stored there. The rooms needed to be cleansed because they were regarded as sacred. Therefore, the presence of an unclean person made the sacred rooms unclean.

Nehemiah further discovers that the portions which had been devoted to the Levites had not been given to them. Without the support of the people, these Levites had returned to their homes. Nehemiah responds to this problem by reprimanding the officials, boldly exclaiming, "Why is the house of God forsaken?" He then gathered the Levites and restored them to their positions in the temple. The scene closes with a brief prayer offered by Nehemiah requesting God to honor his faithfulness.

The second scene describes the unfaithfulness of the remnant in keeping the Sabbath. As Nehemiah journeyed through the rural areas of Judah, he observed men working at their jobs and performing business transactions on the Sabbath.[43] Nehemiah responds to the problem by immediately confronting the Jewish nobility and sharply criticizing their abuse of the Lord's holy day. To ensure that this evil practice would come to an end, Nehemiah takes various steps to restore the sacredness of the day. He first commands that the city gates be closed during the Sabbath. Next, he stations some of his servants at the gates to prevent any wagonloads of goods from entering the city on the Sabbath. The merchants who were thus prevented from entering the city simply set up camp outside the walls. Nehemiah subsequently threatened these traders and merchants with the use of force. The threats of the governor seem to have been sufficient to drive these merchants away. Finally, Nehemiah commissions the Levites to guard the gates of the city on a permanent basis. The scene closes with another prayer offered by Nehemiah, this time asking God to show mercy to him because of his acts of faithfulness.

The third scene describes the unfaithfulness of the remnant in the area of foreign marriages. The nation had once again fallen prey to temptation and intermarried with foreign women (cf. Ezra 9-10; Neh. 6:18; 10:30). The fact that these marriages had produced children indicates that quite some time must have elapsed between Nehemiah's departure for Persia and subsequent return to Jerusalem. The children of these marriages were speaking foreign languages, the languages of their mothers. Unfortunately, it is not only the ordinary people who had committed this transgression, but some of the leaders as well. The grandson of Eliashib, the high priest, married the daughter of Sanballat the Horonite.

Nehemiah responds to the problem by confronting the guilty parties. In the midst of this confrontation, he "cursed" them (13:25). The curse pronounced by Nehemiah here is a reference to the curse of 10:29. The remnant had agreed to accept that curse when they broke the covenant described in chapter ten. That covenant had now been broken. As a result, Nehemiah announces that the curse had now been placed on their heads. Nehemiah even physically assaults some of the lawbreakers, striking them and pulling out their hair. Nehemiah next makes the guilty parties repeat the oath of 10:30, an oath to abstain from intermarriage. Nehemiah then counsels the nation against entering into such unions by describing how these unions negatively impacted the nation in the past, reminding the audience of the tragic example of Solomon (cf. 1 Kings 11).

The final act of Nehemiah recorded in this book is the excommunication of the grandson of Eliashib the high priest. The discussion of intermarriage ends with a prayer by Nehemiah asking God to show justice to those guilty of profaning His name. Verses 30-31 form a concluding summary to the appendix. Nehemiah summarizes the steps taken to purify the remnant and restore the service of the temple. The book closes with a final prayer by Nehemiah, this time asking God to remember his righteous acts. Together, the final three scenes form a resolution of the spiritual conflict detailed in the second half of the book and serve as a continual call to the nation to maintain their purity throughout the intertestamental period.

Study Questions

1. What does the name Nehemiah mean?
2. Why was the occupation of cupbearer so important in the Ancient Near East?
3. Briefly describe the leadership ability of Nehemiah.
4. Who is the Persian monarch during the period of Nehemiah?
5. What two cities serve as the physical setting for the narrative?
6. What are the names of the three governors who oppose Nehemiah?
7. List the ten gates surrounding Jerusalem. Why were these gates the most important segment of the rebuilding project??
8. The list of Nehemiah 7 is found in what other chapter of the Bible?
9. Should 13:1-3 be seen as an introduction to 13:4-31 or as a conclusion to 12:27-47? Defend your answer.?
10. What are the three problems that Nehemiah encounters upon his return from Persia? How does Nehemiah deal with each problem?

CHAPTER 9

Esther

"Then Mordecai told them to reply to Esther, "Do not imagine that you in the king's palace can escape any more than all the Jews. For if you remain silent at this time, relief and deliverance will arise for the Jews from another place and you and your father's house will perish. And who knows whether you have not attained royalty for such a time as this?" (Esther 4:13-14).

The book of Esther is one of the most heavily criticized books in the Bible. The identity of the author is unknown. The date of writing is unknown. The very historicity of the book is questioned. Yet, the book stands as a marvelous testimony of divine providence. The sequence of supposed "coincidences" defies logic, demonstrating the presence of the Lord among his people, even though His name never appears in the book.

Author

Like many Old Testament books (cf. Judges, Ruth, Samuel, Kings, Chronicles, Job), the book of Esther is anonymous and must remain so. Although several individuals have been proposed as the author (e.g., Ezra, Nehemiah, Mordecai), there is no specific evidence supporting any one of them. The author gives no hint whatsoever as to his identity. Whoever the author is, it is highly probable that he lived in Susa since he is aware of the geography of the city and has detailed knowledge of life in the Persian court. If the author of the book is someone named in scripture, Mordecai seems to be the most likely possibility. He lived in Susa, he was well aware of Persian culture, he was a Jew, and he was an eyewitness to the events described in the book. He would also have had intimate knowledge of life in the Persian palace as a result of his own elevated position in the court as well as the fact that the queen was his niece. Josephus, the Jewish historian, and many early Jewish rabbis claimed that Mordecai was the author of the book (Josephus, *Antiquities of the Jews* 11.6.1).[1]

Date

Most modern commentaries date the writing of Esther in the fourth or even third century B.C.[2] The primary argument for such a late date is linguistic. These commentators assert that the language of Esther cannot be dated before 400 B.C. and instead belongs to a later time period.[3] These arguments have been adequately answered by conservative scholarship.[4] In fact, it seems that Esther must have been written prior to Hellenistic expansion because the book contains no Greek words. Gordis explains, "The style indicates a date of composition of approximately 400 B.C.E., only a few decades after the reign of King Xerxes. . . . there is a considerable number of Persian and Aramaic words and idioms. There are, however, no Greek words, a fact which clearly points to a pre-Hellenistic date."[5] While Esther 10:2 demands the passing of some time between the events described in the book and the final composition of the book, the document in its current form could have been written as early as 470 B.C.

Historical Background

The events recorded in this book take place between those recorded in Ezra 1-6 and Ezra 7-10. The events take place between 483 B.C., the third year of the reign of Xerxes (1:3), and 473 B.C., the twelfth year of his reign (cf. 3:7; 9:1). The Ahasuerus of the first verse is the Persian king Khshayarshan. Ahasuerus was his Hebrew name. He is best known by his Greek name Xerxes.[6] Xerxes reigned over the Persian Empire from 486 to 465 B.C. As Esther 1:1 testifies, the Persian Empire stretched from India in the East to Ethiopia in the Southwest. This statement is corroborated by Herodotus (*Histories* 3.94-98; 7:9) and, more importantly, by a foundation tablet found at Persepolis that reads, "Thus speaks King Xerxes; these are the countries—in addition to Persia—over which I am king under the 'shadow' of Ahuramazda: . . . India . . . (and) Kush."[7] India is probably a reference to the area drained by the Indus River, the region of present day Punjab in Pakistan. It is unlikely that Xerxes ruled over peninsular India. Ethiopia was the country directly south of Egypt (currently the northern portion of Sudan), not present day Ethiopia. The northwestern portion of the empire included most of modern day Turkey. The empire was comprised of 127 provinces, each governed by a satrap (cf. 3:12).[8] These satraps were primarily responsible for collecting the tribute owed to the king and for raising the armies needed to defend and expand the empire. Daniel 6:1 identifies the number of satraps appointed by Darius as being 120. The higher number of 127 is probably representative of the additional conquests made by the Persians since the time of Daniel. With more territory comes the need for more satraps.

Xerxes was the son of Darius I Hystaspes (522-486 B.C.), under whose benefaction the Jews were able to complete the rebuilding of the temple in Jerusalem. His mother was Atossa, the daughter of Cyrus. Xerxes gained the throne in November of 486 B.C. at the age of thirty-two. Since he had been designated heir by his father several years previously, Xerxes' ascension to the throne was without contention. The reign of Xerxes ended in early August 465 B.C. when he was assassinated by Artabanus, the captain of the royal bodyguard.

Xerxes is notorious in secular history primarily for his ill-fated invasion of Greece.[9] In 481 B.C. he took an army of 200,000 men and hundreds of ships to Greece to avenge his father Darius' defeat at Marathon in 490 B.C. Initially, Xerxes enjoyed considerable success when the badly divided Greek city-states were unable to achieve an effective coalition.[10] The tide began to turn when the Spartans met this massive invasion force with fierce resistance at the battle of Thermopylae, fighting to the last man. The ill fortune continued for the Persians as their vast navy was destroyed in the battle of Salamis.

Xerxes blamed the defeat on his Phoenician and Egyptian mercenaries, accusing them of cowardice. As a result, these mercenaries abandoned him and returned to their homelands. Xerxes himself left for Persia, leaving his armies under the command of Mardonius. Mardonius suffered a series of setbacks until losing his life in the battle of Plataea. The Persians finally admitted defeat with their loss at Mycale in 479 B.C.

Xerxes is also famous for his building of the royal Persian palace at Persepolis.[11] While Darius I began the construction of the palace complex, it was ultimately finished by Xerxes. The royal buildings at Persepolis are concentrated on a great terrace 40 feet high measuring roughly 1500 feet long by 1000 feet wide, an area of about 33 acres. The buildings are approached through a magnificent double stairway with 111 steps, each rising only 4 inches allowing easy access for mounted horsemen. Immediately past the grand stairway is the Gate of All Nations, guarded by pairs of colossal winged and human-headed bulls. Visitors would wait in this area on black marble benches until called into one of the buildings. Noteworthy buildings on this terrace include the Apadana, a great audience hall that could accommodate a crowd of 10,000, the Palace of Darius, the Treasury, a vast complex of 93 rooms, and the Palace of Xerxes.[12] This beautiful palace was looted and burned by Alexander the Great in 331 B.C.

The narrative of Esther takes place in Susa, the winter capital of the Persian Empire (the summer capital was located at Persepolis). Susa had previously been the capital of Elam. The city of Susa (Hebrew *shushan*, meaning "lily") took its name from the abundance of lilies which grew in its neighborhood. Susa is located in the southwestern portion of modern Iran, about 150 miles north of the Persian Gulf. Its ideal winter climate made it the favorite retreat for the Achaemenid kings. However, the region was brutally oppressive during the summer months with temperatures commonly reaching 140 degrees Fahrenheit. Strabo notes that snakes and lizards crossing the street at noon in the summer heat were roasted to death (15.3.10).[13] Susa is a popular site in biblical literature. Nehemiah served as the king's cupbearer in Susa (cf. Neh. 1) and Daniel pictured himself in Susa in his vision of the ram and male goat (cf. Dan. 8).

The Jews of the southern kingdom of Judah had been carried away into exile by Nebuchadnezzar of Babylon when he conquered the city of Jerusalem in 586 B.C. This exile fulfilled the prophecy of Deuteronomy 28 where the Lord promised to scatter the nation "among all peoples, from one end of the earth to the other end of the earth" (Deut. 28:64) if they failed to obey His commandments. Although the Lord had "stirred up the spirit of Cyrus king of Persia" to issue a proclamation allowing the Jews to return to Judea (538 B.C.; Ezra 1:1), many Jews had chosen to remain in the areas to which they had been exiled. Such was the case with Esther and Mordecai.

The reason why many Jews chose to remain in exile is because they were able to successfully acclimate themselves to their new surroundings. Jewish life in the exile seems to have been fairly pleasant. The Jews frequently enjoyed economic success and were even able to gain positions of considerable influence in the foreign courts (e.g., Daniel, Esther, Mordecai, Nehemiah). This fact is confirmed by the Murashu documents, which further reveal the pleasantry of Jewish life in the Diaspora. There seems to have been little hint of discrimination. Perhaps this is why the entire city of Susa is so shocked at the king's decree calling for the extermination of the Jews (3:15). Rather than being discriminated against, the Jews were actually "engaged in the same types of contractual relationships, at the same interest rates, as their non-Jewish contemporaries" in the Persian Empire of the fifth century B.C.[14] There can be no doubt that the Jews of the Diaspora were able to have a significant impact on the lands in which they lived.

Unfortunately, the lands in which they lived also heavily influenced the Jews of the Diaspora. Merrill explains,

> To argue that the Jews, as committed as they were (and are) to community and tradition, could live under the relatively favorable conditions of Babylonian exile and not absorb them in large measure is naively to assume a stubborn tenacity or rigid isolationism alien to what little is known about Judah in exile. The Jews, ever an adaptable and yet cohesive people, have historically demonstrated a desire to be good citizens of

whatever land they inhabit. This extends to military service, education, culture, and not least, language. It is unreasonable as well as contrary to the evidence to assume that the Jews of Babylonian exile were isolated by either coercion or choice, physically or intellectually. They imbibed deeply of the society in which they lived and yet retained the cherished faith, life, and traditions of their ancestors.[15]

Such was the world of Mordecai and Esther. The fact that Esther was able to acclimate herself to the Persian court without revealing her Jewish identity reveals the degree to which the Jews were able to assimilate their new culture. It would have been impossible for Daniel to have hidden his national identity. The chief difference between the two may have been the fact that Daniel was raised in the Jewish culture of Judah while Esther was raised in the pagan world of Persia. As a result, we should not expect to see the same kind of godly moral behavior on the part of the exiles that we see in the lives of many other great heroes of the Bible. Throughout this book, Esther makes a variety of choices that subvert the Lord's commands. The moral character of Esther must be understood and analyzed in light of her historical setting. Not forgiven or even excused, but understood. In this way, Esther is better compared to other heroes of questionable moral character like Gideon, Jephthah, and Samson, victims of the ungodly times in which they lived.

Audience and Purpose

The book was assuredly written to the Jewish remnant living in Judah. This is the only scenario that accounts for the fact that the book is written in Hebrew. One would have to expect that the book would have been written in Aramaic if it were written to the Jews of the captivity. The very fact that the word "Pur" is translated into the Hebrew seems to settle the issue (3:7; 9:24). The Jews of the captivity would surely have been familiar with the term, especially those living in the region of Persia. Hence, there would have been no need to translate the term. However, the Jews living in Judah had returned with Sheshbazzar in the original return of 538 B.C. and were much more likely to be ignorant of the meaning of the term "Pur," thereby necessitating the translation. The more difficult question is whether the book was written in Judah itself or in Susa and then transported back to Judah. Either scenario is possible and it is impossible to take a firm stand on the issue. Since Mordecai is the most likely candidate for authorship, Susa would naturally be the most likely candidate for place of origination. This would help account for the detailed explanation of the reason why Purim is celebrated on two different days (9:16-19).

Assuming the book was written within about twenty years of 450 B.C. (ca. 470-430 B.C.), it was written to a generation of Jews who were struggling. The Jews who had returned under Sheshbazzar had taken more than twenty years to rebuild the temple of God, and only then under the encouragement of the prophets Haggai and Zechariah. The spiritual condition of the remnant was in desperate need of stimulation. They had intermarried with foreigners (Ezra 9-10). They were withholding tithes from the priests (Neh. 13:10). And they were breaking the Sabbath regulations (Neh. 13:15). As a result, they were once again vulnerable to the judgment of God (cf. Ezra 9:14; Hag. 1:3-11).

This generation was also suffering at the hands of their enemies. Attempts to promote the welfare of the Jews had failed during the reigns of Cyrus, Darius, Xerxes, and Artaxerxes (cf. Ezra 4:5-7). The remnant living in Judah had their own Hamans, opposition leaders like Rehum, Shimshai, Sanballat, Tobiah, and Geshem. Men like Haman, who were so diametrically opposed to the efforts of the Jews to rebuild their nation that they were willing to lie to the Persian king (cf. Ezra 4:12-13; Esth. 3:8). Men like Haman, who were willing to take any steps necessary, including violent slaughter, to rid themselves of the Jewish remnant (cf. Neh. 4:11; Esth. 3:9). This remnant, living in constant fear of their adversaries, was in need of a comforting word from the Lord.

This book would have served to comfort this remnant by reminding them that they could never be destroyed. Even though most of the nation was scattered throughout the known world, God was still watching over them. The Jews had a faithful God who keeps His covenants. The Lord had promised to bless those who bless His people. Accordingly, Xerxes blessed the Jews and his resulting greatness is described in 10:1-2. The Lord had likewise promised to curse those who curse His people. Accordingly, Haman, the enemy of the Jews, is destroyed along with all the other enemies of the Jews. The words of Zeresh summarize well the message of the book, "If Mordecai, before whom you have begun to fall, is of Jewish origin, you will not overcome him, but will surely fall before him" (6:13). The original audience could expect the same judgment to be meted out to their adversaries (Neh. 4:4-5; 6:14).

The book reveals that the reason the audience should have this confidence is because of the absolute sovereignty of their God. Charles Haddon Spurgeon once said "There is no attribute of God more comforting to His children than the doctrine of divine sovereignty."[16] Even though Esther is the only book of the Bible in which the name of God does not appear, His works are manifest in every chapter. The story is "built on an accumulating series of seeming coincidences,[17] all of which are indispensable when the story reaches its moment of peak dramatic tension at the beginning of chapter 6. How 'lucky' the Jews were that Esther was so attractive, that she was chosen over other possible candidates, that Mordecai overheard that assassination plot, that a record of Mordecai's report of the assassination plans was written in the royal chronicles, that Esther had concealed her identity, that the king would have seen her without having called for her, that the king could not sleep that night, that he asked to have the annals read, that the scribe read from that incident several years earlier concerning Mordecai, that the king was wide awake enough to inquire as to whether he had rewarded Mordecai. . . . Luck indeed!"[18] This book was written to emphasize the sovereign providence of God for His people, a sovereignty that should serve to comfort the nation in the midst of their struggles.

A secondary purpose was to explain the origins of the Feast of Purim.[19] The word Purim is the plural form of the Persian word *pur*, meaning "lot." The Persian word is derived from the Old Babylonian word *puru*, meaning "fate" or "lot." The name of the feast refers to the lot cast by Haman to choose the day of Jewish extermination. This feast, celebrated each year, would have been a constant reminder of the sovereignty and providence of God.

Historicity

The historicity of the book of Esther has been doubted for centuries. Luther was so hostile to the book that he "would wish that they [Esther and 2 Maccabees] did not exist at all; for they judaize too greatly and have much pagan impropriety" (*Table Talk*, 24). Writing at the turn of the century, Paton argues, "It is doubtful whether even a historical kernel underlies its narrative."[20] A prominent contemporary Jewish scholar asserts, "If somehow or other the canon were to become open in the twentieth century, I would be among those who would vote to exclude Esther."[21] Adele Berlin, the noted literary analyst, adds, "The story itself is implausible as history and, as many scholars now agree, it is better viewed as imaginative."[22]

Some of the reasons for this doubt include the following: Esther is the only book of the Bible in which the name of God does not appear; the New Testament never quotes from Esther; the book was not found among the Dead Sea scrolls; the Law is never mentioned in the book; the author of the book is not known; prayer is never mentioned in the book; there is no extra-biblical evidence of the existence of Esther; the book records questionable behavior on the part of its heroine.

As a result of these perceived problems, virtually all modern scholars deny the historicity of the book.[23] Many scholars think Esther is simply mythological, a story told to explain the origins of Purim, an originally pagan holiday, in terms acceptable to the Jews. Others see the story as a Jewish adaptation of a Babylonian or Persian religious festival, with Mordecai and Esther representing the Mesopotamian gods Marduk and Ishtar. Still others see the book as representative of the clash between Judaism and Hellenism in the Hasmonean period. A final common interpretation is that the book portrays the conflict between Babylonian religion and a Persian religious cult. According to this view, Mordecai and Esther represent Marduk and Ishtar in their struggle against the Persian cult of Mithra, represented by Haman and Ahasuerus. Each of these views should be strenuously rejected.

Perhaps the most significant problem listed above is the fact that the name of God does not appear in the book.[24] Or does it? Scroggie believes that the name of Yahweh can be seen four times in acrostic form in the book, a phenomenon that he claims is beyond the realm of mere coincidence. He suggests that the omission of God's name is intentional, thereby protecting the book from pagan plagiarization and the substitution of the name of a heathen god.[25] Weiland offers additional explanations for the absence of God's name:

> First, the hidden nature of divine providence may partially explain why the author did not mention God. Divine providence does not necessitate observable intervention. God may work quietly outside the realm of human purview as well as openly and visible to human eyes. Second, in Esther the historical situation of the captivity may explain why God is hidden from view. These Jews elected not to return to the land of Israel where God continued to work out His plan for the nation. Mordecai originally preferred anonymity (2:10, 20), possibly implying at some level a disassociation with the God of the Jews. Third, omitting any reference to the Lord's visible activity adds to the rhetorical irony the author employed in his story. Fourth, not mentioning God's name helps emphasize that His providential care does not alleviate the necessity of human action and responsibility.[26]

In any event, the absence of God's name is more than compensated for by the presence of His power and grace in the deliverance of His people, a fact that gives canonical worth to the book (cf. Esther 4:14; 9:20-22).[27]

Even though the problems of Esther are many, they were not strong enough to keep the book from making it into the Old Testament canon, a fact that argues strongly for the historicity of the account. Many of the Church Fathers had reservations, however, and the book of Esther was placed among the Antilegomena writings ("those spoken against;" i.e., Song of Solomon, Ecclesiastes, Esther, Ezekiel, and Proverbs). Christ Himself seems to validate the Hebrew canon, and subsequently the book of Esther, when He refers to the Old Testament with the phrase "from the blood of righteous Abel to the blood of Zechariah, the son of Berechiah, whom you murdered between the temple and the altar" (Mat 23:35). This reference alludes to the books of Genesis and 2 Chronicles, the first and last books of the Hebrew canon. Beckwith summarizes the historical evidence in support of the canonicity of Esther when he writes,

> Josephus's attestation of Esther is direct. He tells us that the 22 canonical books [the Hebrew equivalent of our Protestant canon] trace the course of history from the Creation to the time of Artaxerxes the successor of Xerxes, whom he identifies with the Ahasuerus who married Esther. . . . Esther was in the canon of Aquila, and it was probably accepted in the Western Christian church from the beginning. . . . It is quoted in the Mishnah and the other tannaitic literature, in the latter case with the standard formulas for citing Scripture.[28]

Another strong argument supporting the historicity of Esther is the accuracy of its portrayal of the Persian court. The author's familiarity with both general and specific features of Persian life during the Achaemenian period lends credence to the story as does his intimate knowledge of Persian court etiquette and public administration.[29] The author knows details of topography, customs, protocol, and chronology. The book's portrayal of Ahasuerus is especially accurate. Barucq maintains that Esther's account "conforms perfectly to Xerxes as we know from Herodotus."[30] Talmon concludes, "there is a fairly universal agreement among scholars that the author of the Esther-story generally shows an intimate knowledge of the Persian court-etiquette and public administration. . . . If his tale does not mirror historical reality, it is indeed well imagined."[31]

A final argument supporting the historicity of the book is its genre. The book is historical narrative and reads as such.[32] The account begins with a Hebrew waw-consecutive with the verb "to be" ("Now it took place"). This form is followed by a temporal clause characteristically employed to initiate a historical account.[33] This fact places the book squarely among other Old Testament historical narratives, the historicity of which is commonly accepted (e.g., Joshua, Judges, Ruth, 2 Samuel). The book also contains numerous chronological references (e.g., 1:1, 3; 2:16; 3:7). These chronological details testify to the historicity of the story. In fact, "the basis for the celebration of Purim is the historic moment during which the Jews were delivered from their enemies. If the story does not report this historical incident with a certain measure of accuracy, then Purim is only a celebration of a legendary victory."[34] Finally, the book includes three implicit invitations to search the historical records (2:23; 6:1; 10:2), a feature common in historical narrative, especially prevalent in the book of Chronicles (e.g., 1 Chron. 29:29; 2 Chron. 16:11; 20:34; 25:26; 35:27). This invitation would scarcely have been given if the book were not historically accurate. Obviously, the author of Esther considered his narrative to be just as accurate as the other biblical accounts.[35]

While there is no extra-biblical evidence for Esther, there may be some for Mordecai. Mordecai is probably to be identified with the *Marduka* who is listed as a *sipir* (accountant) in a tablet from Borsippa in Mesopotamia. The tablet details an inspection tour of Susa led by Marduka during the latter part of the reign of Darius I or the early years of Xerxes. It is also possible that Mordecai is to be identified with one of the individuals named Marduka in the Elamite tablets from Persepolis, dated between 505 and 499 B.C. Nevertheless, this is an argument from silence. It is possible that evidence is forthcoming. After all, liberal scholars denied the existence of Belshazzar until the Cylinder Inscription of Nabonidus was discovered, identifying Belshazzar as the son of Nabonidus.

Structure and Outline

The book of Esther is naturally divided into six sections. The first section relates the story of how Esther replaced Vashti as queen of Persia (1:1-2:23). The second section reveals the plot of Haman to destroy the Jews (3:1-15). The third section describes the efforts of Esther and Mordecai to save the Jews (4:1-7:10). The fourth section is an account of how the plans of Haman were thwarted (8:1-9:19). The fifth section explains the origins of the Feast of Purim (9:20-32). The sixth section is an appendix describing the greatness of Mordecai (10:1-3).

In an attempt to reconcile some of the noteworthy problems mentioned earlier, the Greek version of the Book of Esther (LXX) contains six major additions to the narrative. Esther 11:1-12:5 in the

LXX describes a dream that Mordecai had on Nisan 1 in the second year of the reign of Artaxerxes the Great. Esther 12:6-13:6 in the LXX provides a copy of the letter written by Haman calling for the extermination of the Jews (cf. 3:12). Esther 13:7-18 in the LXX records the prayer of Mordecai offered to the Lord upon hearing of the decree of Haman. Esther 14:1-15:15 in the LXX details the prayer of Esther offered to the Lord upon hearing of the decree of Haman. Esther 16:1-23 in the LXX supplies a copy of the letter written by Mordecai allowing the Jews to defend themselves on Adar 13 (cf. 7:9-10). Esther 10:4-13 in the LXX reveals the interpretation of Mordecai's dream described in the first addition. These additions should be regarded as uninspired attempts to fill in some of the noticeable gaps in the inspired version of the story. This practice is common among the apocryphal writers (cf. e.g., Baruch, Epistle of Jeremiah, Prayer of Azariah, Prayer of Manasseh).

Outline
I. Esther Replaces Vashti as Queen (1:1-2:23)
    A. The King's Banquets (1:1-9)
        1. King Ahasuerus Introduced (1:1)
        2. The Banquet for the Nobles (1:2-4)
        3. The Banquet for the People of Susa (1:5-8)
        4. The Banquet for the Palace Women (1:9)
    B. Queen Vashti Deposed (1:10-22)
        1. The King's Command (1:10-11)
        2. The Queen's Defiance (1:12)
        3. The King Seeks Counsel (1:13-15)
        4. Memucan's Advice (1:16-20)
        5. The King's Decision (1:21-22)
    C. The Search for a Successor (2:1-11)
        1. The Plan to Replace Vashti (2:1-4)
        2. Mordecai and Esther (2:5-7)
        3. Esther Pleases Hegai (2:8-11)
    D. The Contest (2:12-16)
        1. The Preparation of the Virgins (2:12)
        2. The Parameters of the Contest (2:13-14)
        3. Esther Takes Her Turn (2:15-16)

E. Esther Chosen as Queen (2:17-23)
1. Esther Pleases the King (2:17-18)
2. Mordecai Sits at the King's Gate (2:19-20)
3. Mordecai Saves the King's Life (2:21-23)
II. Haman Plots the Destruction of the Jews (3:1-15)
A. Mordecai Disrespects Haman (3:1-6)
1. Haman the Agagite (3:1)
2. Mordecai's Rebuff (3:2-4)
3. Haman's Response (3:5-6)
B. The Plot of Haman (3:7-15)
1. Haman Casts the Lot (3:7)
2. Haman's Request (3:8-9)
3. The King's Response (3:10-15)
III. Esther Saves Her People (4:1-7:10)
A. Mordecai's Instruction (4:1-12)
1. The Reaction of the Jews (4:1-3)
2. The Request of Mordecai (4:4-8)
3. The Reply of Esther (4:9-12)
B. The Decision to Act (4:13-17)
1. The Rebuke by Mordecai (4:13-14)
2. The Resolve of Esther (4:15-17)
C. Esther's Intervention (5:1-14)
1. Esther Visits the King (5:1-4)
2. The First Banquet (5:5-8)
3. Haman's Pride (5:9-14)
D. The King Honors Mordecai (6:1-14)
1. The King's Insomnia (6:1-3)
2. Haman's Recommendation (6:4-9)
3. Mordecai's Exaltation (6:10-14)
E. Haman's Execution (7:1-10)
1. Esther's Plea (7:1-6)
2. Haman's Fate (7:7-10)
IV. The Plot Reversed (8:1-9:19)
A. The King's Decree (8:1-17)
1. Mordecai's Promotion (8:1-2)
2. Esther's Petition (8:3-8)
3. The King's Proclamation (8:9-14)

Summary of Contents

Esther Replaces Vashti as Queen (1:1-2:23)

The book begins with the traditional Hebrew formula *hayah* ("Now it took place;" cf. Joshua, Judges, Ruth, 1 Samuel, 2 Samuel). The initial events of the book of Esther take place in an exotic location. The reader is immediately thrust into the midst of an extravagant banquet in the gardens of the king's palace in the capital city of the most powerful nation on earth. In 483 B.C., the third year of Xerxes' reign, he decided to give a banquet for the chief administrators of his empire. On festive occasions the Persian kings would hold huge banquets. Ctesias records that these banquets would accommodate as many as 15,000 guests.[36] For six months (180 days) the king entertained his guests. His guests included his princes (probably his closest relatives), his attendants (oftentimes his closest confidants), his army officers (his military leaders), the nobles (probably the wealthy landowners), and the satraps ("princes of his provinces;" 1:3).

In light of the length of the banquet (180 days) and the roster of invitees, this may well have been the military planning session for Xerxes' invasion of Greece the following year. Certainly the parties involved would be included in the planning of such an ambitious mission. The princes and attendants were his closest advisors, the military leaders would plan the campaign, the nobles were needed to help finance the operation, and the satraps would be responsible for raising the necessary supplies and manpower.

This banquet is the first of many mentioned throughout Esther. In fact, the first chapter of Esther alone describes three different banquets. Banqueting is a central theme throughout the book.[37] The king throws a banquet for Esther after she is named queen (2:18). Esther prepares a banquet for the king and Haman in 5:4. Esther holds another banquet for the king and Haman in 7:2. The Jews celebrate the news of Xerxes' decree by feasting in 8:17. The Jews celebrate their victory over their enemies by feasting in 9:18-19. And finally, the Jews commit to celebrating the Feast of Purim annually on Adar 14-15 (9:20-22).

At the end of the banquet for the leadership of the empire, the king hosted a banquet for the entire city of Susa. This banquet lasted seven days and was probably a way of repaying the residents of the city, many of whom had no doubt provided the services needed during the first banquet. The emphasis in the passage is on the limitless resources of the king (cf. 1:4, 7). To be able to host a weeklong banquet for the entire city of Susa required an enormous amount of resources, especially in light of the fact that the 180-day banquet for the aristocracy had just ended.

This banquet was held in the court of the garden of the king's palace. The entire area was decorated in white and violet, the royal colors of Persia. The aesthetic appeal was further enhanced by the abundance of gold, silver, marble, and precious stones. As one would expect, the principal activity during this banquet was the drinking of wine. This wine was in abundance and was served in gold vessels. Due to the significance of the occasion, the king made a law allowing everyone to drink according to their own wishes.[38]

While Xerxes was giving his banquet in the garden, his wife Vashti[39] was giving a banquet for the women in the palace itself. The text never reveals why there were two separate banquets. It was not customary for Persian men and women to eat separately. For example, in chapter seven, the king and Haman are seen as participating in a banquet with Esther. It is possible that the sheer number of guests demanded a second location. It is also possible that Vashti's banquet was for the women of the harem. These women would never have been allowed to mingle with the public, thus necessitating a second banquet in the privacy of the palace.

After a week of continual drinking, the king had become quite intoxicated.[40] Ahasuerus called his closest attendants[41] and asked them to bring Queen Vashti to the king's banquet so all could witness her beauty. The public exhibition of the queen was part of the king's presentation of the glory and splendor of his majesty (cf. 1:4). The stunningly beautiful Queen Vashti served as a sort of living trophy; the king's most prized possession. The exhibition of the royal queen would have served as a fitting climax to the celebration. Certainly her appearance would have inspired patriotism and loyalty on the part of the subjects, critical attributes for men about to embark on a great war.

When the attendants came to get Vashti, the queen refused to accompany them back to the king. The text never states why Vashti refused the king's order. Perhaps she was pregnant with Artaxerxes who was born about this time. Perhaps she had recently given birth to Artaxerxes and lacked confidence in her post-natal appearance. Perhaps she was ill. Perhaps the king required her to appear in the nude. Perhaps she felt her responsibilities were to the women of her own banquet. Perhaps she was simply not in the mood to be gawked at by thousands of drunken revelers. According to the Talmud, the queen refused to come because the angel Gabriel had smitten her with leprosy. Whatever the reason, the queen's refusal to obey the king's command was a serious breach of court etiquette and opened the door for a massive revolt on the part of the king's subjects, particularly the women. This great king who ruled the whole world could not rule his own wife. The queen's refusal infuriated the king. It was a great humiliation and would not go unpunished.

Before making a decision concerning Vashti, the king sought the advice of his council. The king asked his closest advisors whether or not there was a law in place which applied to the situation at hand, that is, the punishment of Vashti for refusing the king's order. Evidently there was no law already in place as the king's counselors instead offered their advice. It is likely that no Persian queen had ever publicly refused her husband prior to this time.

The king's advisors believed that Vashti's defiance would lead to a revolt by the leading women of the empire against the authority of their husbands. Memucan, speaking on behalf of the king's council, warns the king about the possible effects Vashti's behavior could have on the nation as a whole. By identifying the matter as an issue of national concern, Memucan succeeds in persuading the king. This is the same tactic Haman will use in 3:8 as part of his plan for the extermination of the Jews.

To resolve this situation, Memucan recommends that the king issue a decree deposing Queen Vashti. Vashti's sentence was not execution; she was simply demoted within the harem. As a result, she lost her prestigious title, her position of influence in the court, and the chance to gain the favor of the king. Note that verse nineteen is the first reference to Vashti without her title queen. Prior to this verse, she is always identified as Queen Vashti (1:9, 11, 12, 15, 16, 17). From this point on, she is simply identified as Vashti (1:19, 2:1, 4, 17). The punishment of Vashti fits her crime. Since she would not come at the king's request, she would no longer be allowed to come into the king's presence at all.

Memucan further advises the king to choose a new queen, one that is "more worthy" (1:19) than Vashti. The same Hebrew word utilized here (*tob*) is used in 1 Samuel 15:28 to describe God's choice of David as a "better" king than Saul. David was a "better" man because of his obedience to the Lord (cf. 1 Sam. 15:22-26). Here in Esther, the phrase is used similarly, referring to one who will obey the king's commands. It is likely that the king's decree would be structured in such a way as to allow any husband whose wife disobeys him to have her punished (cf. 1:22). The anticipated effect of the decree is that women throughout the nation would respect and honor their husband's wishes. The decrees of the Persians could not be repealed once they became official (cf. 8:8; Dan. 6:8).[42]

Memucan's advice pleased the king and he followed the recommendation of his council. Xerxes issued the decree and sent letters[43] throughout his kingdom. Each province received letters written in their native language, a statement that reveals the truly international and multicultural constitution of the Persian Empire. It is likely that the decree was also written in Aramaic, the official international language of the Persian Empire.

At some point subsequent to the events of chapter one, the king's anger subsided and he remembered his former queen. The events of this passage take place two or three years after the banquet described in chapter one. In the meantime, Xerxes has invaded Greece and been repulsed. One gets the sense from 2:1 that the king regrets his decision to depose Vashti. However, her punishment has been decreed and could not be repealed. His attendants sought to appease him by reminding him that he needed to select a new queen. The opportunity to pick a new queen from all the beautiful virgins in the empire would likely have removed Xerxes' reservations about deposing Vashti. As one would expect, the suggestion of his attendants pleased the king.

In an effort to get as many women as possible involved in the contest, the advisors of Ahasuerus recommend that the king appoint overseers in each of the provinces of the kingdom. These overseers were given the responsibility of gathering the most beautiful young virgins in their respective provinces and transporting them to Susa. The king's counselors further recommend that the maidens who were to participate in the contest be placed under the authority of Hegai, the eunuch who was in charge of the women. These women were not yet regarded as concubines since the concubines were in the care of Shaashgaz, a different eunuch.

A parenthetical passage (2:5-7) is now introduced into the story, disrupting the flow of the narrative. The disruption involves the identification of two characters that will play significant roles in the unfolding of the plot, Mordecai and Esther. Mordecai is identified as a Jew[44] from the tribe of Benjamin living in the capital city of Susa. Mordecai's great-grandfather Kish had been taken into exile at the same time as Jeconiah (Jehoiachin). This exile took place in 597 B.C. The name Mordecai is derived from the name of the Babylonian storm god Marduk and means "worshiper of Marduk."

Esther's name is Persian and means "star." It is derived from the Akkadian name Ishtar, the Mesopotamian goddess of love, war, and the planet Venus. Esther's Hebrew name is Hadassah, which comes from the word for myrtle, a beautiful fragrant tree. The use of her Persian name would help Esther keep her national identity a secret. It was common for the Jews of the exile to receive and use pagan names (cf. Ezra 1:8; Dan. 1:7).

Esther is described as "beautiful[45] of form and face" (2:7). In Hebrew literature, the epithets included in the narrative at a character's first introduction invariably prove crucial to the plot (e.g. Judg. 3:15; Ruth 2:1; 1 Sam. 16:12; 2 Sam. 11:2).[46] Such is the case with Esther. Her beauty will allow her the opportunity to become the queen of Persia. It will take a "beautiful" woman to replace the "beautiful" Vashti (cf. 1:11). Esther had been adopted by Mordecai, her cousin, when her parents died. Mordecai provided her with a family and regarded her as his own daughter.

In 2:8, the writer resumes the story from 2:1-4. Esther was taken to Susa and placed in the custody of Hegai. Hegai was immediately smitten with Esther. He demonstrates his affection for Esther by providing her with seven maids and by assigning her the best place in the harem. The text reveals that Esther did not make known the fact that she was a Jew. In an attempt to keep her national identity a secret, Esther certainly would have partaken of unclean food (Lev. 11:46-47) and broken a number of other ceremonial regulations, including laws of separation and worship. It would have been impossible in this situation for a faithful Jew to keep their ethnic heritage hidden while still fulfilling the obligations of the Mosaic Law. The text fails to specifically condemn Esther for her actions. This lack of moral judgment is common in biblical narratives.

Mordecai obviously has great affection for his cousin Esther. He nervously visits the harem each day in order to find out news about Esther. If anti-Semitism has already become prevalent in the Persian court, then he may be worried for Esther's safety. In 2:21 the reader is informed that Mordecai has a position of authority in the king's court ("sitting at the king's gate").

Each woman who was to spend a night with the king spent twelve months preparing for her opportunity. This preparation would have involved elaborate beauty treatments, a prescribed diet, and courses in court etiquette. The elaborate beauty treatment given each of the virgins is detailed in this passage. Each contestant spent six months with oil of myrrh.[47] Each contestant spent another six months with a variety of other perfumes and cosmetics. The Persians were famous for their spices and perfumes.

2:13-14 describes the parameters of the contest. The king would sleep with a different virgin whenever he wanted to. There can be no doubt that this was a sexual contest, not simply a beauty contest. When a virgin's opportunity was presented, she would go to the king's chambers in the evening and spend the night with him. Each woman was allowed to bring anything she wanted to. Following her night with the king, each maiden would be placed into the care of Shaashgaz, the king's eunuch who was in charge of the concubines. Shaashgaz would then give her a place in the harem.

Esther's opportunity finally arrives as she is taken to the king's palace in the month Tebeth (late December, early January) of the seventh year of Xerxes' reign. The young maiden follows the advice of Hegai and only takes with her whatever he recommends. Esther's night with the king had such an impact on him that he loved Esther more than all the other virgins and chose her as his new queen.

Esther became queen in the winter of 479-478 B.C. Esther was coronated four years after Vashti had been deposed. The king himself takes the royal crown and sets it on Esther's head. In celebration of the queen's coronation, the king pronounced a holiday for the entire kingdom. The text notes that at this time Mordecai was "sitting at the king's gate" (2:19). This phrase meant that he was in a position of authority at the court.

While sitting at the king's gate, Mordecai learns of a plot against the king by Bigthan and Teresh. Like a true patriot, Mordecai quickly informs Esther of his discovery and she in turn notifies the king, being sure to give the credit to Mordecai. This marks the second of four important collaborative efforts between Mordecai and Esther recorded in this book (i.e., the contest, the assassination attempt, the rescue of the Jews, the institution of Purim). After verifying the claims of Mordecai, the king has both conspirators executed. He then recorded the event in the official records of his reign.

Haman Plots the Destruction of the Jews (3:1-15)

The events of chapter three take place just over four years after Esther was named queen (cf. 2:16; 3:7). At this point in the narrative a new character, Haman, is introduced. Haman is identified as the son of Hammedatha the Agagite. The identification of Haman as an

Agagite is a deliberate attempt to classify him as the modern incarnation of an ancient enemy of the Jews. Agag was the name of the Amalekite king Saul failed to execute, despite the fact that he was directly ordered to do so by the Lord through the words of Samuel, "Now go and strike Amalek and utterly destroy all that he has, and do not spare him; but put to death both man and woman, child and infant, ox and sheep, camel and donkey" (1 Sam. 15:3). Mordecai was identified in 2:5 as the son of Kish, surely an allusion to the Kish that was the father of Saul and also of the tribe of Benjamin.

Haman is promoted by Xerxes and placed in a position of authority over all the princes. Haman was probably the chief administrator in the empire, second only to the king and perhaps the crown prince. His title was likely that of "prime minister" or "vizier." The position of this passage in the overall narrative is worthy of note. One might have expected Mordecai to be elevated in this passage in light of his heroics detailed at the end of chapter two. Instead, it is Haman, Mordecai's future enemy, who gets promoted while Mordecai gets forgotten. This won't be the last time that the roles of Haman and Mordecai are reversed in the narrative.

The nature of Haman's new position was such that he was now worthy of the respect of all he came in contact with. All the king's servants were commanded to bow before Haman whenever he passed by them. It is highly unlikely that these Persian officials were asked to actually worship Haman. Paying homage simply meant to give him the respect due him because of his exalted position. Nevertheless, Mordecai refused to bow before Haman whenever he passed by. When the rest of the king's servants who sat at the gate inquired as to the reason why he refused to follow the king's decree, Mordecai responded by appealing to his ethnicity, the fact that he was a Jew. Therefore, Mordecai's refusal to bow before Haman may have been due to the ancient antagonism between the Jews and the Amalekites rather than to religious conviction.

Mordecai's actions strike a major blow to the ego of Haman and he is filled with rage at this sign of disrespect. The anger of Haman leads him to take rash steps to appease his pride. Instead of simply laying hands on Mordecai, he decides to get his revenge by plotting to kill all the Jews in the empire. Haman becomes aware of the national identity of Mordecai when some of the king's officials inform him that he is a Jew.

Haman, putting his plan into action, casts the lot (the Persian word *pur* means "lot") to determine the best day to seek vengeance upon the Jews. Quite often, the lot was cast during the first month of the year in order to determine which dates were best for important events. By casting the lot, Haman is leaving this monumental decision up to his god.

Having determined the best day to enact vengeance on the Jews, Haman now moves to the second part of his plan, that is, gaining the king's permission for his scheme. He approaches the king and brings an accusation against a "certain people" (3:8). Haman describes these people as scattered throughout all the provinces of the kingdom. This scattering of the Jews was a result of the deportations prescribed for the conquered nations of Israel and Judah by the Assyrians and Babylonians. Haman claims that these people do not observe the king's laws, a very serious offense in ancient times.

In hopes of gaining the king's approval, Haman offers to make a donation to the king's treasury. Haman was evidently a very wealthy man. The 10,000 talents offered by Haman was a considerable amount. Perhaps Haman expected to recompense some of this money by confiscating the possessions of the Jews. The offer of 10,000 talents would have greatly enticed the king since his treasury had recently been depleted thanks to his recent wars with the Egyptians and Greeks.

Finding no good reason to deny the petition, the king grants Haman's request. The edict is given on Nisan 13, the day before Passover, which celebrated the Jews' redemption from slavery in Egypt. The date is April 17, 474 B.C. God had previously delivered his people from the hands of the Egyptian Pharaoh. Now, His people were again in need of deliverance from a foreign monarch. As part of his permission, the king gives Haman his signet ring. The imprint of the king's signet ring essentially served as his signature. Haman uses the king's signet ring to write his decree and send it throughout the empire. The decree called for the extermination of the Jews. The date on which the Jews could be attacked was March 7, 473 B.C. (Adar 13). All Jews, regardless of age or gender, were the focus of the edict. There is a striking contrast in 3:15. While the king and Haman celebrated, the city was in confusion. No doubt the common citizen could not believe such a decree had been issued.

Esther Saves Her People (4:1-7:10)

When the Jews heard the decree of Haman they were understandably distraught. Their distress was communicated throughout the city as they immediately engaged themselves in a variety of visible forms of mourning. The first form mentioned is that of tearing one's clothes.[48] Since many individuals of this time period likely only owned one pair of clothes, this action took on great significance and was perhaps the most popular form of visible mourning. It was an outward illustration of the grief that was tearing one apart inside. The second form of mourning mentioned is that of the use of sackcloth and ashes.[49] Sackcloth is made of goat or camel hair, thus making it coarse and uncomfortable. The piece of sackcloth clothing used in mourning usually took the form of a loincloth. The third form of mourning mentioned is that of wailing.[50] This form seems to be commonly associated with death and is probably designed to picture a parent's uncontrollable cries of anguish over the loss of a child. The fourth form of mourning mentioned is that of fasting.[51] Fasting usually accompanies a time of great anxiety. The fifth and final form of mourning mentioned in these verses is that of weeping.[52] Weeping usually signifies the loss of a loved one.

Mordecai especially is cut to the heart. It is on his account that the Jewish people are endangered. Because he refused to bow to Haman, his countrymen are condemned. Esther's maidens and eunuchs witnessed Mordecai's anguish and rushed at once to inform the queen. Evidently, they were aware that Esther and Mordecai had some sort of relationship with each other. Maidens and eunuchs were the two categories of temple personnel at the queen's disposal. Esther obviously had great trust in them and used them to relay information both to and from Mordecai (cf. 4:5, 9, 12, 13, 15).

The news of Mordecai's behavior caused Esther great despair and consternation. She immediately sends clothes to Mordecai to replace the sackcloth that he had begun to wear. Mordecai refuses to change his appearance. Perhaps he was trying to gain the attention of the king. When Esther learns that Mordecai has refused the clothing she offered, she sends Hathach, her chief eunuch, to find out why Mordecai was acting so peculiarly. The queen was so isolated from general affairs in her harem that she knew nothing of the decree that had electrified the city.[53]

Hathach meets with Mordecai in the city square. This square was located in front of the palace gate and was a customary meeting spot. Mordecai tells Hathach everything that has happened, being sure to make special mention of Haman's promise of payment. Mordecai asks him to tell Esther to use her exalted position to influence the king to deliver her people. He even supplies Hathach with a copy of the king's edict in case there was any doubt as to the accuracy of his information.

Hathach immediately relays Mordecai's message to Esther. Esther's response is one of apprehension. She explains that if she approaches the king unannounced it could result in her death. Access to the king was strictly governed. One could not normally go before the king unannounced. This custom helped to prevent attempts on the king's life. It also served to separate him from those whom he did not wish to see. The correct protocol was to send a messenger requesting an audience. The king would then respond, either granting or denying the request. Esther notes that she had not been called into the king's presence for thirty days. After five years of marriage, the king's desire for her had obviously cooled. Once again, Hathach rushes off to faithfully relay Esther's message to Mordecai.

Mordecai's response to Esther is one of rebuke. He informs Esther that she will not escape the decree even though she holds a high position in the palace. The decree of Haman called for the death of "all" Jews (3:13). Surely Haman's hatred was such that he would be willing even to take the life of the queen. While appearing before the king unannounced might jeopardize her life, her fate is certain if she decides to do nothing.

Of primary significance in this passage is Mordecai's belief that the Jews would be delivered somehow. He is convinced that "deliverance will arise for the Jews from another place." Even if Esther chooses to do nothing, the Jews will surely survive. Although the name of God is not mentioned, He is clearly the inspiration for

Mordecai's confidence. As a result, Mordecai's rebuke is critical in the attempt to understand the book as a whole. Although most of the nation was scattered throughout the known world, God was still watching over them, making sure that they would never be destroyed. The Jews had a faithful God who keeps His covenants (cf. Gen. 12:2-3). The reason for Mordecai's confidence is the absolute sovereignty of God. He will deliver His people. The book of Esther was written to emphasize the sovereign providence of God for His people, a fact at once apparent in Mordecai's rebuke.

Mordecai also remarks "who knows whether you have not attained royalty for such a time as this?" (4:14). Mordecai evidently realizes that the selection of Esther as queen was providential. His words suggest the possibility that everything that has happened in their lives has been a prelude to this moment. Perhaps Esther was serendipitously chosen as queen in order to be in a position to save her people when the opportunity arose. That moment has now arrived.

After hearing the words of Mordecai, the queen tells her representatives to send her reply. Esther calls for a fast among the Jews for three days. This fast included both food and drink and was to be held both night and day. Having prepared herself spiritually, the queen resolves to approach the king in an effort to save her people. It is at this point that Esther utters the immortal words, "if I perish, I perish" (4:16). Esther's statement is one of courageous resolve, not an expression of resignation to her inevitable fate (cf. Gen. 43:14).[6] From this point forward, Esther takes the lead in the effort to deliver her people. The text notes this shift by stating that Mordecai did "just as Esther had commanded him." Mordecai never again gives Esther a command.

On the third day of the fast Esther decided to put her plan to save the Jews into action. She prepares to see the king by getting dressed in her royal robes. Esther approaches the king's throne room and stands in the inner court. This would have been a serious breech of court etiquette and Esther does indeed put her life on the line (cf. 4:16).[54]

The king soon observes Esther standing in the court and extends his golden scepter to her. The extending of the scepter was a sign for Esther to approach the king. Royal protocol demanded that the one to whom the scepter was pointed was to approach the throne and touch the end of the scepter. After Esther had touched the end of the scepter the king questions her concerning her actions. Xerxes evidently realizes that something is weighing heavily on the queen's mind. Wishing to put her mind at ease, the king reassures her that any reasonable request would be granted.

Esther's request is for the king's presence at a banquet so that she can make her request to the king in a less formal setting. The throne room would have been very formal. The king was certain to be surrounded by his cupbearer and other attendants. Guards were also assuredly present. Esther further requests the presence of Haman at the banquet.

The king immediately summons Haman so that he could fulfill Esther's request. Esther had already prepared the food so the parties could eat without delay (5:4). The king evidently realized that Esther's request was not simply that they come to her banquet since he again questions her concerning her petition upon the completion of the meal. In replying to the king, Esther again puts off her request, this time asking the king and Haman to come to another meal.

The queen's second invitation to a banquet had the effect of stimulating the arrogance of Haman. He leaves the palace "glad and pleased of heart" (5:9). As Haman gleefully passes through the gate of the palace, Mordecai again refuses to pay homage to him. Haman's joy quickly turns to fury. Even with all of his greatness, Haman is dismayed because one person refuses to give him the honor he thinks he deserves. Despite Mordecai's insubordination, Haman is able to control himself, likely because he believes that his revenge will soon come to fruition when the extermination of the Jews is accomplished.

Upon arriving at his home, Haman calls for his wife Zeresh and his closest friends so that they can listen to him complain and commiserate with his problem. Haman begins by recounting his greatness. A significant part of Haman's importance was his great wealth. Another significant part of Mordecai's greatness was the fact that he had many sons. The Persians placed great value on having many sons. We learn in 9:10 that Haman has ten sons. A final indication of the importance of Haman is the nature of his position in the Persian court. He was probably the highest ruler of the empire outside the family of King Xerxes. However, in the eyes of Haman all that he has gained is worthless in light of the insubordination of Mordecai.

As part of his description of his own greatness, Haman informs his confidants that the queen had invited him to a special banquet earlier that day. He further reveals that she has invited him to another banquet on the following day. Haman is so taken with his own importance that he never even suspects Esther's ulterior motive in inviting him to her banquets.

After listening to his lament, Haman's wife Zeresh offers a solution. She tells Haman to build a gallows and simply get the king's permission to hang Mordecai. If Haman is able to get the king's permission to exterminate an entire race, then surely he is capable of getting the king's permission to kill a single individual. Note the cold heart of Zeresh – have Mordecai hanged, then go joyfully!

Following the queen's banquet, the king has a difficult time sleeping and asks for the "book of records" (6:1) to be read to him. The "book of records" was a detailed listing of the daily activities of the king. It was the official record of the proceedings of the Persian Empire (cf. 10:2). The king's servant who was reading to him chose to read from the events that occurred during the seventh year of his reign (cf. 2:16, 21). Upon hearing of the heroic exploits of Mordecai in the matter of Bigthana and Teresh, the king questioned his attendants concerning the nature of the honor that had been granted him. The king was no doubt surprised to hear that nothing had been done for Mordecai. The king normally rewarded those who helped him. Mordecai's heroic actions had taken place almost five years earlier.

Throughout the narrative, Xerxes consistently seeks counsel from his officials. Such is the case in this passage as the king questions his attendants as to who is present in the court. The attendants inform the king that Haman is in the court. The king, seeking to reward Mordecai, calls for Haman and questions him concerning the nature of an appropriate reward for one whom the king wished to honor. Haman, believing that he was the one that the king was referencing, realizes that he cannot ask for a promotion since he has already achieved the highest position possible. The only thing that would be even greater than his current position would be to be treated like the king himself. Haman's recommendation, quoting the king's own words, is that "the man whom the king desires to honor" (6:7) be treated as if he were the king.

Haman's recommended treatment involved three elements. First, the one deserving of honor was to be allowed to wear a royal robe worn previously by the king. Wearing the king's robe was a mark of special favor in the Ancient Near East (cf. Herodotus, *Histories* 9.109-112). Second, the one deserving of honor was to be allowed to ride upon the king's horse. Third, the one deserving of honor was to be led on horseback throughout the streets of the city by one of the king's "most noble princes" (6:9). While leading this procession, the prince was to proclaim "Thus it shall be done to the man whom the king desires to honor" (6:9).

Haman's answer delights the king and he immediately instructs Haman to do exactly as he himself had recommended. However, Haman was to play the part of the "most noble prince" while Mordecai was to be "the man whom the king desires to honor." Haman, following the orders of the king, takes the robe and the horse and gives them to Mordecai. He then leads Mordecai throughout the city proclaiming, "Thus it shall be done to the man whom the king desires to honor." This parade probably lasted for hours and would have been observed by the entire population. One can only imagine the shame and humiliation heaped upon Haman as he led his arch-enemy throughout the streets of the city. When the triumphal procession had been completed, Mordecai returned to his place at the king's gate while Haman rushed home with his head covered. Covering one's head was a traditional form of mourning in the Ancient Near East (cf. 2 Sam. 15:30; Jer. 14:3-4). The practice was designed to depict shame and humiliation.

This surprising turn of events foreshadows the greater turn of events that is about to unfold. Even Haman's friends could see that destiny was against him as he recounted to them the events that had just transpired. They inform Haman that his plot is destined for failure because Mordecai is a Jew. They evidently realize that providence is on the side of the Jews. While Haman is still talking to his confidants, the king's eunuchs arrive to take him to Esther's banquet.

Just like the king's eunuchs rushing Haman to the banquet (6:14), the events of chapter seven move with breathtaking speed, the effect surely enhanced by the reader's anxiety to see how the events of the narrative unfold. When Haman arrived at the court, he and the king went to Esther's banquet. While they were drinking wine the king asks Esther to make known her request. This is now the third time that the king has asked his queen this question (cf. 5:3, 6).

Esther replies to the king with a plea for her life. She explains that her life is in danger because the Jews have been marked for extinction. Esther asserts that she would have kept quiet if her people had simply been sold as slaves. If that had been the case, then the issue would not have been significant enough to bring before the king.

The king's response to Esther's plea is one of rage. The king immediately demands to know who is responsible for endangering the life of his queen. Esther responds to the king's forceful demands by identifying Haman as the guilty party, characterizing him as a "foe" and an "enemy" (7:6). Haman's response is predictable; he becomes terrified as he stands before the king and queen. No doubt he can scarcely believe the turn of events.

Esther's words enrage the king and he storms off into the palace garden. Haman remains behind to beg for his life. He is obviously aware that the king is furious. His only chance to escape death is to beg Esther to plead with the king to be merciful to him. Royal protocol demanded that no one remain alone in the presence of the queen. In fact, a man was not allowed to approach closer than seven steps when speaking with a woman of the palace.[55] Haman's behavior is unimaginable. He actually fell on the couch where Esther was reclining. In Persian culture, it was traditional to recline on cushions while partaking of after-dinner wine.

It is at precisely this moment that Xerxes returns to the banquet room. Seeing Haman lying prostrate at the queen's side, the king naturally assumes that he is assaulting the queen. An assault on the queen was viewed as synonymous to an assault on the throne (cf. 2 Sam. 16:21-22). The king gasps at this breach of conduct and says to himself, "Will he even assault the queen with me in the house?"

(7:8). Xerxes immediately orders the execution of his prime minister. The king's attendants rush in and seize Haman. The prime minister is hanged on the same gallows he meant for Mordecai.

The Plot Reversed (8:1-9:19)

On the very same day that Haman was executed, the king gave his estate to Queen Esther. When Esther makes the nature of her relationship to Mordecai known to Ahasuerus, the king responds by granting him a promotion. Mordecai is elevated to a high position in the empire, perhaps even second in authority only to the king. Mordecai's position of influence in the kingdom is evidenced by the fact that the king gives him the signet ring previously worn by Haman. The reversal of roles between Mordecai and Haman is now complete, as Mordecai has inherited Haman's position and Haman has taken Mordecai's place on the gallows.

Esther once again approaches the king to plead for her people. The decree calling for the extermination of the Jews is still in effect. Esther falls at the feet of Xerxes and implores him to take steps to avert the upcoming massacre. Ahasuerus answers Esther by taking credit for having dealt with the author of the original decree, in effect making himself the savior of the Jews. He further solidifies himself in that role by allowing another decree to be written, this time offering protection for the Jews. Since he cannot change his original decree, the king realizes that the only solution to the problem is to write another decree to counter the effects of the first one. The king tells Esther and Mordecai to write this decree and seal it with his signet ring.

The king's royal scribes are summoned just as they had been a little over two months earlier with Haman's original decree (cf. 3:12). While the first decree allowing for the extermination of the Jews was given on April 17, 474 B.C., this decree allowing the Jews to defend themselves is given on June 25, 474 B.C. The date on which the enemies of the Jews could attack them is March 7, 473 B.C. The Jews still have almost a year to prepare to defend themselves against their enemies.

The decree of Mordecai is addressed to the same recipients of Haman's decree, that is, the satraps, governors, and princes of each province in the empire. However, Mordecai's decree is also addressed to the Jews. In fact, the Jews are mentioned first in the list. This notation serves to empower the Jews, allowing them to take steps to fulfill the stipulations of the decree. Mordecai writes his decree in the name of King Ahasuerus, sealing it with the king's own signet ring. The decree was then sent throughout the empire.

The content of the decree is provided in 8:11-12. The decree essentially allows the Jews to defend themselves by whatever means necessary. While Haman's decree emphasized the right to kill the Jews, Mordecai's decree emphasizes the right to live on the part of the Jews. Haman's decree called on the inhabitants of the empire to "destroy," "kill," and "annihilate" all of the Jews (3:13). Mordecai's decree allows the Jews to "destroy," "kill," and "annihilate" all who attack them. Like Haman's decree, Mordecai's decree was posted throughout the city of Susa (cf. 3:15).

The reaction of the Jews to the first decree was great mourning. The reaction to this second decree is great joy and celebration. Mordecai himself comes from the presence of the king wearing royal robes of blue and white. He is also clothed in fine linen and purple. Completing the ensemble is a crown of gold. This is a marked contrast from 4:1-2 where Mordecai is pictured as wearing sackcloth and ashes, thereby preventing him from being in the king's presence.

Mordecai's joy is echoed throughout the city of Susa. The people respond with great rejoicing. In every province of the empire, the Jews responded to the news with joy and gladness. They also feasted and celebrated a holiday. The impact of the celebration was such that many Jews became proselytes as a result of the decree. A proselyte was a gentile who completely submitted to the regulations of the Mosaic Law, including circumcision, and lived as a Jew. This is the only mention in the Old Testament that Gentiles became Jews.

Almost nine months after the decree of Mordecai, and eleven months after the decree of Haman, the fateful day arrived. The date is March 7 (Adar 13), 473 B.C. The text begins by foreshadowing the end result. This was supposed to be the day on which the enemies of the Jews triumphed over them. Instead, it was a day of Jewish revenge. The plans of the enemies were "turned to the contrary" (9:1). This phrase is the most explicit statement regarding the theme of role-reversal so prevalent in this book. The verb used here (Hebrew *hapak*; cf. 9:22) occurs throughout the Old Testament in reference to the actions of the Lord in overturning His enemies. Balaam's curse was "turned" into a blessing (Deut. 23:5; Neh. 13:2). The water of the Nile was "turned" to blood (Ex. 7:17:20). The wicked are "overthrown" (Prov. 12:7). God "overthrew" Sodom and Gomorrah (Amos 4:11). And finally, the Lord will "overthrow" the thrones of the nations (Hag. 2:22).

Throughout the empire, the Jews assembled in their cities. Individual Jews remained in grave danger; the original edict allowing anyone to attack them and plunder their goods was still in effect. The power of the assembled Jews was such that no one could stand before them. The most significant reason for the turnaround of the Jewish plight was the presence of Mordecai in the king's court. Since the execution of Haman, Mordecai had grown in stature and authority.

The Jews throughout the empire exacted revenge on all who came against them.[56] In Susa alone five hundred men were killed. Those killed in the region of Susa included the ten sons of Haman. The text identifies Haman's sons by name (9:7-9). These names were certainly viewed as significant by the Hebrew scribes. The names are listed in the Hebrew text with only two names per line with the margin justified and indented. The only other place this occurs is in Joshua 12:9-24, a passage which lists the Canaanite kings who were defeated by the children of Israel in their initial conquest of the land.

The number of the casualties in Susa was reported to the king. It is at this time that Esther approached the king with another request. The original decree of Mordecai limited the Jewish revenge to Adar 13. Esther's request is that Adar 14 be given to Jewish revenge as well. Evidently, this edict only applied to the city of Susa. As a result of the extension, three hundred more men of Susa are killed on Adar 14. Esther further asks that the sons of Haman be hanged on the gallows. The purpose of hanging Haman's sons on the gallows was to discourage other enemies of the Jews from attacking them.

9:16-19 summarizes the effects of Mordecai's decree. The total number killed by the Jews was 75,000. To celebrate their great victory, the Jews throughout the empire feasted and rejoiced on Adar 14. The only exception was the city of Susa. There the celebration was delayed until Adar 15 because of Esther's request that the slaughter of the enemies continue through Adar 14.

The Feast of Purim Instituted (9:20-32)

Mordecai recorded the events of 9:1-19 and sent letters to the Jews who lived in each province. These letters called on the Jews to celebrate annually on Adar 14 and 15. There is to be one day of celebration each for two groups of people, Adar 14 for the rural Jews and Adar 15 for the urban Jews (those who lived in walled cities; cf. 9:17-19). Almost all modern Jews celebrate Purim on the evening of Adar 14. The exceptions are the Jews in the cities that were traditionally considered walled in the days of Joshua, including Jerusalem, Hebron, and Jericho, where Purim is celebrated on Adar 15.[57]

Purim is the plural form of the Persian word *pur*, meaning "lot." The name refers to the "lot" that was cast by Haman to determine the best day to seek vengeance upon the Jews (3:7). The Jews commit to celebrating the Feast of Purim according to its regulations without fail. This is one commitment where the Jews have proved faithful to their God. Modern Jews around the world are still celebrating the Feast of Purim.

Today, Purim is the most festive and popular Jewish holiday. The people put on masks and use noisemakers. "In some places, it is even customary to chalk the name of the wicked vizier |Haman| upon the soles of one's shoes so that it may be literally trodden underfoot and blotted out. Children are permitted special license on this occasion and what would normally be regarded as an interference with the decorum of divine worship is on this day not only tolerated but actively encouraged."[58] It is a day of hearty singing and heavy drinking. In fact, the Talmud gives the following instruction: "A person is obligated to become inebriated on Purim until he doesn't know the difference between cursed is Haman and blessed is Mordecai" (*Megillah* 7b). During Purim, the book of Esther is read in the synagogues. While the book is being read, the audience cheers whenever Mordecai's name is mentioned and boos and hisses at the name of Haman. The holiday is still celebrated by sending gifts to friends and family.

Esther herself issues an edict in 9:29-32. Her full title is used in this passage. She is "Queen Esther, daughter of Abihail" (9:29). Esther's decree further validates the day of Purim as a holiday for the Jews. Evidently, the queen had more authority than Mordecai. Since the verb is in the feminine singular form, Esther should be regarded as the sole author of the decree. She writes to validate what Mordecai had already written. This is confirmed in 9:32 where the text notes that the "command" of Esther "established" (or "validated") the Purim customs inaugurated by the letters of Mordecai. The regulations and customs pertaining to the Feast of Purim were written in the "book" (9:32), most likely the official records of the king (cf. 6:1).

The Greatness of Mordecai (10:1-3)

This postscript begins with a reference to the fact that the king imposed a tax on his empire. The ability to impose this tax revealed the power of the king. The details of Mordecai's accomplishments were written in the official records of the Medes and Persians. The appeal to these records lends credibility to the historicity of the events detailed in the Book of Esther. One could easily check the official records for the accuracy of the claims made in the Book of Esther.

The book closes with a final description of the greatness of Mordecai. Mordecai was second in authority only to the king himself. Mordecai did not simply serve the king; he also promoted the position of the Jews in the empire, striving continuously for their "welfare" (Hebrew *shalom*; 10:3). Throughout the book, the lives of Mordecai and his people were in grave danger. In the end, however, Mordecai is exonerated and the Jews are vindicated.

Study Questions
1. Who do you think wrote the book of Esther?
2. Why do many modern commentators date the writing of the book of Esther in the fourth or even third century B.C.?

3. What is the Greek name of King Ahasuerus?
4. Why was the book of Esther written?
5. Why did many Jews choose to remain in exile after being given permission to return to Judah?
6. Give several reasons why many scholars doubt the historicity of the book.
7. Do you think the narrative of Esther is a true story? Why or why not?
8. Mordecai is named after what Babylonian god?
9. Esther is named after what Mesopotamian goddess??
10. What is the Persian word meaning "lot?"?
11. How are the names of the sons of Haman recorded in the Hebrew text?
12. Describe the Feast of Purim as it is celebrated today.

The Relationship between Chronicles, Ezra, and Nehemiah

Before the interpreter can perform a satisfactory analysis of the books of Chronicles, Ezra, and Nehemiah, it is essential that the boundaries of the narratives be firmly and accurately established. The proper identification of the boundaries of a book and, subsequently, the unity of a book, are crucial elements in literary analysis. One must be aware of the complete text of a narrative account before one can effectively examine the literary nature of that composition. Obviously, if a text is not complete the chances of misinterpretation are greatly multiplied. One must also be confident that a single author composed the complete text of a narrative for that narrative to have a unified and distinct message. A variety of authors results in a variety of purposes and messages and makes accurate literary analysis virtually impossible. The collective similarities between the books of Ezra and Nehemiah and the book of Chronicles have led many scholars to incorporate all three books into a single unified work attributed to the "Chronicler." The discussion which follows examines the arguments presented by these scholars and evaluates the relationship between these books.

Introduction

For the past 170 years the majority of scholars have held that the books of Chronicles, Ezra, and Nehemiah were originally part of a single work composed by the "Chronicler."[1] This view was originally defined and presented by L. Zunz[2] in 1832. Zunz's work convinced the majority of scholars and the view has persisted to the modern day.[3] Scholars have held to the unity of all three books for several reasons. Their arguments largely rest on the following four points: a) Thematic similarities; b) Linguistic similarities; c) The overlap of 2 Chronicles 36:22-23 and Ezra 1:1-3a; d) The evidence of 1 Esdras.

While it is freely admitted that there is a chronological continuation between the three books and that they do indeed treat similar themes and ideas, it does not necessarily follow that the books should be seen as a literary unit. Throughout the remainder of this chapter, each of the main arguments presented by scholars adhering to the unity of all three books is reviewed and evaluated as to the extent that it supports the unity and common authorship of all three books. It will be shown that these arguments are not nearly as strong as some scholars suppose. In fact, these very same arguments can be used to disprove the original unity of the books. In conclusion, an additional argument based on the formation of the canon is supplied to support the opinion that the books of Ezra and Nehemiah should be regarded as separate from Chronicles.

Supposed Thematic Similarities

Several scholars around the turn of the century performed ideological and thematic studies of Chronicles-Ezra-Nehemiah in hopes of proving the common authorship of all three books.[4] While these scholars arrange their findings in various manners, their arguments largely rest on the following four points: 1) an emphasis on David and his dynasty; 2) an emphasis on the cult; 3) the use of genealogies; and 4) an anti-Samaritan polemic. Each of these arguments is reviewed and evaluated as to the extent that they support the unity and common authorship of all three books. Furthermore, two additional arguments, based on the Chronicler's doctrine of retribution and the inclusion of a literary device called a Levitical Sermon, are supplied which show major thematic elements which differ between the books.

Emphasis on David and his Dynasty

David is the central figure in the book of Chronicles. Fully one-third of Chronicles (1 Chron. 11-2 Chron. 9) is devoted to David and his son Solomon. North notes that "the person and dynasty of David forms the heartbeat of all the Chronicler's theology."[5] Clines goes into even more detail,

> Already in the genealogies of 1 Chron. 1-9 it is plain that for him the whole movement of the history of salvation has been towards the election of the Davidic state: Judah takes first place among the sons of Jacob (1 Chron. 2:3; cf. 5:1f.) and little attention is paid to Ephraim and Manasseh (7:14-27). The story proper starts, not with Patriarchs, Exodus, Sinai, or Conquest, but with the establishment of the Davidic dynasty at Jerusalem and the organisation [sic] of the whole structure of Israelite society and worship by David.[6]

David is idealized throughout Chronicles, receiving credit for many of the important successes in the history of Israel, including the building of the temple. It is David's devotion to the cult which becomes the standard by which his successors are evaluated (e.g., 2 Chron. 28:1; 29:2).[7] Overlooked are the various blemishes which serve to tarnish his reputation throughout the books of Samuel and Kings. For example, there is no mention of his adultery with Bathsheba and murder of Uriah, a pivotal event in Samuel, nor of the murder of his son Amnon and the subsequent rebellions of his sons Absalom and Adonijah. And it is not just David who receives the glowing report of the Chronicler. Consistently throughout the historical account, the Chronicler portrays the entire dynasty of David in a positive light. Perhaps the most notable example of this fact is the inclusion of the repentance of Manasseh (2 Chron. 33:12-16), an event completely ignored in Kings where Manasseh is portrayed as one of the most ungodly of all the southern kings.

However, David and his dynasty are relatively unimportant in both Ezra and Nehemiah.[8] In the majestic recounting of Israel's history in Nehemiah 9 there is no mention of David or the building of the temple. Freedman correctly observes that "this constitutes a complete reversal of the Chronicler's treatment of the tradition."[9] Furthermore, Solomon is mentioned in Nehemiah as a paradigm of sin with regards to his relationship with foreign women (Neh. 13:26), a fact completely overlooked in the Chronicler's treatment of Solomon.[10] The Chronicler tends to treat Solomon in quite the opposite manner. In fact, when the subject of Solomon's foreign wife is addressed in 2 Chronicles 8:11, Solomon is seen as attempting to preserve the purity of the cult in Israel, removing his Egyptian wife from Jerusalem to her own palace because his wife "shall not dwell in the house of David king of Israel, because the places are holy where the ark of the Lord has entered." Although Solomon evidently realizes that his marriage to an Egyptian wife is detrimental to the cultic worship of the nation, he is quite unwilling to take the steps of ultimate separation called for in Ezra and Nehemiah. If the Chronicler is the author of all three books, it is worth noting that he neglects to mention this fact in his treatment of Solomon.

Yet perhaps the most remarkable neglect of David's dynasty is found in Ezra's treatment of the character of Zerubbabel. Zerubbabel's Davidic lineage is completely absent from the book. He is merely "son of Shealtiel" (Ezra 3:2), rather than son of David (e.g., 2 Chron. 28:1; 29:2).[11] This is especially noteworthy in a book that seems to place a high degree of emphasis on pedigrees (cf. Ezra 7:1-5). Zerubbabel is never once portrayed as a Davidic ruler and in one passage is not even credited with the successful completion of the rebuilt temple (Ezra 6:14; cf. Zech. 4:9). These observations demonstrate that the authors of Ezra and Nehemiah portrayed the Davidic dynasty in a far different manner than did the author of Chronicles. Eskenazi writes, "All of this points to a drastic difference between Chronicles and Ezra-Nehemiah on the importance of David and his dynasty. This difference is so pronounced that it constitutes, in my judgment, a decisive contrast between the two books and renders common authorship implausible."[12] These striking contrasts, as Eskenazi points out, raise considerable doubts as to the plausibility of the common authorship view.[13]

Emphasis on the Cult

It is readily apparent that the books of Chronicles, Ezra, and Nehemiah all demonstrate an extensive affinity for the cultic worship of Israel. All three books recognize the centrality of the temple and the priority of the Levites and other spiritual leaders, including singers and musicians.[14] Nevertheless, it seems that this emphasis on cultic worship was quite common during this period. It should be remembered that the glory of God was physically present in the nation prior to the Babylonian exile but not after the nation's return to Israel (cf. Ezek. 10 and 43). Without the glory of God present in the temple, it seems as if the restored nation focuses more on the leaders of worship and the act of worship than on the one being worshipped. The exilic book of Ezekiel places a considerable focus on cultic practices as do the postexilic books of Haggai, Zechariah and Malachi. Ezekiel spends several chapters describing the future temple and the worship which will be performed therein (e.g., Ezek. 40–44). Haggai and Zechariah are both instrumental in the reconstruction of the temple during the time of Zerubbabel. Haggai sharply criticizes the returned remnant for failing to finish the rebuilding project (Hag. 1:2-11). Zechariah focuses on the religious leadership in the land (cf. Zech. 3:1-9; 6:9-15). Malachi harshly condemns the failures of the religious leadership in his day (cf. Mal. 2:1-9) and the faulty worship practices of the populace (cf. Mal. 1:6-14; 3:6-18). So it can readily be seen that all of the postexilic books emphasize a return to the proper worship of God on the part of the nation and its spiritual leadership. A worship which focuses on God rather than men. A worship which focuses on attitude, not ceremonial actions. Therefore it should not surprise us that the books of Chronicles, Ezra and Nehemiah all emphasize these cultic practices as well.

However, the cultic details in these books do not always agree. For example, the Chronicler emphasizes that it is in the building of the temple that the Davidic covenant has its initial fulfillment (see 1 Chron. 22:7-19, 28:2-10, and 29:1-10). Conversely, in the books of Ezra and Nehemiah we see no such emphasis on or even mention of the Davidic covenant. Surely the Chronicler would have alluded to the Davidic covenant and its continuity when the temple is rebuilt had he written Ezra. Eskenazi further points out several differences in the treatment of Levites, singers, and gatekeepers between the books.[15] These noteworthy differences again raise considerable doubt as to the validity of the common authorship view.

Genealogies

It is at once obvious that the books of Chronicles, Ezra, and Nehemiah all utilize genealogies to supplement their historical accounts. However, there are subtle differences in both the style and purpose of the genealogies recorded in each book. Many of the genealogies in Chronicles are called "genealogies" (Hebrew, *toledotim*; e.g., 1 Chron. 1:29), a term that is not found in Ezra and Nehemiah. Eskenazi observes that the genealogies recorded in Chronicles are typically segmented (e.g., 1 Chron. 1:5-16), whereas the books of Ezra and Nehemiah have no segmented genealogies, only linear ones.[16] Johnson shows that the genealogies of Chronicles utilize military terminology and focus on the twelve tribes while those of Ezra and Nehemiah do not.[17] And Johnson further points out crucial differences in the purpose of genealogies in each book, concluding that the books of Ezra and Nehemiah are concerned with legitimation while Chronicles is more concerned with history.[18] These various stylistic differences serve to argue for the independent authorship of each book.

Anti-Samaritan Polemic

It is generally acknowledged that an anti-Samaritan polemic permeates the books of Ezra and Nehemiah.[19] The Samaritans, after initially being rejected from participating in the rebuilding process, actively and persistently resist the building activities of the returned remnant. The position of both Ezra and Nehemiah on these people is clear. They are considered ungodly foreigners and dangerous adversaries. Ezra and Nehemiah strongly oppose the nation's intermingling with these individuals, especially in the union of marriage. As a result, the Samaritans are not even allowed to participate in the community of Israel or to partake in the religious liturgical activities of the temple.

There is no evidence, however, that the author of Chronicles is engaged in an anti-Samaritan polemic or even an anti-foreigner polemic. In fact, the book of Chronicles fails even to recognize the presence of foreigners in the territory of Israel. Newsome observes, "Notice should be taken here of the fact that the Chronicler writes almost as if no other people but the Jerusalem community were in existence. . . . Only when foreigners are necessary to his story of the ongoing life of the Jerusalem community does he mention them, such as in 2 Chron. 12:2-12 (Shishak), 2 Chron. 32:1-23 (Sennacherib), and the like. Rarely does his introduction of a foreign principal have theological significance, except as part of the mechanics for the unfolding of the historical drama itself."[20] This is a significantly different portrayal of foreigners than that of Ezra and Nehemiah. Williamson shares the same convictions regarding this inconsistency and adds further,

> In 2 Kings 17, we are told at length of the apostasy of the northerners that led to their defeat and deportation, and how the king of Assyria settled foreigners in their stead. Surely, if the author of Chronicles shared the negative view of Ezra and Nehemiah toward the inhabitants of the former northern kingdom of Israel, he would have included in Chronicles the material from 2 Kings 17 in his recounting of Israelite history, since this was obviously available to him, as we know from the many instances in which he copied the account in Kings almost verbatim. How remarkable it is, then, to find that Chronicles completely omits any reference to 2 Kings 17, the very chapter that would have given the historical background to the ideological stance so strongly represented in Ezra/Nehemiah. Indeed, in Chronicles, we find instead that the good kings of Judah (the southern kingdom) who ruled after the fall of Israel to the Assyrians (kings of Judah such as Hezekiah and Josiah) go out of their way to woo back all those northerners who had not been deported by the Assyrian king (2 Chronicles 30 and 34:9), while no mention whatever is made of foreigners having been brought into the former kingdom of Israel.[21]

Instead of being engaged in an anti-Samaritan polemic or even an anti-foreigner polemic, it seems that the Chronicler is somewhat inclusivistic when it comes to foreigners participating in the worship at the temple. After an analysis of 2 Chronicles 6:32-33 and 30:1-9, Newsome concludes, "The attitude of Chronicles reflects a certain internationalism, but the outlook of Ezra-Nehemiah is unyieldingly separatist . . . It is the Chronicler's view that all peoples, including northerners and Gentiles, are welcome to be participants in the Temple cult, the only condition being that they come in an attitude of reverence and piety."[22] This inclusivistic attitude on the part of the Chronicler towards apostates and foreigners contrasts sharply with the separatistic attitudes of Ezra (Ezra 9:1-15) and Nehemiah (Neh. 13:1-3, 23-27).

Doctrine of Retribution

It has long been acknowledged that one of the most noticeable and characteristic features of the Chronicler's theology is his emphasis upon the doctrine of immediate retribution.[23] Individuals are characterized as successful or unsuccessful, good or bad, right or wrong, depending upon how faithfully they adhere to the revealed will of God. Williamson explains, "The fortunes of the individual monarchs (and through them usually, though not invariably, those of the people) are directly related to their obedience to the law of God. Often, a change for evil or repentance from wickedness causes a dramatic change of status. The basis of this doctrine is furnished by 2 Chron. 7:14, which establishes the vocabulary through which its development may be traced in Chron, and shows that it is intended to be generally applicable to the people and not just reserved for certain specific cases."[24] This doctrine of retribution is found throughout Chronicles. Every step of the way, individuals succeed or fail because of their religious devotion. In fact, for the Chronicler it seems as if all history unfolds in terms of retribution. Braun observes, "it is difficult to find an addition which the Chronicler has made to his *Vorlage* which does not function in these terms."[25]

Of special note concerning the doctrine of retribution so prevalent in Chronicles is the role played by the prophets. The prophet in Chronicles was the individual who revealed God's will to the sovereign. Consistently we see the prophet serving as God's mouthpiece and delivering His messages. Eskenazi elaborates on the crucial role of the prophets in the doctrine of retribution: "The role of the prophets in Chronicles is particularly significant and carefully stressed. The role of the prophets turns out to be central in Chronicles' distinctive exegesis and structure. Chronicles has more prophets than do its sources. These prophets play a crucial role as mediators between Israel and God. They are the cornerstone of Chronicles' carefully worked out retribution. The fate of kings and nation in Chronicles depends directly on how they respond to the prophetic message."[26]

However, it is apparent that this doctrine is largely absent from the books of Ezra and Nehemiah. Nowhere do we find success or failure conditional upon obedience to God's word. In fact, just the opposite holds true; the more faithful the activities of the remnant and its leadership, the greater the increase in opposition. Williamson rightly concludes,

It is noteworthy, therefore, that no trace of this doctrine is to be found in Ezr.-Neh. The piety of the leaders and/or the people is not reflected in sudden up-turns of fortune, but on the contrary may entail an increase of opposition (Ezr. 4, Neh. 4), neither is there any indication that confession of sin leads to restoration (Ezr. 9, Neh. 9). Rather, the problems of mixed marriages, tithing and Sabbath profanation seem merely to recur regardless (Neh. 13). The characteristic vocabulary of 2 Chron. 7:14 does not hold the programmatic significance that it clearly does in Chron. This contrast is hard to explain if these books are indeed all part of a single work.[27]

It is equally apparent that the crucial role played by the prophets in this doctrine of retribution is likewise absent in Ezra and Nehemiah. Haggai and Zechariah, the prominent prophets mentioned in Ezra, neither warn the people nor deliver promises. This marks a sharp contrast from the style of the Chronicler. And this ideological and theological difference strongly argues for independent authorship of the books.

Levitical Sermon

A feature unique to the book of Chronicles is the "Levitical sermon." This literary form was first identified and described by Von Rad in an essay entitled "The Levitical Sermon in I and II Chronicles." In his essay, Von Rad identified the following elements which appear either in whole or in fragmented form: 1) the quotation of an ancient source, often prophetic, 2) the application of the theological principle of that quotation to some aspect of Israel's past, and 3) its application to the present, i.e., a call to faith and action on the part of the auditors.[28] Newsome identifies a fourth characteristic of the "Levitical sermon," observing that the sermon "was usually bracketed by a stylized salutation and by a no less stylized summons to faith and action."[29] These "Levitical sermons" are used by the Chronicler to "draw out the lessons of the historical narrative for the reader."[30]

While the "Levitical sermon" was a favorite form of address in the book of Chronicles, it is completely lacking in Ezra and Nehemiah. This is admittedly an argument from silence. However, there seems to have been a number of pivotal occasions in Ezra and Nehemiah where the "Levitical sermon" could have been used effectively, especially the times when Ezra and Nehemiah are calling on the nation to change its conduct. The situations regarding the separation of the remnant from foreigners seem tailor-made for a "Levitical sermon." It can therefore be assumed that had the Chronicler written these books, he probably would have employed this form of address throughout the narratives.

Conclusion

After a careful and detailed analysis of the supposed thematic similarities between the books of Chronicles, Ezra, and Nehemiah it must be concluded that they do not offer solid evidence for the common authorship view. Quite the contrary, it seems as if they constitute ideological contrasts between the books, thus making the common authorship view quite improbable. While the Chronicler strongly emphasizes David and his dynasty, they are of little interest to Ezra and Nehemiah. Although all three books emphasize the cultic worship of Israel, there are subtle differences in style and terminology between the books. Although all three books contain genealogies, they are recorded in different styles and are utilized for different purposes. The inclusivistic attitude of the Chronicler toward apostates and foreigners contrasts sharply with the separatism advanced in Ezra and Nehemiah. The doctrine of retribution administered through prophetic influence so prevalent in Chronicles is virtually ignored in Ezra and Nehemiah. And finally, the "Levitical sermon" so common in Chronicles is nowhere to be found in Ezra and Nehemiah. The logical conclusion to these arguments, therefore, is that the author of the book of Chronicles, the so-called Chronicler, did not write the books of Ezra and Nehemiah.

Supposed Linguistic Similarities

Several scholars around the turn of the century performed linguistic studies of the books of Chronicles, Ezra, and Nehemiah in hopes of proving the common authorship of the books.[31] These studies analyzed the books in terms of common vocabulary, similar syntax, and stylistic peculiarities. These studies have recently been reinvestigated and evaluated as to their validity. This reinvestigation began with an extensive article by Sara Japhet.[32] Japhet arranged her article around three categories of evidence which revealed the differences between the books: 1) Linguistic opposition; 2) Specific technical terms; and 3) Peculiarities of style. In each case, noteworthy differences were brought to light. Japhet concludes her article by stating: "Certain parts of the material discussed revealed conspicuous stylistic differences between Ezr.-Neh. and Chron Other parts exhibit actual opposition between the two. From the linguistic point of view the book of Chron deviates in some important points from the tendencies and phenomena of . . . Ezr.-Neh. Our investigation of the differences between the two books, which was restricted to one field, has proven that the books could not have been written or compiled by the same author."[33]

This study by Japhet was followed by an examination performed by Hugh G. M. Williamson.[34] While Japhet concentrated on the differences between the books of Chronicles and Ezra and Nehemiah, Williamson focused on the alleged similarities between the books. Williamson proposed a set of criteria by which to measure the unity of authorship. Having compared the results of his examination to his set of criteria, Williamson concludes,

> Having now presented all the evidence relating to the two lists in Dr [Driver] and CM [Curtis and Madsen], we may briefly summarize by observing that for the specific purpose of demonstrating the unity of authorship of Chron and Ezr.-Neh. on the basis of style, the large majority of the entries are found to be irrelevant or quite inconclusive. Of the remainder, most in fact favour diversity of authorship, and serious questions can be raised about at least four of the six items that might favour unity. . . . As far as the argument from style is concerned, the onus now rests on those who favour unity of authorship to produce more compelling new arguments to support their position.[35]

Williamson's challenge was taken up by David Talshir, who vigorously criticized the findings of both Japhet and Williamson and supplied further linguistic evidence supporting common authorship of the books,[36] and Polzin, who analyzed the Hebrew of each book and concluded that there is a very close linguistic relationship between the books.[37] The present state of linguistic analysis in the area of the books of Chronicles, Ezra, and Nehemiah may fairly be regarded as inconclusive. Throntveit writes, "I do not think linguistic analysis is capable of providing definite proof either way. Perhaps the safest course would be to take seriously the *a priori* assumption of separate authorship and investigate both works individually from a theological point of view, leaving the question of authorship open until the intent and message of both are better understood."[38] Ackroyd agrees and further adds, "the discussions of linguistic evidence for uniting or separating Chronicles and Ezra-Nehemiah have, on the whole, reached an inconclusive position."[39]

While it seems that these linguistic analyses cannot prove or disprove the common authorship of the books, they are sufficient to demonstrate the tenuous nature of this argument. Both sides use similar arguments in support of their respective views. In any event, it should be noted that linguistic studies in general have an inherent flaw. The presence of similar linguistic usage does not demand common authorship. It merely indicates that the authors came from a similar time period, where a comparable style of writing and word usage existed. Likewise, the lack of similar linguistic usage does not automatically demand that authors came from different chronological eras. In the vast majority of instances, there is simply not enough evidence to conclusively prove either position.

The Overlap of 2 Chronicles 36:22-23 and Ezra 1:1-3a

The overlap of 2 Chronicles 36:22-23 and Ezra 1:1-3a has been taken as a conclusive indication of the original unity of the books. Whether ascribing this phenomenon to deliberate literary style[40] or to scribal error,[41] many scholars assert that this parallel constitutes the most decisive evidence for the unity of the books.[42] However, a scribal error of this magnitude is highly improbable and difficult to accept. Eskenazi observes, "the kind of monumental error by a scribe, which Batten envisions, and the perpetuation of such an error are difficult to accept. It is of course quite credible that scribal errors have crept into the received texts. But the very obviousness of this one makes it seem unlikely that it would have gone undetected and uncorrected."[43] The suggested literary arguments are likewise unconvincing. If this phenomenon is a deliberate literary element it is unique in the Old Testament, despite the fact that it would work well in some instances (e.g., Pentateuch, Samuel, Kings). In fact, the presence of the overlap has been taken by some to conclude that the books were originally separate. Welch contends that "men do not take the trouble to stitch together two documents, unless they have been originally separate."[44]

Additionally, scholars have yet to give a persuasive reason for the seemingly deliberate abbreviation of Cyrus' decree in 2 Chronicles. It should not be surprising that both authors utilize the Cyrus decree, for it is a crucial event for the message of both books. However, it is quite surprising that the Chronicler abbreviates the decree. This author believes that the major purpose in appending Cyrus' decree to the end of Chronicles was to provide a hopeful conclusion to the book.[45] The decree is intentionally abbreviated to encourage the remnant and returnees to remain in the land and the exiles to return to the land. Therefore, the final words an Israelite would read in the book of Chronicles ("and let him go up [to Jerusalem]") would be an exhortation to remain in or return to the land. The decree naturally begins the book of Ezra as it is the logical starting place for a book whose major theme is the returns to the land on the part of the exilic community.

The Evidence of 1 Esdras

First Esdras includes portions of all three books (2 Chron. 35:1-36:23; Ezra; Neh. 7:73b-8:13a). This fact has been used by scholars to assert that this evidence confirms the common author-ship of Chronicles-Ezra-Nehemiah. Existing theories on the relation of 1 Esdras to Chronicles, Ezra, and Nehemiah can be divided into two basic positions: the Compilation Hypothesis and the Fragment Hypothesis. The Compilation Hypothesis asserts the priority of Chronicles, Ezra, and Nehemiah and argues that 1 Esdras is a late compilation of material from these three books. In other words, the author of 1 Esdras took portions from each of the three books and arranged them into a cohesive story. The Fragment Hypothesis main-tains that 1 Esdras is a actual fragment out of the original work of the Chronicler. This view holds that Chronicles, Ezra, and Nehemiah were thus created by taking various parts of the original work of the Chronicler and separating them into individual books.

A leading proponent of the Fragment Hypothesis is K. F. Pohlmann.[46] Pohlmann's arguments, however, rest largely on silence. Pohlmann makes the assumption that the Chronicler borrowed the material from 1 Esdras and then attempts to show how the Chronicler composed his work combining 1 Esdras and other sources. While this scenario is possible, it is not the most probable. It is far more likely that 1 Esdras is a later compilation of material from the books of Chronicles, Ezra, and Nehemiah. Myers has effectively shown that the Greek 1 Esdras shows marked signs of Egyptian coloring, thereby concluding that the historical account probably originated in Alexandria in the second century B.C.[47] Williamson also performs an extensive study on 1 Esdras and determines that 1 Esdras 1:21-22 is integral to the text of 1 Esdras, but was never part of the Masoretic Text. Williamson thus concludes that 1 Esdras is not a fragment of the original LXX of Chronicles-Ezra-Nehemiah.[48] These two studies together show that 1 Esdras is a compilation of material from the books of Chronicles, Ezra, and Nehemiah rather than a fragment from the Chronicler's original work. It seems best to regard the evidence of 1 Esdras as supporting the independent authorship of Chronicles, Ezra, and Nehemiah.

Place in the Canon

An additional argument which supports the conclusion that Ezra and Nehemiah should be regarded as separate from Chronicles is the fact that Ezra and Nehemiah directly precede Chronicles in the Hebrew canon.[49] Scholars have attempted to prove that Ezra and Nehemiah originally closed the canon by asserting that Chronicles was intentionally moved because it represents the whole sacred history[50] or because it provides an optimistic ending for the Old Testament canon.[51] They further assert that the decree of Cyrus is repeated to point readers back to Ezra and Nehemiah. However, the fact that the Hebrew canonical order is original seems to be inferred in Matthew 23:35. In this verse, Christ uses the murders of Abel and Zechariah as representative of all the righteous blood shed on earth. Abel's murder is the first recorded in the Old Testament (Gen. 4:8) while Zechariah's is the last (2 Chron. 24:20-22). Christ here indirectly attests the canonical order which places Chronicles last among the Writings.

If this order is original, then the question as to why the books are arranged in this manner if the Chronicler is the author of all three books must be answered. Fensham has suggested that the order may be due to the likelihood that Ezra and Nehemiah were accepted into the canon before Chronicles.[52] However, he goes on to argue that the books of Chronicles, Ezra, and Nehemiah were originally one work composed by the Chronicler.[53] It seems quite unlikely that Ezra and Nehemiah would have been accepted into the canon before Chronicles if all three books were originally one work composed by the same author.

Conclusion

After reviewing the key evidence, it must be concluded that the books of Chronicles, Ezra, and Nehemiah were never meant to be regarded as a unified piece of literature. The arguments which many scholars believe lead to the conclusion that the original work consisted of all three books (thematic similarities, linguistic similarities, the overlap of 2 Chron. 36:22-23 and Ezra 1:1-3a, and the evidence of 1 Esdras) have been reviewed and evaluated as to the extent that they support the unity and common authorship of the books. It was found that these arguments are faulty and at times even point to the separate authorship of the books. The final argument presented, concerning the place of Chronicles in the Hebrew canon, serves to further support the conclusion that Ezra and Nehemiah should be regarded as separate from Chronicles.

Study Questions

1. How does the portrait of Zerubbabel differ between Chronicles and Ezra and Nehemiah?
2. How do the exilic and postexilic prophets emphasize worship?
3. What is the doctrine of retribution?
4. What is a Levitical Sermon?
5. Do you hold to the Compilation Hypothesis or the Fragment Hypothesis? Be sure to explain your answer.
6. In your opinion, what is the most convincing argument for separating Chronicles, Ezra, and Nehemiah?

Introduction: Ezra-Nehemiah or Ezra and Nehemiah?

Introduction

Ezra's extensive similarities to Nehemiah have called into question its independence from that book, thus leading many scholars to regard the two books as one unified work. As a result, scholarly analysis of Ezra has tended to focus on identifying the various sources which the author used in compiling his historical narrative rather than analyzing the literary text of the book to determine the author's original purpose in writing.

Primarily due to the fact that the books have been preserved in the Masoretic Text as a single book, scholarship has largely assumed that Ezra and Nehemiah should be viewed as a literary unit.[1] Several other factors point to the conclusion that the books are a unit. First, the LXX records Ezra-Nehemiah as a single work entitled Εσδρασ β. Second, the rabbis consider it one book (e.g., *Babylonian Talmud, Baba Batra,* 14b, 15a).[2] Third, the oldest extant Hebrew manuscripts record Ezra-Nehemiah as a single book (e.g., the Aleppo Codex, dated c. A.D. 930). In fact, when the Masoretes calculated the number of verses in the book (685), they did so for the combined Ezra-Nehemiah. They also identified Nehemiah 3:32 as the center of the book. Further indication that the Masoretes viewed the books as a unit lies in the fact that they included their notes on both books after Nehemiah, rather than after each book. Fourth, the earliest church fathers regarded the books as a unit (e.g., Melito of Sardis; Eusebius *Historia Ecclesiastica* 4.26.14). This arrangement also seems to be inferred from Josephus' enumeration of the biblical books (*Contra Apion* 40). It should be noted at this point that each of these arguments arises as a result of the fact that the Hebrew Bible records the two narratives as a literary unit. Fifth, numerous studies have pointed out key stylistic, theological, and epistemological similarities between the two books.[3] Finally, some literary investigations have concluded that structural analysis supports the original unity of the books.[4] While these arguments are certainly compelling, there are nevertheless several reasons why the books should be viewed as separate works.

Nehemiah's Introduction

Nehemiah's book is introduced with the superscription: "The words of Nehemiah the son of Hacaliah." This introduction clearly states that the words contained in the book are the product of Nehemiah himself. Similarly, the extensive use of the first person throughout the book strongly indicates that Nehemiah should be seen as the sole author. The first-person is used in reference to the person of Nehemiah 110 times while Nehemiah is mentioned by name only five times, usually in a general sense (once to identify the author, once in a list, twice to denote the time period "days of Nehemiah," and once to describe the work of Ezra and Nehemiah).

Some scholars have argued that Nehemiah 12:26 and 12:47 indicate that Nehemiah could not have written this section.[5] In these verses the phrase "in the days of Nehemiah" is used to denote that period during which Nehemiah is governor. The use of this phrase, it is argued, indicates that this time period had already passed. Harrison answers this objection: "This is not a serious objection, for the phrase was being used to designate specific eras or periods such as those of Jehoiakim or Zerubbabel. Consistency suggests that the same usage would extend quite naturally to Nehemiah also, since it might have appeared somewhat strange had he employed a different style of reference to the period of his own activity. It should also be noted in passing that these verses are completely irrelevant as far as chronological considerations are concerned, since Nehemiah in his capacity as *tirshatha* or royal commissioner would certainly take priority over others in his own memoirs."[6]

It is also possible that Nehemiah shifts to the use of the third person to emphasize the work of others, especially the priesthood. During the early part of the narrative, there is no question that Nehemiah was the instigator of the work. In the latter half of the book, however, Nehemiah seems to be reporting on events as they occur rather than actually instigating those events. Consequently, he appropriately allows other religious leaders to take the foreground in the narrative. It should also be noted that Nehemiah was not present in Jerusalem for the whole period covered in the latter half of the book (cf. Neh. 13:6). It is quite possible that some events may have occurred while he was absent. The author's return to the first person in chapter 13 helps form an inclusio with the first half of the narrative, indicating his authorship of everything in between.

The Repeated List in Ezra 2 and Nehemiah 7

Ezra 2 includes an extensive list of the original returnees. An almost identical list occurs in Nehemiah 7. This repeated list is somewhat redundant if the two books are composed by a single author.[7] Young writes, "The two books are indeed closely related, but the repetition of Ezra 2 in Nehemiah 7:6-70 shows that they were not one originally."[8] Another problem for the common authorship view is the way in which the list is used in each narrative. VanderKam explains,

> In Ezra one reads, 'When the seventh month came and the sons of Israel were in the towns, the people gathered as one man to Jerusalem' [Ezra 3:1]. It then continues with events of the seventh month—the episode of Joshua, Zerubbabel and construction of the altar during Cyrus's reign (therefore between 538 and 530). The parallel in Nehemiah reads, 'And when the seventh month had come, the children of Israel were in their towns. And all the people gathered as one man into the square before the Water Gate . . .' [Neh. 7:73b-8:1a]. The book then continues with what happened in the seventh

month mentioned in it: the reading of the law by Ezra which occurred no earlier than the twentieth year of Artaxerxes (445 or perhaps somewhat later). There is, therefore, a gap of about 90 years between the events of the seventh month in the two books, although the reference to the seventh month is quoted from the same document in each. If the same editor inserted the list into both Ezra 2 and Nehemiah 7, then he would be interpreting the seventh month of the text in one case to refer to a year in Cyrus's reign and in the other to a year in Artaxerxes' reign—a sizable historical blunder.[9]

If Ezra and Nehemiah are regarded as independent literary accounts written by different authors, then the recurring list would not present an imposing problem for the interpreter. Each author simply includes this extensive list because it suits their individual purposes. Ezra uses the list to identify the various groups and individuals who returned in the time of Cyrus while Nehemiah uses the list as the basis for his effort to repopulate the city of Jerusalem. Kraemer elaborates, "The list in Ezra is introduced simply by identifying those included as the ones who returned. But it is followed by speaking of those who came to the house of the LORD in Jerusalem and volunteered to support the rebuilding project (vv. 68-69); the return leads to rebuilding. In contrast, in Nehemiah the list is framed in such a way as to make clear that return leads to rebuilding and repopulation of the city (see 7:4-5 and 69-71), where 'the work' for which donations are made is, given the context, clearly the rebuilding and repopulation effort."[10] Obviously, the repeated list strongly argues for the original separation of the books.

The Omission of Ezra's Activities in Nehemiah 1-7

Another argument which favors the independence of the books is the fact that Nehemiah 1-7 makes no mention of Ezra's activities. While this is admittedly an argument from silence, it nevertheless poses many problems for scholars who hold to the unity of the books. Since Ezra is the main character in the second half of his book, one would assume that he would remain a key character throughout Nehemiah. However, there is no mention of Ezra during

Nehemiah's building narrative. One would expect that Nehemiah would seek out Ezra immediately upon entering Jerusalem. One would further expect that Nehemiah would ask for Ezra's aid in building the walls of the city, especially when internal problems arose. This omission, however, can be easily explained if separate authors wrote the books, for Ezra does not appear in Nehemiah until it serves Nehemiah's purpose.

Furthermore, the accounts characterizing Ezra differ radically between the two books. In the book of Ezra, he is introduced as both a priest and a scribe, accompanied by a lengthy and detailed genealogical pedigree (7:1-6). Throughout the narrative, it is Ezra's priestly concerns which dominate as he is concerned with the temple and the religious cult. He is also concerned about the purity of those who worship in the temple as we see in the matter of intermarriages among the people. Kraemer rightly observes, "In the book of Ezra, Ezra is a well-connected priest whose exclusive concern is the strengthening and purification of the cult. His primary activity involves the elimination of intermarriages, an offense that is newly and uniquely described in priestly terms. As befits the emphasis of the book as a whole, Ezra is a man of the priesthood."[11]

The portrait of Ezra in the book of Nehemiah is somewhat different. Here Ezra is related exclusively in the third person and is restricted primarily to chapter eight, though he does make a ceremonial appearance in chapter twelve. While Ezra is introduced as both a priest and scribe (Neh. 8:1-2), he functions exclusively as a scribe throughout the narrative. In fact, Ezra's other introductions demonstrate that he is regarded primarily as a scribe in the book of Nehemiah. Four times he is spoken of as a scribe alone (Neh. 8:1, 4, 13; 12:36), twice he is named as both a scribe and priest (Neh. 8:9; 12:26), while only in the one passage is he described simply as a priest (Neh. 8:2). His priestly pedigree, so crucial in Ezra (cf. 7:1-5), is completely ignored. Nowhere do we see Ezra performing ritual sacrifices or other priestly functions. He devotes himself to the public reading of Torah and the instruction of the people. Noting this striking contrast, Kraemer concludes, "Thus, the Ezra remembered in Ezra is not the Ezra known in Nehemiah. In Ezra, Ezra is a priest, a man concerned with the cult and its purity, while in Nehemiah he is a scribe, a man of the book, who is entirely unconcerned with the Temple or sacrifices. These are two different Ezras, the one bearing little relationship to the other. The disparate portraits do, however, bear powerful relationship with the ideological bents of the books in which they appear."[12] These vastly different portraits of the character of Ezra throughout the narratives strongly point to the original separation of the books.

Stylistic and Linguistic Differences

A stylistic and linguistic analysis of the two books supports independent authorship. First, Ezra usually writes in first person in Ezra while he is referred to in the third person in Nehemiah. This poses quite a problem if one views Ezra as the author of both books. Second, Ezra uses Aramaic and Hebrew in composing his narrative while Nehemiah uses only Hebrew. While this is admittedly an argument from silence, the question as to why there is no Aramaic in Nehemiah must be addressed. Third, Nehemiah tends to include short prayers while Ezra records lengthy prayers. Fourth, both Ezra and Nehemiah refer to the temple as the "house of God" (Hebrew, *bet elohim*; e.g., Ezra 3:8; Neh. 12:40), but Ezra alone calls it the "house of the Lord" (Hebrew, *bet yahweh*; e.g., 3:11). Fifth, Ezra routinely employs the divine title "God of Israel" (Hebrew, *elohim yisrael*; 1:3; 3:2; 4:1, 3; 5:1; 6:14, 22; 7:6, 15; 9:4, 15) while it is not attested in Nehemiah. Sixth, though Sukkot is observed in both books, Ezra regards it as a holiday of sacrifices, neglecting to even mention booths, while in Nehemiah it is a holiday of booths and there is no mention of sacrifices. While each of these arguments is insufficient to prove independent authorship, the collective weight of these stylistic differences lends support to the independent authorship view.

Theological Differences

The main focus of the book of Ezra is the restoration of the temple and its cult. The book is built upon priestly concerns. Ezra 6:14 supplies the reader with a succinct, yet comprehensive, thematic statement for the entire book. The people, represented by their elders, successfully complete the rebuilding project through the motivation of the prophets under the protection of the Persian sovereigns. Many scholars who view the books of Ezra and Nehemiah as a unit have incorrectly made this the thematic statement for the collective work, thereby transferring the place of God from the temple to the city and downplaying the role of God's chosen leader in Nehemiah.[13] However, it is clear that Nehemiah maintains a strong distinction between the house of God and the city of Jerusalem (e.g., Neh. 6:10; 8:16; 10:32-39; 11:11, 16, 22; 13:4, 7, 9, 11, 14). Furthermore, rather than Nehemiah's role as leader being diminished throughout the book of Nehemiah, it is actually magnified, even to the extent that many contemporary expositors believe the book to be a manual for leadership principles.[14]

Historical Opinion

At least by the time of Origen (A.D. 185-253) some held that Ezra and Nehemiah should be viewed as separate. Origen was the first to divide the books into two and regarded the books as First and Second Ezra (Eusebius, *Historia Ecclesiastica* 6.25.2). Jerome (A.D. 342-420) introduced the division into the Vulgate, entitling the books "Book of Ezra" and "Book of Nehemiah." A Hebrew manuscript dated A.D. 1448 adopted the division and it was similarly utilized by the Bomberg Bible in A.D. 1525. The books remained divided thereafter in most printed editions. Following this line of evidence, Kraemer rightly concludes, "Whatever the antiquity of such an opinion, its wisdom has to be weighed seriously."[15]

Conclusion

While Ezra and Nehemiah record consecutive historical periods, they do so from significantly different perspectives. After reviewing the evidence, it must be concluded that Ezra and Nehemiah should not be regarded as a single unified work. Several arguments have been presented to demonstrate that the books should be regarded as separate (i.e., Nehemiah's introduction, the repeated list in Ezra 2 and Nehemiah 7, the omission of Ezra's activities in Nehemiah 1-7, stylistic differences, theological differences, and historical opinion). The collective weight of these arguments is overwhelming.

Study Questions

1. Why do many scholars view the books of Ezra and Nehemiah as one book?
2. In your opinion, what is the most convincing argument for regarding the books of Ezra and Nehemiah as one book?
3. Why does Nehemiah switch between first person and third person narration?
4. The list of Ezra 2 is repeated in what chapter of Nehemiah?
5. How does the portrait of Ezra differ between the two books?
6. What are some of the stylistic differences between the two books?
7. Who was the first Church Father to divide Ezra-Nehemiah into two books?
8. In your opinion, what is the most convincing argument for separating Ezra-Nehemiah into two books?

NOTES

Introduction

1. Leland Ryken, *Words of Delight: A Literary Introduction to the Bible* (Grand Rapids: Baker Books, 1974), 31.
2. Tremper Longman III, *Literary Approaches to Biblical Interpretation* (Grand Rapids: Zondervan Publishing House, 1987), 68-71.
3. Longman lists five pitfalls in the literary approach: 1) The first difficulty with the literary approach is that the field of secular theory and the related discipline of linguistics are divided among themselves. 2) The second pitfall follows from the first: Literary theory is often obscurantist. 3) The next danger is that of imposing modern western concepts and categories on ancient Semitic literature. 4) The next pitfall is the danger of moving completely away from any concept of authorial intent and determinant meaning of a text. 5) The last pitfall is indeed the one about which I have the most concern. Along with the move away from the author in contemporary theory one can also note the tendency to deny or severely limit any referential function to literature (Tremper Longman III, "The Literary Approach to the Study of the Old Testament," *Journal of the Evangelical Theological Society* 28 [October 1985]: 387-92). Ryken adds his own list: 1) One of the fallacies that is prevalent is the assumption that everything in the Bible is literary in nature and amenable to the ordinary tools of literary criticism. 2) A second fallacy is the premise that what Bible scholars have traditionally called literary criticism of the Bible is, in fact, the kind of literary criti-

cism that teachers of literature perform and constitutes a large body of *bona fide* criticism on biblical literature. 3) Another common fallacy is the claim that biblical literature is virtually unique and cannot be adequately studied with the familiar tools of literary criticism or compared with Western literature. 4) Moving on to another fallacy, the main effect of the various types of biblical criticism has been to divide the Bible into fragments and to claim that the fragments contradict each other. 5) There is a lurking and regrettably widespread suspicion that the Bible cannot be taught as literature and should therefore be taught as something else. 6) It is a fallacy of literary criticism to regard the supernatural element in biblical literature as something to be discarded. 7) A final fallacy is the view that it is futile to look for a high degree of literary artistry in the Bible (Leland Ryken, "Literary Criticism of the Bible: Some Fallacies," in *Literary Interpretations of Biblical Narratives*, vol. 1, ed. Kenneth R. R. Gros Louis [Nashville: Abingdon Press, 1974, 1982], 24-39). While these pitfalls and fallacies are not sufficient to discredit the field of literary analysis, they are nonetheless sufficient to demonstrate the problems facing the literary analyst who investigates the biblical text.

4. Shimon Bar-Efrat, *Narrative Art in the Bible*, trans. Dorothea Shefer-Vanson, Journal for the Study of the Old Testament Supplement Series, ed. David J. A. Clines and Philip R. Davies, no. 70 (Sheffield: Almond Press, 1989).
5. Meir Sternberg, *The Poetics of Biblical Narrative* (Bloomington, IN: Indiana University Press, 1985).
6. Robert Alter, *The Art of Biblical Narrative* (New York: Basic Books, 1981).
7. Sternberg, *The Poetics of Biblical Narrative*, 39.
8. This listing is adapted from the list provided by Bar-Efrat. Bar-Efrat's five categories are narrator, characters, plot, time and space, and style. Bar-Efrat's category of narrator is synonymous with my category of point of view while his category of time and space is closely related to my category of setting. Bar-Efrat, *Narrative Art in the Bible*, 13-223.

9. Leland Ryken, *How to Read the Bible as Literature* (Grand Rapids: Zondervan Publishing House, 1984), 35.
10. Steve L. Reynolds, "A Literary Analysis of Nehemiah" (Ph.D. diss., Bob Jones University, 1994), 47.
11. Bar-Efrat, *Narrative Art in the Bible*, 47.
12. Harry Shaw, *Dictionary of Literary Terms* (New York: McGraw-Hill Book Company, 1972), 71.
13. Reynolds, "A Literary Analysis of Nehemiah," 47.
14. Ryken, *How to Read the Bible as Literature*, 39.
15. Reynolds, "A Literary Analysis of Nehemiah," 47.
16. Sternberg, *The Poetics of Biblical Narrative*, 349-54.
17. Ryken identifies five ways in which characters are portrayed: 1) Direct description by the storyteller; 2) Other character's responses; 3) A character's words or thoughts; 4) Self-characterization; and 5) A character's actions (Ryken, *How to Read the Bible as Literature*, 37-38). Sternberg also identifies five levels of characterization, using 1 Samuel 16:18 to illustrate his categories: 1) Physical ("a fine-looking man"); 2) Social ("a son of Jesse of Bethlehem"); 3) Singular or concretizing ("who knows how to play the harp"); 4) Moral and ideological ("the Lord is with him"); and 5) Psychological in a wide sense ("a brave man, a warrior, he speaks well"). For a full explanation of these levels of characterization, see Sternberg, *The Poetics of Biblical Narrative*, 326.
18. Shlomith Rimmon-Kenan, *Narrative Fiction: Contemporary Poetics* (London: Methuen, 1983), 60.
19. Tamara C. Eskenazi, *In an Age of Prose: A Literary Approach to Ezra-Nehemiah*, The Society of Biblical Literature Monograph Series, ed. Adela Yarbro Collins, no. 36 (Atlanta, GA: Scholars Press, 1988), 128. This can be vividly seen in the account of Ehud in Judges 3:12-30. Ehud is characterized as "a left-handed man" while Eglon is characterized as "a very fat man." Both epithets will play a crucial role in the narrative that follows. Because Ehud is "a left-handed man" he is able to smuggle a weapon past Eglon's guards. Because Eglon is "a very fat man" he is unable to pull out the sword that has pierced his belly.
20. Rimmon-Kenan, *Narrative Fiction*, 70.

21. Berlin takes a different approach to the classification of characters. She writes, "in literary criticism, it is customary to distinguish flat characters and round characters. Flat characters, or types, are built around a single quality or trait. They do not stand out as individuals. Round characters, on the other hand, are much more complex, manifesting a multitude of traits, and appearing as 'real people'" (Adele Berlin, *Poetics and Interpretation of Biblical Narrative* (Sheffield: Almond Press, 1983; reprint, Winona Lake, IN: Eisenbrauns, 1994), 23 (page citations are to the reprint edition). She later adds a third category of character which she calls an agent. Agents, according to Berlin, "serve as mere functionaries and are not characterized at all" (ibid.). Berlin goes on to identify the women in David's life as examples of the three categories. Michal and Bathsheba are round characters, having a wide variety of personality traits. Abigail is a flat character, typifying the perfect wife. Finally, Abishag is an agent, serving only a single function (ibid.). Reynolds, arguing against Berlin's classification of a third category, asserts that Abigail should properly be viewed as a round character while Abishag should be viewed as a flat character. He writes, "All of Berlin's arguments about Abigail . . . are purely subjective. The text does not clearly indicate that Abigail is a type of the perfect wife. She is a deeper character who serves several functions in the text. She prevents a mistake by David, encourages him in his perseverance, and becomes the first wife that the Lord gives to David as a reward for obedience. Berlin's idea causes too much confusion" (Reynolds, "A Literary Analysis of Nehemiah," 49).
22. Leland Ryken, *Words of Delight: A Literary Introduction to the Bible*, 2d ed. (Grand Rapids: Baker Book House, 1992), 26.
23. Northrop Frye, *Anatomy of Criticism* (Princeton: Princeton University Press, 1957), 99.
24. Leland Ryken, *The Literature of the Bible* (Grand Rapids: Zondervan Publishing House, 1974), 26.
25. Frye, *Anatomy of Criticism*, 315-16.
26. Bar-Efrat, *Narrative Art in the Bible*, 93.
27. Alter writes, "a proper narrative event occurs when the narrative tempo slows down enough for us to discriminate a partic-

ular scene; to have the illusion of the scene's 'presence' as it unfolds; to be able to imagine the interaction of personages or sometimes personages and groups, together with the freight of motivations, ulterior aims, character traits, political, social, or religious constraints, moral and theological meanings, borne by their speech, gestures, and acts" (Alter, *The Art of Biblical Narrative*, 63).

28. Bar-Efrat writes, "In addition to the structure consisting of a factual outline of the plot development, narratives possess what may be designated as dramatic structure. Dramatic structure involves the building up and relaxation of tension. Many biblical narratives are organized in this respect so as to exhibit the classical pyramid pattern. From a peaceful initial situation the action rises towards the climax where the decisive step determining the outcome of the conflict is taken, and from there it drops again to a more or less tranquil situation at the end" (Bar-Efrat, "Some Observations on the Analysis of Structure in Biblical Narrative," 165).

29. Ryken, *How to Read the Bible as Literature*, 40.

30. Sternberg elaborates on the element of suspense in a narrative, "In art, as in life, suspense derives from incomplete knowledge about a conflict (or some other contingency) looming in the future. Located at some point in the present, we know enough to expect a struggle but not to predict its course, and above all its outcome, with certitude. Hence a discontinuity that extends from the moment of prospection on the unknown to the moment of enactment and release. Hence also the state of mind that characterizes the intermediate phase (expectant restlessness, awareness of gaps, gap-filling inference along alternative lines) with the attention thrown forward to the point in time that will resolve it all and establish closure by supplying the desired information. Often, moreover, we have a stake (ethical, emotional, practical, doctrinal) in the event that hangs in the balance. The play of expectations then escalates into a clash of hope and fear, which engenders the sharpest form of suspense, because these rival hypotheses about the outcome are both loaded (hope with a

positive charge, fear with a negative) and mutually exclusive" (Sternberg, *The Poetics of Biblical Narrative*, 264).

31. Ryken, *Words of Delight: A Literary Introduction to the Bible*, 49.
32. Ibid., 50.
33. Bar-Efrat, "Some Observations on the Analysis of Structure in Biblical Narrative," 163.
34. Berlin writes, "it is impossible to discuss character without reference to point of view, for, after all, a character is not perceived by the reader directly, but rather mediated or filtered through the telling of the (implied) author, the narrator, or another character" (Berlin, *Poetics and Interpretation of Biblical Narrative*, 43).
35. Bar-Efrat explains the significance of point of view: "First of all, the point of view is one of the factors according unity to a work of literature, which naturally involves diffuseness and variety as regards characters, events, places and times. It has been said that the narrator's point of view is the 'fourth unity' (after Aristotle's three: unity of time, place and plot), because it blends the multiplicity of viewpoints of the characters within one general vista. Secondly, the point of view which has been selected dictates what will be narrated and how, what will be related from afar and what from close to. The narrator is like a photographer who decides what will and will not be included in a picture, from what distance and angle, with what degree of sharpness and in what light. Just as the nature of a film is dependent on the position of the camera and the way it is operated, the nature of the narrative depends on the point of view from which the events are presented. Thirdly, the appropriate point of view can make a crucial contribution to enhancing the interest or suspense of the narrative. The narrative should be moulded in such a fashion that it will be interesting, even gripping if possible, in order to enthrall the reader and make him or her share in what is happening. . . . Fourthly, the point of view is one of the means by which the narrative influences the reader, leading to the absorption of its implicit values and attitudes. Naturally, the reader's attitude to what is being related is dependent to a considerable extent on values and ideas which are held beforehand, but the author can

also influence these judgments." Bar-Efrat, *Narrative Art in the Bible*, 15-16.

36. Ibid., 13-14.

37. Howard identifies five different points of view in narratives: "First, from a psychological perspective, an omniscient narrator can tell us of the internal thoughts and feelings of the characters. Second, from an evaluative or ideological perspective, narrators will occasionally insert themselves into the text itself with a direct comment on the action or situation. Third, from a spatial perspective, biblical narrators can be anywhere. Fourth, from a temporal perspective, narrators can tell the story in strict chronological order with a limited temporal perspective, or they can tell of events from a less time-bound perspective. Fifth, from a phraseology perspective, the narrator can use linguistic symbols to indicate whose point of view is being taken at any one time" (David M. Howard, Jr. *An Introduction to the Old Testament Historical Books* [Chicago: Moody Press, 1993], 51-52).

38. Sternberg, *The Poetics of Biblical Narrative*, 53.

39. Ryken classifies four modes of narration: direct narrative, dramatic narrative, description, and commentary. He elaborates, "in *direct narrative*, storytellers simply report events, telling us in their own voice what happened. In *dramatic narrative*, writers dramatize a scene as though it were in a play, quoting the speeches or dialogue of characters and noting the surrounding context. In *description*, writers describe the details of setting or character. *Commentary* consists of explanations by storytellers about details in the story, background information, or the overall meaning of the story." Ryken, *Words of Delight: A Literary Introduction to the Bible*, 43.

40. Sternberg has provided a useful list identifying the various narrative intrusions: 1. *Expositional antecedents*, like the preliminaries concerning Job or the delayed mention of the Gibeonites (2 Sam 21:1-3). The exposition may unfold specific or general (Judg 16:4) information about the world, relate to individuals or groups, consist in external accounts or 2. *Character sketches*, usually in the form of one or two epithets, e.g., 'Esau was a skillful hunter, a man of the field; Jacob was a quiet man, dwelling in

tents' (Gen 25:27). More variable in length are 3. *Descriptions of objects*, whose upper limit is the meticulous picture drawn of the tabernacle in Exodus and the Temple in Kings. 4. *Interscenic summary*: 'He mourned for his son many days' (Gen 37:34), 'Absalom dwelt two full years in Jerusalem' (2 Sam 14:28). 5. *Retrospects*: 'And this is the reason why Joshua circumcised them: . . . all the people that were born on the way in the wilderness after they had come out of Egypt had not been circumcised' (Josh 5:4-5). 6. *Prospects*: 'Samuel did not see Saul again until the day of his death' (1 Sam 15:35). 7. *Genealogies and catalogues*, from 'the book of the generations of man' (Gen 5) to the interminable lists in Chronicles. 8. *Identifications*: 'Then Jerubaal (that is, Gideon) and all the people who were with him rose early' (Judg 7:1). 9. *Value judgments*: of agents, like 'the men of Sodom were wicked, great sinners against the Lord' (Gen 13:13), or actions, 'Thus God requited the crime of Abimelech' (Judg 9:56). 10. *Telescoped inside views*: 'Moses hid his face, for he was afraid to look at God' (Exod 3:6), 'He went away in a rage' (2 Kgs 5:12). 11. *Notes and stage directions in dialogue*: 'All the people answered with one voice' (Exod 24:3), 'Michal the daughter of Saul came out to meet David and said' (2 Sam 6:20). 12. *Intrusions into direct discourse*: 'He said, Thus and so he spoke to me' (2 Kgs 9:12). 13. *Bibliographical references*: 'David lamented with this lamentation over Saul and Jonathan. . . . Behold, it is written in the Book of Yashar' (2 Sam 1:17). 14. *Temporal or cultural bridging*, of special interest in this connection: 'He arrived opposite Jebus, that is, Jerusalem' (Judg 19:10)." Sternberg, *The Poetics of Biblical Narrative*, 120-21.

41. Whereas repetition, dialogue, and wordplay frequently involve the verbal elements of a story, parallelism, chiasm, and inclusio by definition involve the structure of a narrative. Bar-Efrat elaborates, "A distinction should be made . . . between the analysis of structure on a verbal level and the analysis of texture. Texture is structure looked at through a magnifying glass. It consists of the small-scale relations among the subordinate and generally proximate parts of the narrative, whereas structure proper consists of the relatively large-scale relations among the main and possibly

distant parts. Structural analysis, even if it is based on words or phrases, does not usually concern itself with texture (the investigation of texture is carried out by means of stylistic analysis)" (Bar-Efrat, "Some Observations on the Analysis of Structure in Biblical Narrative," 158).

42. Alter delineates five common areas of repetition in biblical narrative. First, *Leitwort* is the repetition of a verbal word-root. This involves the reoccurrence of key words as well as their verbal and phonetic relatives (e.g. the verb *to see* and its poetic synonyms in the Balaam story). Second, Motif is the recurrence of concrete images, sensory qualities, actions or objects. These elements have no meaning in themselves without the defining context of the narrative (e.g. water in the Mosaic narrative). Third, Theme is the reappearance of an idea which is part of the value-system of the narrative. This idea may be moral, legal, social, psychological, or theological and is often associated with one or more *Leitwörter* (e.g. obedience versus rebellion in the Wilderness stories). Fourth, Sequence of Actions is the reappearance of themes or ideas with some intensification or increment from one occurrence to the next, usually concluding either in a climax or a reversal (e.g. the three catastrophes that destroy Job's possessions, followed by a fourth in which his children are killed). Finally, Type-scene is an episode occurring at a portentous moment in the career of the hero which is composed of a fixed sequence of motifs (e.g. the annunciation of the birth of the hero). Robert Alter, *The Art of Biblical Narrative*, 95-96. Sternberg adds five kinds of deviations commonly found in biblical repetition: 1) Expansion or addition. 2) Truncation or ellipsis. 3) Change of order. 4) Grammatical transformation. 5) Substitution (Sternberg, *The Poetics of Biblical Narrative*, 392-93).

43. David M. Gunn and Danna Nolan Fewell, *Narrative in the Hebrew Bible*, The Oxford Bible Series, ed. P. R. Ackroyd and G. N. Stanton (New York: Oxford University Press, 1993), 148. Alter comments on the biblical use of repetition, "One of the most imposing barriers that stands between the modern reader and the imaginative subtlety of biblical narrative is the extraordinary

prominence of verbatim repetition in the Bible. Accustomed as we are to modes of narration in which elements of repetition are made to seem far less obtrusive, this habit of constantly restating material is bound to give us trouble, especially in a narrative that otherwise adheres so evidently to the strictest economy of means" (Alter, *The Art of Biblical Narrative*, 88).

44. Reynolds, "A Literary Analysis of Nehemiah," 44. Reynolds continues, "There is no logical reason why a text that normally specializes in economy should exhibit waste without a reason. Critics use this idea to argue for dual authorship, but a better alternative exists. The text has an internal purpose for the features" (ibid.). Sternberg adds, "From a broader viewpoint, neither the reticence of biblical narrative, nor the ubiquity of informational gaps, nor the miniature scale, nor the reign of economy, nor the combinatory artfulness, nor the demand for alertness—none of these accords with a wasteful handling of the structure of repetition. Hence a prima facie case, even better than usual, for a functional approach" (Sternberg, *The Poetics of Biblical Narrative*, 369).

45. Allen P. Ross, "The Literary Analysis," unpublished class notes in 103 Introduction to Hebrew Exegesis, Dallas Theological Seminary, Fall 1995.

46. Allen P. Ross, *Creation and Blessing* (Grand Rapids: Baker Book House, 1988), 191.

47. Howard, *An Introduction to the Old Testament Historical Books*, 57.

48. Sternberg explains, "Curiosity has much in common with suspense. Both are interests that derive from a felt lack of information about the world, give rise to a play of hypotheses framed to supply the missing link, and generate expectations of stable closure. The various modes of foreshadowing are in principle options and intensifiers rather than necessary conditions. To produce curiosity, on the other hand, the artist must perceptibly deform the chronological order, suppress and entangle and delay information in order to open gaps about what has already come to pass in terms of the natural time-line. In terms of the Bible's world view, the inferential movement back and forth along the

plot line even assumes the status of a rule, for to be in suspense about what looms ahead is to be curious about the divine scenario for it" (Sternberg, *The Poetics of Biblical Narrative*, 283-84). Martin identifies five categories of what he calls "dischronologized" material: 1) Where the effect is mentioned before the cause (e.g. 2 Kgs 24:7). 2) Where the end is mentioned before the beginning (e.g. 2 Sam 12:26ff.). 3) When the present state is mentioned before the past (e.g. 1 Kgs 9:15ff.). 4) The later is mentioned before the earlier (e.g. 1 Kgs 2:7ff.). 5) Where a consequence is mentioned before its antecedent (e.g. 2 Sam 4:4ff.). Commenting on the possible reasons for these shifts, he later writes, "in some cases nothing more seems to be involved than the reversal of the chronological order as a concession to memory. Or the purpose might be to arrange incidents according to their geographical distribution. A writer, on the other hand, might wish to subordinate and arrange incidents according to their relative importance. The major consideration with any writer of literary talent would be to present his material so organized as to stimulate attention and to communicate it effectively" (W. J. Martin, "Dischronologized Narrative in the Old Testament," in *Congress Volume: Rome, 1968*, Supplements to Vetus Testamentum, ed. G. W. Anderson et al., vol. 17 [Leiden: E. J. Brill, 1969], 181-82, 186).

Chapter One

1. Raymond B. Dillard and Tremper Longman III, *An Introduction to the Old Testament* (Grand Rapids: Zondervan Publishing House, 1994), 107.

2. While the Babylonian Talmud (*Baba Bathra* 15a) and some rabbis, including Rashi and David Kimchi, attributed the book to Joshua, Avravanel attributed it to Samuel, due especially to the phrase "to this day" (4:9; 5:9; 6:25; 7:26, etc.; David M. Howard, Jr., *An Introduction to the Old Testament Historical Books* [Chicago: Moody Press, 1993], 60).

3. Almost all dates cited in this book are taken from Eugene H. Merrill, *Kingdom of Priests: A History of Old Testament Israel* (Grand Rapids: Baker Books, 1987).

4. Nelson Glueck, "Explorations in Eastern Palestine and the Negev," *Bulletin of the American Schools of Oriental Research* 55 (1934): 3-21; 86 (1942): 14-24.

5. The excavation of Jericho has become particularly important in the dating of the Exodus. John Garstang, an early excavator of Jericho, dated the end of his "City IV" to 1400 B.C. Garstang's findings were disputed by Kathleen Kenyon, who dated the end of City IV to 1550 B.C. Kenyon argued that Jericho was largely unoccupied from 1550-1100 B.C. More recently, Bryant Wood has refuted Kenyon's claims, thus reaffirming the dating of Garstang. Wood argues that Kenyon mistakenly based her dating on imported pottery found largely in tombs rather than on the more common, local pottery found more widely throughout the Jericho mound. For a full discussion of this issue, see Howard, *An Introduction to the Old Testament Historical Books*, 84-85.

6. For the evidence, see Kathleen Kenyon, *Archaeology in the Holy Land* (New York: Praeger, 1960).

7. For a notable example, see Gerald L. Mattingly, "The Exodus-Conquest and the Archaeology of Transjordan: New Light on an Old Problem," *Grace Theological Journal* 4 (1983): 245-62.

8. Merrill, *Kingdom of Priests*, 71.

9. Much of this information, including the titles of the different views, is taken from Howard, *An Introduction to the Old Testament Historical Books*, 66-68.

10. For a defense of this view, see A. Alt, *Essays on Old Testament History and Religion* (Oxford: Blackwell, 1966).

11. For a defense of this view, see G. E. Mendenhall, "The Hebrew Conquest of Palestine," *Biblical Archaeology* 25 (1962): 66-87 or N. K. Gottwald, *The Tribes of Yahweh: A Sociology of the Religion of Liberated Israel, 1250-1050 B.C.E.* (Maryknoll, NY: Orbis, 1979).

12. It is also possible that the pharaoh who enslaved the Israelites was a Hyksos ruler in the Nile Delta region (John Rea, "Joshua," in *The Wycliffe Bible Commentary*, ed. Charles F. Pfeiffer and Everett F. Harrison [Chicago: Moody Press, 1962], 206).

13. Merrill F. Unger, *Unger's Bible Dictionary* (Chicago: Moody Press, 1966), 493.

14. Merrill, *Kingdom of Priests*, 97.
15. Ibid.
16. Keith N. Schoville, "Canaanites and Amorites," in *Peoples of the Old Testament World*, ed. Alfred J. Hoerth, Gerald L. Mattingly, and Edwin M. Yamauchi (Grand Rapids: Baker Books, 1974), 178.
17. Donald K. Campbell, "Joshua," in *The Bible Knowledge Commentary: Old Testament*, ed. John F. Walvoord and Roy B. Zuck (Colorado Springs: Victor Books, 1985), 326.
18. Thomas L. Constable, "A Theology of Joshua, Judges, and Ruth," in *A Biblical Theology of the Old Testament*, ed. Roy B. Zuck (Chicago: Moody Press, 1991), 105.
19. Our knowledge of the fertility cult practices of the Canaanites was greatly enhanced with the 1929 discovery of the Ras Shamra (Ugarit) tablets. These tablets were written in a cuneiform script based on an alphabet and provide significant information on the social, political, economical, and religious practices of the Canaanites.
20. Earl D. Radmacher, Ronald B. Allen, H. Wayne House, ed., *Nelson's New Illustrated Bible Commentary* (Nashville: Thomas Nelson Publishers, 1999), 272.
21. Dillard and Longman, *An Introduction to the Old Testament*, 113.
22. Although Moses had two sons, Gershom and Eliezer, neither one seems destined for leadership, perhaps because their mother was Zipporah, a Midianite.
23. It is also possible that the city was named after the moon (*yareach*) since it was the center of Canaanite moon worship.
24. Some have suggested that the word *zonah* describes Rahab as an innkeeper rather than as a prostitute (D. J. Wiseman, "Rahab of Jericho," *Tyndale Bulletin* 14 [1964]: 8-11; see also Josephus, *Antiquities of the Jews* 5.7-8). While the Hebrew term is admittedly somewhat ambiguous, there is no such ambiguity in the Greek word used to identify Rahab in Hebrews 11:31, *porne* (from which we get the word pornography), a term that clearly portrays Rahab as an actual prostitute.

25. Stephen L. Harris and Robert L. Platzner, *The Old Testament: An Introduction to the Hebrew Bible*, 2d ed. (New York: McGraw-Hill, 2008), 203.
26. Campbell, "Joshua," 364.

Chapter Two

1. The Greek (Septuagint) title for the book is *Kritai* while the Latin (Vulgate) title is *Judicum*, both of which mean the same thing as the Hebrew title *shophetim* ("judges").
2. Stephen L. Harris and Robert L. Platzner, *The Old Testament: An Introduction to the Hebrew Bible*, 2d ed. (New York: McGraw-Hill, 2008), 206.
3. David Noel Freedman, *Pottery, Poetry, and Prophecy* (Winona Lake, IN: Eisenbrauns, 1980), 167-78.
4. John E. McKenna, "Judges," in *Old Testament Survey: The Message, Form, and Background of the Old Testament*, 2d ed., ed. William Sanford Lasor, David Allan Hubbard, and Frederic William Bush (Grand Rapids: William B. Eerdmans Publishing Company, 1996), 161.
5. E.g., Victor P. Hamilton, *Handbook on the Historical Books* (Grand Rapids: Baker Academic, 2001), 98. Many scholars believe that the "book of the law" found by Hilkiah the high priest during the reign of Josiah was the book of Deuteronomy. Following Wellhausen, they date the books reviewing the early history of Israel through the lens of Deuteronomy to this period as well. For a full discussion of the view, see Julius H. Wellhausen, *Prolegomena to the History of Ancient Israel* (New York: Meridian, 1878, 1957). Howard, who holds to a sixth century B.C. date for the final edition of Judges, believes that an early form of the book, minus the prologue (1:1-2:5) and appendixes (chaps. 17-21) was written in the seventh century B.C. (David M. Howard, Jr. *An Introduction to the Old Testament Historical Books* [Chicago: Moody Press, 1993], 101).
6. E.g., ibid., 100.
7. Dillard and Longman believe the book was written after the schism between the northern and southern kingdoms of Israel. They suggest that the story of Micah's idols and the migration

of the Danites was used to show that the northern tribes were always prone to false worship and idolatry (Raymond B. Dillard and Tremper Longman III, *An Introduction to the Old Testament* [Grand Rapids: Zondervan Publishing House, 1994], 121).

8. Merrill identifies the forty years of Philistine oppression (Jud. 13:1) as taking place from 1124-1084 B.C. Since Samson did not live to see the end of the Philistine oppression, he probably died shortly before Samuel subdued the Philistines at Mizpah (Eugene H. Merrill, *Kingdom of Priests: A History of Old Testament Israel* [Grand Rapids: Baker Books, 1987], 149).

9. Some scholars have applied the Greek concept of "amphictyony" to Israel during the period of the Judges (for a notable example, see Martin Noth, *The History of Israel*, 2d. ed. [New York: Harper & Row, 1960], 85-109). The term describes a very loose association of twelve tribes unified only by the single sanctuary located at Shiloh (McKenna, "Judges," 160). This concept has little bearing on Judges, however, as the sanctuary at Shiloh is completely ignored in this book. The major similarity between the Greek amphictyony and the nation of Israel is the lack of any intertribal organization or central government. The classic example of Greek amphictyony "comes from Delphi in central Greece, dating to ca. 600 B.C. This was a religious association of twelve members revolving around a shrine at Delphi, pledged to a peaceful coexistence and a common defense against outside aggression; it met yearly for religious assemblies and affirmations of the ties that bound it together" (Howard, *An Introduction to the Old Testament Historical Books*, 108).

10. Merrill, *Kingdom of Priests*, 159.

11. Ibid., 161.

12. Ibid., 154.

13. For the complete text of the Merneptah Stele, see James B. Pritchard, ed., *Ancient Near Eastern Texts Relating to the Old Testament*, 3d ed. (Princeton: Princeton University Press, 1969), 376-78.

14. William C. Gwaltney Jr., "Assyrians," in *Peoples of the Old Testament World*, ed. Alfred J. Hoerth, Gerald L. Mattingly, and Edwin M. Yamauchi (Grand Rapids: Baker Books, 1974), 78.

15. Ibid., 103.
16. The term "Philistine" comes from the Hebrew *pelistim*, which occurs 288 times in the Old Testament. Its original derivation or meaning is unknown. In modern English, "philistine" has come to mean "boorish" or "uncultured." Information taken from David M. Howard Jr., "Philistines," in *Peoples of the Old Testament World*, ed. Alfred J. Hoerth, Gerald L. Mattingly, and Edwin M. Yamauchi (Grand Rapids: Baker Books, 1974), 231.
17. The reasons for this exodus are unclear. It is possible that a variety of factors were involved, including foreign invasion, political turmoil, famine, and natural disaster.
18. The Egyptian account of Rameses' battle with the "Sea Peoples" is the first extrabiblical reference to the Philistines, where they are identified as the "Peleset."
19. The Philistines of the book of Judges should not be confused with the Philistines of the book of Genesis, even though they probably shared the same ancestry and place of origin. The Philistines of Genesis migrated to Canaan around 2100 B.C.
20. Howard, "Philistines," 244.
21. Eugene H. Merrill, "1 Samuel," in *The Bible Knowledge Commentary: Old Testament*, ed. John F. Walvoord and Roy B. Zuck (Colorado Springs: Victor Books, 1985), 436.
22. Ashtoreth is the counterpart of the Babylonian goddess Ishtar and the Greek goddess Aphrodite.
23. The book "contains no record of annual celebrations of the Passover or the great feasts of Firstfruits, Pentecost, Trumpets, or Tabernacles, or of the observance of the Day of Atonement. This resulted in a downward spiral of religion and moral conditions" (Howard F. Vos, *Nelson's New Illustrated Bible Manners and Customs* [Nashville: Thomas Nelson Publishers, 1999], 115).
24. Andrew E. Hill and John H. Walton, *A Survey of the Old Testament* (Grand Rapids: Zondervan Publishing House, 1991), 176.
25. Dillard and Longman, *An Introduction to the Old Testament*, 125.
26. Ibid.
27. The phrase "inquired of the Lord" (1:1) may be a reference to the seeking of the will of God by the use of the Urim and Thummim,

two small objects that could be thrown like dice to solicit a response from God (Hamilton, *Handbook on the Historical Books*, 2001), 101.

28. Merrill, *Kingdom of Priests*, 144.

29. Lindsey identifies the Angel of the Lord as the preincarnate Jesus Christ, the second Person of the Trinity in visible and bodily form (F. Duane Lindsey, "Judges," in *The Bible Knowledge Commentary: Old Testament*, ed. John F. Walvoord and Roy B. Zuck [Colorado Springs: Victor Books, 1985], 381). This view is somewhat problematic in light of the repeated references to Yahweh in the Angel of the Lord passages. The New Testament, which routinely associates Jesus Christ with Old Testament figures (e.g., Prophet, Priest, King, Messiah, Son of Man, Word, Lamb), never identifies Jesus Christ as the Old Testament "Angel of the Lord."

30. Many scholars see the duplication of material as the result of the convergence of independent traditions (e.g., J. Alberto Soggin, *Judges: A Commentary* [Philadelphia: Westminster Press, 1981], 20, 40-42). Cundall views verse 1a, "Now it came about after the death of Joshua," as the title to the entire book and thus regards the contents of chapter one as taking place before the death of Joshua (Arthur E. Cundall, *Judges: An Introduction and Commentary* [Downers Grove: InterVarsity Press, 1968], 19, 51). Howard correctly observes that "the reference in 2:6-10 about Joshua's death is out of place chronologically. It is a 'flash-back' inserted at the beginning of the second section of the book (2:6-3:6). It duplicates Joshua 24:28-31 almost word for word, and its purpose is to tie closely the material that follows to the book of Joshua" (Howard, *An Introduction to the Old Testament Historical Books*, 113).

31. Each cultic center had their own local Baal (e.g., Baal-Peor, Baal-Zebub, Baal-Gad, Baal-Hermon, Baal-Berith, etc.).

32. All dates given in this section are very general approximations.

33. Ehud's weapon was different from the normal sword of the period, which was curved and would be used to slash instead of thrust (Yigael Yadin, *The Art of Warfare in the Biblical Lands*

According to Archaeological Finds [New York: McGraw Hill, 1963], 254-55).

34. It is possible that Anath is named for Anat (Anath), the Canaanite goddess and sister of Baal.

35. Wood believes that Jephthah's vow covers both options. He translates the latter part of 11:31 as "shall surely be the Lord's [human] or I will offer it up for a burnt offering [animal]" (Leon Wood, *A Survey of Israel's History* [Grand Rapids: Zondervan Publishing House, 1970], 223-24).

36. E.g., Robert G. Boling, *Judges*, Anchor Bible 6A (Garden City, NY: Doubleday & Company, 1975), 208.

37. E.g., C. J. Goslinga, *Joshua, Judges, Ruth*, trans. R. Togtman, Bible Student's Commentary (Grand Rapids: Zondervan Publishing House, 1986), 388. Howard, *An Introduction to the Old Testament Historical Books*, 116.

38. Hamilton believes that Jephthah did indeed anticipate that his daughter would be the one to greet him upon his return (Hamilton, *Handbook on the Historical Books*, 145). This view fails to take into account Jephthah's grief upon seeing his daughter come out of the house (cf. 11:35).

39. Howard, *An Introduction to the Old Testament Historical Books*, 117.

40. Hamilton, *Handbook on the Historical Books*, 153.

41. Lindsey translates the meaning of her name as "devoted" and suggests that she may have been a temple prostitute (Lindsey, "Judges," 407).

42. E.g., Radmacher, Allen, and House, *Nelson's New Illustrated Bible Commentary*, 330.

Chapter Three

1. An early Hebrew tradition places Ruth before Psalms (*Baba Bathra* 14b). Howard comments, "This [placement] is eminently understandable, since the book would thus function as an introduction to the Psalter or as a memoir of its 'author,' David. Since the major purpose of the book has to do with showing God's hand in the lives of people who were David's ancestors and with introducing David himself, this placement has much to commend

it" (David M. Howard, Jr. *An Introduction to the Old Testament Historical Books* [Chicago: Moody Press, 1993], 130).

2. N. M. Tischler, "Ruth," in *A Complete Literary Guide to the Bible*, ed. Leland Ryken and Tremper Longman III (Grand Rapids: Zondervan Publishing House, 1993). See also Robert L. Hubbard, Jr. *The Book of Ruth*, New International Commentary on the Old Testament, ed. R. K. Harrison (Grand Rapids: William B. Eerdmans Publishing Company, 1988), 24.

3. Earl D. Radmacher, Ronald B. Allen, H. Wayne House, ed., *Nelson's New Illustrated Bible Commentary* (Nashville: Thomas Nelson Publishers, 1999), 337.

4. Thomas L. Constable, "A Theology of Joshua, Judges, and Ruth," in *A Biblical Theology of the Old Testament*, ed. Roy B. Zuck (Chicago: Moody Press, 1991), 109.

5. Hubbard, *The Book of Ruth*, 42.

6. Howard, *An Introduction to the Old Testament Historical Books*, 133.

7. John W. Reed, "Ruth," in *The Bible Knowledge Commentary: Old Testament*, ed. John F. Walvoord and Roy B. Zuck (Colorado Springs: Victor Books, 1985), 417.

8. Andrew E. Hill and John H. Walton, *A Survey of the Old Testament* (Grand Rapids: Zondervan Publishing House, 1991), 184.

9. Hubbard, *The Book of Ruth*, 45.

10. Howard, *An Introduction to the Old Testament Historical Books*, 126-27.

11. Hill and Walton, *A Survey of the Old Testament*, 184.

12. Jack M. Sasson, *Ruth: A New Translation with a Philological Commentary and a Formalist-Folklorist Interpretation* (Baltimore: John Hopkins University Press, 1979), 215.

13. Edward F. Campbell, Jr., *Ruth*, Anchor Bible, ed. William F. Albright and David N. Freedman, vol. 7 (Garden City, NY: Doubleday & Company, 1975), 3.

14. Stephen L. Harris and Robert L. Platzner, *The Old Testament: An Introduction to the Hebrew Bible*, 2d ed. (New York: McGraw-Hill, 2008), 342.

15. Reed, "Ruth," 420-21.

16. Ronald L. Hubbard, Jr., "Ruth," in *Old Testament Survey: The Message, Form, and Background of the Old Testament*, 2d ed., ed. William Sanford Lasor, David Allan Hubbard, and Frederic William Bush (Grand Rapids: William B. Eerdmans Publishing Company, 1996), 524.

17. Howard, *An Introduction to the Old Testament Historical Books*, 128.

18. Radmacher, Allen, and House, *Nelson's New Illustrated Bible Commentary*, 338.

19. Reed, "Ruth," 420-21.

20. Naomi's silence has been interpreted by some as anger at Ruth (D. N. Fewell and D. M. Gunn, "'A Son is Born to Naomi!' Literary Allusion and Interpretation in the Book of Ruth" *Journal for the Study of the Old Testament* 40 [1988]: 100).

21. Grant calls this statement "the nadir of the Ruth narrative" (R. Grant, "Literary Structure in the Book of Ruth," *Bibliotheca Sacra* 148 [July-September 1991]: 431).

22. Radmacher, Allen, and House, *Nelson's New Illustrated Bible Commentary*, 340.

23. Much of the information in this paragraph is taken from Charles P. Baylis, "Naomi in the Book of Ruth in Light of the Mosaic Covenant," *Bibliotheca Sacra* 161 (October-December 2004): 428-31.

24. Howard, *An Introduction to the Old Testament Historical Books*, 137.

25. Reed, "Ruth," 425.

26. Ibid., 426.

27. Howard, *An Introduction to the Old Testament Historical Books*, 138.

28. Victor P. Hamilton, *Handbook on the Historical Books* (Grand Rapids: Baker Academic, 2001), 200.

29. The Babylonian Talmud records a tradition that Boaz was previously married, but his wife died on the same day that Ruth and Naomi arrived in Bethlehem (*Baba Batra* 91a).

30. Hamilton, *Handbook on the Historical Books*, 192.

Chapter Four

1. Andrew E. Hill and John H. Walton, *A Survey of the Old Testament* (Grand Rapids: Zondervan Publishing House, 1991), 187.
2. David M. Howard, Jr. *An Introduction to the Old Testament Historical Books* (Chicago: Moody Press, 1993), 142.
3. A. Kirk Grayson, *Assyrian Royal Inscriptions*, vol. 2 (Wiesbaden: Harrassowitz, 1976), #97.
4. Pitard disagrees with the traditional view. He asserts, "It seems quite unlikely that the Arameans were immigrants into Syria and Upper Mesopotamia at all, but rather that they were the West Semitic-speaking peoples who had lived in that area throughout the second millennium, some as pastoralists and some in villages, towns, and cities. During the period following the collapse of the Hittite Empire, this West Semitic element of the population slowly became politically dominant in several areas, and it is this element, then, that begins to appear in the sources in the late twelfth century" (Wayne T. Pitard, "Arameans," in *Peoples of the Old Testament World*, ed. Alfred J. Hoerth, Gerald L. Mattingly, and Edwin M. Yamauchi [Grand Rapids: Baker Books, 1974], 209-10).
5. There are several different Aramean states. The Aramean states that play a major role in the Old Testament are Aram-Zobah and Aram-Damascus. Aram-Zobah was located in the central part of the Lebanon valley between the Lebanon and Anti-Lebanon mountain ranges. Other notable Aramean states include Aram-Naharayim (Padan Aram; Gen. 25:20; located in northern Mesopotamia), Beth-Rehob (located north of Dan), Geshur (located in the Golan Heights), Aram-Maacah (also located in the Golan Heights), and Tob (located in the northern Transjordan east of Gilead). For a full discussion of the Arameans, see J. A. Lund, "Aram, Damascus and Syria," in *Dictionary of the Old Testament Historical Books*, ed. Bill T. Arnold and H. B. M. Williamson (Downers Grove, IL: InterVarsity Press, 2005), 41-50.
6. Other Semitic languages include the East Semitic language Akkadian, an umbrella term covering both Babylonian and Assyrian, and the South Semitic languages Arabic, Ancient South

Arabian, and classical Ethiopic, i.e., Geez (J. A. Lund, "Aramaic Language," in *Dictionary of the Old Testament Historical Books*, ed. Bill T. Arnold and H. B. M. Williamson [Downers Grove, IL: InterVarsity Press, 2005], 50).

7. Pitard, "Arameans," 227.

8. Ibid., 228.

9. The term "Philistine" comes from the Hebrew *pelistim*, which occurs 288 times in the Old Testament. Its original derivation or meaning is unknown. In modern English, "philistine" has come to mean "boorish" or "uncultured." Information taken from David M. Howard Jr., "Philistines," in *Peoples of the Old Testament World*, ed. Alfred J. Hoerth, Gerald L. Mattingly, and Edwin M. Yamauchi (Grand Rapids: Baker Books, 1974), 231.

10. The reasons for this exodus are unclear. It is possible that a variety of factors were involved, including foreign invasion, political turmoil, famine, and natural disaster.

11. The Egyptian account of Rameses' battle with the "Sea Peoples" is the first extrabiblical reference to the Philistines, where they are identified as the "Peleset."

12. The Philistines of the book of Judges should not be confused with the Philistines of the book of Genesis, even though they probably shared the same ancestry and place of origin. The Philistines of Genesis migrated to Canaan around 2100 B.C.

13. Howard, "Philistines," 244.

14. Eugene H. Merrill, "1 Samuel," in *The Bible Knowledge Commentary: Old Testament*, ed. John F. Walvoord and Roy B. Zuck (Colorado Springs: Victor Books, 1985), 436.

15. Ashtoreth is the counterpart of the Babylonian goddess Ishtar and the Greek goddess Aphrodite.

16. Earl D. Radmacher, Ronald B. Allen, H. Wayne House, ed., *Nelson's New Illustrated Bible Commentary* (Nashville: Thomas Nelson Publishers, 1999), 344.

17. Hill and Walton, *A Survey of the Old Testament*, 197.

18. Julius H. Wellhausen, *Der Text der Bucher Samuelis untersucht* (Gottingen: Vandenhoeck und Ruprecht, 1871). See also Julius H. Wellhausen, *Prolegomena to the History of Ancient Israel* (New York: Meridian, 1878, 1957).

19. Information taken from Howard, *An Introduction to the Old Testament Historical Books*, 143.
20. The Deuteronomistic theory is the belief that most of the material recorded in the Old Testament historical books came from one document supposedly written during the reign of Josiah. For a defense of the view, see Martin Noth, *The History of Israel*, 2d. ed. (New York: Harper & Row, 1960).
21. Listing taken from Howard, *An Introduction to the Old Testament Historical Books*, 144.
22. For a notable example of a study that presents the book as a unified work, see J. P. Fokkelman, *Narrative Art and Poetry in the Books of Samuel*, 2 vols. (Assen, The Netherlands: Van Gorcum, 1981, 1986).
23. An animal's horn was the ultimate symbol of its strength since it was used for both offensive and defensive actions.
24. Merrill, "1 Samuel," 433.
25. The Law required all male Hebrew adults to appear at the tabernacle three times yearly for the Feasts of Unleavened Bread, Pentecost (Weeks), and Tabernacles (Booths; cf. Deut. 16:16).
26. A Nazirite was a person who was to be disciplined in his appetite (no wine or grapes), distinctive in his appearance (no haircut), and discreet in his associations (no contact with a dead body; cf. Num. 6:2-6; Victor P. Hamilton, *Handbook on the Historical Books* [Grand Rapids: Baker Academic, 2001], 512).
27. Cf. 2 Macc. 7:27.
28. Hannah's prayer recorded in 1 Samuel 2:1-10 probably served as the inspiration for Mary's Magnificat (Luke 1:46-55). It also appears to have been the model for Psalm 113.
29. As such, the children are a perfect illustration of the difference between the righteous and godly spoken of in Hannah's prayer (1 Sam. 2:1-10).
30. Eli is a descendant of Ithamar. However, the last high priest mentioned before him is Phinehas, the son of Eleazar (Jud. 20:28). It is not known how or why the office of high priest switched from the family of Eleazar to the family of Ithamar.
31. The ultimate fulfillment of this prophecy is the Lord Jesus Christ who will ultimately serve as both Priest and King. The sons of

Zadok will serve as His priests in the millennial temple (Ezek. 44:15).

32. Eugene H. Merrill, *Kingdom of Priests: A History of Old Testament Israel* (Grand Rapids: Baker Books, 1987), 149.

33. Ibid., 176.

34. The Ark of the Covenant was the most significant piece of furniture in the tabernacle. It was crafted by Bezalel and Oholiab out of acacia wood overlaid with gold (cf. Ex. 25:10-11; 31:1-11). The Ark of the Covenant contained a golden pot full of manna, Aaron's rod that budded, and the tablets of the covenant (Heb. 9:4). It resided in the Holy of Holies in the tabernacle and, subsequently, the temple (Heb. 9:3-4).

35. The transcript of 1 Samuel 13:1 is the victim of severe textual corruption. The text literally reads, "Saul was [illegible] years old when he became king, and he reigned over Israel two years." Obviously, it is impossible to fit all the events of Saul's reign into two years so there must be another missing number. The NASB reads, "Saul was forty years old when he began to reign, and he reigned thirty-two years over Israel." The NIV reads, "Saul was thirty years old when he became king, and he reigned over Israel forty-two years." The NKJV reads, "Saul reigned one year, and when he had reigned two years over Israel. . . ." The NRSV does not even try to solve the problem, reading "Saul was . . . years old when he began to reign; and he reigned . . . and two years over Israel." According to Merrill, the best reading is "Saul was [forty] years old when he began to reign. When he had reigned for two years. . . ." (Merrill, *Kingdom of Priests*, 193). Merrill explains the reasoning behind his suggestion, "In support of Paul's statement that Saul ruled for forty years [Acts 13:21] is the fact that Ish-Bosheth, the son of Saul who succeeded him as king, was forty when he began to reign (2 Sam. 2:10) and yet was not born until after Saul ascended Israel's throne. This is clear from a comparison of the list of Saul's sons in the earliest years of his reign (1 Sam. 14:47-51) and the list of all his sons (1 Chron. 8:33; 9:39). The former names Jonathan, Ishvi, and Malki-Shua, and the latter Jonathan, Malki-Shua, Abinadab, and Esh-Baal. Esh-Baal is identical to Ish-Bosheth, and Abinadab

is presumably another name for Ishvi (see 1 Chron. 10:2). When Saul was slain by the Philistines, his three sons Jonathan, Abinadab, and Malki-Shua died with him (1 Sam. 31:2). Since Ish-Bosheth survived, he obviously was not Abinadab" (ibid., 193-194).

36. Edwin R. Thiele, *The Mysterious Numbers of the Hebrew Kings* (Grand Rapids: William B. Eerdmans Publishing Company, 1965), 51-52.

37. The king's command is in the form of an oath. According to Hamilton, "An oath in the Old Testament, to be distinguished from a conditionally stated vow, comes in one of two forms. First, there is what we shall call the 'oath of purgation,' whose purpose is to clear the accused of a charge. Examples of this kind are Gen. 14:22-23; Exod. 22:8; Lev. 6:3-5; Num. 5:19; Rom. 1:9. The second kind of an oath is what we shall call a 'promissory oath,' which imposes some kind of an obligation on the oath taker. Examples are Abraham's servant who takes an oath to get a wife for Isaac from the Canaanites (Gen. 24:2-4); Joseph, who takes an oath that he will bury his father in Canaan rather than leave his corpse behind in Egypt (Gen. 47:29-31; 50:5); David, who by oath, which he is now asked to honor, allegedly promised that Solomon would succeed him as King (1 Kings 1:13, 17, 30). Of course, by definition a covenant is a promissory oath. Saul's oath is the latter type. It imposes a fast on his soldiers. If there are instances in the Old Testament of oath taking that spring from the sublime and solemn, Saul's oath is an instance of a noble institution used trivially and irrationally. The rigors of battle are debilitating enough, especially when one is up against a superior foe, and now add to that abstinence from food" (Hamilton, *Handbook on the Historical Books*, 246-47).

38. Merrill, "1 Samuel," 451.

39. The Jebusites were the descendants of Canaan, the son of Ham (Gen. 10:16).

40. Merrill, *Kingdom of Priests*, 236.

41. Radmacher, Allen, and House, *Nelson's New Illustrated Bible Commentary*, 395.

42. Merrill, *Kingdom of Priests*, 234.

43. Since Hiram ruled Tyre from 980-947 B.C., this project must have taken place in the latter years of David's reign.

44. David appears to serve as a priest throughout Samuel and Chronicles. He wears the linen ephod as the Ark is taken to Jerusalem (2 Sam. 6:14), he offers burnt offerings and peace offerings (2 Sam. 6:17; 24:25), he appoints the religious personnel at the tabernacle (1 Chron. 16:4-6), and he separates the Levites into divisions (1 Chron. 23-25).

45. Merrill, *Kingdom of Priests*, 275.

Chapter Five

1. Another argument against Jeremiah's authorship is the stylistic differences between the books of Jeremiah and Lamentations and the book of Kings. Of special note is the differences in the use of the names of Judah's kings.

2. The Deuteronomistic theory is the belief that most of the material recorded in the Old Testament historical books came from one document supposedly written during the reign of Josiah. For a defense of the view, see Martin Noth, *The History of Israel*, 2d. ed. (New York: Harper & Row, 1960).

3. For a defense of the double-redaction hypothesis, see F. M. Cross, *Canaanite Myth and Hebrew Epic* (Harvard University Press, 1973), 274-89.

4. Stephen L. Harris and Robert L. Platzner, *The Old Testament: An Introduction to the Hebrew Bible*, 2d ed. (New York: McGraw-Hill, 2008), 222.

5. Ibid.

6. Eugene H. Merrill, *Kingdom of Priests: A History of Old Testament Israel* (Grand Rapids: Baker Books, 1987), 292.

7. Tiglath-Pileser III is also called Pul in the Old Testament (cf. 1 Chron. 5:26).

8. For the Assyrian text, see James B. Pritchard, *Ancient Near Eastern Texts Relating to the Old Testament*, 2d ed. (Princeton: Princeton University Press, 1955), 283a.

9. For the Assyrian text, see ibid., 284b.

10. Andrew E. Hill and John H. Walton, *A Survey of the Old Testament* (Grand Rapids: Zondervan Publishing House, 1991), 397.

11. Raymond B. Dillard and Tremper Longman III, *An Introduction to the Old Testament* (Grand Rapids: Zondervan Publishing House, 1994), 161.

12. Ibid., 165.

13. Much of the material in this paragraph, including vocabulary, is taken from David M. Howard, Jr. *An Introduction to the Old Testament Historical Books* (Chicago: Moody Press, 1993), 176-77.

14. Dillard and Longman, *An Introduction to the Old Testament*, 160.

15. Howard, *An Introduction to the Old Testament Historical Books*, 178.

16. The idea for a bull may have been borrowed from Egypt, where the Apis cult of Memphis symbolized their god with an image of a bull.

17. Thomas L. Constable, "1 Kings," in *The Bible Knowledge Commentary: Old Testament*, ed. John F. Walvoord and Roy B. Zuck (Colorado Springs: Victor Books, 1985), 515.

18. There are several indications that this Absalom is not the son of David. First, the daughter of David's son Absalom was named Tamar (2 Sam. 14:27). Second, 1 Kings 15:2, 10, has Abishalom rather than Absalom. Third, Maacah's father is elsewhere called "Uriel of Gibeah" (2 Chron. 13:2). This listing is taken from Merrill, *Kingdom of Priests*, 321.

19. There is considerable debate as to the proper chronological structure of the reign of Asa. For a full discussion of the issue, see ibid., 332-34.

20. For a full discussion of the pattern of coregency among the Hebrew kings, see Edwin R. Thiele, "Coregencies and Overlapping Reigns Among the Hebrew Kings," *Journal of Biblical Literature* 93 (1974): 174-200.

21. For a translation of the text, see James B. Pritchard, *Ancient Near Eastern Texts Relating to the Old Testament*, 2d ed. (Princeton: Princeton University Press, 1955), 320-22. Merrill, *Kingdom of Priests*, 366-67.

23. Ibid., 393.

24. The chronology of the reign of Pekah is notoriously difficult. It appears that he spent the first twelve years of his reign as ruler over a pro-Samaria, anti-Assyrian element in Israel. For a full discussion of this hypothesis, see ibid., 397-98.
25. Pritchard, *Ancient Near Eastern Texts Relating to the Old Testament*, 288..

Chapter Six

1. Williamson, who holds that different authors wrote Chronicles and Ezra, believes that the appendage occurred for liturgical considerations. He explains that "there was a desire not to end a reading on too negative a note." As a result, "instead of finishing with the Chronicler's original ending at 2 Chronicles 36:21, it became normal to read a short passage from the beginning of Ezra, which of course in one sense continues the story where the Chronicler left off. And so in time this habit came to be reflected in the written form of the text" (Hugh G. M. Williamson, "Did the Author of Chronicles Also Write the Books of Ezra and Nehemiah?" *Bible Review* 3 [spring 1987]: 59). Williamson, however, gives no explanation as to why Cyrus' decree is abbreviated in Chronicles.
2. Eugene H. Merrill, "A Theology of Chronicles," in *A Biblical Theology of the Old Testament*, ed. Roy B. Zuck (Chicago: Moody Press, 1991), 158.
3. Andrew E. Hill, *The NIV Application Commentary: 1 & 2 Chronicles* (Grand Rapids: Zondervan Publishing House, 2003), 38.
4. Listing taken from Andrew E. Hill and John H. Walton, *A Survey of the Old Testament* (Grand Rapids: Zondervan Publishing House, 1991), 218.
5. C. C. Torrey, *The Composition and Historical Value of Ezra-Nehemiah* (Giessen: J. Rickersche, 1896), 252, 274, as cited in David M. Howard, Jr., *An Introduction to the Old Testament Historical Books* (Chicago: Moody Press, 1993), 232.
6. Hill and Walton, *A Survey of the Old Testament*, 218-19.
7. For a chart of these differences, see Hill, *The NIV Application Commentary: 1 & 2 Chronicles*, 31.

8. Hill and Walton, *A Survey of the Old Testament*, 222.
9. Hill, *The NIV Application Commentary: 1 & 2 Chronicles*, 27.
10. Ibid.
11. Robert North, "Theology of the Chronicler," *Journal of Biblical Literature* 82 (December 1963): 376.
12. David J. A. Clines, *Ezra, Nehemiah, Esther*, New Century Bible Commentary, ed. Ronald E. Clements and Matthew Black (Grand Rapids: William B. Eerdmans Publishing Company, 1984), 25.
13. Ibid., 26.
14. Stephen L. Harris and Robert L. Platzner, *The Old Testament: An Introduction to the Hebrew Bible*, 2d ed. (New York: McGraw-Hill, 2008), 353.
15. Raymond B. Dillard and Tremper Longman III, *An Introduction to the Old Testament* (Grand Rapids: Zondervan Publishing House, 1994), 174.
16. Ibid., 175.
17. M. D. Johnson, *The Purpose of the Biblical Genealogies*, 2d ed. (Cambridge: Cambridge University Press, 1988), 77-82. Cited by Howard, *An Introduction to the Old Testament Historical Books*, 250-51.
18. Harris and Platzner, *The Old Testament: An Introduction to the Hebrew Bible*, 353.
19. Hill and Walton, *A Survey of the Old Testament*, 224.

Chapter Seven
1. Edwin M. Yamauchi, "Persians," in *Peoples of the Old Testament World*, ed. Edward J. Hoerth, Gerald D. Mattingly, and Edwin M. Yamauchi (Grand Rapids: Baker Books, 1994), 110.
2. Ibid.
3. David M. Howard, Jr., *An Introduction to the Old Testament Historical Books* (Chicago: Moody Press, 1993), 285.
4. Many scholars have advanced the view that Gubaru is to be identified as the "Darius the Mede" figure referenced in the Book of Daniel (e.g., 5:31; 6:9, 25, 28; 9:1). Howard maintains, "The details of 'Darius the Mede's' life fit those of Gaubaruwa [Gubaru] very closely, and 'Darius the Mede' may simply have been an alternate title for him" (David M. Howard, Jr., *An*

Introduction to the Old Testament Historical Books [Chicago: Moody Press, 1993], 285. For a full explanation of this view, see W. H. Shea, "Darius the Mede: An Update," *Andrews University Seminary Studies* 20 (autumn 1982): 229-48. An alternative view identifies Cyrus II as "Darius the Mede." According to this view, the last portion of Daniel 6:28, "So Daniel prospered during the reign of Darius and the reign of Cyrus the Persian," should be understood to mean "the reign of Darius, that is, the reign of Cyrus" (see NIV margin note). For a full explanation of this view, see B. E. Colless, "Cyrus the Persian as Darius the Mede in the Book of Daniel," *Journal for the Study of the Old Testament* 56 (December 1992): 113-26.

5. For a full listing of these battles and their dates, see Edwin M. Yamauchi, *Persia and the Bible* (Grand Rapids: Baker Books, 1990), 146.

6. Eugene H. Merrill, *Kingdom of Priests: A History of Old Testament Israel* (Grand Rapids: Baker Books, 1987), 498.

7. Edwin M. Yamauchi, "The Archaeological Background of Nehemiah," *Bibliotheca Sacra* 137 (October-December 1980): 291.

8. Another possible fulfillment of the words of Jeremiah is Jeremiah 51:1, 11. In these verses, the Lord announces the destruction of Babylon. This view is based on the close relationship between the phrases "the Lord stirred up the spirit of Cyrus king of Persia" in Ezra 1:1 and "the Lord has aroused the spirit of the kings of the Medes" in Jeremiah 51:11. Allen explains the logic of this view: "The narrative provides its own clue [as to the fulfillment of Jeremiah's prophecy] in the phrase 'the Lord stirred up the spirit.' Jeremiah 51:1, 11 uses the same language in an oracle about the future destruction of Babylon. The latter verse is especially significant, with its statement that 'The Lord has stirred up the spirit of the kings of the Medes.' Cyrus, king of Anshan and Persia, became king of the Medes by conquest in 549 B.C. before pressing on to capture Babylon in 539. This capture of Babylon made it possible for him to release the Judeans exiled to Babylonia, in the year 538. The narrator probably associated Jeremiah 51 with the even more relevant passages in Second

Isaiah, which proclaim that Israel's God 'stirred up' Cyrus in Isaiah 41:2, 25; 45:13. In these first two cases it was to conquer nations and in the last case to rebuild Jerusalem. In Isaiah 44:28, although the verb 'stir up' is not used, the divine role given to Cyrus actually includes laying the temple foundations. There was therefore ample material to substantiate the narrative's appeal to prophetic prediction" (Leslie C. Allen, "Ezra," in *Ezra, Nehemiah, Esther*, New International Biblical Commentary [Peabody, MA: Hendrickson Publishers, Inc., 2003], 15-16). A significant problem with this view is that the proclamation issued by Cyrus deals with the remnant's ability to return to their homeland. No mention is made of the destruction of Babylon, a noteworthy omission if this is the fulfillment that Ezra had in mind.

9. Ezra later records the work of the Lord to put it into the heart of Artaxerxes to allow Ezra to return to the Promised Land (7:27). He further writes that the Lord had "turned the heart of the king of Assyria [Darius] toward them [the Jewish remnant] to encourage them in the work of the house of God, the God of Israel" (6:22). Nehemiah consistently gives God the credit for his success (cf. Neh. 2:20; 6:16), even seeing Him as responsible for causing Artaxerxes to allow Nehemiah to return to Judah (cf. Neh. 2:4, 8). The very fact that both Ezra and Nehemiah consistently pray to the Lord demonstrates their belief in His sovereignty. Even though the name of God is not mentioned in the book of Esther, the major theme of the entire narrative is the sovereign providence of God. Like a puppet master pulling the strings of his marionettes, it is the Lord who orchestrates the succession of events that begin with the demotion of Vashti and promotion of Esther and result in the salvation of the Jews during the time of Xerxes. In each of these books, God is seen as completely sovereign, even over Cyrus, Darius, Xerxes, and Artaxerxes, the kings of the most powerful empire on earth.

10. Throughout the postexilic historical books, there is a strong emphasis on the fact that the Persian kings wrote their decrees (cf. Ezra 6:2; Esth. 3:12; 8:9). The edicts of the Persian kings were written down and recorded because they were seen as

irrevocable (Esth. 1:19; 8:8; Dan. 6:15). This decree was likely written in the Book of the Chronicles of the Kings of Media and Persia (cf. Esth. 10:2). The fact that this decree was written down allowed Darius to confirm its authenticity in chapter six. Of interest is the fact that this proclamation is the only official document in Ezra not written in Aramaic.

11. The postal system of the Persians was world-renowned. Herodotus, who traveled in Western Persia shortly after the reign of Xerxes, writes "Nothing mortal travels so fast as these Persian messengers. The entire plan is a Persian invention; and this is the method of it. Along the whole line of road there are men (they say) stationed with horses, in number equal to the number of days which the journey takes, allowing a man and horse to each day; and these men will not be hindered from accomplishing at their best speed the distance which they have to go, either by snow or rain, or heat, or by the darkness of night. The first rider delivers his dispatch to the second, and the second passes it to the third; and so it is borne from hand to hand along the whole line, like the light in the torch-race, which the Greeks celebrate to Vulcan. The Persians give the riding post in this manner, the name of 'Angarum'" (*Histories* 8.98).

12. The exact nature of this offering is unknown. It is doubtful that the reference is to money since silver and gold has already been mentioned. It is also unlikely that the reference is to meal or grain offerings since these might have spoiled or rotted prior to the time of sacrifice. The offering probably consisted of a herd of animals to be sacrificed on the rebuilt altar. In 3:5, the same word is used to denote the freewill offerings of the remnant which were burnt on the altar.

13. Dozeman comments on this phrase, "The author of Ezra-Nehemiah employs the geopolitical meaning of *Abar Naharah* [beyond the river] to advance three social and religious arguments about the nature of Persian rule and its impact on Yahwism. First, the Persian monarchs in general, and Artaxerxes in particular, are idealized as kings who uphold the law in *Abar Naharah* and are restricted by it. Second, not only Persian kings but Persian law itself is represented as an ideal in Ezra-

Nehemiah. It is impartial and equally binding for Persians and Judeans. Third, the author of Ezra-Nehemiah advocates a form of environmental determinism in the region of *Abar Naharah*. The Persian rule of law in *Abar Naharah* provides the environment (i.e., the *nomos*) for the transformation of Yahwism from a messianic religion centered in a monarchy to a religion of law, constituted in the Torah of Moses" (Thomas B. Dozeman, "Geography and History in Herodotus and in Ezra-Nehemiah," *Journal of Biblical Literature* 122 [July 2003]: 459).

14. The Southern Kingdom of Judah had rebelled against the Assyrians in the days of Hezekiah (2 Kin. 18:7). They rebelled against the Babylonian Nebuchadnezzar in the days of Jehoiakim (597 B.C.; 2 Kin. 24:1). And finally, they again rebelled against Nebuchadnezzar in the days of Zedekiah (588 B.C.; 2 Kin. 24:20).

15. Derek Kidner, *Ezra and Nehemiah*, Tyndale Old Testament Commentaries (Downers Grove, IL: InterVarsity Press, 1979), 55.

16. For a full discussion of the relationship between these two documents, see E. J. Bickerman, "The Edict of Cyrus in Ezra 1," *Journal of Biblical Literature* 65 (1946): 259-275.

17. The Canaanites lived along the eastern Mediterranean coastal regions from the River of Egypt to the area of Lebanon (Num. 13:29). The Canaanites, caught between the cumbersome writings of Mesopotamian cuneiform and Egyptian hieroglyphics, were the inventors of a simplified method of writing, the alphabet. Biblical Hebrew is derived from the Canaanite language. The Canaanites were also known as artisans, bronze metallurgists, potters, and merchants. However, their most significant impact on Israel came in the area of religion. The Canaanite fertility cult was perhaps the most immoral and vile religion known to man. The chief god of the Canaanites was Baal, god of thunder and lightning. Other gods included El, the patriarchal deity who was the father of Baal; Yam, the god of the sea; Asherah, the wife of El; Mot, the god of the underworld; and Anat, the sister of Baal. The Canaanites worshipped their gods by engaging in sexual immorality involving male and female prostitutes and sacrificing

their children. The Canaanite religion proved to be too attractive for the Hebrews to resist. Israel's worship of Baal seems to have been the most significant sin among those that led to the nation's deportation (cf. Jer. 11:17; Hos. 2:1-13; 11:2; Zeph. 1:4).

18. Many scholars consider the Hittites as the third most influential people group of the Ancient Near East, rivaling the Egyptians and the Mesopotamians.[3] The Hittites dominated Asia Minor, their capital located on the Halys River at a place called Boghaz-keui in central Anatolia. Groups of Hittites migrated south, eventually settling in the hill country of Canaan near the city of Hebron (Gen. 23:19; Num. 13:29). Notable Hittites include Ephron, from whom Abraham purchased a burial site (Gen. 23), and Uriah, one of the mighty men of David (2 Sam. 23:39). Esau married two Hittites (Gen. 26:34) and Solomon had Hittite women in his harem (1 Kin. 11:1).

19. The Jebusites lived in the hill country (Num. 13:29) and were the original inhabitants of Jerusalem. Jebusite Jerusalem was taken by King David in about 1004 B.C. (cf. 2 Sam. 5:5-8). The Jebusites are identified in Deuteronomy as one of the seven nations in the Promised Land "greater and stronger" than Israel (Deut. 7:1). During the period of the judges they lived in the general region of Jerusalem in the territory allotted to the tribes of Judah and Benjamin (cf. Josh. 15:63; Judg. 1:21). It should be remembered that Jerusalem was among the cities allotted to the tribe of Benjamin (Josh. 18:28). Notable Jebusites include Adoni-zedek, the King of Jerusalem who formed the alliance against Gibeon (Josh. 10:1-4), and Araunah (also known as Ornan), from whom David bought the threshing floor which would become the site of Solomon's temple (2 Sam. 24:16-24; 1 Chron. 21:14-27). If Salem is identified as Jerusalem, then Melchizedek may have been a Jebusite (cf. Gen. 14:18).

20. The Ammonites lived on the eastern side of the Jordan River. The nation's territory was essentially surrounded by the Jabbok River and its tributaries. As a result, the border of Ammonite territory was referred to simply as the Jabbok River (Deut. 3:16; Josh. 12:2). The sources of the Jabbok River are near modern Amman, Jordan. This territory had previously belonged to the Rephaim,

an ancient people who were displaced by the Ammonites (Deut. 2:20-21). The earliest documentation of hostilities between the Ammonites and the Children of Israel is the record of Judges 3:12-14, where the Ammonites join the coalition formed by Eglon, king of Moab. Jephthah later defeats an unnamed king of Ammon (Judg. 11). Notable Ammonites include Naamah, the wife of Solomon and mother of Rehoboam (1 Kin. 14:21, 31; 2 Chron. 12:13), and Tobiah, one of the major antagonists of Nehemiah (Neh. 2:19; 4:3). Solomon built a sanctuary for Molech, the "detestable" chief god of the Ammonites, on the Mount of Olives (1 Kin. 11:7). Child sacrifice was a significant part of the Ammonite Molech cult (Lev. 18:21; 20:2-5; 2 Kin. 23:10; Jer. 32:35).

21. The Moabites lived on the eastern side of the Jordan River and the Dead Sea, just to the south of the Ammonites. The land of Moab was famous for its pasturage. 2 Kings 3:4 testifies to the agricultural wealth of the area, "Now Mesha king of Moab was a sheep breeder, and used to pay the king of Israel 100,000 lambs and the wool of 100,000 rams." The climate of Moab also allowed for the growing of wheat, barley, vineyards, and fruit trees. The chief god of the Moabites was Chemosh (1 Kin. 11:7, 33). The worship of Chemosh included a priesthood (Jer. 48:7) and a sacrificial system (Num. 22:40; 25:2). Solomon married Moabite women and built a sanctuary for Chemosh on the Mount of Olives (1 Kin. 11:1, 7). Notable Moabites include the following: Balak, the king who hired Balaam to curse the Children of Israel (Num. 22-24); Eglon, the king who was assassinated by Ehud (Judg. 3:15-30); Ruth, the widow of Mahlon and wife of Boaz (Ruth 4:10, 13); and Mesha, the king who rebelled against King Jehoram of Israel (2 Kin. 3). Mesha is of special significance thanks to the archaeological discovery of the thirty-four-line Mesha Inscription, also known as the Moabite Stone. The Mesha Inscription dates to approximately 830 B.C. and commemorates Mesha's achievements, especially his overthrow of Omride oppression after the death of Omri. The text specifically names Omri king of Israel. It also specifically names Yahweh in the statement that Mesha, having captured an Israelite

town, "took from there the vessels of Yahweh and dragged them before Chemosh" (lines 17-18).

22. The land of Egypt is strategically located at the northeastern tip of Africa, forming a land bridge to the continent of Asia. The most significant feature of the land of Egypt is the Nile River. In fact, Egypt is often called "the gift of the Nile." Because the Nile River flows from south to north, southern Egypt is known as Upper Egypt while northern Egypt is known as Lower Egypt. The chief god of the Egyptians was Ra, the sun god. However, many other gods were routinely worshipped including Osiris, god of the Nile, and Isis, goddess of children. These gods were shown to be inferior to Yahweh through the ten plagues sent upon Egypt, thus demonstrating that the God of Israel is the most powerful Being in the universe. While the various gods were certainly important to the Egyptians, the single most significant ingredient of Egyptian religion was the pharaoh. Notable Egyptians include Shishak, the pharaoh who invaded Israel during the reign of Rehoboam (1 Kin. 14:25-26), and Neco, the pharaoh of the army who met Josiah in battle at Megiddo, a battle in which Josiah was fatally shot by the Egyptian archers (2 Kin. 23:29; 2 Chron. 35:22-23).

23. The Amorites lived to the west of Mesopotamia and thus were called "westerners." The name Amorites is derived from the Akkadian *Amurru*, meaning "west." The Amorites had their origins in Syria and migrated south into the land of Canaan. They were so numerous that the land of Canaan is called *Amurri* in the Amarna letters. The Amorites are identified in Deuteronomy as one of the seven nations in the Promised Land "greater and stronger" than Israel (Deut. 7:1). The Amorites lived in the hill country on both sides of the Jordan River (Num. 13:29; Josh. 5:1). The so-called King's Highway traversed their territory (Num. 21:21-22). They were largely nomadic shepherds, supplying sheep and goats to the Canaanite cities. Notable Amorites include Sihon and Og, two Kings who were defeated by the Israelites on their way to the promised land (Num. 21).

24. F. Charles Fensham, *The Books of Ezra and Nehemiah*, New International Commentary on the Old Testament, ed. R. K.

Harrison (Grand Rapids: William B. Eerdmans Publishing Company, 1982), 129.

25. John A. Martin, "Ezra," in *The Bible Knowledge Commentary, Old Testament*, ed. John F. Walvoord and Roy B. Zuck (Colorado Springs: Victor Books, 1985), 671.

26. A. Philip Brown II, "Nehemiah and Narrative Order in the Book of Ezra," *Bibliotheca Sacra* 162 (April-June 2005): 192.

Chapter Eight

1. Edwin M. Yamauchi, "The Archaeological Background of Nehemiah," *Bibliotheca Sacra* 137 (October-December 1980): 296-97.

2. W. Rudolph, *Esra und Nehemia*, Handbuch zum Alten Testament, ed. Otto Eissfeldt, vol. 20 (Tübingen: J. C. B. Mohr, 1949), 103; Jacob M. Myers, *Ezra, Nehemiah*, Anchor Bible, ed. William F. Albright and David N. Freedman, vol. 14 (Garden City, NY: Doubleday & Company, 1965), 96; Edwin M. Yamauchi, "Was Nehemiah the Cupbearer a Eunuch?," *Zeitschrift für die alttestamentliche Wissenschaft* 92 (1980): 132-42. Both the Codex Vaticanus and the Codex Sinaiticus have *eunouchos* ("eunuch") in place of the *oinochoos* ("cupbearer") of the Codex Alexandrinus. However, this is most probably an error for the latter word (Yamauchi, "The Archaeological Background of Nehemiah," 297).

3. Yamauchi, "The Archaeological Background of Nehemiah," 298.

4. While this author believes that the book of Nehemiah portrays the character of Nehemiah in an extremely pious and godly light, some scholars believe just the opposite to be the case. Kellermann speaks of the "degradation" of Nehemiah (U. Kellermann, *Nehemia—Quellen, Überlieferung, und Geschichte*. Beihefte zur Zeitschrift für die alttestamentliche Wissenschaft, ed. Georg Fohrer, vol. 102 [Berlin: Töpelmann, 1967], 92) and lists numerous parallels and contrasts between Ezra and Nehemiah which serve to elevate Ezra over Nehemiah (ibid., 95). Eskenazi consistently portrays Nehemiah in a negative light, finding fault in even his most pious acts (Tamara C. Eskenazi, *In an Age of*

Prose: A Literary Approach to Ezra-Nehemiah, The Society of Biblical Literature Monograph Series, ed. Adela Yarbro Collins, no. 36 [Atlanta, GA: Scholars Press, 1988], 144-52).

5. Steve L. Reynolds, "A Literary Analysis of Nehemiah" (Ph.D. diss., Bob Jones University, 1994), 212-13.

6. This extensive inventory of Nehemiah's attributes is generated from this author's investigation as well as taken from the following sources: Cyril J. Barber, *Nehemiah and the Dynamics of Effective Leadership* (Neptune, NJ: Loizeaux Brothers, 1991); Raymond Brown, *The Message of Nehemiah*, The Bible Speaks Today, ed. J. A. Motyer and John R. W. Stott (Downers Grove, IL: Inter-Varsity Press, 1998); Donald K. Campbell, *Nehemiah: Man in Charge* (Wheaton, IL: Victor Books, 1979); Joseph Maciariello, "Lessons in Leadership and Management from Nehemiah." *Theology Today* 60 (2003):397-407; Richard H. Seume, *Nehemiah: God's Builder* (Chicago: Moody Press, 1978); Charles R. Swindoll, *Hand Me Another Brick,* rev. ed. (Nashville: Word Publishing, 1990); Edwin M. Yamauchi, "The Archaeological Background of Nehemiah," *Bibliotheca Sacra* 137 (October-December 1980): 304; and Edwin M. Yamauchi, "Nehemiah: Master of Business Administration," *His* (January 1979): 8-10.

7. Eskenazi interprets Nehemiah's actions to aid his people as completely self-serving. She writes, "Nehemiah in his memoirs portrays himself as a liberator in all areas of life—social, military, economic, and cultic. His zeal is reminiscent of one who will help the elderly person across the street, whether that elderly person wants this or not. It is not at all clear that his subjects—and other people are consistently cast by him in that role of 'subjects' (i.e. inferiors to be manipulated)—appreciate being 'liberated.' His direct intervention on behalf of the perceived oppressed (whether they wish it or not) is apparent in Neh 13:4, 13:10, 13:15, 13:23, 13:28. Some of the negative consequences of his liberation emerge in Nehemiah chapter 5. In most cases he seems to be up against other established authorities among the Judeans" (Eskenazi, *In an Age of Prose*, 146).

8. Eskenazi interprets Nehemiah's prayers and actions as extremely self-serving rather than arising out of a strong sense of duty to God. She writes, "He [Nehemiah] asks God's support . . . Requests typify him. His most ardent request—that he be remembered—punctuates the book (Neh 1:8, 5:19, 13:14, 22, 31). All of Nehemiah's requests keep him at the center. Even when concern for his people motivates him to journey to Jerusalem, his own vested interests are not neglected" (ibid., 145).

9. Eskenazi questions the extent of the opposition faced by Nehemiah in the narrative. She asserts, "Less clear is the magnitude of the obstacles, especially in view of his claimed royal support. It remains plausible that Nehemiah exaggerates these, much as he exaggerates his own importance" (ibid., 145).

10. Neither Eskenazi (Eskenazi, *In an Age of Prose*, 127) nor Reynolds (Reynolds, "A Literary Analysis of Nehemiah," 172-94) views God as a principal character in their literary treatments of the narrative.

11. It must be admitted that due to this author's belief in the sovereignty of God and the divine inspiration of Scripture, it could be argued that God is actually the chief character in the narrative. As Fee and Stuart note, "In the final analysis, God is the hero of all biblical narratives" (Gordon Fee and Douglas Stuart, *How to Read the Bible for All Its Worth*, 3d ed. [Grand Rapids: Zondervan Publishing House, 2003], 106). However, a literary analysis of the book indicates that the narrative pictures Nehemiah as the protagonist and God as aiding him throughout his ministry. While God sovereignly governs all of the action in the book, the story is told from man's viewpoint.

12. Yamauchi, "The Archaeological Background of Nehemiah," 291.

13. Edwin M. Yamauchi, "Persians," in *Peoples of the Old Testament World*, ed. Edward J. Hoerth, Gerald D. Mattingly, and Edwin M. Yamauchi (Grand Rapids: Baker Books, 1994), 110.

14. Ibid.

15. David M. Howard, Jr., *An Introduction to the Old Testament Historical Books* (Chicago: Moody Press, 1993), 285.

16. It is quite likely that the rebuilt walls around Nehemiah's Jerusalem may have been somewhat smaller than those around Hezekiah's Jerusalem. Howard notes, "there is no archaeological evidence for occupation of the western hill during the Persian period (nor even the later Hellenistic period for that matter); thus, the scholarly consensus today holds that Nehemiah's city was smaller than the preexilic city" (ibid., 290).

17. Joseph Blenkinsopp, *Ezra-Nehemiah*, Old Testament Library, ed. Peter Ackroyd, James Barr, Bernhard W. Anderson, and James L. Mays (Philadelphia: Westminster Press, 1988), 66.

18. F. Charles Fensham, *The Books of Ezra and Nehemiah*, New International Commentary on the Old Testament, ed. R. K. Harrison (Grand Rapids: William B. Eerdmans Publishing Company, 1982), 152.

19. Brown writes, "Holiness is more important than even the closest of human relationships: marriage. Although divorce is hateful to God, this episode reinforces the principle taught in Deuteronomy 13 that unswerving loyalty to Yahweh is of far greater importance than the continuance of marriage. The Lord regards His people's relationship to Himself as the preeminent priority of their lives" (A. Philip Brown II, "The Problem of Mixed Marriages in Ezra 9-10," *Bibliotheca Sacra* 162 [October-December 2005]: 458).

20. 1. Note also the similar phrase "The word of the Lord which came to Hosea" (cf. Joel, Jonah, Micah, Zephaniah, and Zechariah).

21. Hanani was probably an actual brother of Nehemiah (cf. 7:2), although "brother" could refer to "kinsman" (L. H. Brockington, *Ezra, Nehemiah and Esther*, The Century Bible, ed. H. H. Rowley [London: Thomas Nelson and Sons Ltd., 1969], 104).

22. Batten believes that Hanani, like Nehemiah, had never been to Jerusalem but is simply delivering a report he has received from a recent pilgrim (L. W. A. Batten, *A Critical and Exegetical Commentary on the Books of Ezra and Nehemiah*, International Critical Commentary [New York: Charles Scribner's Sons, 1913], 183. Fensham represents the traditional view that Hanani himself had just returned from Jerusalem (F. Charles Fensham, *The Books of Ezra and Nehemiah*, New International Commentary on the

Old Testament, ed. R. K. Harrison [Grand Rapids: William B. Eerdmans Publishing Company, 1982], 151).

23. Holmgren, attempting to emphasize Nehemiah's need to wait for the right occasion to approach the king, asserts that Nehemiah "initiates a plan to secure the support of the king for the rebuilding program" (Fredrick Carlson Holmgren, *Israel Alive Again: A Commentary on the Books of Ezra and Nehemiah*, International Theological Commentary, ed. George A. F. Knight and Fredrick Carlson Holmgren [Grand Rapids: William B. Eerdmans Publishing Company, 1987], 95). However, this statement clearly misinterprets the events of the scene. According to the text, King Artaxerxes makes the initial move, evidently motivated by his close relationship to Nehemiah, noticing Nehemiah's downcast appearance and questioning him as to his sad countenance. Holmgren places the emphasis on Nehemiah's actions rather than on the king's.

24. The events of Daniel 9 are predicated upon Daniel's prayer to the Lord regarding Jeremiah's prophecies that Israel would serve the king of Babylon for seventy years (Jer. 25:11-12; 29:10). The angel Gabriel appears to Daniel to give him the Lord's response. Gabriel does not directly address the specific request by Daniel, rather he gives him a new prophecy related to the idea of a period of "seventy" being decreed for the nation. Daniel is told that there will be seventy "weeks" between the decree of Artaxerxes and the destruction of the "prince who is to come." The angel also reveals that there will be sixty-nine "weeks" between the decree of Artaxerxes and the time when the messiah will be "cut off." Since the Hebrew word for "week" (*shavu'*) literally means "period of seven," it seems best to identify these "weeks" as periods of seven years. The idea of years has already been introduced in the chapter by Daniel's request (Dan. 9:2). Since this is such an important piece of the chronological timetable of eschatology, it is imperative that the date of Artaxerxes' decree be ascertained. If one sees the decree as having been given on the first day of the month Nisan in Artaxerxes' twentieth year, the date can be calculated as falling on March 5, 444 B.C.[6] Thus, using a prophetic year of 360 days (cf. Rev. 11:2-3), 69

groups of 7 years would total 173,880 days. Exactly 173,880 days after Nisan 1, 444 B.C., Christ made his triumphal entry into Jerusalem on Nisan 10, A.D. 33 (March 30). Only four days later, on Nisan 14, A.D. 33 (April 3), Christ was crucified. The seventieth week of Daniel's prophecy still awaits future fulfillment (cf. Matt. 24; Rev. 6-19).

25. Sanballat's name is derived from the Akkadian *Sin-uballit*, meaning "Sin (the moon god) has given life." The epithet "Horonite" identifies him as coming from one of three possible areas: 1. Hauran east of the Sea of Galilee; 2. Horonaim in Moab (cf. Jer. 48:34); or 3. upper or lower Beth-Horon, two key cities located twelve miles northwest of Jerusalem (cf. Josh. 10:10; 16:3,5). The third option is the most probable.[1] He is evidently the leader of Samaria (cf. 4:2), the region directly north of Jerusalem. This fact is substantiated by the Elephantine papyri, which identify Sanballat as the governor of Samaria.

26. Tobiah's name is Hebrew, meaning "The Lord is good." He is further identified as an Ammonite. The Ammonites were the descendants of Ben-Ammi, the child born as a result of Lot's incestuous relationship with his youngest daughter. The region of Ammon was located directly east of Samaria. Tobiah was married to the daughter of Shecaniah (cf. 6:18) while his son Jehohanan was married to the daughter of Meshullam, the son of Berechiah. Meshullam was among those who helped rebuild the walls of Jerusalem (cf. 3:4).

27. Geshem's name is derived from the Arabic name *Jasuma*, meaning "bulky" or "stout." The fact that he is identified as an Arab indicates not only his ancestry but also the fact that he controlled the Arab regions east and south of Judah. Geshem ruled a league of Arabian tribes which took control of northern Arabia, Moab, and Edom.

28. Burrows represents the maximalist position. For a full discussion of his view see M. Burrows, "Nehemiah's Tour of Inspection," *Bulletin of the American Schools of Oriental Research* 64 (December 1936), 12.

29. Kenyon represents the minimalist position. For a full discussion of her view see Kathleen Kenyon, *Jerusalem: Excavating 3000 Years of History* (New York: McGraw-Hill, 1967), 107-8.
30. Clines identifies this date as October 2, 445 B.C. He further identifies the start of the rebuilding project as August 11 if Sabbaths are included in the total. For a full discussion of the dates, see Clines, *Ezra, Nehemiah, Esther*, 176.
31. Allrik provides a table listing twenty-nine differences between the lists of Nehemiah 7 and Ezra 2 out of the 153 individual numerals or ciphers (H. L. Allrik, "The Lists of Zerubbabel [Nehemiah 7 and Ezra 2] and the Hebrew Numeral Notation," *Bulletin of the American Schools of Oriental Research* 136 [December 1954]: 22). He believes the discrepancies between the lists to be the result of scribal error (ibid., 21-27). Reynolds lists nineteen numerical differences between the two lists (Steve L. Reynolds, "A Literary Analysis of Nehemiah" [Ph.D. diss., Bob Jones University, 1994], 235). He sees the reading of this list as an indictment upon the people for their carelessness in preserving their genealogies. He asserts that "any interested Jew would see the glaring mistakes and be more careful" (ibid., 159).
32. F. Charles Fensham, *The Books of Ezra and Nehemiah*, New International Commentary on the Old Testament, ed. R. K. Harrison (Grand Rapids: William B. Eerdmans Publishing Company, 1982), 214; Jacob M. Myers, *Ezra, Nehemiah*, Anchor Bible, ed. William F. Albright and David N. Freedman, vol. 14 (Garden City, NY: Doubleday & Company, 1965), 146. Eskenazi adds, "social and political, as well as economic, concerns most likely lurked in the background and explain their [the lists of Nehemiah 7 and Ezra 2] origin" (Eskenazi, "The Structure of Ezra-Nehemiah and the Integrity of the Book," 645).
33. Hugh G. M. Williamson, *Ezra, Nehemiah*, Word Biblical Commentary (Waco, TX: Word Books, Publisher, 1985), 281-82. Regarding the structure of this scene, Fensham observes, "we may have here a careful description of the liturgical ritual of public worship in the postexilic times, namely, the people coming to form a congregation, the request to read the law,

opening of the book of the law, the rising of the congregation, the benediction of the congregation, reply of the congregation, kneeling down to hear the word . . ., the sermon . . ., reading from the law, oral transmission by translation, and dismissal for a festival" (F. Charles Fensham, *The Books of Ezra and Nehemiah*, New International Commentary on the Old Testament, ed. R. K. Harrison [Grand Rapids: William B. Eerdmans Publishing Company, 1982], 215).

34. Hamilton believes that the phrase "the joy of the Lord is your strength" (8:10) should be taken as a subjective genitive (the joy the Lord experiences in His people; Victor P. Hamilton, *Handbook on the Historical Books* [Grand Rapids: Baker Academic, 2001], 512). This is unlikely since the phrase is in apposition to "do not be grieved." It is best to see the phrase as an objective genitive (the joy we experience in the Lord).

35. For a full description of the Exodus imagery in Ezra see Melody D. Knowles, "Pilgrimage Imagery in the Returns in Ezra," *Journal of Biblical Literature* 123 (March 2004): 57-74.

36. There is considerable debate among scholars as to the precise place of Nehemiah 9 in the Books of Ezra and Nehemiah. According to some scholars it should be placed after Ezra 10 (e.g., W. Rudolph, *Esra und Nehemia*, Handbuch zum Alten Testament, ed. Otto Eissfeldt, vol. 20 (Tübingen: J. C. B. Mohr, 1949), 154; Jacob M. Myers, *Ezra, Nehemiah*, Anchor Bible, ed. William F. Albright and David N. Freedman, vol. 14 [Garden City, NY: Doubleday & Company, 1965], 165). Others point out the dangers of trying to solve the problems of this chapter by regarding it as displaced (e.g., F. Charles Fensham, *The Books of Ezra and Nehemiah*, New International Commentary on the Old Testament, ed. R. K. Harrison (Grand Rapids: William B. Eerdmans Publishing Company, 1982), 222; T. W. In der Smitten, *Esra—Quellen, Überlieferung, und Geschichte*, Studia Semitica Neerlandica 15 [Assen: Van Gorcum, 1973], 48). It seems best to regard the present placement of the chapter as genuine. For a satisfactory refutation of the major arguments used in support of displacement, see Fensham, *The Books of Ezra and Nehemiah*, 222-23.

37. Throntveit and Reynolds believe this psalm to have a chiasmic structure. Throntveit's chiasm is as follows:
a Praise (9:5b)
  b Confession in the form of historical retrospect (9:6-31)
    c Petition (9:32)
  b´ Confession of present sin (9:33-35)
a´ Lament (9:36-37)
For a full discussion of Throntveit's rationale, see Mark A. Throntveit, *Ezra, Nehemiah*, Interpretation, ed. James Luther Mays (Louisville: John Knox Press, 1992), 102. Reynolds' chiasm is as follows:
a God's provision for Israel in the past (9:6-15)
  b God's response to Israel's continual rebellion (9:16-31)
    c Request for God's attention (9:32)
  b´ The justice of God's actions (9:33-35)
a´ The need for God's provisions (9:36-37)
For a full discussion of his rationale, see Steve L. Reynolds, "A Literary Analysis of Nehemiah" (Ph.D. diss., Bob Jones University, 1994), 105-6.

38. Lipschits mistakenly makes the city the central element in the passage, not the remnant. He writes, "This chapter is particularly solemn and tendentious, intending to emphasize the renewed centrality of the holy city, the ancient capital of the nation. The emphasis here is on the utopian and ideological aspects of the author's perceptions. The fortification and repopulating of the city are both described as the initial stages in the process of the city's restoration to the fame and glory known during the monarchic period" (Oded Lipschits, "Literary and Ideological Aspects of Nehemiah 11," *Journal of Biblical Literature* 121 [September 2002]: 424).

39. M. Broshi, "La population de l'ancienne Jerusalem," *Revue Biblique* 92 (1975): 9-10.

40. D. E. Gowan, *Bridge Between the Testaments* (Pittsburgh: Pickwick, 1976), 20.

41. Rudolph asserts that the list includes names to well after 400 B.C., thereby announcing that Nehemiah was not the author of the entire book (Rudolph, *Esra und Nehemia*, 193). However, it is

certainly possible that Eliashib's great-grandson was born while Nehemiah was still living. For a comprehensive discussion of the problems of this list, see Harold H. Rowley, "Sanballat and the Samaritan Temple," *Bulletin of the John Rylands University Library of Manchester* 38 (September 1955): 166-98 and Myers, *Ezra, Nehemiah*, 196.

42. Warren W. Wiersbe, *The Bible Exposition Commentary: Old Testament History* (Colorado Springs: Victor Books, 2003), 690.

43. Fensham notes that "the Sabbath was celebrated to show that man's existence as a creation was more important than his fight for survival. It was one of the significant phenomena which distinguished the Jews from other nations. Because of their need, the Jews were conducting their business on that day like the neighboring heathen" (F. Charles Fensham, *The Books of Ezra and Nehemiah*, New International Commentary on the Old Testament, ed. R. K. Harrison [Grand Rapids: William B. Eerdmans Publishing Company, 1982], 263-64).

Chapter Nine

1. R. K. Harrison, *Introduction to the Old Testament* (Grand Rapids: Wm. B. Eerdmans Publishing Co., 1969), 1087.

2. Examples include the following: Frederic Bush, *Ruth, Esther*, Word Biblical Commentary (Dallas: Word Books, 1996); Jon D. Levenson, *Esther: A Commentary*, Old Testament Library (Louisville: Westminster/John Knox, 1997); and Michael V. Fox, *Character and Ideology in the Book of Esther* (Columbia, SC: Univ. of South Carolina Press, 1991).

3. For a detailed linguistic analysis of the Hebrew in Esther, see Ronald L. Bergey, "Post-Exilic Hebrew Linguistic Developments in Esther: A Diochronic Approach," *Journal of the Evangelical Theological Society* 31:2 (June 1988): 161-68.

4. Carey A Moore, *Esther*, Anchor Bible (Garden City, NY: Doubleday & Company, 1971). Note also S. Talmon, "'Wisdom' in the Book of Esther," *Vetus Testamentum* 13 (1963): 419-55.

5. R. Gordis, *Megillat Esther* (New York: KTAV Publishing House, 1974), 8.

6. Ezra 4:5-7 reveals that Ahasuerus reigned after Cyrus and Darius and before Artaxerxes. The only possible identification is Xerxes.

7. James B. Pritchard, ed., *Ancient Near Eastern Texts Relating to the Old Testament*, 3d ed. (Princeton: Princeton University Press, 1969), 316.

8. Herodotus lists only twenty satrapies for Darius I (*Histories* 3.89-94). However, he was referring to larger taxation units such as the fifth satrapy, which included all of Phoenicia, Palestine, Syria, and Cyprus (*Histories* 3.91).

9. This invasion was predicted in Daniel 11:2 ("And now I will tell you the truth. Behold, three more kings are going to arise in Persia |Cambyses, Pseudo-Smerdis, Darius|. Then a fourth |Xerxes| will gain far more riches than all of them; as soon as he becomes strong through his riches, he will arouse the whole empire against the realm of Greece").

10. Eugene H. Merrill, *Kingdom of Priests: A History of Old Testament Israel* (Grand Rapids: Baker Books, 1987), 498.

11. Although a number of Greek historians picture Xerxes as an incompetent ruler (e.g. Herodotus, Ctesias, Xenophon, Strabo, Plutarch), the fact is that Xerxes was far more successful than the Greek portrait shows. He had a number of military victories, accumulated great wealth, and built the impressive palace at Persepolis.

12. For a full description of the palace complex at Persepolis, see Edwin M. Yamauchi, *Persia and the Bible* (Grand Rapids: Baker Books, 1990), 342-68.

13. Ibid., 281.

14. Michael D. Coogan, "Life in the Diaspora: Jews at Nippur in the Fifth Century B.C." *Biblical Archaeology* 37 (1974): 9-10.

15. Merrill, *Kingdom of Priests*, 473.

16. Warren W. Wiersbe, *The Bible Exposition Commentary: Old Testament History* (Colorado Springs: Victor Books, 2003), 712.

17. Weiland comments, In the book of Esther the heroic and comic features and the use of irony and satire, communicated through the unexpected twists in the story, lead the interpreter to surmise

that the narrative was pointing out something paradoxical about these Jews, something deplorable about the hatred of their enemies, and something mysteriously wonderful about God" (Forrest S. Weiland, "Literary Clues to God's Providence in the Book of Esther," *Bibliotheca Sacra* 160 [January–March 2003]: 36).

18. Raymond B. Dillard and Tremper Longman, III, *An Introduction to the Old Testament* (Grand Rapids: Zondervan Publishing House, 1994), 196.

19. Laniak mistakenly makes this the primary purpose of the book. He characterizes Esther as a festival etiology. He asserts, "The story in its present form is most clearly constructed to provide the historical background (and therefore legitimization) for the feast of Purim. Esther is thus a festival etiology (that is, an explanation of the origin of Purim) that follows the conflict story pattern" (Timothy S. Laniak, "Esther," in *Ezra, Nehemiah, Esther*, New International Biblical Commentary [Peabody, MA: Hendrickson Publishers, Inc., 2003], 174).

20. Lewis Baytes Paton, *A Critical and Exegetical Commentary on the Book of Esther*, International Critical Commentary (Edinburgh: Clark, 1908), 75. Paton's list of objections includes four major ones: 1) The chief personages of the book are unknown in history (e.g., Vashti, Haman, Esther, Mordecai); 2) The statement that the laws of the Medes and the Persians could not be altered is unconfirmed by any ancient evidence; 3) Esther could never have been Xerxes' queen, for the testimony of Herodotus 3.84 is that the Queen might be selected only from seven of the noblest Persian families; 4) The book is full of improbable statements (e.g., 1:4; 2:12; 3:9; 9:16). Ibid., 65ff. Each of these arguments has been refuted by conservative scholars.

21. S. Sandmel et al., "A Symposium on the Canon of Scripture," *Catholic Biblical Quarterly* 28 (1966): 205.

22. Adele Berlin, *Esther*, JPS Bible Commentary (Philadelphia: Jewish Publication Society, 2001), xv.

23. Johnson consistently refers to the book as a work of fiction as she compares the book to Greek novels. She writes, "There can be no doubt that texts such as Esther engage in a deliberate fiction-

alizing of the past that is strikingly reminiscent of the fictional historical grounding of many Greek novels" (Sara R. Johnson, "Novelistic Elements in Esther: Persian or Hellenistic, Jewish or Greek?" *Catholic Biblical Quarterly* 67 |October 2005|: 573).

24. Wiersbe writes, "When you consider the backslidden state of the Jewish nation at that time, the disobedience of the Jewish remnant in the Persian Empire, and the unspiritual lifestyle of Mordecai and Esther, is it any wonder that the name of God is absent from this book? Would you want to identify your holy name with such an unholy people" (Warren W. Wiersbe, *The Bible Exposition Commentary: Old Testament History* |Colorado Springs: Victor Books, 2003|, 713). By contrast, Whitcomb observes that a reference is made to the Persian king 190 times in Esther's 167 verses (John C. Whitcomb, *Esther: Triumph of God's Sovereignty*, Everyman's Bible Commentary |Chicago: Moody Press, 1979|, 20).

25. W. Graham Scroggie, *Know Your Bible*, 2 vols. (London: Pickering & Inglis, n.d.), 1:96.

26. Forrest S. Weiland, "Literary Conventions in the Book of Esther," *Bibliotheca Sacra* 159 (October–December 2002): 429.

27. Norman L. Geisler and William E. Nix, *A General Introduction to the Bible*, rev. ed. (Chicago: Moody Press, 1986), 260.

28. Roger Beckwith, *The Old Testament Canon of the New Testament Church and Its Background in Early Judaism* (Grand Rapids: Wm. B. Eerdmans Publishing Co., 1986), 322.

29. Sandra Beth Berg, *The Book of Esther: Motifs, Themes, and Structure*. SBLDS (Missoula, MT: Scholars Press, 1979), 2.

30. A. Barucq, "Esther et la cour de Suse," *Bible et Terre Sainte* 39 (1961): 3.

31. Talmon, "'Wisdom' in the Book of Esther," 422.

32. Whitcomb raises some penetrating questions, "Would an author who knew so much about the court of Susa in the days of Xerxes have deliberately conjured up a nonexistent queen as one of the key persons in his story? Would the Jewish community throughout the Medo-Persian Empire have accepted as canonical a book that was tainted with such colossal historical blunders when they labeled as apocryphal such works as 1 Maccabees,

Tobit, and Judith? Did not the Jewish leaders of that day have at least as much knowledge of their Persian overlords as did the Gentiles of that same time?" (Whitcomb, *Esther: Triumph of God's Sovereignty*, 55).

33. Robert B. Chisholm Jr., *From Exegesis to Exposition: A Practical Guide to Using Biblical Hebrew* (Grand Rapids: Baker Books, 1998), 120.

34. Laniak, "Esther," 178.

35. For a full discussion of the arguments concerning the genre of Esther, see Forrest S. Weiland, "Historicity, Genre, and Narrative Design in the Book of Esther," *Bibliotheca Sacra* 159 (April–June 2002): 151-65.

36. For a description of a Persian banquet, see Xenophon, *Cyropaedia* 8.4.1-27.

37. 10. Levenson has organized the book in a chiastic structure based on the themes of banquets and plot reversals (Jon D. Levenson, *Esther: A Commentary*, Old Testament Library [Louisville: Westminster/John Knox, 1997], 8). His chiasm is as follows:

A[1] Greatness of Ahasuerus (1:1-8)
  B[1] Two Banquets of the Persians (1:1-8)
    C[1] Esther Identifies as a Gentile (2:10-20)
      D[1] Elevation of Haman (3:1)
        E[1] Anti-Jewish Edict (3:12-15)
          F[1] Fateful Exchange of Mordecai and Esther (ch. 4)
            G[1] First Banquet of Threesome (5:5-8)
              H Royal Procession (ch. 6)
            G[2] Second Banquet of Threesome (7:1-6)
          F[2] Fateful Exchange of Xerxes and Esther (7:1-6)
        E[2] Pro-Jewish Edict (8:9-14)
      D[2] Elevation of Mordecai (8:15)
    C[2] Gentiles Identify as Jews (8:17)
  B[2] Two Banquets of the Jews (9:17-19)
A[2] Greatness of Ahasuerus and Mordecai (10:1-3)

38. Verse eight has produced problems for both interpreters and translators. The text seems to claim that the drinking was done according to the law. However, it further asserts that individuals were free to drink in whatever manner they wished. These

statements would at first glance appear to be in contradiction to each other. According to Herodotus and Josephus, the Medes and Persians had a law that whenever the king drank, everyone drank.[15] The reference in this verse may be to the negation of this law since the text records "there was no compulsion." Conversely, the NIV translates the verse "By the king's command each guest was allowed to drink in his own way, for the king instructed all the wine stewards to serve each man what he wished." This is similar to the NET rendering, "There were no restrictions on the drinking, for the king had instructed all of his supervisors that they should do as everyone so desired." These translations interpret the word "law" in the sense of order or command rather than law or decree. A probable solution lies in the NKJV translation, which reads "In accordance with the law, the drinking was not compulsory; for so the king had ordered all the officers of his household, that they should do according to each man's pleasure." This rendering gives the impression that the law referred to in the verse had just been decreed by the king. Therefore, the "law" is that anyone can drink however they want to.

39. One of the most serious attacks on the historicity of the book of Esther surrounds the book's identification of Xerxes' queen as Vashti. Herodotus indicates that Xerxes' queen was Amestris, daughter of Otanes (*Histories* 7.61). Herodotus pictures Amestris as a powerful and vindictive woman (he recounts the story that the queen once ordered eighteen noble Persian youths to be buried alive as a thank offering [Herodotus, *Histories* 7.113-14]). Her vengeful nature is revealed in her reaction to one of Xerxes' affairs. When Xerxes took a trip to Sardis, he fell in love with Artaynta, the daughter of his brother's wife. Amestris had woven with her own hands a long robe of many colors which she presented to her husband as a gift. Xerxes put it on and wore it to visit Artaynta. Artaynta pleased him so much that day that Xerxes promised her that he would grant her whatever she wished. Artaynta immediately asked for the robe. Xerxes tried all possible means to avoid the gift, offering her cities instead, and heaps of gold, and an army which should obey no other leader. However, nothing could get Artaynta to change her mind and at

last he gave her the robe. Artaynta was very excited and often wore the garment, being quite proud of it. In a short time, Amestris found out that the robe she had given Xerxes had been given to Artaynta. Upon discovering this affair, Amestris confronted Xerxes at his birthday banquet, demanding the mother of Artaynta as a gift. She then mutilated the mother of Artaynta by cutting off her breasts, nose, ears and lips and feeding them to dogs (Herodotus, *Histories* 9.109-112). The alleged difficulty in identifying Vashti with Amestris is the fact that Amestris continues to yield considerable influence in the kingdom until the death of Xerxes. In fact, Amestris' son Artaxerxes I gains the throne after Xerxes. However, the text never states that Vashti was killed or even divorced; it simply implies that Vashti was demoted in the royal harem. Furthermore, if Vashti was Amestris, it gives plausible reasons as to why Vashti is defiant enough to disobey the king's order and why Xerxes is so quick to demote her. As a result, it seems best to view Vashti and Amestris as one and the same; Vashti, meaning "the beloved," or "the desired one," being her Persian name while Amestris was her Greek name. Wright and Shea have shown how the name "Vashti" could be a transliteration of "Amestris." For their rationale, see J. Stafford Wright, "The Historicity of Esther," in *New Perspectives on the Old Testament*, ed. J. Barton Payne (Waco: Word, 1970): 37-47, and William H. Shea, "Esther and History," *Andrews University Seminary Studies* 14, no. 1 (Spring 1976): 227-46.

40. Excessive drinking was an essential part of the king's war council. The Persians believed intoxication gave them better access to the spirit world. As a result, it was customary for the Persians to deliberate important matters of state while intoxicated. Herodotus writes, "It is also their [the Persians] general practice to deliberate upon affairs of weight when they are drunk; and then on the morrow, when they are sober, the decision to which they came the night before is put before them by the master of the house in which it was made; and if it is then approved of, they act on it; if not, they set it aside. Sometimes, however, they are sober at their first deliberation, but in this case

they always reconsider the matter under the influence of wine" (*Histories* 1.133).

41. The king's attendants are identified as eunuchs. A eunuch is a man who has been castrated and is therefore incapable of reproduction. Eunuchs were invaluable to the Persian kings. Queens of ancient times rarely left the palace area. When they did leave the palace they were always accompanied by eunuchs responsible for their care. Kings were notoriously distrustful of their wives and often castrated all those who had contact with the queen. This was done to ensure that any child born to the queen was the progeny of the king. The Persians valued eunuchs so highly that they often included young boys among the tribute required of vassal states so that they could castrate them and train them for service as government officials. Eunuchs were also among the most trusted subjects of the king because they rarely became involved in conspiracies against the throne due to the fact that they were not able to produce an heir to sit on the throne.

42. This custom is corroborated by Diodorus Siculus (17.30) who relates the account of Darius III (335-331 B.C.) and Charidemus. Darius, in a fit of anger, condemned Charidemus to death. When his anger abated, the king repented and tried to undo his mistake but it was not possible because the royal edicts could not be undone.

43. The postal system of the Persians was world-renowned. Herodotus, who traveled in Western Persia shortly after the reign of Xerxes, writes "Nothing mortal travels so fast as these Persian messengers. The entire plan is a Persian invention; and this is the method of it. Along the whole line of road there are men (they say) stationed with horses, in number equal to the number of days which the journey takes, allowing a man and horse to each day; and these men will not be hindered from accomplishing at their best speed the distance which they have to go, either by snow or rain, or heat, or by the darkness of night. The first rider delivers his dispatch to the second, and the second passes it to the third; and so it is borne from hand to hand along the whole line, like the light in the torch-race, which the Greeks celebrate to Vulcan. The Persians give the riding post in this manner, the

name of 'Angarum'" (*Histories* 8.98). It has been speculated that there must have been a supply station every twenty miles of so for this postal system to be most effective.

44. The term "Jew" used here became the name of the people of Israel after their exiles throughout Assyria and Babylon. It is the shortened form of the phrase "one from Judah." The word is almost always found in the plural and signifies those from the nation of Israel. In fact, Esther's repeated identification of Mordecai as a Jew (cf. 2:5; 5:13; 6:10; 8:7; 9:29, 31; 10:3) is the only case in the Old Testament where a single member of Israel is identified in this way. The author's frequent use of this epithet serves to establish a contrast between Mordecai the Jew and Haman the Agagite, another character who will figure prominently in the story.

45. The rabbis held that Esther was one of the four most beautiful women in history along with Sarah, Rahab, and Abigail (*Megillah* 15a). Josephus insisted that Esther's beauty surpassed all women in the known world (Josephus, *Antiquities of the Jews* 11.205).

46. Israel Loken, "A Literary Analysis of Nehemiah" (Ph.D. diss., Dallas Theological Seminary, 2001), 60.

47. Myrrh comes from the dried gum of a species of Balsam (Balsamodendron Myrrha). This is a stunted tree resembling the Acacia. It was popular in Arabia and was marked by its light gray bark. The gum resin produced by the tree dries to a rich brown brittle substance that is highly fragrant. It was sometimes used as medicine (cf. Mark 15:23). In Matthew 2:11, Myrrh is brought to Jesus by the Magi from the east, perhaps a reference to Persia. The perfume was also used embalm the body of Christ (John 19:39-40).

48. This traditional form of mourning is observed in every period of Israel's history. Jacob tears his clothes when he thinks his son Joseph has been devoured by a wild beast (Gen. 37:34). Joshua and Caleb tear their clothes when the children of Israel decide not to invade the land of Israel (Num. 14:6). Jephthah tears his clothes upon seeing his daughter in Judges 11:35, knowing that he is going to sacrifice her to the Lord to fulfill his tragic vow.

David mourns for Saul and Jonathan by tearing his clothes (2 Sam. 1:11). And finally, Hezekiah tears his clothes upon hearing of the approach of the armies of Sennacherib, the king of Assyria (2 Kin. 19:1).

49. This form of mourning commonly demonstrated an individual's act of repentance. Jeremiah calls on his people to repent by commanding the nation of Judah to put on sackcloth and ashes in mourning because of the coming of the great nation from the north (Jer. 6:26). Daniel uses sackcloth and ashes as part of his repentance for the sins of the nation (Dan. 9:3). The king of Nineveh uses sackcloth and ashes to demonstrate his repentance upon hearing of the Lord's announcement of imminent judgment (Jon. 3:6). And finally, the Lord reveals that Tyre and Sidon would have repented in sackcloth and ashes if they had witnessed His miracles (Matt. 11:21).

50. This behavior is especially prominent in the Prophetic literature. Throughout the writing of the Prophets, they consistently call on the people to wail in light of their impending judgment, i.e., death (cf. Isa. 13:6; Jer. 4:8; Ezek. 21:12; 30:2; Hos. 7:14; Joel 1:5, 11, 13; Amos 5:16-17; Mic. 1:8; Zeph. 1:10).

51. Fasting, in a sense, is often involuntary. In other words, quite often individuals are too worried or anxious to eat food. Their stomachs are uneasy, resulting in a loss of appetite. David fasts while pleading for the life of his child (2 Sam. 12:16). The inhabitants of Nineveh fast upon hearing news of the imminent judgment announced by the Lord (Jon. 3:5). Nehemiah fasts upon hearing the bad news concerning the state of the city of Jerusalem (Neh. 1:4). And finally, King Darius fasts while Daniel is in the lion's den (Dan. 6:18).

52. Abraham weeps for Sarah (Gen. 23:2). Jacob weeps for Joseph (Gen. 37:35). The Children of Israel weep for Moses (Deut. 34:8). The daughter of Jephthah weeps over her impending death (Judg. 11:37). And finally, David weeps over Absalom (2 Sam. 19:1). Weeping may also signify grief in general. For example, Hannah weeps over her inability to conceive a child (1 Sam. 1:7-10) and Ezra weeps for the disobedient remnant (Ezra 10:1).

53. John C. Whitcomb, *Esther: Triumph of God's Sovereignty*, Everyman's Bible Commentary (Chicago: Moody Press, 1979), 76.
54. Mills writes, "When Esther crosses room thresholds, it is not as wife to husband in a stable partnership but as woman to king, encountering an unknown quantity that is potentially hostile" (Mary E. Mills, "Household and Table: Diasporic Boundaries in Daniel and Esther," *Catholic Biblical Quarterly* 68 [July 2006]: 413).
55. Edwin M. Yamauchi, *Persia and the Bible* (Grand Rapids: Baker Books, 1990), 262.
56. It is interesting to note that archaeological evidence indicates that Samaria and Shechem, two centers of Samaritan opposition, were destroyed about this time. The vengeance described in Esther provides "a possible historical explanation for these archaeological findings" (William H. Shea, "Esther and History," *Andrews University Seminary Studies* 14 [Spring 1976]: 244). See also John C. Whitcomb, *Esther: Triumph of God's Sovereignty*, Everyman's Bible Commentary (Chicago: Moody Press, 1979), 118.
57. Karen H. Jobes, *Esther*, The NIV Application Commentary (Grand Rapids: Zondervan Publishing House, 1999), 214.
58. T. H. Gaster, *Purim and Hanukkah in Custom and Tradition* (New York: Henry Schuman, 1950), 51.

Appendix One
1. Albright advanced the view that the Chronicler was none other than Ezra himself (W. F. Albright, "The Date and Personality of the Chronicler," *Journal of Biblical Literature* 40 [March 1921]: 119-20). Other scholars, such as Cross (Frank Moore Cross, Jr., "A Reconstruction of the Judean Restoration," *Journal of Biblical Literature* 94 [March 1975]: 4-18) and In der Smitten (T. W. In der Smitten, "Die Gründe für die Aufnahme der Nehemiaschrift in das chronistische Geschichtswerk," *Biblische Zeitschrift* 16, no. 2 [1972]: 207-21), hold that the books are the result of a group of editors called the chronistic school rather than the work of a single editor.

2. L. Zunz, *Die gottesdienstlichen Vorträge der Juden, historisch Entwickelt* (Berlin: Louis Lamm, 1832), 12-34.
3. Modern scholars who hold to the unity of all three books include Myers (Jacob M. Myers, *Ezra, Nehemiah,* Anchor Bible, ed. William F. Albright and David N. Freedman, vol. 14 [Garden City, NY: Doubleday & Company, 1965], xlviii), Archer (Gleason L. Archer, *A Survey of Old Testament Introduction,* rev. ed. [Chicago: Moody Press, 1994], 450), Clines (David J. A. Clines, *Ezra, Nehemiah, Esther,* New Century Bible Commentary, ed. Ronald E. Clements and Matthew Black [Grand Rapids: William B. Eerdmans Publishing Company, 1984], 9), and Fensham (F. Charles Fensham, *The Books of Ezra and Nehemiah,* New International Commentary on the Old Testament, ed. R. K. Harrison [Grand Rapids: William B. Eerdmans Publishing Company, 1982], 2-4). Fensham contends that "this view is generally accepted today by conservative as well as critical scholars" (ibid., 2). Haran also holds to the unity of the books and adds, "it is generally recognized among scholars that the two books of Chronicles (originally, one, uninterrupted book) and the Book of Ezra/Nehemiah are the work of a single author, who is often referred to as the Chronicler. The four (actually two) books together are sometimes called the Chronistic Work" (Menahem Haran, "Explaining the Identical Lines at the End of Chronicles and the Beginning of Ezra," *Bible Review* 2 [fall 1986]: 18). Cross (Cross, "A Reconstruction of the Judean Restoration," 4-18) and In der Smitten (In der Smitten, "Die Gründe für die Aufnahme der Nehemiaschrift in das chronistische Geschichtswerk," 207-21) believe that Nehemiah's memoirs were added to the Chronicler's work as a secondary development.
4. The most notable and enduring study is that performed by Torrey (C. C. Torrey, *Ezra Studies* [Chicago: University of Chicago Press, 1910], 240-48). His study was later adopted and expanded by Albright (Albright, "The Date and Personality of the Chronicler," 119).
5. Robert North, "Theology of the Chronicler," *Journal of Biblical Literature* 82 (December 1963): 376.

6. Clines, *Ezra, Nehemiah, Esther*, 25.
7. Ibid., 26.
8. David is mentioned three times in the Book of Ezra (3:10; 8:2, 20) and eight times in the Book of Nehemiah (3:15, 16; 12: 24, 36, 37 |twice|, 45, 46). Five of these citations are in reference to the proper order of worship in the temple (Ezra 3:10; 8:20; Neh. 12:24, 36, 45; e.g., "as prescribed by David"). Four of these references are topographical (Neh. 3:15, 16; 12:37 |twice|; e.g., "city of David"). One of the notations is genealogical (Ezra 8:2; e.g., "of the descendants of David"). The final reference is temporal (Neh. 12:46; e.g., "in the days of David"). David is never mentioned in these books as heir to the dynastic promises found in Chronicles.
9. David N. Freedman, "The Chronicler's Purpose," *Catholic Biblical Quarterly* 23 (October 1961): 440.
10. In dealing with mixed marriages as a whole, the Chronicler differs somewhat from the attitude presented in the Books of Ezra and Nehemiah. Nowhere does the Chronicler condemn mixed marriages. In fact, it appears as if he rather condones them. We find mixed marriages in Chronicles on the part of Judah, David, David's sister Abigail, Solomon, Sheshan, Manasseh, and several others. As Williamson rightly concludes, "it seems hard to believe that the Chronicler condemned mixed marriages with the same vigour as Ezr.-Neh." (Hugh G. M. Williamson, *Israel in the Books of Chronicles* |Cambridge: Cambridge University Press, 1977|, 61).
11. The Chronicler seems to be quite liberal with his genealogies. As North notes "The Chronicler makes Samuel the Ephraimite a son of Levi. He makes Caleb the son and father of all sorts of key people. He sometimes makes a whole town the son or father of an individual or of another town. He puts contemporaries at an equal genealogical remove from persons dozens of generations away" (North, "Theology of the Chronicler," 371). If the Chronicler had written the Book of Ezra it is likely that he would have named Zerubbabel as a son of David.
12. Tamara C. Eskenazi, *In an Age of Prose: A Literary Approach to Ezra-Nehemiah*, The Society of Biblical Literature Monograph

Series, ed. Adela Yarbro Collins, no. 36 (Atlanta, GA: Scholars Press, 1988), 23.

13. Clines admits the discrepancies between the treatment of David in Chronicles versus Ezra and Nehemiah but claims that this is due to the Chronicler's party of interest shifting from the king to the people as a whole. He asserts, "the Chronicler sees in his own time both a failure and a fulfillment of the divine promises: there is no king on the throne of David, and that is how it should be, since the house of David was not faithful to Yahweh; yet the purposes for which the monarchy was established—the building of the temple, the maintenance of worship, the preservation of the state—are all accomplished, and the divine promises have not entirely lacked fulfillment. The Chronicler's community has become the heir of the promises to David" (Clines, *Ezra, Nehemiah, Esther*, 28-29).

14. Blenkinsopp provides an extensive list of the striking similarities between the books regarding religious ideology: 1) Preparations for building the First and the Second Temple are described in parallel ways. 2) In both instances the altar is set up *before* the temple is built, in order to ward off danger. 3) Both temples are endowed by the heads of ancestral houses. 4) Both show great interest in the sacred vessels. 5) Both the order of sacrifices and the enumeration of sacrificial materials are practically identical in the two works |Chronicles and Ezra-Nehemiah|. 6) The descriptions of liturgical music and of musical instruments and who are to play them correspond closely. 7) The same holds for liturgical prayer: the antiphon "for he is good, for his loving-kindness endures for ever," of frequent occurrence in Chronicles, is slipped in at Ezra 3:11; the blessing form at Ezra 7:27-28 ("blessed be YHVH, God of our fathers"), and especially the confessional psalm beginning, exceptionally, with this type of formula at Neh. 9:5-6, is paralleled in 1 Chron. 29:10-19 (Joseph Blenkinsopp, *Ezra-Nehemiah*, Old Testament Library, ed. Peter Ackroyd, James Barr, Bernhard W. Anderson, and James L. Mays |Philadelphia: Westminster Press, 1988|, 53).

15. Eskenazi, *In an Age of Prose*, 24-25.

16. Ibid., 25. For the distinction between segmented and linear gene-alogies, see R. R. Wilson, *Genealogy and History in the Biblical World*, Yale Near Eastern Researches, ed. William W. Hallo, vol. 7 (New Haven: Yale University Press, 1977), 8-10.

17. M. D. Johnson, *The Purpose of Biblical Genealogies with Special Reference to the Setting of the Genealogies of Jesus*, Society for New Testament Studies Monograph Series, ed. Matthew Black, vol. 8 (Cambridge: Cambridge University Press, 1969), 69.

18. Ibid., 76-80.

19. Williamson writes, "we should note that Ezra and Nehemiah take a very harsh, negative view of the inhabitants of the former northern kingdom of Israel" (Hugh G. M. Williamson, "Did the Author of Chronicles Also Write the Books of Ezra and Nehemiah?" *Bible Review* 3 [spring 1987]: 57).

20. James D. Newsome, Jr., "Toward a New Understanding of the Chronicler and His Purposes," *Journal of Biblical Literature* 94 (June 1975): 205-6.

21. Williamson, "Did the Author of Chronicles Also Write the Books of Ezra and Nehemiah?" 57-58.

22. Newsome, "Toward a New Understanding of the Chronicler and His Purposes," 214.

23. Williamson, *Israel in the Books of Chronicles*, 67. See also North, "Theology of the Chronicler," 372-74.

24. Williamson, *Israel in the Books of Chronicles*, 67.

25. Roddy L. Braun, "Chronicles, Ezra, and Nehemiah: Theology and Literary History," in *Studies in the Historical Books of the Old Testament*, Vetus Testamentum Supplement, ed. J. A. Emerton, no. 30 (Leiden: E. J. Brill, 1979), 55.

26. Eskenazi, *In an Age of Prose*, 27.

27. Williamson, *Israel in the Books of Chronicles*, 67-68.

28. G. Von Rad, "The Levitical Sermon in I and II Chronicles," in *The Problem of the Hexateuch: and Other Essays* (London: Oliver & Boyd, 1965), 271. Examples of the "Levitical sermon" are found in 1 Chronicles 22:6-16 and 28:2-10.

29. Newsome, "Toward a New Understanding of the Chronicler and His Purposes," 210-11.

30. Williamson, "Did the Author of Chronicles Also Write the Books of Ezra and Nehemiah?" 57.

31. Noteworthy examples are the thorough studies of Driver (S. R. Driver, *An Introduction to the Literature of the Old Testament*, 9th ed. [New York: Charles Scribner's Sons, 1913], 502-7) and Curtis and Madsen (E. L. Curtis and A. A. Madsen, *A Critical and Exegetical Commentary on the Books of Chronicles*, International Critical Commentary [New York: Charles Scribner's Sons, 1910], 27-36).

32. Sara Japhet, "The Supposed Common Authorship of Chronicles and Ezra-Nehemiah Investigated Anew," *Vetus Testamentum* 18 (July 1968): 330-71.

33. Ibid., 371.

34. Williamson, *Israel in the Books of Chronicles*, 37-59.

35. Ibid., 59.

36. David Talshir, "A Reinvestigation of the Linguistic Relationship Between Chronicles and Ezra-Nehemiah," *Vetus Testamentum* 38 (April 1988): 165-93.

37. R. Polzin, *Late Biblical Hebrew: Toward an Historical Typology of Biblical Hebrew Prose*, Harvard Semitic Monographs, ed. Frank Moore Cross, Jr., vol.12 (Missoula, MT: Scholars Press, 1976), 70.

38. Mark A. Throntveit, "Linguistic Analysis and the Question of Authorship in Chronicles, Ezra and Nehemiah," *Vetus Testamentum* 32 (April 1982): 215.

39. Peter R. Ackroyd, "Chronicles-Ezra-Nehemiah: the Concept of Unity," *Zeitschrift für die alttestamentliche Wissenschaft* 100 supp. (1988): 194.

40. Blenkinsopp suggests that "a break was made at this point to emphasize the new era which opened with the accession of Cyrus (Blenkinsopp, *Ezra-Nehemiah*, 48). Haran argues that the combined composition was too long to fit on a single scroll so it had to be divided (Haran, "Explaining the Identical Lines at the End of Chronicles and the Beginning of Ezra," 19-20).

41. Batten believes that a copyist, working from an older version in which there was still continuity between Ezra-Nehemiah and Chronicles, forgot to stop at the proper place (L. W. A. Batten,

A Critical and Exegetical Commentary on the Books of Ezra and Nehemiah, International Critical Commentary [New York: Charles Scribner's Sons, 1913], 1-2).

42. Freedman writes "the very fact that the books overlap would seem to settle the point: Ezra is the immediate sequel to Chronicles, and together they form part of the same original work" (Freedman, "The Chronicler's Purpose," 436). Haran adds, "the catch-lines that connect Chronicles with Ezra are *decisive evidence* [my emphasis] of the compositional connection between the two works" (Haran, "Explaining the Identical Lines at the End of Chronicles and the Beginning of Ezra," 18).

43. Eskenazi, *In an Age of Prose*, 18.

44. A. C. Welch, *Post-Exilic Judaism* (Edinburgh: Blackwood, 1935), 186.

45. Williamson, who holds that different authors wrote Chronicles and Ezra, believes that the appendage occurred for liturgical considerations. He explains that "there was a desire not to end a reading on too negative a note." As a result, "instead of finishing with the Chronicler's original ending at 2 Chronicles 36:21, it became normal to read a short passage from the beginning of Ezra, which of course in one sense continues the story where the Chronicler left off. And so in time this habit came to be reflected in the written form of the text" (Williamson, "Did the Author of Chronicles Also Write the Books of Ezra and Nehemiah?" 59). Williamson, however, gives no explanation as to why Cyrus' decree is abbreviated in Chronicles.

46. K. F. Pohlmann, *Studien zum dritten Esra*, Forschungen zur Religion und Literatur des Alten und Neuen Testaments, vol. 104 (Göttingen: Vandenhoeck & Ruprecht, 1970).

47. Jacob M. Myers, *I and II Esdras*, Anchor Bible, ed. William F. Albright and David N. Freedman, vol. 42 (Garden City, NY: Doubleday & Company, 1974), 12-13.

48. Williamson, *Israel in the Books of Chronicles*, 13-20.

49. In the majority of Hebrew manuscripts the arrangement is Ezra-Nehemiah-Chronicles. The books never appear in the order Chronicles-Ezra-Nehemiah. On the occasions that Chronicles precedes Ezra-Nehemiah it is separated by others of the Writings.

For the evidence, see Roger Beckwith, *The Old Testament Canon of the New Testament Church* (Grand Rapids: William B. Eerdmans Publishing Company, 1985), 452-64.

50. Shemaryahu Talmon, "Ezra and Nehemiah (Books and Men)," in *The Interpreter's Dictionary of the Bible, Supplementary Volume,* ed. Keith Crim et al. (Nashville: Abingdon Press, 1962), 318. Beckwith adds, "Chronicles is placed last as a recapitulation of the whole biblical story" (Beckwith, *The Old Testament Canon of the New Testament Church,* 159).

51. Holmgren compares the differences between the Jewish canon and the Christian canon, inferring that the Book of Chronicles intentionally concludes the Jewish canon to provide an optimistic ending for the Jewish canon. He writes, "The Jewish canon differs significantly from the Christian canon; whereas the latter canon of the Hebrew Bible ends with the book of Malachi, the Jewish canon ends with 2 Chronicles. For Christians, Malachi (ending with the fervent hope for the Day of the Lord) appears to be longing for some special divine action to take place. The Christian Church has frequently understood Malachi's expectation of the "day of the LORD" to represent the whole OT's hope for the coming of Jesus Christ (Mark 9:12; cf. 1:2). Because in Christian circles the OT ended with Malachi, this interpretation had a special attraction for the Church. But, as we have said, in the Jewish canon the Hebrew Bible ends not with Malachi but with . . . 2 Chronicles. The final verses of 2 Chronicles (36:22-23) contain the announcement that Yahweh *has* intervened on behalf of the Jews in exile. In the midst of their suffering, he is creating a future for them" (Fredrick Carlson Holmgren, *Israel Alive Again: A Commentary on the Books of Ezra and Nehemiah,* International Theological Commentary, ed. George A. F. Knight and Fredrick Carlson Holmgren [Grand Rapids: William B. Eerdmans Publishing Company, 1987], xiv).

52. Fensham, *The Books of Ezra and Nehemiah,* 1.

53. Ibid., 2-4.

Appendix Two
1. Eskenazi writes, "the fact that the MT [Masoretic Text] transmits Ezra-Nehemiah as a single, unified book *decisively* [my emphasis] establishes the perimeters of the book" (Tamara C. Eskenazi, *In an Age of Prose: A Literary Approach to Ezra-Nehemiah*, The Society of Biblical Literature Monograph Series, ed. Adela Yarbro Collins, no. 36 [Atlanta, GA: Scholars Press, 1988], 11).
2. It should be noted, however, that another rabbinical decision contradicts this statement (*Sanhedrin* 93b). In this passage the rabbis assert that Nehemiah was the author of the entire work.
3. For a notable example of such a study, see Eskenazi, *In an Age of Prose*, 37ff.
4. Dorsey writes, "structural analysis strongly supports the compositional unity of these two books. That the two books together have seven parts would by itself support their unity. The interlacing parallel and symmetric structuring schemes that tie the two books together seem to seal the argument" (David A. Dorsey, *The Literary Structure of the Old Testament* [Grand Rapids: Baker Books, 1999], 160). Eskenazi adds, "The complexity of Ezra-Nehemiah gains coherence when one looks at the book's distinctive structure and discerns its major themes" (Eskenazi, *In an Age of Prose*, 37). She goes on to argue that the repeated list of returnees in Ezra 2 and Nehemiah 7 is the key to the structure of the book and serves to unify the work (ibid., 37ff.).
5. David J. A. Clines, *Ezra, Nehemiah, Esther*, New Century Bible Commentary, ed. Ronald E. Clements and Matthew Black (Grand Rapids: William B. Eerdmans Publishing Company, 1984), 228; Joseph Blenkinsopp, *Ezra-Nehemiah*, Old Testament Library, ed. Peter Ackroyd, James Barr, Bernhard W. Anderson, and James L. Mays (Philadelphia: Westminster Press, 1988), 47; Sara Japhet, "Composition and Chronology in the Book of Ezra-Nehemiah," in *Second Temple Studies: 2. Temple Community in the Persian Period*, ed. Tamara C. Eskenazi and Kent H. Richards. Journal for the Study of the Old Testament Supplement Series, ed. David J. A. Clines and Philip R. Davies, no. 175 (Sheffield: JSOT Press, 1994), 193.

6. R. K. Harrison, *Introduction to the Old Testament* (Grand Rapids: William B. Eerdmans Publishing Company, 1969), 1146. Harrison concludes his thoughts on the authorship of Nehemiah by stating "in considering Nehemiah as a whole, there seem to be only highly subjective reasons for not regarding this work as the autobiography of the renowned civil governor of Judaea" (ibid.).

7. Eskenazi disagrees, asserting that the repeated list is the clue to the structure of the Book of Ezra-Nehemiah. She explains, "because Ezra 2 through Nehemiah 7 constitutes ultimately a single event, the grand celebration does not take place after the completion of the Temple in Ezra 6 but awaits and comes only after the completion of the whole project. At that time the completed house of God, Temple, people, walls, are sanctified (Neh. 12:30). Hence, according to Ezra-Nehemiah's structure, all of these developments between Ezra 2 and Nehemiah 7 are necessary elements of the full realization of Cyrus's decree. Only when they have been executed can the great fanfare of the dedication proper take place. Nehemiah 8-13 is that dedication. The repetition of the list is thus the key to Ezra-Nehemiah's structure" (Tamara C. Eskenazi, "The Structure of Ezra-Nehemiah and the Integrity of the Book," *Journal of Biblical Literature* 107 |December 1988|: 647). She also supplies six reasons why the repeated list is foundational to the Book of Ezra-Nehemiah: First, the repeated list unifies the material. Second, the repeated list indicates emphasis. Third, the repeated list expresses Ezra-Nehemiah's view of the wholeness of the people. Fourth, the repeated list bridges past and present. Fifth, the repeated list suggests the broadening of communal participation. And finally, the repeated list implies that the list sets equivalencies between Torah reading and sacrifices (ibid., 646-50). Dorsey agrees that the repeated list is a key to the structure of the unified books. He writes, "the puzzling repetition of the list of returnees under Zerubbabel (Ezra 2; Neh. 7) functions structurally to connect the beginning and end of the work and to reinforce its symmetric design (and to draw attention to the importance of the people who returned" (Dorsey, *The Literary Structure of the Old Testament*, 160-61).

8. Edward J. Young, *An Introduction to the Old Testament* (Grand Rapids: William B. Eerdmans Publishing Company, 1964), 378.

9. James C. VanderKam, "Ezra-Nehemiah or Ezra and Nehemiah?" in *Priests, Prophets and Scribes*, ed. Eugene Ulrich, John W. Wright, Robert P. Carroll, and Philip R. Davies. Journal for the Study of the Old Testament Supplement Series, ed. David J. A. Clines and Philip R. Davies, no. 149 (Sheffield: JSOT Press, 1992), 67-68.

10. David Kraemer, "On the Relationship of the Books of Ezra and Nehemiah," *Journal for the Study of the Old Testament* 59 (September 1993): 84.

11. Ibid., 82.

12. Ibid., 83.

13. One such example is Eskenazi, *In an Age of Prose*, 41ff.

14. For a notable example of such a treatment, see Charles R. Swindoll, *Hand Me Another Brick,* rev. ed. (Nashville: Word Publishing, 1990).

15. David Kraemer, "On the Relationship of the Books of Ezra and Nehemiah," 76.

Selected Bibliography

GENERAL RESOURCES

Aharoni, Yohanan, *The Land of the Bible: A Historical Geography.* Rev. ed. Translated by A. F. Rainey. Philadelphia: Westminster Press, 1979.

Albright, William F. *The Biblical Period from Abraham to Ezra.* 2d ed. New York: Harper & Brothers Publishers, 1963.

Alt, A. *Essays on Old Testament History and Religion* (Oxford: Blackwell, 1966).

Archer, Gleason L. *A Survey of Old Testament Introduction.* Rev. ed. Chicago: Moody Press, 1994.

Arnold, Bill T., and H. B. M. Williamson, ed. *Dictionary of the Old Testament Historical Books.* Downers Grove, IL: InterVarsity Press, 2005.

Barker, Kenneth L., and John R. Kohlenberger III, ed. *Zondervan NIV Bible Commentary, Old Testament.* Grand Rapids: Zondervan Publishing House, 1994.

Baylis, Albert H. *From Creation to the Cross.* Grand Rapids: Zondervan Publishing House, 1996

Beckwith, Roger. *The Old Testament Canon of the New Testament Church and Its Background in Early Judaism.* Grand Rapids: Wm. B. Eerdmans Publishing Co., 1986.

Bright, John A. *A History of Israel.* 3d ed. Philadephia: Westminster Press, 1981.

Darby, J. N. *Synopsis of the Books of the Bible.* Rev. ed. Vol. 2. New York: Loizeaux Brothers, 1942.

Dillard, Raymond B., and Tremper Longman, III. *An Introduction to the Old Testament*. Grand Rapids: Zondervan Publishing House, 1994.

Geisler, Norman L. and William E. Nix. *A General Introduction to the Bible*. Rev. Ed. Chicago: Moody Press, 1986.

Hamilton, Victor P. *Handbook on the Historical Books*. Grand Rapids: Baker Academic, 2004.

Harris, Stephen L. and Robert L. Platzner. *The Old Testament: An Introduction to the Hebrew Bible*, 2d ed. New York: McGraw-Hill, 2008.

Harrison, R. K. *Introduction to the Old Testament*. Grand Rapids: William B. Eerdmans Publishing Company, 1969.

Hill, Andrew E., and John H. Walton. *A Survey of the Old Testament*. Grand Rapids: Zondervan Publishing House, 1991.

Hoerth, Edward J., Gerald D. Mattingly, and Edwin M. Yamauchi, eds. *Peoples of the Old Testament World*. Grand Rapids: Baker Books, 1994.

Howard, Jr., David M. *An Introduction to the Old Testament Historical Books*. Chicago: Moody Press, 1993.

Kenyon, Kathleen. *Archaeology in the Holy Land*. New York: Praeger, 1960.

Kuhl, Curt. *The Old Testament: Its Origins and Composition*. Translated by C. T. M. Herriott. Richmond: John Knox Press, 1961.

Lasor, William Sanford, David Allan Hubbard, and Frederic William Bush, ed. *Old Testament Survey: The Message, Form, and Background of the Old Testament*. 2d ed. Grand Rapids: William B. Eerdmans Publishing Company, 1996.

Merrill, Eugene H. *Kingdom of Priests: A History of Old Testament Israel*. Grand Rapids: Baker Books, 1987.

Noth, Martin. *The History of Israel*. 2d. ed. New York: Harper & Row, 1960.

Pfeiffer, Charles F., and Everett F. Harrison. *The Wycliffe Bible Commentary*. Chicago: Moody Press, 1962.

Pfeiffer, Robert H. *Introduction to the Old Testament*. New York: Harper & Brothers Publishers, 1948.

Pritchard, James B., ed. *Ancient Near Eastern Texts Relating to the Old Testament.* 3d ed. Princeton: Princeton University Press, 1969.

Radmacher, Earl D., Ronald B. Allen, and H. Wayne House, ed. *Nelson's New Illustrated Bible Commentary.* Nashville: Thomas Nelson Publishers, 1999.

Scroggie, W. Graham. *Know Your Bible.* 2 Volumes. London: Pickering & Inglis, No Date.

Terry, M. S. *Biblical Hermeneutics: A Treatise on the Interpretation of the Old and New Testaments.* 1885. Reprint, Grand Rapids: Zondervan Publishing House, 1947.

Thiele, Edwin R. *The Mysterious Numbers of the Hebrew Kings* (Grand Rapids: William B. Eerdmans Publishing Company, 1965.

Unger, Merrill F., ed. *Unger's Bible Dictionary,* 3d ed. Chicago: Moody Press, 1966.

Vaux, R. de. *The Bible and the Ancient Near East.* London: Darton, Longman & Todd, 1971.

Vos, Howard F. *Nelson's New Illustrated Bible Manners and Customs.* Nashville: Thomas Nelson Publishers, 1999.

Walton, John H., Victor H. Matthews, and Mark W. Chavalas. *The IVP Bible Background Commentary: Old Testament.* Downer's Grove, IL: InterVarsity Press, 2000.

Walvoord, John F., and Roy B. Zuck, ed. *The Bible Knowledge Commentary, Old Testament.* Colorado Springs: Victor Books, 1985.

Wellhausen, Julius H. *Prolegomena to the History of Ancient Israel.* New York: Meridian, 1878, 1957.

Wiersbe, Warren W. *The Bible Exposition Commentary: Old Testament History.* Colorado Springs: Victor Books, 2003.

Williamson, Hugh G. M. *Ezra, Nehemiah.* Word Biblical Commentary, ed. David A. Hubbard and Glenn W. Barker, vol. 16. Waco, TX: Word Books, Publisher, 1985.

Wood, Leon. *A Survey of Israel's History.* Grand Rapids: Zondervan Publishing House, 1970.

Yadin, Yigael. *The Art of Warfare in the Biblical Lands According to Archaeological Finds.* New York: McGraw Hill, 1963.

Yamauchi, Edwin M. *Persia and the Bible*. Grand Rapids: Baker Books, 1990.

Young, Edward J. *An Introduction to the Old Testament*. Grand Rapids: William B. Eerdmans Publishing Company, 1964.

Zuck, Roy B. *Basic Bible Interpretation*. Colorado Springs: Victor Books, 1991,

_____, ed. *A Biblical Theology of the Old Testament*. Chicago: Moody Press, 1991.

LITERARY ANALYSIS

Alter, Robert. *The Art of Biblical Narrative*. New York: Basic Books, 1981.

_____. *The World of Biblical Literature*. New York: Basic Books, 1992.

Alter, Robert, and Frank Kermode, eds. *The Literary Guide to the Bible*. Cambridge, MA: Belknap Press of Harvard University Press, 1987.

Bar-Efrat, Shimon. *Narrative Art in the Bible*. Translated by Dorothea Shefer-Vanson. Journal for the Study of the Old Testament Supplement Series, ed. David J. A. Clines and Philip R. Davies, no. 70. Sheffield: Almond Press, 1989.

Berlin, Adele. *Poetics and Interpretation of Biblical Narrative*. Sheffield: Almond Press, 1983. Reprint, Winona Lake, IN: Eisenbrauns, 1994.

Caird, G. B. *The Language and Imagery of the Bible*. Philadelphia: Westminster Press, 1980.

Culley, Robert C. *Studies in the Structure of Hebrew Narrative*. Philadelphia: Fortress Press, 1976.

Dorsey, David A. *The Literary Structure of the Old Testament*. Grand Rapids: Baker Books, 1999.

Driver, S. R. *An Introduction to the Literature of the Old Testament*. 9th ed. New York: Charles Scribner's Sons, 1913.

Exum, J. Cheryl, ed. *Signs and Wonders: Biblical Texts in Literary Focus*. The Society of Biblical Literature Semeia Studies, ed. Edward L. Greenstein. Atlanta, GA: Scholars Press, 1989.

Fee, Gordon, and Douglas Stuart. *How to Read the Bible for All Its Worth.* 2d ed. Grand Rapids: Zondervan Publishing House, 1993.

Fishbane, Michael. *Biblical Text and Texture: Close Readings of Selected Biblical Texts.* Oxford: Oneworld Publications, 1979.

Frye, Northrop. *Anatomy of Criticism.* Princeton: Princeton University Press, 1957.

Gabel, John B., Charles B. Wheeler, and Anthony D. York. *The Bible as Literature: An Introduction.* 3d ed. New York: Oxford University Press, 1996.

Gibson, J. C. L. *Language and Imagery in the Old Testament.* London: Society for Promoting Christian Knowledge, 1998.

Gros Louis, Kenneth R. R., ed. *Literary Interpretations of Biblical Narratives.* 2 vols. Nashville: Abingdon Press, 1974, 1982.

Gunn, David M., and Danna Nolan Fewell. *Narrative in the Hebrew Bible.* The Oxford Bible Series, ed. P. R. Ackroyd and G. N. Stanton. New York: Oxford University Press, 1993.

Licht, J. *Storytelling in the Bible.* Jerusalem: Magnes, Hebrew University Press, 1978.

McConnell, Frank, ed. *The Bible and the Narrative Tradition.* Oxford: Oxford University Press, 1986.

Miller, J. H. *Fiction and Repetition.* Cambridge, MA: Harvard University Press, 1982.

Miscall, P. D. *The Workings of Old Testament Narrative.* Philadelphia: Fortress Press, 1983.

Rimmon-Kenan, Shlomith. *Narrative Fiction: Contemporary Poetics.* London: Methuen, 1983.

Ryken, Leland. *How to Read the Bible as Literature.* Grand Rapids: Zondervan Publishing House, 1984.

_____. *The Literature of the Bible.* Grand Rapids: Zondervan Publishing House, 1974.

_____. *Words of Delight: A Literary Introduction to the Bible.* 2d ed. Grand Rapids: Baker Book House, 1992.

Ryken, Leland, and Tremper Longman III, ed. *A Complete Literary Guide to the Bible.* Grand Rapids: Zondervan Publishing House, 1993.

Sternberg, Meir. *The Poetics of Biblical Narrative*. Bloomington: Indiana University Press, 1985.

Todorov, Tzvetan. *The Poetics of Prose*. Translated by Richard Howard. Ithaca, NY: Cornell University Press, 1977.

JOSHUA

Auld, A. G. *Joshua, Judges, and Ruth*. The Daily Study Bible, ed. John C. L. Gibson. Philadelphia: Westminster Press, 1984.

Boling, Robert G. and G. Ernest Wright. *Joshua*. Anchor Bible. Garden City, NY: Doubleday & Company, 1982.

Butler, Trent C. *Joshua*. Word Biblical Commentary. Waco, TX: Word Books, 1983.

Creach, J. F. D. *Joshua*. Interpretation. Louisville: Westminster John Knox, 2003.

Goslinga, C. J. *Joshua, Judges, Ruth*. Trans. R. Togtman. Bible Student's Commentary. Grand Rapids: Zondervan Publishing House, 1986.

Hawk, L. Daniel. *Joshua*. Berit Olam. Collegeville, MN: Liturgical Press, 2000.

Hess, R. S. *Joshua*. Tyndale Old Testament Commentaries. Downers Grove: InterVarsity Press, 1996.

Howard, Jr., David M. *Joshua*. New American Commentary. Nashville: Broadman & Holman, 1998.

Nelson, R. D. *Joshua*. Old Testament Library. Louisville: Westminster John Knox, 1997.

Woudstra, M. H. *The Book of Joshua*. New International Commentary on the Old Testament, ed. R. K. Harrison. Grand Rapids: William B. Eerdmans Publishing Company, 1981.

JUDGES

Auld, A. G. *Joshua, Judges, and Ruth*. The Daily Study Bible, ed. John C. L. Gibson. Philadelphia: Westminster Press, 1984.

Block, D. I. *Judges, Ruth*. New American Commentary. Nashville: Broadman & Holman, 2002.

Boling, Robert G. *Judges*. Anchor Bible. Garden City, NY: Doubleday & Company, 1975.

Cundall, Arthur E. *Judges: An Introduction and Commentary.* Tyndale Old Testament Commentaries. Downers Grove: InterVarsity Press, 1968.

Enns, Paul P. *Judges.* Bible Study Commentary. Grand Rapids: Zondervan Publishing Company, 1982

Goslinga, C. J. *Joshua, Judges, Ruth.* Trans. R. Togtman. Bible Student's Commentary. Grand Rapids: Zondervan Publishing House, 1986.

Soggin, J. Alberto. *Judges: A Commentary.* Old Testament Library. Philadelphia: Westminster Press, 1981.

Webb, Barry G. *The Book of the Judges: Grace Abounding.* The Bible Speaks Today Series. Leicester: InterVarsity, 1987.

RUTH

Auld, A. G. *Joshua, Judges, and Ruth.* The Daily Study Bible, ed. John C. L. Gibson. Philadelphia: Westminster Press, 1984.

Barber, Cyril J. *Ruth: An Expositional Commentary.* Chicago: Moody Press, 1983.

Block, D. I. *Judges, Ruth.* New American Commentary. Nashville: Broadman & Holman, 2002.

Bush, Frederic. *Ruth, Esther.* Word Biblical Commentary. Dallas: Word Books, 1996.

Campbell, Jr., Edward F. *Ruth.* Anchor Bible. Garden City, NY: Doubleday & Company, 1975.

Goslinga, C. J. *Joshua, Judges, Ruth.* Trans. R. Togtman. Bible Student's Commentary. Grand Rapids: Zondervan Publishing House, 1986.

Hubbard, Jr., Robert L., *The Book of Ruth.* New International Commentary on the Old Testament, ed. R. K. Harrison. Grand Rapids: William B. Eerdmans Publishing Company, 1988.

Nielsen, Kirsten. *Ruth, A Commentary.* Old Testament Library. Louisville: Westminster John Knox, 1997.

Sasson, Jack M. *Ruth: A New Translation with a Philological Commentary and a Formalist-Folklorist Interpretation.* Baltimore: John Hopkins University Press, 1979.

SAMUEL

Anderson, A. A. *2 Samuel.* Word Biblical Commentary. Waco, TX: Word Books, 1989.

Arnold, B. T. *1 and 2 Samuel.* The NIV Application Commentary. Grand Rapids: Zondervan Publishing House, 2003.

Baldwin, J. G. *1 and 2 Samuel.* Tyndale Old Testament Commentaries. Downers Grove: InterVarsity Press, 1988.

Bergen, R. D. *1, 2 Samuel.* New American Commentary. Nashville: Broadman & Holman, 1996.

Brueggemann, W. *First and Second Samuel.* Interpretation. Louisville: Westminster John Knox, 1990.

Evans, M. J. *1 and 2 Samuel.* New International Biblical Commentary: Old Testament. Peabody, MA: Hendrickson, 2000.

Fokkelman, J. P. *Narrative Art and Poetry in the Books of Samuel.* 2 volumes. Assen, The Netherlands: Van Gorcum, 1981, 1986.

Gordon, R. P. *1 and II Samuel: A Commentary.* Library of Biblical Interpretation. Grand Rapids: Zondervan Publishing House, 1986.

Klein, R. W. *1 Samuel.* Word Biblical Commentary. Waco, TX: Word Books, 1983.

McCarter, Jr., P. K. *1 & 2 Samuel.* Anchor Bible. Garden City, NY: Doubleday & Company, 1980, 1984.

KINGS

Brueggemann, W. *1 and 2 Kings.* Smyth and Helwys Bible Commentary. Macon, GA: Smyth & Helwys, 2000.

Cogan, M. *1 Kings.* Anchor Bible. Garden City, NY: Doubleday & Company, 2001.

Cogan, M., and H. Tadmor. *II Kings.* Anchor Bible. Garden City, NY: Doubleday & Company, 1988.

De Vries, S. J. *1 Kings.* Word Biblical Commentary. Waco, TX: Word Books, 1985.

Fretheim, T. E. *First and Second Kings.* Westminster Bible Companion. Louisville: Westminster John Knox, 1999.

Hobbs, T. R. *2 Kings.* Word Biblical Commentary. Waco, TX: Word Books, 1985.

Nelson, R. D. *First and Second Kings.* Interpretation. Louisville: Westminster John Knox, 1987.

Provan, I. W. *1 and 2 Kings.* New International Biblical Commentary. Peabody, MS: Hendrickson Publishers, 2003.

Walsh, J. *1 Kings.* Berit Olam. Collegeville, MN: Liturgical Press, 1996.

CHRONICLES

Ackroyd, Peter R. *I & II Chronicles, Ezra, Nehemiah.* Torch Bible Commentaries, ed. John Marsh and Alan Richardson. London: SCM Press, Ltd., 1973.

Allen, L. C. *1, 2 Chronicles.* Communicator's Commentary. Waco, TX: Word Books, 1987.

Braun, R. *1 Chronicles.* Word Biblical Commentary. Waco, TX: Word Books, 1986.

Curtis, E. L., and A. A. Madsen. *A Critical and Exegetical Commentary on the Books of Chronicles.* International Critical Commentary. New York: Charles Scribner's Sons, 1910.

Dillard, R. B. *2 Chronicles.* Word Biblical Commentary. Waco, TX: Word Books, 1987.

Hooker, P. K. *First and Second Chronicles.* Westminster Bible Companion. Louisville: Westminster John Knox, 2001.

Japhet, Sara. *I and II Chronicles.* Old Testament Library. Louisville: Westminster John Knox, 1993.

Knoppers, G. *1 Chronicles.* Anchor Bible. Garden City, NY: Doubleday & Company, 2002.

McConville, J. G. *I and II Chronicles.* The Daily Study Bible, ed. John C. L. Gibson. Philadelphia: Westminster Press, 1984.

Merrill, E. H. *1, 2 Chronicles.* Bible Study Commentary. Grand Rapids: Zondervan Publishing House, 1988.

Myers, Jacob M. *I Chronicles.* Anchor Bible, ed. William F. Albright and David N. Freedman, vol. 12. Garden City, NY: Doubleday & Company, 1965.

_____. *II Chronicles.* Anchor Bible, ed. William F. Albright and David N. Freedman, vol. 13. Garden City, NY: Doubleday & Company, 1965.

Noth, Martin. *The Chronicler's History*. Translated by H. G. M. Williamson. Journal for the Study of the Old Testament Supplement Series, ed. David J. A. Clines and Philip R. Davies, no. 50. Sheffield: JSOT Press, 1992.

Sailhamer, John. *First and Second Chronicles*. Everyman's Bible Commentary. Chicago: Moody Press, 1983.

Selman, M. J. *1 Chronicles*. Tyndale Old Testament Commentaries. Downers Grove: InterVarsity Press, 1994.

Selman, M. J. *2 Chronicles*. Tyndale Old Testament Commentaries. Downers Grove: InterVarsity Press, 1994.

Thompson, J. A. *1, 2 Chronicles*. New American Commentary. Nashville: Broadman & Holman, 1994.

Tuell, S. S. *First and Second Chronicles*. Interpretation. Louisville: Westminster John Knox, 2001.

Williamson, H. G. M. *I and II Chronicles*. New Century Bible Commentary. Grand Rapids: William B. Eerdmans Publishing Company, 1982.

_____. *Israel in the Books of Chronicles*. Cambridge, MA: Cambridge University Press, 1977.

EZRA

Ackroyd, Peter R. *I & II Chronicles, Ezra, Nehemiah*. Torch Bible Commentaries, ed. John Marsh and Alan Richardson. London: SCM Press, Ltd., 1973.

Allen, Leslie C., and Timothy S. Laniak. *Ezra, Nehemiah, Esther*. New International Biblical Commentary. Peabody, MS: Hendrickson Publishers, 2003.

Batten, L. W. A. *A Critical and Exegetical Commentary on the Books of Ezra and Nehemiah*. International Critical Commentary. New York: Charles Scribner's Sons, 1913.

Blenkinsopp, Joseph. *Ezra-Nehemiah*. Old Testament Library, ed. Peter Ackroyd, James Barr, Bernhard W. Anderson, and James L. Mays. Philadelphia: Westminster Press, 1988.

Bowman, R. A. "The Book of Ezra and the Book of Nehemiah." In *The Interpreter's Bible*. Nashville: Abingdon Publishers, 1954.

Breneman, Mervin. *Ezra, Nehemiah, Esther.* The New American Commentary, ed. E. Ray Clendenen, vol. 10. Nashville: Broadman & Holman Publishers, 1993.

Brockington, L. H. *Ezra, Nehemiah and Esther.* The Century Bible, ed. H. H. Rowley. London: Thomas Nelson and Sons Ltd., 1969.

Clines, David J. A. *Ezra, Nehemiah, Esther.* New Century Bible Commentary, ed. Ronald E. Clements and Matthew Black. Grand Rapids: William B. Eerdmans Publishing Company, 1984.

Coggins, R. J. *The Books of Ezra and Nehemiah.* New York: Cambridge University Press, 1976.

Davies, Gordon F. *Ezra and Nehemiah.* Berit Olam: Studies in Hebrew Narrative & Poetry, ed. David W. Cotter. Collegeville, MN: Liturgical Press, 1999.

Eskenazi, Tamara C. *In an Age of Prose: A Literary Approach to Ezra-Nehemiah.* The Society of Biblical Literature Monograph Series, ed. Adela Yarbro Collins, no. 36. Atlanta, GA: Scholars Press, 1988.

Fensham, F. Charles. *The Books of Ezra and Nehemiah.* New International Commentary on the Old Testament, ed. R. K. Harrison. Grand Rapids: William B. Eerdmans Publishing Company, 1982.

Grabbe, Lester L. *Ezra-Nehemiah.* New York: Routledge, 1998.

Holmgren, Fredrick Carlson. *Israel Alive Again: A Commentary on the Books of Ezra and Nehemiah.* International Theological Commentary, ed. George A. F. Knight and Fredrick Carlson Holmgren. Grand Rapids: William B. Eerdmans Publishing Company, 1987.

In der Smitten, T. W. *Esra—Quellen, Überlieferung, und Geschichte.* Studia Semitica Neerlandica, no. 15. Assen: Van Gorcum, 1973.

Jensen, Irving L. *Ezra, Nehemiah, Esther.* Chicago: The Moody Bible Institute, 1970.

Keil, Carl F. *The Books of Ezra, Nehemiah, and Esther.* Translated by Sophia Taylor. Edinburgh: T. & T. Clark, 1873. Reprint,

Grand Rapids: William B. Eerdmans Publishing Company, 1950.

Kidner, Derek. *Ezra and Nehemiah.* The Tyndale Old Testament Commentaries, ed. D. J. Wiseman. Downers Grove, IL: InterVarsity Press, 1979.

Laney, J. Carl. *Ezra/Nehemiah.* Chicago: Moody Press, 1982.

Loken, Israel P. *Ezra.* Fairfax, VA: Xulon Press, 2007.

McConville, J. G. *Ezra, Nehemiah, and Esther.* The Daily Study Bible, ed. John C. L. Gibson. Philadelphia: Westminster Press, 1985.

Myers, Jacob M., *Ezra, Nehemiah.* Anchor Bible. Garden City, NY: Doubleday & Company, 1965.

Pohlmann, K. F. *Studien zum dritten Esra.* Forschungen zur Religion und Literatur des Alten und Neuen Testaments, vol. 104. Göttingen: Vandenhoeck & Ruprecht, 1970.

Rudolph, W. *Esra und Nehemia.* Handbuch zum Alten Testament, ed. Otto Eissfeldt, vol. 20. Tübingen: J. C. B. Mohr, 1949.

Throntveit, Mark A. *Ezra, Nehemiah.* Interpretation, ed. James Luther Mays. Louisville: John Knox Press, 1992.

Torrey, C. C. *Ezra Studies.* Chicago: University of Chicago Press, 1910.

Williamson, Hugh G. M. *Ezra, Nehemiah.* Word Biblical Commentary, ed. David A. Hubbard and Glenn W. Barker, vol. 16. Waco, TX: Word Books, Publisher, 1985.

NEHEMIAH

Ackroyd, Peter R. *I & II Chronicles, Ezra, Nehemiah.* Torch Bible Commentaries, ed. John Marsh and Alan Richardson. London: SCM Press, Ltd., 1973.

Allen, Leslie C., and Timothy S. Laniak. *Ezra, Nehemiah, Esther.* New International Biblical Commentary. Peabody, MS: Hendrickson Publishers, 2003.

Barber, Cyril J. *Nehemiah and the Dynamics of Effective Leadership.* Neptune, NJ: Loizeaux Brothers, 1991.

Batten, L. W. A. *A Critical and Exegetical Commentary on the Books of Ezra and Nehemiah.* International Critical Commentary. New York: Charles Scribner's Sons, 1913.

Blenkinsopp, Joseph. *Ezra-Nehemiah.* Old Testament Library, ed. Peter Ackroyd, James Barr, Bernhard W. Anderson, and James L. Mays. Philadelphia: Westminster Press, 1988.

Bowman, R. A. "The Book of Ezra and the Book of Nehemiah." In *The Interpreter's Bible.* Nashville: Abingdon Publishers, 1954.

Breneman, Mervin. *Ezra, Nehemiah, Esther.* The New American Commentary, ed. E. Ray Clendenen, vol. 10. Nashville: Broadman & Holman Publishers, 1993.

Brockington, L. H. *Ezra, Nehemiah and Esther.* The Century Bible, ed. H. H. Rowley. London: Thomas Nelson and Sons Ltd., 1969.

Brown, Raymond. *The Message of Nehemiah.* The Bible Speaks Today, ed. J. A. Motyer and John R. W. Stott. Downers Grove, IL: InterVarsity Press, 1998.

Campbell, Donald K. *Nehemiah: Man in Charge.* Wheaton, IL: Victor Books, 1979.

Clines, David J. A. *Ezra, Nehemiah, Esther.* New Century Bible Commentary, ed. Ronald E. Clements and Matthew Black. Grand Rapids: William B. Eerdmans Publishing Company, 1984.

Coggins, R. J. *The Books of Ezra and Nehemiah.* New York: Cambridge University Press, 1976.

Davies, Gordon F. *Ezra and Nehemiah.* Berit Olam: Studies in Hebrew Narrative & Poetry, ed. David W. Cotter. Collegeville, MN: Liturgical Press, 1999.

Eskenazi, Tamara C. *In an Age of Prose: A Literary Approach to Ezra-Nehemiah.* The Society of Biblical Literature Monograph Series, ed. Adela Yarbro Collins, no. 36. Atlanta, GA: Scholars Press, 1988.

Fensham, F. Charles. *The Books of Ezra and Nehemiah.* New International Commentary on the Old Testament, ed. R. K. Harrison. Grand Rapids: William B. Eerdmans Publishing Company, 1982.

Grabbe, Lester L. *Ezra-Nehemiah.* New York: Routledge, 1998.

Holmgren, Fredrick Carlson. *Israel Alive Again: A Commentary on the Books of Ezra and Nehemiah.* International Theological

Commentary, ed. George A. F. Knight and Fredrick Carlson Holmgren. Grand Rapids: William B. Eerdmans Publishing Company, 1987.

Jensen, Irving L. *Ezra, Nehemiah, Esther.* Chicago: The Moody Bible Institute, 1970.

Keil, Carl F. *The Books of Ezra, Nehemiah, and Esther.* Translated by Sophia Taylor. Edinburgh: T. & T. Clark, 1873. Reprint, Grand Rapids: William B. Eerdmans Publishing Company, 1950.

Kellermann, U. *Nehemia—Quellen, Überlieferung, und Geschichte.* Beihefte zur Zeitschrift für die alttestamentliche Wissenschaft, ed. Georg Fohrer, vol. 102. Berlin: Töpelmann, 1967.

Kidner, Derek. *Ezra and Nehemiah.* The Tyndale Old Testament Commentaries, ed. D. J. Wiseman. Downers Grove, IL: InterVarsity Press, 1979.

Laney, J. Carl. *Ezra/Nehemiah.* Chicago: Moody Press, 1982.

Loken, Israel P. "A Literary Analysis of Nehemiah." Ph.D. diss., Dallas Theological Seminary, 2001.

————. *Nehemiah.* Fairfax, VA: Xulon Press, 2007.

McConville, J. G. *Ezra, Nehemiah, and Esther.* The Daily Study Bible, ed. John C. L. Gibson. Philadelphia: Westminster Press, 1985.

Myers, Jacob M., *Ezra, Nehemiah.* Anchor Bible. Garden City, NY: Doubleday & Company, 1965.

Packer, J. I. *A Passion for Faithfulness: Wisdom from the Book of Nehemiah.* London: Hodder & Stoughton, 1995.

Reynolds, Steve L. "A Literary Analysis of Nehemiah." Ph.D. diss., Bob Jones University, 1994.

Rudolph, W. *Esra und Nehemia.* Handbuch zum Alten Testament, ed. Otto Eissfeldt, vol. 20. Tübingen: J. C. B. Mohr, 1949.

Seume, Richard H. *Nehemiah: God's Builder.* Chicago: Moody Press, 1978.

Swindoll, Charles R. *Hand Me Another Brick.* Rev. ed. Nashville: Word Publishing, 1990.

Throntveit, Mark A. *Ezra, Nehemiah.* Interpretation, ed. James Luther Mays. Louisville: John Knox Press, 1992.

Williamson, Hugh G. M. *Ezra, Nehemiah.* Word Biblical Commentary, ed. David A. Hubbard and Glenn W. Barker, vol. 16. Waco, TX: Word Books, Publisher, 1985.

ESTHER

Allen, Leslie C., and Timothy S. Laniak. *Ezra, Nehemiah, Esther.* New International Biblical Commentary. Peabody, MS: Hendrickson Publishers, 2003.

Baker, Carl A. "An Investigation of the Spirituality of Esther." M.Div. thesis, Grace Theological Seminary, 1977.

Baldwin, Joyce G. *Esther.* Tyndale Old Testament Commentaries. Downers Grove, IL: InterVarsity Press, 1984.

Berg, Sandra Beth *The Book of Esther: Motifs, Themes, and Structure.* SBLDS. Missoula, MT: Scholars Press, 1979.

Berlin, Adele. *Esther.* JPS Bible Commentary. Philadelphia: Jewish Publication Society, 2001.

Breneman, Mervin. *Ezra, Nehemiah, Esther.* The New American Commentary, ed. E. Ray Clendenen, vol. 10. Nashville: Broadman & Holman Publishers, 1993.

Brockington, L. H. *Ezra, Nehemiah and Esther.* The Century Bible, ed. H. H. Rowley. London: Thomas Nelson and Sons Ltd., 1969.

Bush, Frederic. *Ruth, Esther.* Word Biblical Commentary. Dallas: Word Books, 1996.

Clines, David J. A. *Ezra, Nehemiah, Esther.* New Century Bible Commentary, ed. Ronald E. Clements and Matthew Black. Grand Rapids: William B. Eerdmans Publishing Company, 1984.

Fox, Michael V. *Character and Ideology in the Book of Esther.* Columbia, SC: Univ. of South Carolina Press, 1991.

Gordis, R. *Megillat Esther.* New York: KTAV Publishing House, 1974.

Jobes, Karen H. *Esther.* The NIV Application Commentary. Grand Rapids: Zondervan Publishing House, 1999.

Keil, Carl F. *The Books of Ezra, Nehemiah, and Esther.* Translated by Sophia Taylor. Edinburgh: T. & T. Clark, 1873. Reprint,

Grand Rapids: William B. Eerdmans Publishing Company, 1950.

Levenson, Jon D. *Esther: A Commentary.* Old Testament Library. Louisville: Westminster/John Knox, 1997.

Loken, Israel P. *Esther.* Fairfax, VA: Xulon Press, 2007.

McConville, J. G. *Ezra, Nehemiah, and Esther.* The Daily Study Bible, ed. John C. L. Gibson. Philadelphia: Westminster Press, 1985.

Moore, Carey A. *Esther.* Anchor Bible. Garden City, NY: Doubleday & Company, 1971.

Paton, Lewis Baytes. *A Critical and Exegetical Commentary on the Book of Esther.* International Critical Commentary. Edinburgh: Clark, 1908.

Whitcomb, John C. *Esther: Triumph of God's Sovereignty.* Everyman's Bible Commentary. Chicago: Moody Press, 1979.

CPSIA information can be obtained at www.ICGtesting.com
Printed in the USA
BVOW05s1434050915

416756BV00001B/56/P